For Jessi – the wonderful girl who endures my obsession with this ridiculous game. And to the fifteen people who I lied to when I said I'd include them in this dedication.

Universe Point

KEVIN CRAMER

FORWARD

IN THE THIRD ROUND OF THE 2006 PITTSBURGH SUMMER LEAGUE DRAFT, I picked a 29 year-old cutter named Cramer. It was my first time captaining and I had already found myself drafting people based on height (at 6'1" Cramer is what you would call "Pittsburgh Tall") and T-shirt size, which usually means you're in for a long and brutal summer. But a collective groan from older captain pairs in the room led me to believe that I may have accidentally stumbled upon a good player. Then someone leaned over in their chair and said, "You're going to like him."

I never could've imagined how right they would be. Playing summer league with Cramer was like working in a story factory. There was the time he threw a behind-the-backer to our biggest, most out-of-shape guy in the pouring rain to take half - the night he enlisted himself as a bodyguard to protect a rattled tournament party DJ from an angry mob throwing shit because not every selection can be from the Hall and Oates catalog - and perhaps most memorably, the afternoon a car full of other ultimate players (that we didn't know) made weird faces at us and Cramer insisted with the conviction of an Uber driver who immediately reveals himself as a 9/11 truther that the only proper retaliation was to speed up and moon them.

Ultimate is full of odd ducks, athletic outliers, and spring break heroes. Cramer's experiences will resonate and conjure up intense nostalgia with anyone who has ever driven twelve hours through the night to play savage or sabotaged themselves professionally to go to a one day hat tournament in Eagle Butte, South Dakota. Like the NHL in the 1980's when dudes were scoring 60+ goals a season, or when Major League Baseball looked the other way on steroids and let Mark McGwire and

Sammy Sosa smack 130 some combined dingers in one year, "Universe Point," reflects what I believe will eventually be remembered as the golden age of ultimate.

Cramer's journey starts at a time when the sport was beginning to see a marked influx of "real" athletes; a game cool enough to pique the interest of NCAA hopefuls that couldn't quite make it, yet niche enough that your best player could still play in a crop top and never wear shoes. With semi pro leagues, high school programs, Olympic recognition, and video on demand, the ultimate community currently knows itself better than it ever has. It is – for better or worse – becoming like other sports. The little biospheres where people first discovered ultimate in college are nearly extinct today...but are still very much alive in this book.

There's ultimate on Sportscenter and you may even see Bob Costas painfully explain self-officiation in a gold medal game in the near future. That's awesome. But as we make strides down the straight and narrow path of legitimacy it's important not only to remember, but also celebrate, ultimate's uniquely ridiculous roots.

Full disclosure: The people that we mooned we really unhappy about it, but I've been playing ultimate long enough to know that they're wrong.

Tad Wissel
2008 Pittsburgh Fall League Champion

INTRODUCTION

"Can dogs play? You should put a dog on the field. How great would that be?"

Eighty-eight percent of people unfamiliar with the sport of ultimate (AKA ultimate Frisbee) make this hilarious joke within the first thirty seconds of hearing about our sport. (By the way, that is the most accurate statistic in the history of statistics.) It comes in many forms, perhaps from Aunt Linda who genuinely believes she's giving fantastic advice on how to make the sport cuter - or from a buzzed frat boy with a red cup full of Natty Light just before he launches into a soliloquy about his mad slow-pitch softball skills. No matter the person, they'll all find themselves immensely clever and original, having zero idea that as an ultimate player, you've had to politely ignore the same exact comment three times since Tuesday, and you'll find yourself giving the same answer as normal....

"Yeah. Dogs. We'll look into it."

I refer to ultimate as "our" sport because I'm going out on a limb to assume that you, the reader are also a member of the miraculously close-knit band of wackos that spend a little too much of our lives chasing around 175 grams of plastic. If you're not an ultimate player (first off, thanks for reading), I hope this book gives you a glimpse into the world and personalities of our sport, a sport played by top-level athletes on a global scale by millions of people, and yet a sport that causes eighty-eight percent of people unfamiliar with it to make the same freaking joke about dogs.

I truly believe there is no sport out there like it. It's a sport where the guy programming code in the cubicle next to you or the girl teaching your kid eighth grade algebra may well be a weekend superstar. In a world where many of our top athletes are celebrated to a point of nausea, ultimate stands out as one of the few remaining pastimes where players truly compete for the sake of the competition. In many ways, it's one of the last pure bastions of sport.

The purpose of this book is not to explain the game of ultimate, its origins, history and great players, nor is it meant to illustrate things like offensive and defensive strategies. All of that has been done before in excellent fashion by the founding fathers (and mothers) of ultimate - players like Eric Simon, Tiina Booth, and Jim Parinella, who actually lived the sport's embryonic stage and built it into what we know today. My goal with this book is rather to take the reader on a journey into the stories that surround ultimate through my own first-person experiences during twenty years of attempting to break the mark. For me, and I assume, my fellow players, ultimate is not simply a game - it's an expe- rience - a way of life. And the stories don't start and stop between the cones. Ultimate is about the people you're with on the long car rides to random soccer fields in a town fourteen hours away that you barely knew existed before you arrived. It's about the parties, the sideline hijinks, the hamstring cramps, the blood, the ER visits, and the way your car smells when you've left your damp cleats behind the passenger seat overnight. Most of all, however, it's about the people. Many of my closest friends, I've met playing this sport. You'll run across a majority of them in one way or another in the coming pages.

To give you some background, I make my living as a writer, so I'm fascinated by the stories of what drives people to become who they are. The question occurred to me, "What is it about ultimate that makes a small group of people dedicate nearly every free minute of their time to something a majority of the country will never hear about?" I began to examine the sport through my own experiences, trying to put my finger on just what it was that kept me coming back for more. This book is written as a personal narrative as I tried to answer that question.

As an ultimate player, I've had a myriad of experiences that I believe everyone who loves the sport, from the casual lunchtime player to the hardcore national competitor can appreciate. I've been through it all, from hideously disorganized pickup games to big time college tournaments - competitive summer leagues to top level club - and even the new pro leagues in three distinct areas of the country with three vastly different styles of play. I've been matched up against some of the best teams and top players the nation has to trot out there and came out of it (relatively) unscathed.

I like to think I was good. Many people will tell you I was much better than that. Even more people will say "Who? Never heard of him." As I look back over my career as it's now coming to an end, I liken myself to a halfway decent utility infielder, one of the best players on your AAA team, but a situational bench guy upon reaching the majors. Or to bring it back to ultimate, on the absolute top club teams in the nation, Condors, Revolver, Ironside, Truckstop, Sockeye - had I lived close enough to play for any of them in my prime, I'd have been about guy number thirteen on the roster. I'll admit right off the bat that I'm not writing this book because I was the best player in history. I'm writing it because I happen to be a writer – and because all the top players have entirely too many stories about winning and winning is fucking boring.

I'd also like to say that I feel fortunate to have played during a very transcendent time in the sport's history. I began playing as an eighteen year old in 1995 when all most people knew about ultimate was through a two-minute scene in the movie PCU starring Jeremy Piven and David Spade. (A scene where now that I think about it, there was a freaking dog on the field…damn it.) I fall into the tail end of the first generation of ultimate players, so I've gotten to watch the sport grow and explode as the kids of the "old guys" that I played with in my late teens and early twenties took the sport over and launched it to new heights. Many of these kids have had a disc, rather than a baseball or football in their hand since they were four. They grew up with the sport that most of my generation discovered in college.

I often run across old photos of teams I've played on in the past. You know the type - half the team is kneeling, the other half standing. One girl in front proudly holds up some admittedly lame trophy as the guy behind her pretends to hump it. Off to the side, a shirtless dude on the end chugs a beer with his back to the camera. Everyone else either looks high or ready to puke. I'm not sure why, but I feel like fifty years from now those will be the pictures hanging in the "The Game Evolves" section of the Ultimate Hall of Fame that will inevitably be built somewhere in New Jersey. Essentially, we were the leather helmet clad football players of the 1930's & 40's – the ones whose picture you see in Canton and go "THOSE GUYS played pro football?"

And yet you have the sinking feeling they probably could've kicked your favorite team's ass. (Especially if you root for the Browns.)

This is the evolution of ultimate as I've seen it. Any dialogue is recalled to the best of my ability and intentionally embellished to make me sound cooler and smarter than I actually am. On this journey, I hope to portray the sport and the people involved in the light they deserve because first and foremost, our sport is a community of (more often than not) top-notch people whose stories have lain dormant for too long. So thanks for coming along for the ride….and no, there won't be any dogs.

ONE

HAD I NOT GONE ON TO PLAY ULTIMATE FOR YEARS, I'M SURE A RANDOM GYM class in September of my junior year of high school would've been long forgotten by now. It was a week or two after I'd transferred to Greensburg Central Catholic High School (about an hour east of Pittsburgh). I wasn't a fan of the public school I'd gone to previously, mainly due to a group of kids who'd ganged up to make walking down the hallway a living hell —and the school was no fan of me due to my trying to light it on fire on two separate occasions. So one sunny day in the fall of 1993, I found myself on the football practice field out behind Greensburg Central with a bunch of guys I'd known for all of two weeks thinking we were probably going to divide up to play soccer or flag football. Then our gym teacher plopped down a mesh sack of Frisbees.

"Ooh, are we playing ultimate?" one kid exclaimed with the kind of enthusiasm usually reserved for dodgeball or floor hockey.

Our gym teacher, a behemoth of a man named Mr. Free who was rumored to have been an offensive lineman for the old Pittsburgh Maulers of the USFL nodded to the enthusiastic kid. "You and Herbie are captains. Start picking teams."

This pained me greatly. I was hoping we were going to play flag football because I didn't really know any of the guys in my class yet and wanted to show off my arm. When I was sixteen, I had a cannon. Nothing gets you immediate respect in Western Pennsylvania, birthplace of Joe Montana, Dan Marino, Joe Namath, and Johnny Unitas quicker than tossing a fifty yard spiral. Being known as *"the new kid who can really chuck a damn football"* was much better than my current moniker *"the scary new kid from the city we think might be a drug dealer."* I could throw a Frisbee about as well as I could throw a lamp.

Before that class, the last time I'd thrown a Frisbee was with my cousin Eric in my grandma and grandpap's tiny backyard in Swissvale, a blue-collar railroad town on a hill above Pittsburgh's Monongahela River. Eric was (and remains) six years older than me, and by the time I got to that gym class at Greensburg Central, he'd already been to Iraq and back with the Marines during the first Gulf War. So, suffice it to say, it had been a while since I had a disc in my hands.

When we were kids, Eric and I invented all kinds of ways to keep ourselves occupied on summer afternoons in Swissvale. Our grandparents kept a cardboard box full of random sports equipment on the back porch – basically stuff grandpap randomly found down by the train tracks or grandma found for a quarter at her church rummage sale. Crammed in there amongst the half chewed rubber balls, whiffleball bats, and ping pong paddles was a bright red WHAM-O Frisbee. I was probably about nine and he was fifteen when we finally decided to get the WHAM-O out of the box - not to have a nice catch in the backyard of course, but to fire it at each other as hard as possible.

The game we invented was simple. It was called Battle Frisbee. Eric would stand next to the crumbly cinderblock wall that kept grandma's garden from spilling into the grass, and I'd stand just in front of the hill that went down into the neighbor's yard. Once we took our positions, we weren't allowed to move. In our minds, the Frisbee was covered in razor sharp blades that immediately sliced clean through whatever they hit. If the disc hit you in the arm, leg, or foot, that appendage was cut off and you couldn't use it the rest of the game. If the Frisbee hit you in the head, neck, chest or stomach, vultures immediately descended on your loser corpse.

Eric spent a lot of the games standing on one leg with his foot amputated cause I always threw it low to avoid having to jump the neighbor's fence to retrieve it if I missed high. I spent a lot of the games getting pegged in the mouth with a red WHAM-O. My grandma later found a Frisbee made of this weird synthetic cloth that flew remarkably well for having zero rigidity. She thought it would be better for Battle Frisbee seeing as we'd be less apt to stumble inside for dinner with welts and fat lips. We tried it for about seven throws then went back to the plastic one. Battle Frisbee was designed to hurt, damn it. That's why it was called "Battle Frisbee" and not "Occasionally Getting Grazed With Something Soft & Nice."

So with all of that in mind, I stepped onto the field for my first ever ultimate frisbee game. Mr. Free explained the rules. Each team tries to score a goal (which at that point we referred to as touchdowns) by passing the Frisbee down the field between players. The objective was to have a teammate catch it in the end zone for one point. If the Frisbee hit the ground, was caught by the other team, or went out of bounds, possession automatically turned over to the other team who then went on offense and tried to score. You weren't allowed to run with the Frisbee and you had ten seconds to throw it once you caught it. And those were the rules.

As we played, I remembered warming up to the game. I was fast and good at intercepting everyone's floaty gym class backhands. I remember being proud that I completed a fifteen-yard pass that actually didn't flop into the ground like a dead goose. When the eight-minute bell rang, the white team and the maroon team were tied. Mr. Free told us that the next touchdown won. Little did I know I was in the middle of my very first universe point. ("Universe point" being the ultimate term for 'tie game and next goal wins.' Essentially whoever scores next controls the universe. It's a pretty big deal.) I only remember how the game ended because this kid named Jason, Central's starting fullback who was like 5'6" and built like a concrete stump, jumped over someone much taller, tipped the disc and caught it as he was falling to the ground for the win. It was spectacular – even if the girls on the adjoining field had already gone inside and couldn't be impressed. It was so insanely heartbreaking for the losing team that they stole Jason's shoes and chucked them into a dumpster, which I'm guessing seemed like pretty sensible retribution in a locker room full of sixteen year olds. In the end, I still wished we'd have played flag football, but I guessed it was way better than soccer, which I was actually worse at than throwing lamps. So all in all, it wasn't a bad

33 minutes.

I have to confess, I thought Mr. Free had invented the game himself one day when he accidentally brought a sack of Frisbees out to the field instead of footballs, then had to wing it. I could envision him standing there in his Polo Shirt and confusingly small cotton gym shorts as he rubbed his beard and stared at the Frisbees.

"Ok, guys, we're gonna play a sport kind of like football….but with a Frisbee."

"So it's tackle?"

"I'm not going to let you guys tackle each other, no. That's a lawsuit waiting to happen."

"Can you run with the Frisbee?"

"Uh….no. You have to pass it."

"What if it hits the ground?"

"Uh….whoever gets to it first and picks it up….nah, you guys will kill each other. How about if it hits the ground, it's a turnover and goes to the other team? Yeah, that sounds reasonable. Ya know what, just start playing. I'll blow the whistle if someone screws up. Get out there. Run. Work up a sweat. Quit being pansies."

At that point, I really did think it was just a gym class game in Greensburg, Pennsylvania. I had no idea that the game had actually been invented by a bunch of high school kids in New Jersey in 1968. I had no idea that the sport was popular on college campuses all over the country and that there'd even been a national championship since the early 1980s. I had no idea that the first-ever collegiate game was played between Princeton and Rutgers, the same two schools that played the inaugural collegiate football game, and on virtually the same field exactly 103 years later. All I knew as I walked toward the locker room that day preparing for 9th period English was that next week we were starting volleyball so I'd probably never play that weird ass game again.

In the summer of 1994, one of the teachers at Woodland Hills High School where my father taught chemistry took her family on a sunny Florida vacation. She had a son named Dan, who is apparently like my third cousin. I only knew him because he was a pretty good left-handed pitcher for Murrysville, the town next to mine, and I'd played baseball against him since I was thirteen. Now normally the family trip of someone you barely know isn't a life-changing event for *you*. It's typically more memorable for the people ya know…actually on the trip. But Dan's family vacation did in fact alter my life because of one tiny detail. They made a side trip to a town that I'd only heard of briefly in a paragraph in my middle school history textbook - the town of St. Augustine, Florida.

During the first half of my senior year, I'd narrowed down my college choices to Ohio University and Penn State. I'd been accepted at both, and I remember leaning toward Penn State enough that I was already making plans to room with a buddy from Greensburg Central once we got up there. That was until Dottie Miller showed my dad some pictures of their Florida trip. The trip included a visit to a tiny liberal arts school with a great baseball team that most people outside of the Sunshine State had never heard of. The school was called Flagler College.

Based on the pictures and a whim, I sent away for their brochure. Based on the brochure and an even bigger whim, we decided to go visit the school over Thanksgiving break of 1994. As we packed the car that Thanksgiving, my parents thought the trip would be a great way to show me how far away Florida actually was. They thought it would be one final nudge that would push me once and for all toward enrolling close to home at Penn State. Then we came over the Bridge of Lions and saw St. Augustine for the first time.

There's a bridge that spans the floodplain going into my hometown of Trafford. It's pure majesty. Off to the left is the old brick Westinghouse Plant that closed in 1990 and looks like a great place to either play paintball or get killed by a psychopath. Straight ahead is the regal town of Trafford, with stunning views of a convenience store, an eight-story old folks home, the police department, and a dive-bar that somehow burns down every December. To the right is a superfund site next to the railroad. A bunch of soccer fields have been built on top of a dump where Westinghouse Electric used to bury drums of industrial waste. The Pittsburgh Ultimate Summer League now plays a handful of games on those fields each year. Whenever we play there, I'm usually involved in this conversation....

"Dude, why didn't you lay out for that?"

"Cause we're playing on a field that five years ago was a pool of lethal toxins. If you could just hit me in stride next time, that'd be awesome."

The Bridge of Lions over the Intercoastal Waterway into St. Augustine was no Trafford Bridge, but it did have sailboats, a marina, palm trees, snowy egrets, diving pelicans, the redoubts of a four-hundred year-old Spanish fort, and the red spires of Flagler College dominating the skyline. It was drizzling and kind of chilly for Florida when we crested the bridge. It didn't matter. The city itself seemed to generate its own light. My family, in a moment of collective consciousness uttered the same profound and simultaneous sound.

"Whoa."

I started at Flagler College that September.

The beauty of the setting aside, I chose Flagler College for two reasons. One, the girl to guy ratio at the time was four to one. Four girls for every guy. I figured with odds like those, even a dumbass like me could stumble into getting laid on occasion. (I told my mom that the communication department really stood out from the rest of the schools I researched.) And two, I wanted to play baseball in Florida.

Like most people who discovered ultimate in college during the 90's, I came to it after training all my life for a completely different sport. With the advent of high school leagues all over the country, some players have been able to focus primarily on ultimate since they were thirteen. Recently, the University of Pittsburgh has created a pipeline from the PHUL (Pittsburgh High School Ultimate League), recruiting the best players in the city- who come to college as freshman already schooled in the game. As a result, Pitt has been consistently ranked in the top ten in the country for the better part of the last decade. (Author's note: Pitt won their first national championship while I was writing chapter 12 of this book.) They aren't forced to recruit the guys who just got cut from the soccer team, still wanted a reason to run after cross country practice, or realized they no longer had time for basketball. As for me, I came to ultimate after a bitter divorce with the sport to which I'd given the first eighteen years of my life.

Throughout high school I'd been a decent pitcher who occasionally showed flashes of brilliance in what was otherwise a giant pile of mediocrity. After transferring to Greensburg Central, I dodged early April snowflakes to shut out the defending section champions from East Allegheny in my very first varsity start.

Then I lost ten games in a row.

It didn't help that my infield averaged about seven errors a game behind me, but I also let their clutzy bumblings bother me enough to give up gap shots like I was throwing underhand. Even so, I was being recruited to play Division I ball at Ohio University because I threw absolute smoke at a camp there the previous summer. After a 6-0 record playing fall ball including a no-hitter against the Butler County All-Stars, I felt pretty good going into my senior year. Then in February, a month before the season, I got a sore throat. I started feeling really tired. Putting on my shoes was enough to make me need a nap. For a while my parents thought I was taking teenage laziness to an absurd new extreme. Turned out I had mono.

If you haven't had the pleasure of mononucleosis, just imagine spending all day in a swimming pool full of cough syrup wearing one of those Sumo Wrestling suits - and then twice a day someone comes along and beats you with a dictionary. It's just a little worse than that. I missed the entire third grading period of my senior year. Instead of dominating on the mound that spring, I labored to get through four unspectacular starts before I had to pack it in all together. The big year I'd planned for myself just wasn't meant to be.

So I decided to walk on at Flagler. About a week after I arrived in Florida, there was a meeting for all guys interested in playing baseball. And I wasn't particularly nervous - until I looked around that room. Every single dude seemed as if they'd been plucked straight out of 1955. Same high and tight haircut. Same clean-shaven face. This did not bode well for the kid with the pointy, death-metal goatee and hair that flew every direction out the back of his hat. In that room, I stuck out like a nine-inch nail. It was the first sign that maybe I was headed down the wrong athletic path.

After shaving and getting a much-needed haircut, I started fall practice with all the other pitchers, throwing bullpen sessions, running, and spending hours working on bunt defense and covering first base. The trouble was, it was Florida. It was hot. It was humid. And the practice was constant. Every day I was going to class, hitching a ride out to the fields, working out in the Florida heat, then coming back to lift weights and study before heading to bed - just to get up and do it all over again the next day. It would have been exhausting even if I hadn't still been trying to flush the mono out of my system. Plus, I was a freshman. Not going to practice for any reason was a no-no, let alone if that reason was "being tired." That fall I got into one game, a scrimmage against Santa Fe Community College. I pitched one inning, the last of a double header, and while I didn't give up any runs and I did strike a guy out when he went fishing for a change up in the dirt, the outing caused our best pitcher to ask me...

"Cramer, can your fastball even hit eighty miles per hour?"

For anyone who hasn't pitched, this is basically the equivalent of someone asking, *"Hey man, so I'm curious. You think you could win a fight with a loaf of bread?"*

"I uh....think so," I said without a lick of certainty.

"Yeah, I'm skeptical," he replied.

For a guy whose fastball had been topping ninety the previous fall, this was not the collegiate debut I was hoping for. As September dragged into October, my body had nothing left. Finally at the end of the fall season, the coaches decided what guys were going to make the team, putting the final roster up on the window outside of Coach Barnett's office. That day, I came back from English Comp, watched a jury acquit OJ Simpson of first-degree murder then hustled down to the athletic office. I'd pitched ok for those six weeks. Not great, but ok. I had no velocity, which was a bit unsettling, but I thought the coaches liked me and saw enough potential to want to keep me around.

I must've read the names on that sheet of paper six times just to make sure I hadn't skipped mine. After that sixth time I was pretty certain it wasn't there. My heart sunk. Since I first played catch with my father when I was five, all I'd ever wanted to do was play baseball and I hadn't even made it through the first semester of my freshman year. Baseball was who I was. Without it, my sense of self damn near flat lined.

I met with our manager Coach Barnett the next Monday. He said while I wasn't on the active roster, he wanted to keep me around to develop for the following year. I ended up throwing so much pregame batting practice that spring, I'm willing to bet I tossed as many pitches as all the other guys on the staff combined. Even so, I could feel the end coming. I didn't want to fade into athletic oblivion at eighteen, destined to be nothing but an intramural superstar. But I didn't think there was much choice.

That all changed on my way to go lift one night. Outside the gym, I ran into a kid named Phil. We got to talking and a year later, I'd have to make a choice between the sport I'd heretofore dedicated my life, and a sport I once played in gym class.

TWO

Phil was the kind of kid that even at 21 had the look of a burned out assistant principal. It wasn't hard to picture him in a short sleeve dress shirt and tie, sighing as he wrote out a detention slip. The night I met him, I was apparently wearing a T-shirt that marked me as a Pennsylvanian, so he stopped me on the sidewalk outside the gym to ask where I was from.

"Just outside of Pittsburgh," I said.

"Oh, cool. I'm from Reading."

It was my first experience with relative distance. If you're in Pennsylvania, Pittsburgh and Reading are nowhere near each other. They're like nineteen dollars apart on the Turnpike. But if you're in Florida, somehow they seem close. I imagine if you're a dude from Boston wandering around Botswana and you run across a girl from Seattle, it's like you're freaking neighbors.

Because of the Pennsylvania connection, we struck up a conversation. We found out we lived at opposite ends of Ponce Hall, which before becoming a dorm, was part of a luxury hotel complex built by railroad baron Henry Flagler just before the turn of the 20th century. If it sounds lavish, it was - in 1889 before there were things like air conditioning and pest control and when five surfers from Cocoa Beach weren't leaving their wetsuits all over your bathroom. Teddy Roosevelt once stayed there. I'm pretty sure his roommate never pissed in the sink.

I must've mentioned to Phil that I'd just gotten cut from the baseball team because his weary, administrative eyes lit up. "You're an athlete? Did you see the signs we put up on the message board by the Coke machine?"

There was currently only one sign on the message board by the Coke machine, so I knew immediately what he was talking about.

Ultimate Frisbee!

2:00 Every Sunday at the Fort

No experience necessary. Just come out and play!

Any questions, see Lew or Phil in Room 9

Phil licks balls!

I'd actually contemplated going out to play before running into Phil, recalling ultimate from gym class and thinking it might be a fun way to spend a Sunday afternoon. Then I'd inevitably remember that Sunday was the only day I didn't have baseball practice and there was no way I was going to spend it running around.

"You should come out and play this Sunday," Phil said before he left.

I nodded. "All right. Sure," I said, waving and walking into the gym. And that's how it began.

In order to truly appreciate the uniqueness of my initiation into ultimate, you need to get a clearer picture of St. Augustine itself. I wasn't just wandering between dorm and classroom buildings to get to a quad or some soccer fields in the middle of campus. I had to weave through a maze of tiny pedestrian-only streets and alleys built by the Spanish in the 1570s. These streets and alleys were anything but empty on a typical St. Augustine Sunday. The way to the field was cluttered with chattering tourists trying to corral their shopping bags, sweaty preachers quoting the Bible, historical reenactors in old conquistador helmets, bellowing hot dog vendors, caricature artists, mimes, puppeteers, unkempt violinists, human statues, a one-man band, biker gangs, hippies walking small alligators - if it was weird, it had a home in the Spanish Quarter. It was like a half-mile long, history-themed freak show. I actually saw four monkeys run past me down the street one day. I am not kidding.

So that was the route I took simply to get to the fields that Sunday in 1995. As I crossed the Avilla de Menendez (Menendez Avenue) toward the fort, I saw a bunch of guys tossing Frisbees. It was an idyllic setting - palm trees swaying in the wind, egrets and ospreys flying overhead, fisherman casting off the from the bayfront, the music of a Jimmy Buffett impersonator drifting over from St. George Street, the looming stone fortress and its cannon-filled turrets in the background, and the smell of grilled seafood everywhere.

As I got there, Phil jogged over to greet me. "Hey man, glad you came out."

"Yeah. You're uh…going to have to refresh me on the rules."

The rules were simple. It was very close to what I remembered from gym class except for one huge exception that didn't make me cringe at the time, but makes all of my organs shiver now. There was no out of bounds. No line of demarcation whatsoever. The only caveat was the disc had to pass through the cones (or more often shoes) at the front goal line or the score didn't count, making each end zone sort of an infinite trapezoid. A regulation ultimate field is a 120-yard by 40-yard rectangle. Ours was more of a constantly shifting amorphous blob. I thought nothing of it at the time.

Phil introduced me to the guys, we picked teams, and we played.

The Sunday game at the fort had originated a few years earlier when the core group of guys who were all now seniors were freshmen. Half the guys I was presently trying to keep up with were on the cross-country team and started the game so they could get in more conditioning on their off day. In other words, at some point they'd looked at each other and said, "Hey guys, we only ran 48 miles this week. I think we could use a little more cardio."

As ultimate players, most of the guys on the field that Sunday were amazing cross-country runners. Every throw was a backhand. (For the non-ultimate players, think of a backhand in tennis. It's the same motion.) There was no strategy. It was run around until you get open offense and a half man, half zone defense that only worked because there weren't many precise throws happening. I don't, however, say there were *no* precise throws happening because of a laid back intellectual from rural Georgia named Lew.

Almost immediately, the guys realized I was pretty fast and told me to go deep a lot. So I did. Somewhere in the middle of the game, the other team pulled to us. (Pulling is the term for when the teams line up at opposite goal lines and one team throws to the other. It's ultimate's version of a kickoff.) The disc landed in our end zone. Phil picked it up and flipped it to Lew. As this was happening, I ran a fly pattern past the dude who was covering me, looking back over my shoulder to see if anyone had noticed. Back at the goal line, Lew had.

It was beautiful. The disc came out of his hand like an egret cutting an elegant path through the sky, ten feet off the ground, flat, never wobbling on its eighty yard journey. I lie. The disc flew better than an egret. Amazed, I kept sprinting. My defender hustled to catch up. He leapt, the disc sailing inches over his outstretched fingers, hitting me just in front of the hip in perfect stride for the goal.

I was blown away. Up until that point, I didn't think throwing a Frisbee was a skill that anyone possessed. But now I'd just seen a guy hit a moving target nearly eighty yards away.

Lew jogged down the field to congratulate me. "Nice run," he said as I flipped him the disc.

"Yeah. Nice freaking throw."

"Eh, it was ok."

Ok? Just ok? His nonchalant reaction pointed to the insane notion that he'd somehow made better throws in previous games. *Better throws than the egret you just launched? Surely that's impossible.*

The whole thing left me dizzy. How could there be people in the world who could throw a Frisbee like Brett Favre could throw a football? And how could I get the whole way to college without finding out about it? When the games were over I limped back through the old Spanish maze - tired, bleeding, and still not one hundred percent certain of the rules.

But the one thing I knew for sure was what I was doing next Sunday.

As much as I enjoyed Sunday afternoons at the fort, my mind was still attached to baseball. During my freshman year, it was my only priority. Before every home game I'd grab my glove, run the two miles out to the baseball field, meet Coach Barnett, lug three buckets of baseballs to the mound and throw about 300 belt-high fastballs for the guys in the lineup that day to rip into the outfield. When batting practice was done, I gathered up the balls, returned them to the equipment room and joined the team in the dugout where I developed some seriously awesome bench chatter.

"Throw him a seat now baby, sit this guy down, toss him a bus pass, hum baby, throw him a Greyhound!"

I just loved being part of the team, being out on the mound, getting to work on my mechanics, and the overall feeling of being a college athlete. To make things better, Coach Barnett loved me because he wasn't the one who had to throw 300 belt-high fastballs before every home game. Next year I was making the team for sure. There was no doubt in my mind. All the ultimate stuff was just a fun distraction.

Even so, I continued to play, not realizing the sport was slowly getting its claws into me. Being from Pittsburgh, I'm a huge Steelers fan. When I say huge, I mean rabid. And by rabid, I mean I salivate incessantly and bite the mailman if they lose to the Ravens. The Steelers were good enough to make the Super Bowl that year. (And would've won it if Neil O'Donnell hadn't thrown the two worst interceptions in NFL history.) The thing was though, as they played important, nationally televised games down the stretch, I found myself watching the first quarter then prying myself away from the TV to jog out to the fort.

If missing football weren't bad enough, many times I'd plan on studying or working on a report until I'd see Lew and Phil tossing disc in the hotel courtyard. I'd run over to join in, telling myself I'd only toss for fifteen minutes then go buckle down on academics. We'd just pass it back and forth around the palm trees, the tourists, and the large, undeniably phallic-looking fountain. It was fun. It was relaxing. And before I knew it, the clock struck midnight and I'd gotten absolutely no work done whatsoever.

Lew was a complete trick shot artist when it came to tossing in the courtyard. There was no shortage of obstacles to throw around and no matter where he was, he managed to have a throw that fit his conundrum.

Trapped behind a palm tree? Put a little curve on it. Hit me right in the chest.

Stuck behind a brick pillar? Put even more curve on it. Hit me right in the chest.

Squeezed by a wall? Skip it off the concrete. Hit me right in the chest.

Tossing in the courtyard with Lew and Phil was the first time I realized a Frisbee didn't always have to be tossed like two drunk dopes on the beach. Between the legs, over the head, behind the back, spin passes, lobs, shit that came at me upside down - I never knew what was coming. I was still in *"desperately trying not to plunk random people in the face"* mode, so I never asked Lew how to actually do any of it. I just stored all his trick throws in the back of my mind and told myself it would be pretty cool to do someday.

To tell you the truth, if the guys who introduced me to ultimate weren't so awesome, I might never have continued playing the game. They were a close-knit bunch of seniors who accepted a freshman into their circle and made me feel comfortable from day one. I felt like I fit in. I didn't know it at the time, but it was very indicative of the type of people that I've found permeate the entire sport. Not to say that the guys on the baseball team were jerks, because they weren't. It's just that they were jocks. They wore polos and dated hot blonde girls. I wore Marilyn Manson T-shirts and occasionally talked to a chick in my math class.

The guys who played ultimate were the guys who didn't care about the rager down the street on Friday night. They were perfectly content to study Greek Literature or play whiffleball in the hallway until 4AM while the rest of campus was out getting hammered. They were the type of guys who stayed up to debate politics and religion, then tipped a water-filled trash can against your door so when you opened it, your feet got soaked. They were the type of guys who figured college would be a hell of a lot more fun if you remembered the experience and came out of it having acquired the knowledge you paid for. They were exactly my type of guys.

Just before the end of the season, we had a cookout at a guy named Dawson's place. Dawson was a perfect representation of the kind of dude who played ultimate with us that year. He wasn't incredibly athletic. He was a stocky guy whose real talent was playing blustery, comedic roles in the main stage plays. But he could kind of throw a backhand thirty yards and didn't mind sweating like crazy on a Florida Sunday, so every weekend you could find him running around out there with the rest of us.

Over burgers and dogs, we all swapped stories about the semester's craziest plays as the seniors slowly began to realize that after four years, they were about to play their final game together. For them, it was the end of an era. They were about to graduate and head back to places like Reading, Pennsylvania, Winter Haven, Florida, Fairfield, Connecticut, and Social Circle, Georgia, most likely never to play together again. They briefly talked of having a reunion game every year with the fervor of guys who were too young to know that time, money, and distance would almost certainly prevent it.

That realization caused them to turn to me and the few other underclassmen in the room. All hopes of their legacy were riding on our shoulders.

"You guys are planning on keeping the game alive next year, right?"

We looked around the room. There were only five of us.

"Actually, I'm transferring," one of the other guys said.

There were four of us.

"I mean, I'll probably be playing baseball next year," I said, "but I mean, if the coaches let me play another sport…"

It was like a flick to the nuts. At least eighty percent of the regular participants in the Sunday game were graduating. What the hell were we going to do next year? What the hell was I going to do with myself if god forbid I didn't make the baseball team again? It was the first time I truly realized how much I was falling in love with ultimate. The prospect of losing it felt like eight hamburgers in my stomach - although realistically, that feeling may well have been due to the eight hamburgers in my stomach.

They handed out awards, top-of-the-line card stock certificates that Phil printed off his computer. Offensive Player of the Year went to a guy named Steve, who to that point was the only person I'd ever seen throw a consistent flick. (The opposite of a backhand, thrown by flicking the wrist, almost like a sidearm baseball throw.) Defensive Player of the Year went to a sophomore male cheerleader named Dustin who could leap over your damn head from a standing position. MVP of the whole thing went to Lew, and I landed Rookie of the Year. I still have that certificate in a folder somewhere in my basement and I'm damn proud of it. I know I'm a nerd, but other than the Samuel Goldwyn Screenwriting Award a decade later, I'm pretty sure the 1996 Flagler College Ultimate Rookie of the Year is the only other award I've ever gotten. Let me enjoy the little things.

And just like that, it was over. Two weeks later, I hitched a ride back to Pittsburgh with the cute girl from my math class and the guys who'd started the game four years prior walked across the stage, shook the president's hand, hugged their families, packed their cars, and left to find the rest of their lives. Flagler College Ultimate teetered on the brink of extinction.

That summer I worked in a warehouse moving around bundles of window and door tracks and played baseball for a semipro team out of Monroeville, PA. We played in a league filled with current college players as well as guys who washed out of the minors but didn't want to give up the game. After fifteen months, I was finally over mono and feeling pretty damn good. It showed. That season I went 6-1, developing a sick change-up, a curve ball that nobody could touch, and on the days I had any idea where my fastball was going, I was just about unhittable.

Our other main pitcher was a giant 28 year old with a beer gut named Ronnie who was a star athlete at Swissvale High School a decade before. He was the type of guy who you swore could crush an entire keg of beer on his forehead. I walked off the mound one night having thrown a pretty good game, only giving up two runs and giving us a great chance to win. All in all I was pretty damn satisfied with myself as I turned the railing and tossed my glove down under the bench.

Ronnie jogged in from left field and scowled at me. "Jesus, Cramer, if I had your stuff, I'd be in the goddamn major leagues."

I smiled. "Thanks, Ronnie."

"That's not a fuckin' compliment," he sneered. "I'm telling you that you're too stupid to get anywhere with what you have, and if the world made any fuckin' sense, *I'd* be the one with your fuckin' arm so as not to fuckin' waste all that talent. Christ I hate dumbass eighteen-year-olds. Don't waste your time sitting down cause I'm knockin' it outta here to win this fuckin' game."

Two pitches later, Ronnie took a fastball over the center field fence to win the fuckin' game.

I only relay this to let you know my mindset upon heading back to college for my sophomore year. I'd spent my summer facing down guys that played in the ACC, the Big Ten, and the Big East, and mowed them all down. Unless my arm dropped off, I was making the team. And not only that, I was going to be good. I couldn't wait to show Coach Barnett what I had.

Even though I was dedicated to baseball, I still felt like I owed it to Phil, Lew, and the other guys to reestablish the ultimate game. So as soon as I got back to Florida that fall, I teamed up with Cheerleader Dustin to put up flyers and recruit players.

We didn't have many guys coming back. We had the two of us, a gangly rock climber named Rick, and a know-it-all ADHD head case named Jon who at that point was squarely in the running for most annoying human being on the planet. I seriously have no idea how he got through high school without getting beaten to death. He was rail thin, wore a bike helmet everywhere, and loudly told everyone he ran across how wrong they were about everything in the screechiest, most ear-piercing voice I've ever heard. It was like a terrified hawk in a room full of chalkboards. To make matters worse, he was the most wretched kind of sports fan - the dreaded Yankees/Cowboys fan. If he'd also rooted for the Lakers, I'm pretty sure you could've used it as a defense to murder him and any sensible jury would've let you off scot-free.

So to get numbers, I did what any self respecting college sophomore would do. I begged and guilt tripped all of my buddies into showing up. I figured if I could just get them out there once, they'd get hooked like I did. To my surprise, it worked. The conversation almost always went like this...

"Hey dude, you coming out to play ultimate at the fort this Sunday?"

"Eh, I don't know. I might have some shit to do."

"Ok, cool. I was just trying to give you a way to shed that freshman fifteen, buddy. I played every weekend last year and didn't put on a pound. Just trying to look out for you, man."

"I didn't....put on weight. Not that much. Like...you seriously noticed I put on weight?"

"Oh, I didn't notice. I just overheard some of the girls talking about how much better you looked at the beginning of last year. Personally, I can't tell the difference. Forget I mentioned it. You got shit to do on Sunday."

"Is Jon going to be there?"

"Uh....I'm not sure. Maybe."

Each friend would stare at the ceiling at this point, contemplating whether looking better for the ladies was worth spending three full hours with Screeching Jon. Inevitably, after a few seconds, they'd nod. "You're gonna have to teach me the rules."

With Cheerleader Dustin and I employing two main strategies, namely bugging our friends and pouncing on athletic-looking sport-unaffiliated freshmen, we somehow walked out to the fort that first Sunday in September to find more players than we'd ever had. I remember standing in the shade of the giant Live Oak beside the field and looking at Dustin just before the game.

"Who the hell are all these kids?" I asked.

"I don't know. But I'm glad they're here," he answered.

The game itself that day was secondary - especially because it was so putridly bad. My buddies ran around in the heat trying to find their abs again, Jon yelled like a dying falcon, and Dustin and I dominated because we were the only ones who almost knew what we were doing. But we had ourselves a Sunday game again. Looking at the eighteen players firing pass after pass into the turf under a beautiful Florida sky that day, (Yup, we played a very crowded 9 on 9) I felt I'd met my obligations to Lew, Phil, and the rest of the guys. I smiled, knowing I could walk away having passed along their legacy. It was a great sense of accomplishment.

I'm not sure why I quit baseball that October. I was throwing better than I ever had. Maybe it was because they'd brought in three freshmen pitchers from the state championship team in Key West to fill the slots in the bullpen I was aiming to take. Maybe it was because as I was throwing gas off the side mounds, all of the coaches were off watching the new guys. Maybe it was because I finally realized that no matter how hard I worked, my arm just wasn't fulfilling the dreams I had at thirteen.

I just remember walking into Coach Barnett's office one Monday before practice and asking him, "Coach, I can do the math. There's no room for me is there?"

"Well," I remember him saying, "to be honest, we got a much better freshman class this year than we anticipated. I really thought there'd be one or two spots open on the staff, but it….didn't turn out that way."

I didn't say anything for a few seconds. I just stared at the clutter of athletic schedules on his desk. "Ok."

"Everybody says you've been throwing great so far. We'd love to have you around. We always have room for a hard worker. Guys get hurt, get homesick, or can't keep their grades up, you never know. It's up to you if you want a second year with no promises of getting a uniform."

He was right. Guys did get hurt. Maybe sometime in the future, I'd be pitching in the World Series and think about that moment - the moment where I stuck with it in the face of overwhelming odds - the moment just before one of the guys from Key West would be ruled academically ineligible or drunkenly break his ankle at an off campus party - the moment that opened the door for me to step in, dominate, and never look back. I continued to stare at the manila folders on Coach Barnett's desk, then stood up and shook his hand.

"Nah, I think it's probably better if I move onto something else."

Coach Barnett nodded. I could tell he was as disappointed as a manager losing his eleventh best pitcher could possibly be. He shook my hand. "Good luck. You work as hard at school as you did for us, you're going to be just fine."

"Thanks for everything."

I shuffled out past the secretary and just like that, my baseball career was over. As I look back on it now, I'm still not quite sure why in the moment I was given the chance to continue playing the sport I'd loved throughout my childhood, I turned it down. Maybe it had to do with what I saw from underneath the Live Oak that Sunday. There were eighteen people running around like frenzied atoms tossing awful backhands that hung in the wind for hours, but they were there because of me. That was *my* game. Looking at it now, I think I walked away from baseball because while trying to pass on a legacy, I'd inadvertently created my own. I didn't know it at the time, but walking back from the athletic office that day, I was now, officially, an ultimate player.

THREE

No one, and I mean no one had a stranger introduction to the sport of ultimate than any of the freshmen attempting to learn the game with us on that narrow strip of Park Service land between the old Spanish Fort and Menendez Avenue. Believe it or not, the closest running water source to fill up our water bottles between games was in the arcade of a Ripley's Believe It or Not Museum. To hydrate, we had to pass by Pac-Man, Dig Dug, a shrunken head, and a freaky picture of some Chinese guy who was born with two pupils in each eye. And that barely scratched the surface of the weirdness. To truly appreciate the insanity of what we considered a normal ultimate game, you have to understand the subtle differences between the fort and a normal field. Read carefully, the variations are so small they may be hard to pick out at first glance.

Shape and Measurements

Normal Ultimate Field: A regular ultimate Field is a rectangle measuring 120 yards by 40 yards. The playing area is 70 yards long with each end zone measuring an additional 25, adding up to the full 120.

The Fort: I guess if it goes into traffic or lands in the bay, it's a turnover.

Slope

Normal Ultimate Field: Flat.

The Fort: Flat except for a gentle hill that started at the left side of midfield and gradually invaded the playing area until one entire end zone resembled a skateboard ramp for toddlers. If you stood at the back (or what passed for the back) of the end zone, and were looking for a toss from the goal line, your knees were pretty much lined up with the thrower's chest. Short guys *loved* the topography of that end zone.

Obstacles

Normal Ultimate Field: None.
The Fort: Screw it. I'm just going to make a list.

Tourists

I played two full *years* of ultimate before I realized that most games weren't constantly interrupted by clueless people from Michigan in fanny packs and flip flops. At minimum, fifteen times a game someone would be forced to shout "Freeze!" And we'd all stop running and hold our positions. For those of you who know the rules of ultimate, it amounted to a pick call. (If a defender can't cover his man because an offensive player has gotten in the way, a pick is called. Everyone on the field stops.) The stoppage of play often happened like this...

(*Italics* are my thoughts)

Ok, got the disc. Jerry's covered. Ron's covered. Oh wait, Ben's open. Nope, that fat guy in the Pistons T-shirt is all over him. Wait, who the fuck is that guy? And who the hell is that chubby lady in the floppy hat? Ah, shit.

"Freeze!"

At this point everyone would stop and look around, finally glimpsing Mr. & Mrs. Oblivious as they slowly dragged their cooler of Twinkies and stupidity right through the middle of the game. And I mean slowly. So slowly, their bipedal motion would completely cease.

"Oh, honey, look at the sky," Mr. Oblivious would say. "I doubt we'll be able to see the sky from anywhere else but right here on this very spot. Let's lay out the blanket. Right here. Right here in the middle of these fourteen sweaty people who are all glaring at us."

"Um, excuse me," I'd say nicely at first.

No response.

"Excuse me!"

Mrs. Oblivious would then spend ten seconds glancing around before finally pointing at her own chest. "Are you talking to us?"

"Yeah, we're actually in the middle of a game here, so…."

At this point, the tourists would look at us with startled terror as if we'd suddenly materialized from a different dimension. They all but perfected the look of Ray Kinsella's brother-in-law when he first sees Shoeless Joe Jackson and the rest of the dead Black Sox appear from the corn. Their embarrassment of course led to them fumbling 60% of the things they were carrying, causing extra delay.

"Oh, we're so sorry. Sorry….." they'd stutter as they tried to pick up all the crap that fell out of their fanny packs.

I'd smile. "No problem. It happens all the time."

Keep moving. Keep freaking moving and…there we go. Finally.

"Ok, game on!"

Damn it, who the hell is this dude with the dog now?

"Freeze!"

Trees

The giant Live Oak we propped our bikes and backpacks against was close enough to the field that it caught the occasional pull or backhand bomb, but the real danger were the huge gnarly roots that crept their way into the playing area. It was like a giant subterranean octopus with wooden tentacles. At least once week, it would reach up and snatch an ankle. Hilarity ensued.

The best tree story, however, involves the skinny little sapling that marked the front corner of the left end zone. Although it was a pretty significant obstacle in the middle of the field, we mostly paid it no mind other than using it to judge whether we'd scored or not. This was until the time I cut from the back of the end zone with Cheerleader Dustin covering me. My roommate Josh, a 6'4" pre-hipster from West Palm Beach threw a late backhand that I swore I was going to catch until my buddy Ben peeled off the guy he'd been covering at the goal line and swatted it away. Seeing the defense, Dustin kept going, trying to take me deep. Ben, a stocky Marine Brat from Havelock, North Carolina flexed his muscles and posed.

"Don't bring that crap in here!" Havelock Ben yelled, jokingly flexing his biceps.

It was about then that I realized the disc was caught at the top of the tree about four feet off the ground. It was about time to exploit a loophole in the rules. As Havelock Ben turned and waved for his teammates to go deep, I deftly slipped over, made sure my feet were in the end zone and picked it out of the branches.

Ben came over to retrieve the disc, still pumped about his defense. I smiled at him with the disc in my hand. "That was a great play, man. But uh….goal."

"What?"

"Disc never hit the ground, buddy. And I am clearly standing here in possession of it in the end zone. So…we're up 7-6."

Ben looked at me as if I'd just slapped his mom. "What the…what the…you can't….that's not a….you can't just pick it out of the fuckin' tree!"

"Again, I reiterate. The disc never hit the ground. The rules state…"

"I know what the rules say!"

By this time, some of the other guys had stopped playing and walked up to see what the argument was about.

"What's going on?"

"Cramer says it's a goal even though it was stuck in the tree for ten seconds."

"Oh yeah. It never hit the ground. Cool. We're up 7-6."

"There's no way that's a goal. The tree is part of the ground."

"I think the tree would beg to differ."

"The roots go into the ground. The tree is part of the ground."

"Trees are not the ground. No kid has ever said, *'Hey mom, I'm going outside to climb the ground.'*"

"Wow, that's a pretty good point."

"That is *not* a good point! Nor does it apply to our current situation."

"How does that example not apply to our current situation? I beg you to tell me how that example does not…."

By the time we'd quit arguing about exactly what constitutes the ground, we had a new rule - if it hits the tree, it's out of play. My team went up on an admittedly cheap goal although we'd wasted so much time that three couples from Michigan spread out blankets in the middle of the field, so we called it a day and headed back to campus.

A Sidewalk

Yeah, you heard me. A freaking sidewalk made a diagonal from the seawall to the street, running between the Live Oak and the skinny little sapling. Now that I think about it, I'm completely amazed that in three years, nobody shattered a kneecap or knocked out any teeth. I mean we had actual concrete in the middle of our field. *Concrete!* One time I leapt to make a D, got undercut, flipped and landed on my shoulder right next to it. Five inches to the left and I'm probably paralyzed. Another time, I laid out shirtless and peeled most of the skin off my rib cage. And yet we didn't pay it much attention until Cheerleader Dustin bombed one over my head in 1997.

I was defending this tall, shaggy-haired senior named Todd who played guitar in a local jam band. The disc was turned over at midfield, and I immediately bolted for the end zone with Jam Band Todd a half step behind. Dustin picked it up and winged it for me to run down. Todd and I were stride for stride, sprinting hard, chasing it as it flew out ahead of us. Just before we hit the sidewalk, we both leapt. Todd made a great play to get a finger on the disc and knock it away. The next thing I remember is a red blur whizzing by underneath me.

I glanced down from midair to see the face of a woman in her early 60's. Three seconds previous, she'd been casually riding her rented bike down the Castillo sidewalk just behind her red-shirted husband on a gorgeous Florida afternoon. Now two large, muscular college students at the end of an all out 40-yard sprint were descending toward her at frightening speed. I can still see her face. It was the face you'd make just before getting eaten by a T-Rex. Bike tires screeched across the concrete.

I still don't know how we missed her. Most of it had to do with her decision to eject just before impact, taking a fortuitous spill into the grass. Todd went sailing over her while I hit the ground at her feet, putting my hand squarely on her ass and doing a miraculous cartwheel over her twisted body, slashing open my shin on the pedal of her bicycle in the process.

When it was over, the three of us crawled back to reality like soldiers who'd been a little too close to a grenade. I stumbled to my feet, still shocked that we hadn't outright killed her.

I extended my hand. "Holy crap, are you ok?"

She let me help her up, but didn't answer. Her arms and legs were vibrating like violin strings. I felt horrible. The last thing in life I ever wanted to do was crush an old lady on a bike. Even though we hadn't outright linebackered her, we'd still caused her to take a nasty tumble.

My guilt soon faded as her jolly, red-shirted husband walked his bike over with the heartiest Texan belly laugh I'd ever heard. Seriously, the dude was cracking the hell up. "You all right, Linda?"

She didn't answer.

"I'm so sorry," I trembled. "People don't normally ride their bikes on this path."

The husband continued to speak for his shaken wife as he picked up her bike. "Eh, it's ok. Toughest woman I know. Little spill ain't gonna set her back." And then, practically tossing Linda to the side, he looks at us and says, "What're y'all playing here? Some kind of Frisbee football?"

"It's called ultimate."

"Hot damn, I'd have never thunk you could play football with a Frisbee. Mind if we watch? Think the missus needs a few minutes to get her head right."

"Uh…sure."

So after we got Linda some water, the couple spent the better part of fifteen minutes resting in the shade of the Live Oak watching the guys who'd almost ended their forty-year marriage run around like idiots. The husband actually cheered at anything cool that happened while his stunned wife continued to stare into the black void of her fears. When our game ended, we shook their hands and they rode off. I can almost hear the husband telling his suburban Dallas card club.…

"Now let me tell y'all about the Frisbee football boys in St. Augustine who almost sent Linda to her maker.…"

If that lady is still alive, I'm positive I show up in her nightmares.

The Moat

Oh wait, you thought it couldn't get worse than the sidewalk? We had a moat. Yes, an actual *moat* just behind the uphill end zone. You see, when the Spanish built the Castillo de San Marcos in the late 1500's, they weren't so much concerned with the safety of any ultimate players that might happen to craft a field out of the land four hundred years in the future - no, they were a tad more concerned about not getting overrun and slaughtered by the French. And so we had a freaking moat.

Often, my ultimate friends from other schools will tell me stories about how crappy their college fields were. It usually goes like this…

"Oh, man, our fields had this one soccer goal that we always had to move."

"Yeah? Ours had a moat."

"Dude, our field was so crappy. There was this one place that would always puddle up."

"Yeah? Ours had a moat."

"We had this one…."

"Moat. Whatever it is you're going to say comes in a distant second to our moat."

When I say we had a moat, it's not like it was filled with wooden pikes and alligators. What it was, in essence, was a sharp eight-foot drop into two inches of liquid malaria. Our only real out of bounds rule incorporated the moat. You weren't allowed to just run into the moat to get open, but if the disc was headed into it anyway, you could take the health risk and follow it. And when I say health risk, I'm not talking about rolling your ankle falling down the hill. I mean when you laid out, you pretty much landed in the tuberculosis epidemic of 1878.

The moat played a major part in the most spectacular catch I've seen in twenty years of playing the game. Cheerleader Dustin was sprinting down the right sideline with his defender, let's just say it was Screeching Jon, right on him. There's an amazing YouTube video of Beau Kittredge from the University of Colorado jumping clean over a San Diego State defender to snag a goal during regionals back in 2006. The SDSU guy is tracking the disc when Beau literally springs over top of him, farts on the dude's hat and catches it before landing at the goal line. It's an absolutely incredible play that highlights the sheer athleticism of one of the best deep receivers to ever play the game.

Beau, however didn't leap from the precipice of a moat.

As Dustin leapt over Jon's back, Jon started to jump, flipping Dustin in the air horizontal over Jon's head. Dustin tipped the disc as he began to plunge headfirst to the ground having flown completely *over* the stumbling defender. Trouble was, Dustin's momentum had carried him far enough forward that the ground was now eight feet below the point from which he'd leapt. So not only was he five feet in the air above the end zone, he was now a full thirteen feet above the bottom of the moat he was about to land in. Just before he disappeared into oblivion *completely upside down*, he reached out and grabbed the disc, which was returning to Earth with him. And then he was gone - eaten by the moat.

I thought it was the last thing he'd ever do as a living being. *Well, buddy, at least it's a hell of a way to go out.* And then like a zombie hand reaching up from the grave, we see a disc. Dustin comes climbing back up the hill and drops it in the end zone.

"Goal," he said nonchalantly like he hadn't made the most spectacular catch in ultimate history.

Whether Dustin actually caught the disc, I have no idea. None of us saw him hit the ground. We were just glad we weren't discovering his deceased body lying in the moat, neck bent back like a fossilized bird. Do I know for a fact he maintained possession? No. Am I going to keep believing he caught the damn thing anyway? You betcha.

Historical Reenactors

Twice a year, we'd show up to play on Sunday only to find an infantry unit camping out in the end zone. The fort itself was captured by the Union in 1862 after the Confederates had completely deserted town. After that, it was used as a prison. Given the history, it probably makes sense that the only thing we ever saw them actually reenact was how to sit around and eat bacon in Victorian era clothing.

There was, however, one amazing game where historical reenactment played a large role. Occasionally, up in the fort, guys dressed as Spanish and English soldiers would do actual weapons demonstrations for large groups of Sunday tourists. Every hour it culminated with them loading and firing a cannon off toward the bay. (Sans cannonball or the people zipping around on jet skis would've been pretty screwed.) We were in our second game of the day, playing to ten. The score was 9-9. Universe point. For a couple minutes, it went back and forth with both teams almost scoring on bomb after bomb. Three points in a row an offensive player laid out only to come up inches short. After six minutes of running back and forth with the score tied, I got the disc at midfield and saw Havelock Ben open in the end zone.

I've found there's a guy on every team that always makes the play even though he doesn't make anything easy. Oh he'll score the goal all right, but it's going to be a show as to how. (Many of you are silently laughing and thinking, 'Yup, that's Jimmy.' If you're not - you're probably Jimmy.) On our team, that guy was Havelock Ben. As he chugged toward the front corner, the backhand I zipped at his chest went straight through his hands. It smacked him in the sternum and popped up in the air allowing his defender to catch up. Fortunately, Havelock Ben was a stocky wall made primarily of muscle and Jello shots. The defender couldn't get around him, instead slamming into his back and falling to the ground. Ben stepped back, tripped over the defender and landed straight on his ass. As he sat there on the ground, the disc landed right in his lap. Goal. We win. Ben pops up and pumps his fist like he hadn't just turned an easy catch into an unnecessary circus. Then as he leaps in celebration….

BOOOOOOM!

The cannons go off. The tourists yell their applause. To this day, I've never seen an ultimate game end with more flair.

Satan

Yup, we occasionally had to battle the devil. The Morning Star himself. Or at least a crazy hobo who was convinced he was Lucifer incarnate. He was pretty harmless - or at least as harmless as a dude who genuinely believed he was the Prince of Darkness could possibly be. Our interactions with him were always pretty similar. All the sudden during a lull in the game, we'd hear a gruff old voice shouting incoherently...

"Bow down at my feet or I'll kill you all! Do you know who I am? I am Satan. Cower before me!"

Then he'd stumble onto the field.

After the first few times, it wasn't shocking anymore so much as kind of annoying. Usually it was left up to Havelock Ben and I to deal with him.

"How's it going, Satan?" I'd say.

"I am Satan!" he'd yell in my face.

"Here's the thing, Satan, we need you to stay off the field."

"I'll rip out your eyes and feed them to the burning dogs of hell!"

"That sounds horrible," Ben would say. "But seriously, this is *our* kingdom. Over here. You can set up a whole kingdom of darkness on that bench over there."

"I am Satan!"

"And as requested, we are cowering in your presence," I'd answer. "But Ben's right. See that bench? Little secret. They only put it there to cover up a portal to hell. So I mean....."

"Off you go," Ben would wave.

Incredibly enough, Satan always listened to us. I mean for the devil, he was surprisingly agreeable. He'd head on over to the bench, yelling at passers by about how he was going to eat the souls of their children. And that would be it. It always ended about a half hour later when some tourist complained to the Park Service and a ranger or local deputy calmly escorted him off the property.

I'm tempted to become a politician just to see if when I die, that guy is there to greet me.

There were many other obstacles that I won't describe in detail including category one hurricanes, fish-dropping ospreys, unfortunately timed sprinklers, hills of construction dirt, WWE wrestling wannabes, and the itchiest damn grass in America, but by now you've gotten the general picture.

Sometime at the beginning of my senior year, the National Park Service decided to start enforcing a rule about not allowing organized sporting events on Park Service land. Our argument for continuing to play on our hallowed ground was basically this...

"If you knew anything about this sport, you'd realize what we're doing is a long way from organized."

They didn't buy it and in early 1999, Flagler Ultimate played its last pickup game at the fort. The next week, we moved three blocks inland to an actual field without trees, tourists or moats. Suddenly, we had rectangular end zones and out of bounds lines. Flagler College Ultimate was all grown up, but I'll always have a soft spot for that quirky little field by the bay.

FOUR

I DON'T EVEN REMEMBER THE KID'S NAME AT THIS POINT. IT MIGHT HAVE been Patrick. It might have been Wally. I'm pretty sure it wasn't Lisa. All I know is he was in town visiting a high school buddy who lived on the opposite end of Ponce Hall. He saw Havelock Ben and I tossing around the palm trees in the Ponce de Leon courtyard and asked if he could join in. To our surprise, he was pretty good. Most of his tosses hit us in the chest as we winged the damn thing over and around the fountain for a half hour or so. We didn't even talk to him. We just wasted the early part of a Thursday night chucking the disc above the heads of frightened hippies, occasionally interrupting their drugged out guitar jam with an errant throw. That particular tossing session ended when I zipped one particularly hard at Havelock Ben.

Beth, the little bundle of brunette energy I was dating at the time was coming back from a club meeting and decided to jump in front of Ben to intercept it. She was one of two girls who actually played pickup with us at the fort on Sunday, so we were a bit surprised when it went through her hands and slashed open the bridge of her nose creating a scar that I'm pretty sure she had to cover with makeup at her wedding seven years later.

Anyway, with Beth crying and bleeding onto my shirt in the first stages of developing raccoon eyes, I finally got a chance to talk to the mysterious Frisbee-loving stranger. He was from Florida Southern University in Lakeland. Florida Southern, like us, had a small but dedicated group of guys who played a semi-organized game every week. As we talked, he told me about this crazy organization called the Ultimate Players Association, which governed college and club ultimate teams.

"Wait a minute. Wait a minute," I said. "There are actual college *Frisbee* teams?"

"Oh yeah," he answered. "Lots of them. My one friend plays at Florida. They travel all over the country."

It was ten o'clock at night, but I swear the sun came out. Suddenly all kind of possibilities flashed through my head. I saw seven of us donning the scarlet and gold of Flagler College as we lined up and waited for the pull against Palm Beach Atlantic or Embry-Riddle Aeronautical or any of our Florida Sun Conference rivals. I optimistically saw fans crowding the bleachers and lining the soccer field to cheer us on. A roar went up as I caught the winning goal. I envisioned people spilling from the stands to celebrate in a collective, joyous mob. The vision I had was glorious. Hopelessly unrealistic, but glorious nonetheless. Only a few months after walking away from what I thought was my only shot to be a collegiate athlete, an opportunity at redemption was now right in front of me.

Next thing I knew, I'd gotten the dude's phone number and we'd scheduled our first intercollegiate games for early April in Lakeland. Now all I had to do was convince the rest of the guys to take the Sunday game and turn it into something much bigger - our very own team. Three or four of the regular Sunday guys shared my enthusiasm for the idea. Unfortunately, you need at least seven to play.

So Havelock Ben, Cheerleader Dustin, and I went to work. Dustin roped in a hyper hippie from Maine who lived across the hall from him. His name was Jerry and he'd been a regular on Sunday. He threw better than any of us even though he played in these eccentric little gloves that we jacked him about constantly. I can't even pee straight with gloves on let alone throw an accurate backhand, yet somehow he stepped right in and became our top handler. (Handler is the term for a player whose main responsibility is to make accurate throws to the receivers.)

Jerry's roommate Ron was a tall, laid-back dude from Savannah with floppy 90's hair and droopy cheeks. We always had to talk him out of going windsurfing before he'd show up on Sundays. Every week was the same. Savannah Ron would sort of disappointedly follow us to the fort and bitch the whole time about the great waves he was missing as he loped up and down the field pretending he wasn't having a blast. Using the same premise, we knew he'd cave if we just bugged him enough.

"But guys, I got like other stuff...."

"Ron, you're playing."

"But guys...."

"Ron....you're playing."

"But guys....c'mon....really.....c'mon...."

"Ron, you're on the team."

"All right. I guess. Fine. You guys suck."

And that's how we got Ron on the team.

Havelock Ben had class with a tall and athletic deaf kid named Fred who was one of the funniest dudes on campus even though he had a hearing aid the size of Jupiter in his left ear. Thinking back, I have zero idea how it didn't fall out when he leapt over someone to catch a goal. A typical conversation with Fred went like this....

Fred: Guys, I'm two feet away, you don't have to shout.

Me: (softer) Oh. Sorry. Were we shouting? I didn't realize we were shouting.

Fred: What?

Ben: (Slightly louder) Sorry, man, we didn't realize we were shouting.

Fred: What? Speak louder.

Me & Ben: (Much louder) We didn't realize we were shouting!

Fred: Guys, I'm two feet away. You don't have to shout.

And then he'd crack the hell up.

Deaf Fred didn't take much convincing. He was on board the first time he heard us ask. So....the fourth time we asked.

In art class, I met a skinny, freckle-faced kid with a buzz cut from Chickamauga, Georgia. He'd just been cut from the baseball team, but was going my route from the previous year and practicing without a jersey. He was a shortstop and I was a pitcher so we didn't really interact much in the two weeks of practice we had together before I quit the team. The first time I talked to him was a week after fall cuts and he was still walking around in a daze. We connected immediately.

"Well, we're trying to start an ultimate frisbee team," I told him.

"You're always welcome to come out and play with us."

"I can't really throw a Frisbee."

"You'd be surprised how little that actually matters right now."

And Chickamauga Jeff rounded out the team.

I was teaching Chickamauga Jeff how to throw when I accidentally figured out how to toss a flick. For a year, I'd been desperately trying to add something other than a backhand to my repertoire of backhands, backhands, and more backhands. For that same year, I watched every attempt I made knife into the ground like a dinner plate.

Chickamauga Jeff and I were tossing in the courtyard just before heading over to Ben's to watch the Packers take on the Patriots in Super Bowl Roman Numeral Something. Jeff threw a floaty lob over my head that I had to chase down into some hedges lining a brick wall. I remember there was a hot girl sitting on a bench nearby, so I was trying like an idiot to get her to notice the spectacular things I was doing. (Because girls are *always* impressed by shirtless guys crashing headfirst into palm trees.) Anyway, I leapt and planned on firing it back to him in midair, but at the last second the disc drifted to the right. I grabbed it and landed on my heels, trying desperately not to tip over into the hedge and look like a moron in front of the hot girl. So I just chucked it back the way I'd grabbed it.

Perfect flick. Hit Chickamauga Jeff right in the chest.

As Jeff scrambled over past the snickering hot girl to help me out of the hedge, he looked at me in awe.

"Wow, how did you throw it like that?"

"I don't know. That's the first time I've ever done it."

Ever have a moment where after an hour of frustration, you stumble upon the little tool that allows you to easily assemble the futon you just bought? *Oh shit, this thing was taped to the inside of the box the whole time? Hell, this makes it much easier.* That's what I felt like. That one happy accident opened up a whole new world. I spent the next twenty minutes trying to recreate the mechanics of my unintentionally awesome throw as the hot girl got up and walked off. I didn't even notice.

"I think you have to keep your wrist from flopping over," I yelled across the sidewalk.

"Yeah," Jeff answered. "You throw it with your wrist. Not your arm. Holy crap."

Next thing I knew, we were both tossing pretty consistent twenty-yard flicks. Granted, they weren't game ready, but I was still excited. It's funny to me now how we had to 'discover' such a basic throw. I help coach a high school team in Pittsburgh and the flick is one of the first things we teach. Five minutes after they show up, our 9th graders know more about how to throw a Frisbee than I learned in my entire first year of trial and error. It just goes to show how far the game has come.

Just after Brett Favre ran off the Superdome field a champion, Havelock Ben and I sprinted down Grenada Street and through the giant iron gate into the Flagler courtyard. He couldn't wait to learn what I'd figured out earlier that afternoon. Ten minutes later, we were tossing flicks over the hippies. It was awesome.

As April approached, we didn't do much different than we'd been doing all year. It never occurred to us to practice. We just kept playing our weird brand of ultimate at the fort once a week and decided that was enough. I also started doing all the boring prerequisite stuff to make Flagler College Ultimate a club sport, getting signatures, writing proposals and all that crap. We were on our way to legitimacy.

In February, Havelock Ben and I went to research as much as we could about college ultimate on this brand spankin' new computer thingy called The Internet. My freshman year, I had to look up literally everything I wanted to know in the card catalog and any communication was done face to face or by letter. Our entire campus had two computers hooked up to the Internet and they were pretty useless because at the time, the web basically consisted of four porn sites and a copy of Seattle's zoning codes. By my sophomore year, the way we gathered information as a society had changed so much that I was shooting emails to my friends back in Pittsburgh and looking up ultimate tournaments in California. Ben and I found the Ultimate Players Association site, which told us of an upcoming college tournament over in Gainesville called Frostbreaker. So one Saturday in early March, Ben and I hopped in his

Mustang of Doom (more on this later) and headed inland through miles of backwoods Florida potato fields to see what real college ultimate was all about.

I can't relay how wide our eyes were as we parked the Mustang that day. Sixteen fields were spread out in front of us, discs flying through the air, the combined din of voices yelling out plays, cheering, and debating foul calls was simultaneously exciting and overwhelming. It was the first time either of us had seen ultimate at its pinnacle. As we stood there fifteen feet from the back of one of the end zones sipping on Gatorades we'd picked up at the Chevron next to the fields, we could barely say anything other than, "Holy shit."

Just then a huck went up in the Georgia vs. Georgia Tech game in front of us. Two guys burned after the disc, bits of sod kicking up from their cleats, the unmistakable sound of pounding feet and straining lungs getting louder as they barreled toward us. The disc hung just before the back of the end zone. The Georgia Tech player leapt. The Georgia player went up with him. For a second, the Tech receiver had his fingertips on the edge of the disc until the Georgia player punched it out from the bottom. It went fluttering out of bounds. The Tech player flipped over the Georgia guy's hip and got whipped headfirst into the ground. Five minutes later, his teammates guided him, woozy and weak-kneed back to their sideline. We continued to sip our Gatorades.

"Holy shit."

As we wandered the fields, we saw one game that even from fifty yards away you could tell was faster, louder, and better than all of the others. We went over and sat down on some bleachers beside a couple other guys.

"Who's playing here?" I asked.

"ECU and NC State. Fucking intense," the guy said without turning away from the action.

In the mid to late 90's, North Carolina State and East Carolina were powerhouses in college ultimate. ECU had won back-to-back championships in 1994 & 1995 and the underclassmen on that NC State team would take the whole thing themselves in 1999. Being only 84 miles apart in eastern North Carolina, they knew each other well. Very well. It was apparent.

Ben and I had never seen ultimate played so crisp, so precise, and so…..fast. ECU would work the disc up the field and score on a brilliant crossfield hammer. NC State would answer with a midfield huck. ECU would make a layout defense. NC State would follow with a layout D of their own. After every goal, the scoring sideline would erupt. Every point was a battle. Every goal mattered.

Ben and I spent the whole game leaning forward mentally dissecting what was happening. At one point, Ben tipped back his Gatorade and squinted. "Does it look like they're running plays?"

"It indeed looks like they have designed plays."

Ben was a basketball guy. During the winter, we'd coached a youth team together in St. Augustine. I could see the wheels turning in his head. "It's like they have a whole offense. They're running a goddamn offense, Cramer."

This was a huge revelation to a couple guys used to just running around in circles to get anywhere we thought might be open. By halftime we'd realized that ECU and NC State were actually playing ultimate. We were just a bunch of guys dicking around beside a moat.

As the Mustang zipped through the potato fields on the way back toward St. Augustine, I turned to Ben. "We got some work to do, don't we?"

"Yeah," he answered. "Yeah we do."

When we got back, we decided our first order of business would be to get uniforms. Not practice or learn anything about the game, mind you, but to outfit the team. I guess we figured if we could manage to look halfway legitimate, everything else would miraculously fall into place. The trouble was, none of us had any money, so one afternoon Havelock Ben and I walked down to the athletic office to visit my old friend Coach Barnett.

"A Frisbee team, huh?" Coach said with skeptical intrigue.

"Yeah, we have a game coming up against Florida Southern in a couple weeks so we figured we should maybe have uniforms."

"A game? Really? Who set it up?"

"Uh, well….we kind of set it up ourselves."

The look on his face was reminiscent of a man witnessing ducks juggle fire. Suddenly there was a new team on campus playing a sport he knew nothing about and as athletic director, had to do no work for. I think the last part was why he gave us the key to the storage closet up by the weight room.

"Don't know what's up there, but we don't need any of it. Take whatever you want. Just bring back the key."

"Thanks, coach," I said practically sprinting out of his office.

So Ben and I spent the afternoon moving around cardboard boxes in a musty old closet that smelled like crap that hadn't been moved since before we were born. Every box was an opportunity. Unfortunately, every box was seemingly filled with old volleyball tops or crappy nut-hugger basketball shorts from 1982. There was nothing of any value whatsoever - which was probably why we thought we'd struck gold with one of the last boxes we ran across.

Our treasure was twenty-one disgustingly heavy polyester baseball uniforms. Out of the bundle, two were relatively clean. The others were covered in dirt and sweat marks like the players had taken them straight off their backs after the last doubleheader of the 1987 season and tossed them directly into the box we were now picking through. Three of them had bafflingly large mustard stains. And yet we were thrilled.

We spent the rest of the afternoon at Ben's mom's house running the uniforms through the wash like eight times. After the treatment, the old white and maroon uniforms were very nearly maroon and white, no longer resembling the smoker's teeth yellow condition in which we'd found them. Hell, most of the mustard was even gone. We were ready to play.

So the Saturday before finals, the seven of us met in the courtyard for the three-hour trip down I-95 and I-4 to Lakeland. As our two cars pulled out of St. Augustine, I was out of my mind with excitement. The little team I'd put together at our tiny ass school was headed on the road to play an actual opponent. I couldn't wait to see how we stacked up. Even more, I couldn't wait for the first moment that an ultimate team representing Flagler College simply put seven on the line and waited for the pull. We spent the whole trip blasting music and debating who was going to score Flagler's first ever goal. I desperately wanted it to be me.

We didn't actually know where we were going, so our plan was to follow the signs toward campus then ask the first person we saw where the intramural fields were. We followed the signs just fine, but unfortunately after 177 miles, we showed up to find an empty Saturday afternoon. The whole campus had the feel of a town recently hit by a mega virus. There was *nobody* around.

We'd expected to see a team warming up somewhere, discs in the air, guys running sprints, anything to let us know we were in the right place. Nope. It was so quiet you could hear the fish breathing in the lake below campus. After circling the school about nine times, we finally decided to take our cleats and our Frisbees and wander toward a gated soccer field. At least we could toss while we waited. Cheerleader Dustin walked over and pulled on the gate.

Locked.

And the fence was fifteen feet high.

So there we were three hours away pissing around a lonely campus not knowing if the chances were better of us playing the games or contracting the plague that had obviously killed everyone in Lakeland.

Havelock Ben punched me in the shoulder. "Cramer, if this is a prank…"

At the time, elaborate jokes were somewhat commonplace for me. Everything coming out of my mouth was suspect, so it wasn't completely out of the question.

"Yeah, Ben. I woke up at 7:30 on a weekend just so I could convince the rest of you to show up at an abandoned field three hours away. Ha, ha….joke's on you."

"Cramer, I'll kill you. I'll seriously kill you."

"I talked to the guy on Thursday. He said they'd be here."

After twenty minutes of crapping around at the edge of the fence, we started to debate whether to just pack up and head for home. Just then, a short, muscular kid came riding up on a bike. He saw the Frisbees and stopped with a smile.

"Are you the guys from Flagler?"

"That'd be us," Dustin said.

"Oh, sweet. We didn't know if you guys were actually showing up or not. Patrick said he got us a game, but no one believed him. I'll go back and get everyone. Patrick has the key. He'll unlock the gate. Awesome. Thanks for coming."

Fifteen minutes later, guys on bikes started arriving from all over campus. The guy I met back at Flagler who may or may not have been named Patrick produced a key. Soon we were inside the fence tossing across a perfectly manicured field of brilliant green turf that unlike the fort grass, didn't make your skin itch for days after a layout. It's still probably the nicest outdoor field I've ever played on. I'm pretty sure Florida Southern is a rich kid school.

We warmed up. We set a start time. All the dreams I'd had of people filling the bleachers were quickly replaced by the reality of six people staring back at us. Three were the dutiful and nearly interested girlfriends of the Florida Southern guys. Our crew consisted of Cheerleader Dustin's girlfriend Mary who spent the whole time with her nose in an economics textbook, Cody, a drugged out blonde who came along to be our stats girl because she had rotating crushes on me and Havelock Ben, and Ron & Jerry's roommate Ed who was there because he had nothing else to do that Saturday and their TV was broken.

We distributed the scarlet and gold-trimmed baseball jerseys. I got #17, Ben #23, Dustin #1 and the other guys took numbers under 25 that I can't recall at the moment. For a few sweet minutes, we looked like a real team and not a bunch of rag-tag doofuses who played on a field bisected by a sidewalk.

The seven of us huddled together just before we took the line.

"Alright, guys," I said. "First game. How cool is this? No matter how long this school has a team, we'll always be the first ones to step on an ultimate field with Flagler across our chests. When you think about it, that's pretty sweet. So let's go."

Havelock Ben chimed in. "Forget that shit, let's kick some ass!"

I nodded. It was a good sentiment. "Fine, let's kick some ass."

And we lined up. Florida Southern took their place at the other end of the field. It was what I'd dreamt about for the better part of a year. I'm pretty sure my smile could be seen back in St. Augustine. Cheerleader Dustin raised his hand. We were ready. The disc went in the air. Flagler Ultimate was official.

About thirty seconds later, we were down 6-0.

We were confused on defense, disorganized on offense, and generally looked like our cleats were filled with sand and coated with tar. It was a complete disaster. As we dejectedly lumbered back to the sidelines after giving up the sixth goal, Ben put his hands on his hips and tried to catch his breath.

"Shit, those guys are fast. All of 'em. All of them are fast. They can't have one fuckin' slow guy?"

Dustin shook his head in confusion. "They're not that much better than us. We should be right with them. I'm not sure what the hell's wrong."

Savannah Ron was already dripping with sweat. He looked like an overworked basset hound as he tried to form words in between heaving breaths. "How critical (inhale) are the jerseys?"

"What do you mean?" I said.

"It's like (inhale) ninety degrees out. We're running around in (inhale) heavy, polyester baseball uniforms. You ask me, that could be a major (inhale) contributing factor to our (inhale) sucking."

It hit me like a punch to the chin. We looked so good. So cohesive. So like an actual athletic team. I loved having the scarlet "Flagler" across my chest, especially since I'd never gotten to wear it on the baseball field. Unfortunately, Savannah Ron was onto something. We might as well have been running around in festive holiday sweaters.

"Damn it, Ron, you're right. These things are pretty awful."

"I vote we (inhale) ditch them."

Ben was appalled. "Ditch the uniforms? We can't ditch the uniforms! Do you know how much laundry we had to do to get these things presentable? It was like an entire afternoon."

Ron squinted. "Are you (inhale) comfortable?"

Ben clutched his knees trying not to dry heave to the goal line. "Yeah, I'm fine. Great. Kind of. It's tolerable. I mean it's not horrible. I'm not comfortable at all, no," he said as he inhaled, stood up and yelled across the field. "Southern! Time-out!"

We returned to the field having changed into the various T-shirts we normally wore at pickup.

With each of us three pounds lighter and sweat able to escape our skin, we took the field and went on a run. On the point following our timeout, Dustin lofted a backhand from midfield toward Chickamauga Jeff that sailed over his head and into the waiting hands of Deaf Fred who'd lost his defender in the back of the end zone. It was Flagler's first ever goal. I didn't even care that I wasn't the one to catch it. I was just glad we were on the board.

Now that we were sporting similar apparel, we found we were pretty evenly matched. Both teams had one or two guys who threw nervous flicks if they were wide open, but the game was dominated by backhands.

I leapt high over my defender to grab a lob from Savannah Ron along the sideline, doing a somersault toward the goal line upon landing that I'm pretty sure was a blatant travel. From my knees I flipped a two-foot pass to Chickamauga Jeff to close it to 6-4. A few points later, I intercepted a pass and fired an immediate 45-yard backhand to Jerry Gloves in the back right corner of the end zone. We'd somehow erased our early deficit and brought the score to 7-7.

The game went back and forth. We didn't take a halftime. We were playing to ten, win by two, and we took leads of 10-9, 11-10, and 12-11. Our tenth goal is still one of the most awkwardly exciting plays I've ever witnessed. On stall nine, (The player holding the disc has ten seconds to get rid of it before it becomes a turnover. This is called a stall count. The term "stall nine" refers to the ninth second I held the disc.) I lofted a dead backhand toward Chickamauga Jeff that was without a doubt my worst throw of the game. It wobbled like a confused bee toward the sideline and handcuffed him as he sprinted toward me. The disc bounced straight off both of his hands and popped into the air. After completely flubbing the initial catch, Jeff pulled a move only a bumbling freshman would even attempt. Hopping on one foot to avoid touching the sideline, he twisted to grab the disc, straddling the chalk with one foot on the ground and the other in the air. Blissfully unaware of the rule that says once he gained possession of the disc with one foot in bounds, he could reestablish position should he topple out of play, Jeff decided he needed to get the damn thing out of his hands with all possible haste. With arms and legs flailing like a broken pinwheel, he spun around to wing a 50-yard blind crossfield huck just before he fell on his ass out of bounds. Dustin, cutting toward the right sideline saw it go up and sprinted the entire way across the front of the end zone, laying out like a fighter jet, catching the disc five feet out of bounds along the left sideline, managing to drag both of his toes about a millimeter inside the line for the point. We erupted. We'd broken physics twice on one play to take an incredible one-goal lead.

It was turning into an epic game. Needing only to force a turnover and score to win, we were feeling pretty damn good. Unfortunately as we played defense on the next point, Deaf Fred rolled his ankle covering his guy away from the disc. The dude he was covering showed great sportsmanship and didn't take off deep. He called timeout as Fred sat on the ground trying to flex it out.

Havelock Ben and I rushed over to him. Watching Fred clutch at his ankle was the first time any of us even considered the possibility of injury. We'd only brought seven players and now one of them was grimacing. This wasn't good.

"Can you walk it off, man?" I asked desperately.

Fred stood up. He put a little bit of pressure on his leg and his ankle buckled like he'd been hit with a pool stick. "I'm gonna need a few minutes."

"Well this sucks, we only have six guys now," Ben said.

"I don't want to play six on six. That's not a regulation game, ya know."

As Fred propped his ankle up on the bleachers, Ben and I surveyed our options. Mary was still neck deep in her textbook and had next to no interest in what we were doing, Ed was presently leaning against the side of the bleachers smoking a cigarette, and Cody was flipping a disc in the air decked out in a sports bra, running shoes and gym shorts looking ready to....

Wait a minute...

With one exception, Cody was everything you were looking for in a girl. She was hot, amazingly nice, and always smiling. She was also a high school basketball star from West Virginia who was faster than everyone on the team but me and Dustin, so she was a perfect option to go into the game. It amazes me that we hadn't thought of having her sub in earlier. Some guys might've minded having a girl on their team. We were not those guys.

So what was the exception you ask? All the drugs she did in high school had basically turned her mind into an invention from 1911 that constantly had to sputter and clunk its way toward a cohesive thought.

"Cody, we need you in the game," I said.

Cody's eyes bugged out like we'd just asked her to kill a puppy. "Oh no, I can't. I can't go in the game. No....no way."

"Fred's hurt. We don't have anybody else. You have to play."

Cody stared at us, then out at the field, then back at us. "I....came to watch."

It was about that time that Ed stomped his cigarette out in the grass. "I'll play."

Ben and I turned toward him with the same appalled squint. This was definitely not a fortuitous turn of events.

Ed was a short, pudgy dude from Long Island who according to legend had been kicked out of his last school for throwing a toaster at his roommate to disrupt some amorous activity he didn't feel like being witness to one morning. We all believed the tale because Ed was the type of guy you could easily picture throwing a toaster at someone. He was presently wearing a backwards Yankees cap, a wife beater and jeans. And he was walking toward our line.

"Cody, we're begging you."

She shook like a cornered mouse. "No....no....Ed can play. He's a boy."

Ben sighed and looked at me. "We're up 12-11. One more point and we win. We can cover for Ed for one point, right?"

"Yeah, we'll figure something out."

Final score:

Florida Southern 14

Flagler 12

The second game was a mirror image of the first. Deaf Fred worked out his ankle issues and returned to the field, sending Ed back to the bleachers with his Marlboro Lights. It went back and forth with neither team taking more than a two-goal lead. I got clotheslined across the face as I dove for a goal at the front cone, but managed to hold on to make the score 8-8. Then, like déjà vu, as we played defense, Jerry Gloves tweaked his calf. He came up limping and called time out to hobble to the bench. Once again Ben and I approached Cody, this time with more urgency, knowing exactly how Ed would destroy all that was good in the world should he happen to be forced into the game.

"Cody, we need you for two points. Two points. That's it. Please. If we were certain our legs would allow us to stand up again, we'd be on our knees here."

"You don't want me to play. I'm....not that good."

"Cody, you're better than Ron and he's been on the field all day."

"Hey!" Ron yelled with his hands on his knees, still gasping for air.

"Dude, she'd run right past you."

Ron looked down at his shoes. "Yeah, I know."

Cody started chewing on her fingernail. "Guys, I can't."

Almost before the words were out of her mouth, Ed put out his cigarette. "All right, let's do this shit."

Florida Southern 10

Flagler 8

On the last point, I ran up to cover Ed's guy while he and his jeans ran around after the Frisbee like the world's stupidest dog. This let my guy behind me. Southern put up a pass toward the sideline that I turned and chased. And I would've totally made the D if I could've generated the energy to lay out. But after forty-three straight points that wasn't happening. I stretched out but missed the disc by an inch. My guy caught the winning goal along the sideline.

We were disappointed, but not overly so. We'd traveled three hours as a team, faced down an actual opponent, rallied from a 6-0 deficit to come within a point of victory, and if not for having to put an out of shape smoker wearing jeans on the field, probably would've swept the day. If nothing else, it was a hell of a launching point for next year. We concentrated so much on reliving the games on the way back that we almost ran out of gas on I-95. Luckily, Ben noticed just before disaster struck and coasted his mom's minivan into a Sunoco in Palm Coast. A week later, we all said goodbye for the summer and went our separate ways. Deaf Fred, who caught the first goal in Flagler history would end up transferring, but the rest of the guys would be back. At the time, I didn't know how much better I'd be when I returned to Florida.

FIVE

In early May, I got a crappy warehouse job packing Swedish flooring displays that were shipped to Home Depots all over the country. (This all but mandated that I drive my bosses insane by talking in a bad Scandinavian accent all day.) The only saving grace of the summer was something my mom found on that shiny new information superhighway. Apparently she'd done some research on the sport of ultimate before I came home so that she'd have any idea what the hell I was talking about at dinner. In a related note, my mom is awesome.

Like most players who discovered ultimate in college in the 80's & 90's, I had to desperately try and convince my parents that I was playing an actual sport and not just inventing something on which to blame my mediocre grades. To them, ultimate was a sport from the same realm as hackey sack or competitive eating. And my parents were anything but sports neophytes. My dad was a high school basketball coach. My mom yells at the TV when the refs miss a pass interference call. Ultimate just hadn't even made it to the periphery of the national conversation yet.

It wasn't that my parents disapproved, it was that they didn't yet have a working knowledge of the game. At first, I think it was tough for my dad when he'd meet his friends down at the local bar. (The world renowned Trafford Polish Club) I imagine the conversations went something like this….

"Ya know, Billy made eleven tackles against Youngstown State last week. How's your son doing, Paul? Is he still playing baseball down in Florida?"

"Well…no. He gave it up to play Frisbee."

"Frisbee? He gave up baseball to play Frisbee?"

"Yeah. He seems to love it."

Long pause. "So he throws to dogs or what?"

"Hell if I know. Kevin marches to a drummer no one else can hear."

"That's a shame. He had a hell of a curve ball."

For a while, that seemed to be the slogan for most ultimate parents….

Ultimate Frisbee: It's a shame - your kid was so good at something else.

For that first year, I could tell my parents were just nodding in semi-confused support every time I mentioned it. But once I formed the team at Flagler, they figured it must not be a teenage phase. When I got home that summer my mom already had a manila envelope waiting. In it was all the information I'd need to sign up for the Pittsburgh Ultimate Summer League. All I had to do was answer a few questions about my experience, tell them my T-shirt size, mail them a check for twenty-five bucks and I was in. Thank God my mom had the ambition to do the research herself because I was nineteen and well….much too lazy to figure it out on my own.

In 1997, the Pittsburgh Summer League began with a hat tournament. You showed up, registered, and were put on a temporary team for the day. It let the captains see the new talent play a few times before the draft - so one Saturday in early June, I showed up at the Turner Valley Soccer Complex, a sprawling 20-field monstrosity in an isolated hollow next to the Youghiogheny (Yock-oh-ganie) River a half hour east of downtown Pittsburgh.

I wound down the hill and parked my truck during a ridiculous thunderstorm, taking a nap as everyone who was there for the tournament waited out the rain. I was pretty nervous. I was well aware that I was a great player amongst guys who had zero idea what they were doing. Now I was about to find out if I was even moderately decent around people who did. The thunderstorm let me think about it for a while.

I'm going to look like a complete doofus out there. I've been playing for two years and somehow know almost nothing about this game. How is that possible? Maybe I should just go home. Ah, crap. I already paid them. I don't want to be out twenty-five bucks.

Eventually the downpour turned to a drizzle and the familiar echo of slamming car doors told me it was time to get out and wander around. Reluctantly, I threw on my cleats, walked to the pavilion to check out what team I was on and trudged over toward the fields. There wasn't a single familiar face to even ask where to go. I just sort of hovered at the edge of the parking lot until a couple guys walking by said…..

"Got some serious athletes coming out this year. Hell yeah."

I didn't realize they were talking about me until one of them gave me a high five. At the time I was 6'2", 170 pounds with three percent body fat and 15-inch biceps. I just wasn't consciously aware of it. Only two years before, I was a gangly awkward geek coming off mono. Spending every night at the Flagler gym had paid off. Apparently I *looked* like I was good. That was a start.

I found out that my team was captained by the one and only player I'd actually heard of - a brick wall of a guy with a scrubby mustache and long black hair who looked like some sort of Sioux Warrior. (Even though I'm pretty sure he was Polish.) His name was Iron Mike and he was the captain of some really good Carnegie-Mellon teams in the early 90's. Iron Mike had a web page about ultimate back when there were all of two web pages devoted to ultimate - which was why I'd heard of him.

Up to that point, I'd never seen someone so intense on the field. Iron Mike barely said anything the whole day. He just stared at everyone with these quiet, menacing eyes that seemed to say, *"If you drop this pass, they won't find your body."* But man, he was good. Every one of his pulls landed in the very back of the end zone. He could get off an 80-yard backhand huck against an angry grizzly bear. It was amazing to watch. He was like Lew on steroids.

We were up 2-0 when I first got on the field. On my first point in the Pittsburgh Summer League, Iron Mike pinned the other team deep off the pull. I sprinted down on defense, cut in front of my guy to pick off the initial pass out of the end zone, and before the thrower knew it was a turnover, rifled a ten-yard flick into the chest of my teammate as he turned around from his mark. That opened some eyes. I heard a couple people ask, "Jesus, who the hell is that guy?" Any nerves I had at the beginning of the game quickly went away. Maybe I could just fake my way through the day by being faster than everyone else.

Iron Mike came jogging down the field and held his hand out for the disc.

"Nice play," he said, barely looking at me.

"You bet," I said, nodding like I did it all the time. I figured I'd leave out the part about it being the first flick I'd ever completed in a game.

After the hat tournament, I ended up getting drafted onto a team captained by a girl named Suzy who looked like a grown-up version of the Wendy's fast food mascot. To say Suzy was kind of good would be like saying Texas is kind of big. There are supermodels who wish they looked as good on the runway as Suzy did making an in-cut. A few years later, she played on the first USA co-ed national team at the World Games in Japan. So yeah, she was decent.

Our team would eventually be named T.O.F.U. (Team Of Fun Ultimate) which let's face it, is the type of summer league name you submit six weeks into the season because everybody's sick of being called "Team 15" or "the Yellow Team."

Just before the first game, we all introduced ourselves. Our main players other than Suzy were old vets. Sammy B was a short, quick bald guy with glasses who was always open and always on the move. He played at Georgia when they went to nationals in 1986 when nationals themselves were in their infancy. We also had a loud guy named Troy who was virtually the same player as Sammy B only with slightly more hair and a voice that always suggested he just got back from a rock concert. And I'd be completely remiss not to mention one of the most interesting guys I've ever played with. He was a chubby Asian doctor named Paul who wore braces on both knees due to earlier ACL tears. He couldn't outrun the grass he stood on, but if you lined up fifty yards away and told him what eyelash to hit, he could do it - with either hand. The dude was phenomenal. So we had our fair share of handlers. What we lacked was size, speed, and ups.

Which was apparently where I came in.

Just before we took the field for the first game, Suzy came up and sat next to me as I was stretching.

"Hey," she said. "Are you comfortable going deep?"

If I knew her better I'd probably have made the sort of crude joke that old auto mechanics make, but I didn't. "Yeah. Whatever you guys need me to do."

"I saw you play last week. That's why I drafted you. I needed a deep guy."

"Then I'm your man."

"Great. You said you play in college?"

"Yeah. In Florida."

"Cool. So I assume you're familiar with force defense?"

"Uh…you've probably made better assumptions."

Her face resembled someone who'd just stepped in a puddle. "Oh. How about vertical stack?"

"Try again."

"Really? I saw you play last week."

"Yeah, I kind of faked my way through all that."

"Well you sure fooled me," she said, standing up with an intrigued chuckle. "Seems like we have a lot to teach you. For now, when you get on the field, just guard their biggest, fastest guy and shut him down. And go deep when we tell you to go deep."

"I think I can do that."

And that's pretty much what I did the whole summer.

I learned a million little things from the veterans that year. Watching Sammy B, Suzy, and Troy, I learned how to set up a cut. I learned that hopping around with my hand in the air did not constitute open. I wasn't going to get the disc unless I was in motion. Knee-Brace Paul showed me how to throw a consistent flick, the grip, the wrist and the hip action needed to throw it fast and solid.

All that stuff would come in really handy when I went back to Flagler. But for now, I was there to break deep and play D. I think it takes getting older to realize just how athletic you were at nineteen. Because there's shit that I did without thinking about it back then that would outright kill me now. During a team practice on the lawn beneath the University of Pittsburgh's behemoth soot-stained cathedral, they taught me how to play zone defense. They put me back as the deep safety and said…

"When the disc is in the air, you go get it."

So I did. All summer. I remember many times playing the deep in the zone, sprinting the entire way across the field to knock a huck out of bounds, then taking off for the end zone. As soon as I'd reach the goal line, we'd turn it, and I'd sprint back down the field to my deep safety position. We'd force a turn and I'd make another deep cut. I happily did this all game, every game without getting tired. Eventually, one team would score and someone would jog out to the line.

"Cramer, you should take a break."

"Nah, I'm good."

"I counted. You just sprinted up and down the entire length of the field thirteen times. Trust me. You probably need some water."

I was like a border collie happily chasing a stick. "Ok, but I'm good if you need me."

I don't know where that energy comes from when you're nineteen. Or where it goes so damn quickly. Years of beating the crap out of my body on the ultimate field have occasionally made getting up the stairs a chore, let alone completing thirteen consecutive seventy-yard sprints. I just wish I could go back into that body for an hour with the knowledge I have now so I could actually appreciate how awesome it was.

Apparently I'd been doing shit like that all year. At nineteen, I just thought it was normal, but people were noticing. One of the coolest ultimate conversations I've ever been a part of originated with Knee-Brace Paul on the sidelines between games one day. Back in his younger days he played for the Stanford team that won the first ever collegiate national championship. In fact, while doing research for this particular paragraph, I came across an amazing photo of him from the 1984 title game against UMass - a much skinnier guy with better knees than the one I knew. In the picture, he's two yards in front of a defender whose left leg is in the process of buckling from the sick juke Paul just threw. You can tell he's going to be wide open at the goal line as the uncovered thrower in the foreground winds up a backhand. There's two hippies and a cop curiously watching the action from in front of a graffiti-covered frat house just behind the end zone. No cameras. No real crowd. The ultimate national championships have come a long way in thirty years.

Paul was talking on the sideline about the early days of college ultimate in the Bay Area, and where all his teammates were, which ones were lawyers, businessmen, professors, etc. Then he grinned. "Actually, my most famous teammate is in the NFL."

"The NFL?" Sammy B asked.

"Yeah, he plays quarterback for the Broncos."

"John Elway plays quarterback for the Broncos."

Paul nodded.

"No shit?"

"When he was at Stanford, he and his roommate used to come out and practice with us all the time. He just couldn't play on the actual team because he had football and baseball scholarships, but yeah, he'd be out there when he could be. He loved it."

One of the other rookies on the team dribbled some Gatorade onto his shirt in stunned amazement. "Elway played with you guys?"

Paul nodded. "I always wished we could've played one actual game with him. It would've been a massacre."

"Was he good?"

I was stretching off to the side, listening in when I heard Paul chuckle. "Was he good? Ya know, we come out here and we run around and play this game and call ourselves athletes. We fool ourselves into thinking we're in some kind of elite class. But none of us compare. None of us are even close to someone like Elway."

I will never forget the caveat he added. He laughed and then randomly looked over at me as I stretched outside the semicircle that had gathered around to hear his stories.

"Well, except Cramer."

I almost dislocated a vertebrae popping my head off the ground. "Huh, what now?"

"He was a little bit bigger, but other than that, watch Cramer and you'll know what Elway was like out there."

Mouth open, I squinted at him. "Wait, Paul, cause I'm not quite processing this. Did you just compare me to John Elway?"

Paul smiled and got up to flex out his aching knees. "Don't let it go to your head."

Suffice it to say that by that point, I was glad I didn't decide to drive back home during that initial thunderstorm. After being compared to perhaps the best quarterback of the era (and he hadn't even won his two Super Bowls yet) by someone who legitimately knew what he was talking about, I felt like I belonged on the field with anybody. I started sprinting out to the line instead of cautiously looking around hoping for someone to nod their approval.

The best moment of that year came in one of our last regular season games. After telling my dad about hucks and flicks all summer, he decided to come out and see for himself just what the hell had me so excited. We were playing a halfway decent team called The Mountaineers who were captained by a dude named Evan who looked like a big, athletic version of every 90's vegan rock front man. At halftime, I saw my dad hanging out on the wooden pedestrian bridge that spanned the little stream that bisected the Turner Valley Complex. He stood there in the shade by the corner of the end zone and watched - no doubt trying to piece together the rules as the second half commenced.

We were up 14-8 when Sammy B got open about thirty yards from the end zone. I saw he was going to get the disc, so I broke deep with their captain Evan right on my hip. I'm sure Sammy wanted to loft the disc over both of us toward the back corner so I could run it down for the score. Unfortunately, what came off his hand was a flat flick straight at the back of my defender's head. Evan slowed and turned around to grab the disc near the goal line. Sammy B slapped his hands in disgust and started looking for someone to cover. Evan had me completely boxed out. I couldn't get around him. It was going to be a turnover.

Unless I went over him. Hell, it was worth a shot.

Evan was a foot or so in the air when I jumped from directly behind him. The disc was an inch from hitting his palms when I stretched my right arm over the top of his head, reached down and snagged it from in between his hands, ripping it away with a flourish, somehow landing on two feet behind him without so much as grazing his body.

No foul. Catch. Score. End of game.

A roar went up from everyone who saw it. Evan turned and shook his head, still staring at the hands he expected to be holding the disc.

He stuck out his hand to shake. "Are you kidding me?" he said, half pissed and half deferential. "How the hell did you do that?"

I'm pretty sure I shrugged and answered with a fart noise of uncertainty. "Uh, pffffffttt."

Not only had I gone over a guy, I'd gone over a club guy who was one of the best players in the city. Holy shit.

Sammy B came sprinting toward me with a look of stunned disbelief. "Thanks for bailing me out on that piece of shit throw." He slapped me on the back. "Unbelievable catch, man."

Most ultimate players have those select few sick layouts, skies, or throws that they can recount on command - and probably will ad nauseam if given the chance. A lot of players are nodding right now saying, *"If I have to hear about Trevor's full field hammer one more time...."* But some of them are special for a reason. For me, this one ranks near the top because I'd done it to end the first game my dad had ever seen.

I remember the beaming smile on his face as I walked over and shook his hand. "So what do you think? Different than you thought?"

"Yeah," my dad said, scanning the seven other games that were going on around us. "I'd have never thought the league was so big."

"Yeah, it surprised me at first too."

"So if it hits the ground, the other team gets to go on offense I take it?"

"Yup."

"That's what I thought," he said. "I had no idea you could jump like that."

"To tell you the truth, dad, I didn't either. There's not a lot of jumping in baseball."

"As a pitcher, no. Jumping does not come into play much," he laughed.

"It looked good, huh?"

"Your whole chest was above his head," he said, patting me on the back. "You gonna be home for dinner?"

"I will probably be home for dinner. Yeah."

Now I could finally picture him at the bar surrounded by his buddies and a couple cold ones.

"Billy had two fumble recoveries against Temple on Saturday. Last one sealed the game. How's Kevin doing with his uh....Frisbee?"

I could see him taking a sip of Iron City Beer from a pint glass. "I saw him play this summer. He jumped clear over a guy to grab the Frisbee for the winning touchdown. Ya know he plays for their team down at Flagler? He's the captain. Tell ya what, you've got to be an athlete to play that sport. Let me tell ya a little about it...."

The best part about that summer? I'd hooked my parents.

As for TOFU, we came in eighth place in the sixteen-team league. I was voted to the league-wide all rookie team, which I have to admit was pretty damn cool. I think I got a special disc that I've since lost at a tournament or on a random roof somewhere.

I have no idea where Suzy and Paul ended up. I saw them around occasionally, then they sort of disappeared from the ultimate circle. Sammy and Troy played well into their 40's and continued to be bad asses. I'll always be grateful to the lot of them for actually teaching me the game.

Now it was time to bring that knowledge back down south.

SIX

I GOT BACK TO FLORIDA FOR MY JUNIOR YEAR READY TO TAKE THE ULTIMATE team to the next level. Unfortunately, it took a while for the administration of the whole thing to catch up. We had to write bylaws, raise funds, get approved by the Student Government Association, get colonoscopies, go on a vision quest out in the swamp - it took most of the first semester.

In the mean time, to get myself in shape for the season, I joined the cross-country team. And when I say my motivation was to get in shape for the ultimate season, what I really mean is a ridiculously hot blonde girl on the women's team suggested I come out to practice and I obliged. Her name was Sue and I knew her because she was in class with a bunch of my buddies from the tennis team. She ate dinner with us a couple times a week. In between munching on cheap cafeteria salad, she said to us....

"Any of you guys want to run cross-country?"

"Isn't it the middle of the season already?" I asked.

"Right now we only have four healthy guys. Everybody has stress fractures or pulled things. We need five in order to have a team at the next meet. Cramer, I see you out running all the time."

"Yeah, like three miles. Not twelve."

"It's not like you have to learn plays or something. You just come out and run."

"I don't know. That sounds like a hell of a commitment."

"I'll let you run behind me as much as you want."

"Yeah, as tempting as that is…"

She stood and bent over to get a fork she'd intentionally knocked off the table. I was at practice the next day.

My very first day, we ran 14.5 miles, starting and finishing in the parking lot of a Pizza Hut, a sadistically cruel joke I've since found that only a cross-country coach can muster. The practices only got more ridiculous from there. We ran hill sprints at the county landfill in a tropical depression. We did mile repeats in soft sand during eye-stinging red tides. Our coach would drop us off at the other end of the ghetto just before dark and say, "I were you guys, I'd get back to campus before the sun sets." Yet through all the physical and mental torture, I continued.

Sue had a really nice ass.

I was as good a cross-country runner as Principal Phil and the rest of the guys were at ultimate. My best 8K time that year was at the University of South Florida meet where I ran a 37:52. In a race of nearly 200 runners, I think I beat eight of them. The guy who won finished a full twelve minutes ahead of me. That's an entire quarter of NBA basketball. Put a Frisbee in front of me and I knew why I was running. Put five miles of golf course ahead of me and I didn't have a clue.

Either way, the mile repeats, the stairs, the bridge sprints, and the slow ten milers got me into a shape I'd never been before. By November, I was a freaking machine.

As for ultimate, we barely had to recruit. Three weeks into the first semester, the Flagler College TV News Magazine wanted to run a story on us. Word leaked out and anyone who'd ever played or thought about playing showed up at the fort that day so they could be on TV. The program was on like Channel 93 at 6:30 on Sunday nights. I'm pretty sure it was preceded by a dog trainer and followed by an infomercial for roach traps and yet the prospect of a brief moment of local fame brought out so many players that we had to break off into two games.

Of course, most of the three-minute segment was Cheerleader Dustin's talking head explaining the rules along with occasional clips of the game, which mainly showed us pissing around after a turnover or lining up before a pull. Imagine if Sportscenter decided to make their entire NFL highlight package out of nothing but guys jogging back to the huddle after an incompletion and you'll have a fairly accurate understanding of what we watched that night. But even though the finished product wasn't exactly the highlight reel we were gunning for, the overall experience raised the visibility of the team to new heights. People on campus now actually knew we existed.

To top things off, the school newspaper ran a recap of our games against Florida Southern in the first sports page of the year. Since the newspaper hadn't sent anyone down to Lakeland to cover it, I wrote the damn thing myself under a pseudonym doing my best to make us sound like a legitimate sport, penning sentences like…

"A midfield strike from Kevin Cramer to Jerry Garvin tied the game 7-7," and, *"The most brilliant play of the game came when an off balance Jeff Anderson fired a pass on which Dustin Nova made an acrobatic diving maneuver in the end zone to catch the disc and still keep his feet in bounds."*

I left out things like…

"Ed Catavagno, fresh off a menthol cigarette stumbled onto the field in jeans without knowing the rules."

I was going for the illusion that we were a sport in the same way the soccer, basketball, and baseball teams were sports. I figured giving the readers access to the unabashed truth might seriously hinder our desperate attempt at respectability.

The other thing that raised the profile of the team was the fact that we averaged three hours a day just chucking the disc around campus. Every day we needed our fix. I'm not sure what it is about winding up and letting go of a disc that makes you crave the experience like an opiate addict. On nice days, I retained almost no information from class as I counted down the minutes until I could get outside to toss.

Recently, there have been all kind of YouTube videos from guys on college campuses doing crazy trick throws, skipping the disc off buildings and into trash cans, completing all sorts of ridiculous passes through a crazy maze of obstacles. A former University of Florida player named Brodie Smith has even managed to make a career out of it. (His trick shots are so phenomenal, he's been in commercials for State Farm, Hewlett-Packard, Dr. Pepper, and Subaru among others.) As for us, we just didn't have YouTube or a camera. To try and get it over and around all the hippies, tourists, hedges, and palm trees in the courtyard, we constantly had to invent throws. Scoobers, hammers, behind the backers, overheads, thumbers, behind the headers, high release lobs, through the leggers, I developed them all out of necessity. I even got pretty good at skipping it off the second tier of the fountain, which looked awesome as the disc caught a comet trail of water before sailing the final ten yards into the receiver's hands. Curiously, that throw also tended to soak people I didn't like who happened to be walking by.

"Whoops. Sorry! My fault!"

The best thing about constantly tossing in the courtyard was that the sheer volume of throws we made in close proximity to people who weren't involved in any way led to some memorable moments. Even guys who weren't on the ultimate team got involved in the stupidity. I was tossing with my good friend Jason, a soccer-playing artist from Cleveland who fell desperately in love with a different girl every week. The other guy we were tossing with was our giant Polish buddy Tomasz, a rock-hard and sometimes rock-headed 6'5" tennis player who'd later transfer to Clemson and win the 2000 ACC indoor singles title. His serve pretty much always went exactly where he wanted it to go. His Frisbee throws did not.

The girl Jason was in love with that week was a petite volleyball player who, like most of the girls he was in love with, was way out of his league and he'd spoken to briefly once. As we were tossing one Thursday night, she happened to come through the doors from the main hotel, making her way down the center sidewalk and past the fountain. Jason saw her, forgot what he was doing, and tried to smile and play it cool. He waved. She smiled and gave a polite wave back. The encounter was actually going pretty well for him.

Until a Frisbee cracked her in the back of the head.

I don't even think she said anything. She just gave Jason the kind of disgusted scowl that only an angry woman can muster as she rubbed her head, briefly glared back in the direction of Tomasz, and stormed off.

As soon as she'd passed through the giant iron gate that led out toward King Street, Tomasz yelled toward Jason in a heavy Polish accent.

"Jason, what the hell are you doing?"

Jason snapped out of his mortified haze, pressing his hands into his temples. "What am I doing? What the hell are *you* doing? You gunned it at the back of her head!"

"You're supposed to leap in and save her! Then you're her hero! But you stood there like a moron! This is why you never get laid."

"Doesn't that seem like something you should have alerted me to *before* you let go of the Frisbee?"

"She'd hear the plan! If she knows what we're doing, it ruins it."

"It also ruins it if *I* don't know the plan and she gets pegged in the head while I stand there like a dork!"

On the other side of the fountain, I was laughing so hard I could barely breathe. "You realize that in almost two years, that's the first time Tomasz actually hit what he was aiming at, right?"

Both of them turned to me simultaneously. "Shut up, Cramer."

Miraculously enough, we never actually belted a tourist with a disc the whole time I was there. Not a single unlucky soul ever got their bell rung out of the hordes who descended on the Ponce de Leon Hotel each day to marvel at our trick throws and maybe take a brief look at the Tiffany Glass windows and intricate wood carvings.

That doesn't mean some of them weren't grazed on occasion.

One sunny afternoon, spunky little Beth, who I was now dating every other week tried to clock me in the ribs with a flick for being the delightful jackass she both couldn't stand and couldn't resist. She missed and knocked off some woman's glasses – just sent them spiraling off the lady's face and right into her husband's lap. Incredibly, there was no damage to anything except our already complicated relationship. But in four years, that was about as close as any of us ever came to a lawsuit.

There was, however, one incident that inadvertently turned pretty dangerous. Coming back from the gym, I passed through the gate to find Havelock Ben and Chickamauga Jeff staring up at a tall, skinny palm tree. Beside them was a new guy, a local who'd begun taking classes at Flagler. A rail thin, 6'7" guy with a Johnny Bravo haircut and charm that radiated for miles, the dude we'd go on to know as Tall Andy bore a striking resemblance to the palm tree he presently stood beneath. The three of them had a problem. Ben's favorite disc was stuck in the palm fronds about thirty feet off the ground. So were two of Jeff's baseballs. And Tall Andy's football.

I wandered up to them. By this time, a small crowd had gathered. Small crowds tended to gather in the courtyard because let's face it, most students at liberal arts colleges think they have a lot to do – when they don't really have a hell of a lot to do. They can spend an hour watching people try to get a Frisbee down from a palm tree and suffer no setback whatsoever to their schedule.

"Disc stuck in the tree?" I asked Ben, squinting up into the sun.

"Among other things."

"It's like a sporting goods store up there," Tall Andy said.

"We need something heavier," Ben said. "Something that won't get stuck."

Tall Andy looked around. There were half pieces of brick laying in some of the landscaping along the wall. He brought one over. It was about as big as his hand. "What about this?"

"Bricks are definitely heavy," Ben said.

Andy looked to the crowd with an authoritative smile. "All right folks. Let's get back."

Ben glanced up at the tree. Then back at Tall Andy. Then back at the tree. "Actually, Andy, I don't know if we should be throwing...."

Ignoring Ben, Andy launched the brick up into the tree. It didn't come down.

"What the fuck?" Ben yelled. "What the hell is this tree made of?"

I stared upward, slack-jawed. "Anybody else concerned that we just put a brick in a tree?"

"Yeah, we should really try to get that down," Jeff said.

Ben was incredulous. "The only thing we have left to throw is more...."

Andy cut him off by launching another brick into the tree. Once again, it failed to return to Earth.

"Jesus, now there's *two* bricks in the tree!" Ben shouted. "Quit throwing bricks into the tree!"

"Yeah," I said. "I'm thinking maybe you should knock this off before you put a whole fuckin' house up there."

The four of us stared at the tree for a good minute, waiting for either of the bricks to wiggle free and drop. They didn't. Unable to come up with a solution, we shrugged our shoulders and headed to dinner.

For days, every time we happened to see someone studying or playing guitar beneath that tree, one of us would rush over and usher them elsewhere, telling them about how we'd just been attacked by fire ants in that very same spot. If there's one thing I've learned in life, it's that if you want to get people to hustle, tell them you just saw fire ants…or a skunk. Or a fire skunk.

Luckily, a tropical storm blew through about two weeks later. When everyone emerged from their dorms, two baseballs, a football, a Frisbee, and a brick lie at the foot of the tree. We collected them and breathed a sigh of relief. Though we never accounted for the second brick, we figured if it rode out a tropical depression, it was probably in there for good. Although I still occasionally have nightmares about the NBC Nightly News anchor turning toward the camera and announcing…

"In other news, a tourist from Grand Rapids, Michigan was killed in a freak accident at Flagler College in St. Augustine, Florida today when a piece of brick fell thirty feet from a palm tree and struck him on the head. Witnesses say…."

I still don't go anywhere near that tree when I go back and visit.

So our throws had gotten a ton better. In a couple of months, most of us had graduated from wobbly backhands to a pretty full arsenal. It was about time to pull those throws out of the courtyard and back onto an honest to god field.

The game at the fort had gotten big enough that players were starting to come down from Jacksonville. A few of the guys who made the trip down I-95 every other Sunday were on the newly formed team at the University of North Florida. What started off as a pickup game for Students for Christ had turned into an actual club up there and now they were looking for their first games. We were happy to oblige, so one Saturday in late November, we took the team on the road once again.

Unlike Lakeland, when we showed up, campus was bustling with activity. They told us to find the aquatic center, and when we did, the girl at the front desk actually said, "Oh, you're the ultimate team from Flagler? Let me show you to the locker room. When you're ready, they're waiting for you on the intramural field just behind the building." I still can't believe how giddy we were that people were expecting us.

We'd even improved our numbers from the year before. Instead of playing savage, we had *eight* guys make the trip. There'd be no putting in Ed this year. Hell no. We had a sub if a guy got hurt. A freaking sub! We had vastly improved throws, a couple new players, and the ability to rest on occasion if the situation warranted. There was an outside shot we might actually get a win. We were really pumped.

Then their captain came over to greet us.

He was a massive individual, 6'7" and somewhere in the neighborhood of 270 pounds. Everyone called him Big Tim. We'd find out later he was a power forward for Florida Southern before coming to grad school at UNF.

I have big hands. I can palm a basketball rather easily. His swallowed mine as he came over to shake. "Thanks for coming," he said. "Just let us know when you're ready and we'll start."

"Yeah," I said, watching Cheerleader Dustin's hand disappear into the dude's palm as well. "Give us fifteen minutes or so and we should be good to go."

He lumbered off. I looked at Dustin. "So I was pretty confident about things until just now."

"Maybe he gets tired quickly."

"Yes, maybe he gets….I really hope he gets tired quickly."

As we returned, our whole huddle seemed to be watching Big Tim with the same hesitant gaze. "Please tell me that guy's just their coach and he's not playing."

"Nah, he's their captain," I said, trying not to let the intimidation in my brain come out in my voice. "We'll just uh….avoid him….as much as possible."

"How are we going to avoid him?" Havelock Ben said. "He takes up most of the field."

"We're hoping he gets tired quickly."

"And if he doesn't?"

"Let's uh….not think about that."

Ben sighed. "I don't think he could fit in my apartment."

Along with me, Dustin, Ben, Chickamauga Jeff, and Jerry Gloves, we had three new guys. We had a ridiculously fast junior transfer named Brad who lived across the hall from me and looked like a Christian soap-opera star, a pudgy guy from Tampa named Todd who was and still is squarely in the running for nicest human on the planet, and a freshman from Cherry Hill, New Jersey named Ryan who wore big brown accountant glasses and was built like a delivery truck.

And so on another brilliant day, we put on our Flagler whites and went to battle against UNF in blue. They had a lot of really good athletes. Incredibly good athletes. We were definitely having trouble keeping up. Much like the Florida Southern games, we found ourselves down early. And much like the Florida Southern games, we managed to battle back.

We realized that while their average player was bigger and faster than ours, our throws were much, much better. Down 4-2, we forced a turn. I picked it up and threaded a 25-yard flick between two defenders that hit Dustin in the chest as he leapt across the center of the end zone.

On the next point, Big Tim hucked one deep. It sailed just past the receiver's outstretched hand, landing a few yards in front of the goal line. Jerry Gloves recovered the disc and flipped a dump to me as I rotated behind him. I caught it and bombed a 75 yard backhand toward Ben that he caught just over the opposite goal line to tie it up 4-4. We'd charged back to tie it. Suddenly, we weren't intimidated anymore.

The first reason we did so well that day is simple. One of the guys on their team told me after the games….

What you guys call a forehand, we call WOW!

The second reason we did so well that day occurred just before half time. I was cutting down the right sideline being covered by Big Tim. Jerry Gloves lofted a perfect floaty backhand toward the end zone. Let me rephrase that. It *would've* been perfect if a giant wasn't running a half step behind me. Neither of us broke stride. The disc was way up there.

I'm positive that being 6'7", Big Tim figured he could just reach up and swat the damn thing away. I'm sure he figured I had absolutely no play on the disc. To tell you the truth, he should've been right.

I still have no idea how I went over him. I remember that leap, feeling like I hit a trampoline as I took off, then getting a rocket boost halfway in the air. His massive arm was up and ready to snatch away the disc when I came over his shoulder and grabbed it with my right hand. I landed in the back corner of the end zone for the score to take half 8-5.

Big Tim was so stunned at not being in possession of the disc that he toppled awkwardly out the back of the end zone, landing hard on his shoulder. He got up flexing his arm. We found out later that he'd broken his collarbone. He always insisted he'd done it diving for a bad dump on the first point of the second half, which is probably the truth. It's just not as good of a story. Anyway, with Big Tim absent, we really felt like we could take the game.

Our strategy was to pressure the disc, especially when it got to one of their athletic but accuracy-challenged players. Using that strategy, we forced a lot of turns and maintained a pretty safe lead. The second half was highlighted by plays like Chickamauga Jeff juggling the disc the entire way from the center of the field to the sideline. He looked like part of the Blue Man Group as he and two defenders tipped the disc off various parts of his body twelve times before he finally laid out and grabbed it six inches from the sideline.

Later on, Dustin pulled an amazing fake on a hanging huck, jab stepping toward the center of the end zone, throwing his hands down like he was about to leap. Seeing it, the defender spun and jumped. The guy was a foot in the air before he realized the disc was actually coming down in the back right corner. Dustin casually jogged over and caught the goal uncontested. That put us up 14-11 in our game to 15. We were one point away from our first victory.

I don't remember much about that final point except for the way it ended. I was charging in for a dump toss when Jerry Gloves whipped a ten-yard flick to the center of the end zone for Transfer Brad. A UNF defender dropped off his man to lay out and get a finger on it. The disc ricocheted off Brad's shoulder and popped up toward the back of the end zone. Havelock Ben was returning to the stack after making a cut to the front cone. He saw the disc jump off Brad's shoulder and trucked toward it from the left. A big UNF defender peeled off Tampa Todd and barreled in from the right. It was like two trains chugging toward each other on the same track.

Right along the back line, Ben jumped, getting two hands on the disc....

BOOM!

The dude slammed into his ribs, tacoing the disc against Ben's sternum. His feet hit an inch inside of the line just before he back-smacked to the ground with an "Oof" that set off nearby car alarms. From his back, he raised the disc and let it drop to the ground. Goal number fifteen. We'd won!

Those of us not presently lying half conscious in the back of the end zone leapt in collective joy at the first win in Flagler history. We stormed Ben, expecting him to pop up with the disc and do a stupid Havelock Ben style dance. Quite frankly, his reaction to the victory sucked. It was just him laying on the ground twitching. Considering the circumstances, it was pretty lame. I sprinted toward him.

"That's how to end the first win! That's how to end it!" I shouted as my shadow bounced across him.

His eyes sort of drifted off to the left. "Was I in?"

"You bet your ass you were in," I yelled, thwapping him in the ribs. "You are a legend!"

"Not the ribs, don't....please not the ribs," Ben grunted with deflated lungs. "Give me a minute to...lay here and try not to die."

"Hell yeah....hell....oh, shit....you serious?" I said, pulling back on my excited punches. "You're actually fucked up?"

"There's a reason....I'm still not with the.....up."

About five minutes later, we got Ben to a sitting position. He blinked a few times, vomited up some water, staggered to his feet and yelled like he'd just caught the disc. With most of the players now milling about on the sidelines, Ben finally exploded.

"Yeah! We got a win, baby! We got a win!" he shouted, holding up the disc and sprinting in to tackle the rest of us.

For the guys who'd seen the team go from disorganized pickup through to legitimacy, it was a really cool moment. The team we'd created hadn't just stepped on the field against another team. We'd actually won.

Our second victory came about an hour and a half later. With only one sub, we were wearing down in the Florida heat. Their throws were getting better as the games wore on. UNF was all over us, up 12-11 when the soft cap went on. (The soft cap is a time restraint whereby the game is played to a score two points beyond the winning team's current score.) We were now playing to fourteen. We turned the disc and were about to go down by two when Transfer Brad sprinted the entire way across the end zone to swat away a pass to a wide-open UNF receiver. It was the spark we needed. Next thing we knew, we were up 13-12 and one point from victory.

Dustin pinned them deep on the pull and the guy I was charging down to guard caught the first pass about five yards out of his own end zone. I forced him hard flick. Nearing a stall, he threw a bladey ten-yard backhand under my arm toward a guy he thought would be open.

To realize how amazing the play I'm about to describe actually is, you have to realize that Cherry Hill Ryan hadn't touched the disc one time all day. He'd been on the field for 7/8ths of the points in a freaking doubleheader for God's sake. According to my calculations, that's a full 45 points. And he hadn't made a defense, hadn't caught a two-foot flip, hadn't snagged an overthrow, hell, the disc hadn't even randomly been deflected into his leg at any point. That's damn near impossible. It takes a unique combination of rookie cluelessness, lack of speed, and pure bad luck to be on the field that often and not once be involved in the game. It's tantamount to a swimmer getting the entire way to the finish line without getting wet.

Despite the history, I turned around to see Cherry Hill Ryan clomping in toward that bladey backhand. He cut in front of his guy and got his full palm on the disc, swatting it forward. I remember thinking, *"Oh fuck, I forgot Ryan was here,"* as I took off for the end zone. The disc rolled ten yards or so toward the goal line. Dustin and I turned and sprinted side by side trying to catch up to it.

"Go!" he yelled, picking up the rolling disc.

I did as I was told and peeled off for the end zone. It was our easiest goal of the game. A two-yard uncontested flip for the win. I pumped my fist and held up the disc. We were 2-0.

We were tired, bruised and sunburnt as we headed back down I-95. None of us cared. We had two wins under our belt. That night, Ben and I hit the Internet. It was time to see how we stacked up to the big boys.

SEVEN

Mardis Gras. The name alone was all Havelock Ben and I needed to know before deciding where to make Flagler Ultimate's tournament debut. We told the guys at Sunday pickup of our plan and they unanimously approved. We set a roster with the UPA. We scraped together the entry fee. Everyone was excited. And they continued to be excited - until it came time to pony up gas money and invest an entire weekend of their lives. The Sunday before the tournament, we had thirteen guys going. And then…..

"Oh, hey dude, I have a Western Civ paper due on Monday, so…."

"Amy and I had this big fight about me going to Mardis Gras, so…."

"I'm kind of short on cash right now, so…."

"I'm not technically allowed in Louisiana, so…"

By Thursday, we were down to seven. Seven freaking guys. My beard had gone gray in four days. We'd put so much work into getting a legitimate team together only to see it absolutely decimated by lame excuses. I was bitching about the situation after cross country practice on Thursday night when one of our top runners, a little vegan stoner named Dan rolled over to stretch his quad.

"You guys are going to Mardis Gras?" he asked.

"Maybe. I don't know now. We barely have enough guys."

Vegan Dan nodded as he counted silently in his head. "I'll go. See what that shit's all about."

"Really?" I exclaimed, almost popping my hamstring in the process. "You'd have to play like five or six games of ultimate."

"Cool," he nodded. "Teach me the rules on the way. Mardis Gras. Sweet," he said, rolling over to stretch the other quad.

And so we had a sub. He'd never played a point of ultimate in his life, but he was a human rabbit who never got tired. There were worse dudes to randomly throw onto the field and pretend were Savannah Ron.

We gathered in the lobby of one of the dorms at noon the next day, watching Congress vote on President Clinton's impeachment before heading out on the ten-hour drive. The plan was simple. Cheerleader Dustin and Jerry Gloves would be leaving in Dustin's girlfriend's car once he was done taking a test. The rest of us would pile into Havelock Mom's minivan and get a ninety-minute head start. The rooms at the Motel 6 in Baton Rouge were under Dustin's name, but it wouldn't matter because we'd just get there and snag something to eat while we waited for them to catch up. Very simple. Simple like calculus.

As we threw our stuff into the van, I noticed Havelock Ben's little brother, a fifteen-year-old high school tennis player sitting in the front seat flipping through CDs. I'm pretty sure he should've been in biology class.

Havelock Ben jumped into the front seat, excited like normal. "We ready to roll?"

"Is your brother coming with us?" I asked, curiously pointing to the front seat.

"No," Ben said. "This is Tampa Todd. At least until Monday."

Havelock Brother put in a CD and waved.

On the bright side, we now had two subs. Granted, one was a gangly teenager who not only didn't go to our school, but we couldn't pass off as a college freshman without a Hollywood-level fake beard. In the end though, we figured no one would be taking DNA samples and he didn't really look any younger than Chickamauga Jeff, so we'd probably be all right.

I-10 through the panhandle of Florida might be the most boring interstate in America. It's basically five hours of the same tree until you hit Pensacola. Then come the weird little feet of Alabama and Mississippi before you cross into Louisiana. Around ten hours after we'd left, I saw the Mississippi River for the first time in my life when we took a wrong turn looking for the Siegen Lane exit off of I-10. After a twenty-minute detour, we found the Motel 6 and got out to stretch our legs in the parking lot. No doubt Dustin's car was just behind us. After a long drive, we'd soon be comfortably resting up for the next day's games.

And so we waited. And waited. And waited. Five years later and all of us would've had cell phones, but this was 1998 and those were reserved for stockbrokers and run of the mill d-bags, so we just sort of waited around the parking lot blind.

At about two hours, a couple of us got out discs and started to throw just to pass the time. Somewhere around midnight, a bunch of dudes in University of Maryland gear came stumbling out of the woods next to the hotel like they'd been ingesting things that might cause you to come stumbling out of the woods. They saw us tossing and made their way over.

"Whasup," said a dude in a gray hoodie. "You guys here for the tournament?"

"Yup," I said.

"Right on," he said, nodding like Phish was jamming behind my head. "What school?"

"Flagler College."

"Right on. Right on. Where?"

"Small school in Florida nobody's ever heard of. I assume you guys are from Maryland?"

I'd just blown the guy's mind. "Whoa, yeah. How'd you know?"

"Your hoodie says University of Maryland."

"Oh, right on. Right on. Space Bastards Ultimate," he said, looking around. I could see the light bulb actually turn on inside his eyes. "Hey Flagler College, we should like…play a game. Like right now. Like a warm up for tomorrow."

I squinted at him. I scanned the parking lot. We were seven guys delirious from a ten-hour drive and bored to death from two hours of waiting in a parking lot. They were seven guys delirious from an eighteen-hour drive and stoned out of their minds. We were all in jeans and sneakers. There was nowhere to play but a vaguely field-sized square of asphalt with a rather large drainage grate at midfield. It was pitch black except for a few random patches that were lit by street lamps. The only thing we could possibly do was get hurt, damage a car, or get in trouble. This was a terrible idea.

"Hey guys," I shouted. "Get on the line, we're playing Maryland!"

Needless to say, it was not the most precise game ever. Being as we could only see the disc in a few select places, there were a lot of drops. They went up 1-0 when a guy got behind Cherry Hill Ryan. We tied the game when Chickamauga Jeff fired a backhand toward Havelock Ben that was a good two or three feet out of bounds. Luckily for us, it deflected off the back of the Ford Windstar we were using as the goal line and bounced back into play. Ben skinned up his knee and his pants diving on the blacktop to grab it for the goal. The Space Bastards were way too baked to care that it was technically a turnover.

Ben leapt up ready to make his case for the goal. "That should count. Parking lot rules. We never said anything about deflections off cars. I'm bleeding and my pants are torn, that effort needs to be reward…."

"Ben, they're not arguing. At all."

Ben watched them jog/walk/stagger back to their line. "Oh. Sweet. I'm pulling."

They were up 2-1 and we were in the middle of a point when a friendly security guard acted as the final horn. In typical night security guard fashion, he rolled up and yelled. "Hey, it's midnight! Knock this shit off. We'll have you all arrested."

"We're just playing a friendly game here man," the Maryland dude said, attempting to shake the guy's hand. "With new friends from like some college in Florida. It's all cool."

"I'm not telling you again. You have ten seconds to disperse."

We listened. We dispersed. So the Motel 6 game had reached its inevitable conclusion. To tell you the truth, I can't believe we got in three whole points. The best thing about the game was that back in '98, the UPA had a system whereby if both captains reported the score of a game, it would count towards the UPA rankings. I ran across their sober-ish captain later and we agreed to report the score as a neutral site game since it would give them a victory and us points for a close loss to a pretty good team. So we reported it.

Maryland 2 Flagler 1.

Since this ended up being an official game, there are two things I'd like to point out. First of all, I'm betting that the three combined goals make it the lowest scoring game in the history of college ultimate. Second of all, I'm relatively certain that via that sweet assist to Ben, that minivan is the only inanimate object to ever appear on the score sheet of a game that actually counted.

Once that was over, we continued to wait. And wait. And wait. We began to think we may have driven over six hundred miles only to play a three point game in a parking lot. If those two guys had ditched us or run into something worse, we were back down to seven and would barely be able to field a team the next day. At about 2:30AM, a couple of us, now very concerned about Dustin and Jerry's well being, crawled into Havelock Mom's minivan and dozed off while the others hit up Waffle House. We'd been homeless in Louisiana for the better part of five hours.

I was completely asleep when I felt a spotlight frying my eyelids.

Thunk-thunk-thunk….

"What the…."

After a few seconds, the thunking turned into an out and out pounding.

POUND- POUND- POUND….

I opened my eyes to see the lights of what equated to an alien spacecraft burning into my face. In the other seats, Havelock Ben and Vegan Dan were slowly waking up to a cold voice.

"Please step out of the vehicle."

Ben wiped his eyes. "What?"

"Step out of the vehicle. *Now.*"

I squinted toward the front of the van. There was a light in Ben's face. Vegan Dan lit up for a second before the light zapped back in my eyes. I could barely make out the backlit shadow of a cop as he said…

"Out of the vehicle. Let's go. Show us your hands."

I wasn't totally sure whether I was awake or not as the three of us cautiously exited the van with our hands above our heads. This was not exactly the way I'd hoped to begin our first tournament. Two of our guys might well have been at the bottom of the Gulf of Mexico and the rest of us seemed to be on the verge of arrest. The dudes who'd come up with lame excuses to stay home for the weekend suddenly looked brilliant.

The cops looked us up and down as we turned and assumed frisking position against the van. "What is it that you're all doing here?"

"Uh....sleeping," I said.

"Yup, sleeping," Ben reiterated.

The cops gave us the skeptical eye. "There's four perfectly good motels within eyesight, boys."

"We're uh....supposed to be in this Motel 6 here, sir," I said. "We're coming from Florida. Playing in an ultimate frisbee tournament this weekend. But the guy who reserved the rooms was supposed to show up like four hours ago and he hasn't. They won't let us in without his credit card. And it's booked solid. We checked."

The cop nodded. "We've been having some break-ins around here the last couple weeks. Waffle House over there got robbed."

"Well, it wasn't us," Ben said. "That would be a long drive just to rob a Waffle House."

"There's a Waffle House back in St. Augustine," I said, my exhausted mind desperately trying to process what I was saying. "Not that we would rob it. We're an ultimate frisbee team. We have no desire to rob a Waffle House."

"We do not rob Waffle Houses," Ben said in agreement as Vegan Dan tried to stifle a delirious laugh.

The cops pondered a moment as we stood there frozen against the van.

"If we see something suspicious, we'll let you know," I said.

"All right," the cop said, no doubt realizing we were pretty harmless. "But you can't sleep out here. Your buddy doesn't show up in the next hour, find yourself some lodging."

"Yes sir," the three of us answered, thrilled that we weren't in handcuffs.

Our hearts still pounding from being jolted awake by the police, we stood outside the van and pissed around some more, desperately hoping our teammates weren't in a morgue outside of Pascagoula. With each tick of the clock, we grew more and more concerned until around 3:30 AM, a car we'd never seen before rolled into the lot. Out stepped Dustin, Jerry, and girlfriend Mary. Apparently, Mary's car had died on I-295 on the west side of Jacksonville less than an hour into the trip. They'd had it towed and then somehow convinced Hertz to rent them a Chevy Malibu for the weekend even though Mary and Dustin were both only 21. I didn't care how they pulled it off, just that they were alive, we weren't on our way to jail, and I finally had a floor to pass out on.

Luckily, we had a first round bye the next day and got a glorious extra hour and a half of sleep. We all woke up, gathered our cleats, threw on our new uniforms, and headed out to get some breakfast.

Yes, by this time we had uniforms. Actual uniforms that didn't make you feel like you were hiding inside a stove. They were white and Red T-shirts that Havelock Ben got made up at a local St. Augustine print shop with numbers on the back and our brand spankin' new logo on the front.

The logo of the Flagler College Fightin' Amish.

I have no idea why I named us the Fightin' Amish. Or why everyone went along with it. There was literally nothing about St. Augustine or Flagler College that had anything to do with those loveable butter churning, barn builders up north. Years later when I lived in eastern Pennsylvania, the team from Franklin & Marshall College in Lancaster, PA was called the Huckin' Amish. This made sense because it's Lancaster freaking Pennsylvania where you stare at the reflective orange triangle on the back of a plodding horse and buggy every day on your way to work. I'm pretty sure the nearest Amish person to St. Augustine lives somewhere in southern Ohio.

We could've been any number of things that actually applied to our team. *Fanny Pack - Malaria Pit – Spanish Fly - Lighthouse Ghost –Conquistodorks* - in retrospect, all of them were much better names. But one night, I saw a Dave Letterman Top Ten List of Rejected NFL Team Names and thought #3 was really funny. So our logo ended up being dude with a pitchfork and a beard ready to kick some ass.

Now getting breakfast before a tournament isn't usually an adventure in waiting. Most times, you walk over to the McDonald's, eat, walk back, pack the car and go. Well, we walked over to the McDonald's, ate, and walked back all right. But as we got set to leave, we realized Vegan Dan was missing. Being a vegan, he hadn't accompanied us to McDonald's for obvious reasons. Instead, he'd hit up the Chevron next door for a bunch of granola bars. We didn't know this, however, so as the rest of the guys packed the van, I took Ben's little brother off on a search for him.

To better understand what happened, you have to picture the exit at I-10 and Siegen Lane just outside of Baton Rouge. Siegen Lane is actually six lanes of traffic with a turn lane in the middle and a stoplight that lets traffic turn into the Motel 6, the Budgetel, the Waffle House and the Chevron. Across those seven lanes of traffic are a Days Inn, a McDonalds and a huge Race-Trac gas station. All the while, cars and trucks are zipping by getting on and off the interstate. The whole place is the exact opposite of a nice day on the lake.

To our surprise, Vegan Dan wasn't hard to find. He was standing in the shade of the Chevron overhang just sort of chilling with an orange juice and his granola bars.

I jogged over. "We were wondering where you went. Game's in like a half hour. We really gotta get on the road."

"Just grabbing a little grub here, man. Give me a second," he said, holding his finger up, starting to chug his orange juice.

"Dude, you can eat in the..."

It was one of the worst sounds I've ever heard – like a flock of geese in a meat grinder followed by….

BAM!

Our necks swung around to see a tiny Geo Metro do a 360 into the middle of the road and a giant Buick careen up a grassy little hill, take out a lottery sign and slam into the curb in front of the Chevron.

Havelock Brother and I took off toward the crash immediately as Vegan Dan desperately tried to down the rest of his orange juice. For some reason we sprinted right past the Buick and into the middle of the street to check on the Metro, whose driver door was completely caved in, window shattered, mirror lying in the middle of the street. The girl inside was probably twenty-five or so and looked to be on her way to a bridal shower or something.

"Hey, are you ok? We're going to flag down some help," I said through the busted window.

She was dazed. Her eyes were floating around. Her head fell back against the headrest. "Ok," she said, barely conscious.

Then from behind me, I heard Havelock Brother yell. "Oh shit!"

I turned to see him take off up the little hill toward the Buick. The entire front end was smashed as it sat there on top of the crushed lottery sign. The woman inside was probably in her sixties and just as dazed as the girl she'd slammed into. Her car wasn't in quite as bad a shape as the destroyed little Metro, but unfortunately, the impact had started a small engine fire. White smoke was already seeping through the vents and into the car as the half conscious woman tried to regain her faculties.

Fifteen-year-old Havelock Brother ran up to the car and threw open the driver's side door, smoke escaping (I'd hesitate to say billowing. That'd probably be an exaggeration) from the inside. For a second, he ducked inside to try and turn the car off, but didn't want to reach over the woman, so he ran around to the other side as she coughed and choked from breathing in the smoke. He ducked in the passenger door and turned the car off as I reached in and unbuckled the lady's seat belt.

"Hey, can you stand? We're gonna get you out," I said trying not to inhale.

She nodded. By this time Dan was right beside me. We each took one of her hands and helped her out of the smoky car, her knees wobbly as she sat down in the grass.

Havelock Brother came around the trunk and walked toward the woman, who was still trying to flush out her lungs. "Here's your car key."

She held up her hand and took it. "Thank you," she said, coughing.

With the older woman safely out of her smoking car, we turned back to the younger girl. We slowly approached as a guy in a red truck pulled over to help as well. He came out with a cell phone, surprising us because he didn't seem to be a stockbroker or a d-bag.

"I've got a phone. I'll call 911," he said in the middle of dialing.

I kicked some car parts out of the way and returned to the girl. She wasn't in good shape. "We got some help. A guy is calling an ambulance. It won't be long," I said.

She looked at me and mumbled something incoherent.

I tried the door. There was no getting it open. It was smashed beyond recognition, jagged pieces of metal sticking out in weird directions. As I peered in the shattered window, talking to her, I realized we weren't getting her out. Without describing it in detail, it was going to take someone with much more medical experience than any of us had to get her left arm away from the door.

Luckily at that point, another dude who happened to be an EMT pulled over. He had a medical kit in his truck. He walked up to the lady we pulled from the car. "How's she doing?" he asked us.

"Pretty good," Havelock Brother answered. "She just breathed in a lot of smoke."

"Fresh air's the best thing," he said. "The girl in the other car?"

"Left arm's bleeding pretty good," I answered.

The guy nodded, set his medical kit down in the grass and started pulling out supplies as red truck guy started putting out the engine fire with a tiny portable extinguisher. The three of us looked around, for the first time since the accident realizing our original intent was to find Dan so we could get to the fields.

"So," I said to the EMT, "we uh….actually have to get going. We have a game."

"Oh yeah, fine. Go if you need to go. I got it covered until the ambulance comes. Looks like you've done enough for them already."

Havelock Brother waved to the lady we'd pulled from the car. "Uh, hope you… feel better."

She held up her hand as a thank you as she tried to catch her breath. I can hear her later telling her kids, "And then these three boys with boxing Amish men on their chests came out of nowhere and pulled me from the car."

We picked up Vegan Dan's granola bar back at the pumps and returned to the Motel 6 where Havelock Ben was having a conniption next to the van.

"Where the hell were you guys?" he yelled. "We have less than a half hour until the first game. Quit pissing around."

"We were off saving lives, Ben. Calm down."

"What?"

"Just pulled a lady from a burning car," Dan said, munching on his granola bar.

"Probably get like some kind of humanitarian award from the city of Baton Rouge." I added.

"Shut up."

"Ask your brother."

Havelock Brother smiled and nodded. "I hope we get a medal and not just some dumb certificate."

The way we described it to the other guys on the way over, we risked life and limb to pull this woman from a car fully engulfed in flames. The more and more agitated that Ben got at having missed it, the more and more we embellished.

Whether we actually saved the woman's life is up for debate. Serious debate. If we hadn't been there, someone would've eventually come along to do precisely what we ended up doing. But another two minutes trapped in her car breathing smoke probably wouldn't have been the best thing that ever happened to her lungs. So I'll continue to go on believing we saved her life. Besides, rescuing someone from a burning car and then saying, "We'd stick around but we got a game to get to," is the kind of superhero shit you don't often get to experience in real life.

So in less than a day, we'd been homeless for hours in a state we'd never been to, played a three point official game in a parking lot, nearly got arrested, and saved a stranger's life. The trip was already legendary and we hadn't even played a point yet.

EIGHT

Our first ever tournament game was against Miami of Ohio. As we stepped onto the field that morning, we hadn't yet come to despise them, hadn't yet been victimized by their numerous and recurrent crappy calls, and had no reason to turn their college into an insult, i.e. *"Quit acting like an asshole, man. You don't go to Miami of Ohio."* They weren't yet the rival that two years of randomly being tossed into the same pool at every tournament would bring. (More on this later) They were just the first opponent.

The nine we brought to the field that day were me, Cheerleader Dustin, Havelock Ben, Chickamauga Jeff, Jerry Gloves, Cherry Hill Ryan, Vegan Dan, Havelock Brother, and a 6'3" guy named Bryan with a big 90's pompadour who looked like he should be doing nothing in life but lifting weights on the beach. He played pickup with us most Sundays and was a great guy in addition to being large and athletic. Big Bryan would've also been an incredibly good ultimate player if his hands were made of anything other than granite. Seriously, if he patted you on the shoulder, it was advisable to go get checked for radon poisoning. But he was actually cool enough to not make up a lame excuse to get out of the trip to Baton Rouge and thus ended up rounding out our nine.

So on a bright, sunny Louisiana day we took the line in our white and red jerseys. True to tradition, we immediately went down by multiple scores as we tried to run a legitimate vertical stack with about four guys who actually understood the concept. As Miami pulled to us at 3-0, I decided to switch up our strategy to take advantage of the one thing we actually did well.

"Screw this stack shit," I said. "Jerry, pick up the pull. I'm going deep down the left sideline. Dustin, go deep down the right sideline. Just huck the fuckin' thing. One of us will come down with it. Everyone else follow us to the end zone."

Amazingly enough, it worked. When the pull landed, Dustin and I took off. Jerry picked it up and launched a big, hanging backhand. Fifty yards downfield, I went up in between three guys to grab it as they pin-balled me in the air a couple yards in front of the goal line. I stumbled to my knees, realizing that two of the three defenders were now on their asses on either side of me and the one who remained on his feet was hastily retreating to cover Havelock Ben. He didn't get there. From my knees I put a backhand into Ben's chest. Goal. 3-1.

We all let out a sigh of relief. Truth was until that point we'd been optimistic, but none of us really knew if we could compete against better teams who did crazy things like practice. At least we weren't going to get skunked. On the next point, we forced a turn and I caught a lob from Ben to cut it to 3-2, but without a lot of great handlers, the rest of the game featured a bunch of throws that I'll nicely describe as "iffy at best." Despite a great three point run just after halftime, we ended up falling 13-6. In the end though, we were pretty happy with the result. In our first tournament game, we'd given a pretty good game to a state school that had approximately 15,000 more students.

Speaking of more students, our next opponent was a little school called the University of Texas.

1998 Student Enrollment:

University of Texas: 64,500

Flagler College: 1,250

Apparently, Los Chupacabras Ultimate had a tradition whereby their captain would share a good luck shot with the other team's captain be-fore the game. I'm thinking this tradition very well may have been invent-ed earlier in the day when they passed by an ABC Liquors on their way to the fields. Their captain at the time was a lanky hippie who handed me a flask as the other guys flipped for pull.

"Good luck shot, man," he said. "Pregame bonding."

Now at the time I didn't drink and for good reason. I did a lot of shit sober that most people wouldn't consider while drunk. Freshman year, I scaled the outside of a hotel in Daytona Beach to try and get to a party on the seventh floor. I was dead sober. And very nearly dead. Sober.

"Oh, no thanks, man. I don't drink," I said. "I appreciate the offer though."

"It's tradition. Captains always share a shot before the game."

Hearing the word "shot" Havelock Ben immediately leapt to his feet. "Cramer just pretends to be the captain. I'm the guy you're looking for. What's in the flask?"

"Vodka."

"Nice."

Now Ben was known for his love of spirits, so what happened next didn't surprise us in any way. The Texas guys, however, watched in awe, reverence, and shock as Ben took the flask and tipped it back. It was so smooth. No involuntary facial contortions, no shakes, no pursing of the lips, nothing. He might as well have been chugging a Gatorade. He simply wiped his chin and said, "Aaah," as he handed it back to the guy.

The Texas captain squinted and then brought the flask up to his own mouth to complete the ritual. He tipped it back. Nothing.

"Shit….this is empty. You drank it *all*?"

Ben was genuinely surprised. "Yeah. Why? Was I not supposed to?"

"Well…no. It was, ya know….we *each* do a shot. That's how…." he said, tapping on the hollow flask. "Jesus, this is all gone."

"Oh, I thought you were offering me what was in the flask. Oh fuck. I'm sorry."

The Texas guy yelled back to his sideline. "Hey, we need more vodka!"

The sideline yelled back. "*More* vodka?"

"Their guy drank it all!"

"*All* of it?"

"All of it!"

Ben yelled back at them. "Sorry! I didn't understand the ground rules!"

Soon another one of their guys came jogging over with the bottle. He handed it to their captain, who completed his shot and then shook our hands sort of awkwardly, still curiously squinting at Ben.

As their captain got around to me, I smiled. "His liver can bench press the van we came in."

"We thought this bottle would last the day. We still have two more games," he said, half impressed and half irritated just before heading off.

I tapped Ben on the back. "You going to be ok to play?"

Ben looked at me like I'd just asked him if he knew how to walk. "Yeah. Why?"

"All right then. Let's hit the field."

Jerry Gloves launched the opening pull halfway into the Texas end zone. Their handler picked it up and fired a crisp backhand toward his uncovered teammate. Just before the receiver turned around, however, I think he noticed me speeding toward him like a Pamplona bull. Obviously concerned that I wasn't going to stop, he took his eye off the disc as I closed on him. It caused him to fumble an easy pass that otherwise hit him right in the chest. Turnover. I all but picked it off his foot, saw Dustin streaking toward the end zone and zipped a crossfield flick parallel to the goal line for the score.

Flagler 1

Texas 0

As the two Texas handlers began to argue heading back to their line, I threw a smirk toward Dustin. "Well that was slightly easier than I anticipated."

"Let's get another," Dustin said.

Just before Jerry pulled, I turned to the team. "Guys, I'm pretty sure this isn't going to last, but uh....right now, as of this moment.... we're beating Texas."

I was right. It didn't last. We did manage to tie it 2-2 before they realized all we were doing was hucking it to me or Dustin. Like any smart team will do in that situation, they started dropping an extra guy off Cherry Hill Ryan or Vegan Dan to help deep. Next thing we knew, it was 12-4. And that's when I may well have chopped a few branches off one of their family trees.

After receiving the pull, we worked it to midfield, at which point I peeled out of the stack and went deep. I got behind their safety and with my defender trailing me, I sprang up to grab it in the center of the end zone. Unfortunately, as the dude guarding me tried to stop, his feet slid out from under him like his cleats had hit a frozen pond. In the air above him, I watched him wipe out. It was like a slow motion horror scene. My foot was coming down. His torso was sliding right underneath it. I really had no ability to alter my landing spot so I basically had two options....

Step on his nuts with my left foot or....step on his nuts with my right foot.

It was a groan I'm pretty sure they heard in Shreveport as he grabbed himself and started rolling around. His teammates came rushing over as he curled into a fetal position and grunted a divot into the end zone.

"So I'm pretty sure I stepped on his nuts," I said as they knelt beside him.

"Yes!" he yelled. "You stepped on my fucking nuts. Fuck, I got cleated in the dick!"

"I'm sorry, dude. I wasn't trying to...."

"I know....I know.....shit, fuck.....aaaaah!"

His buddies were just the right mix of concerned and amused as he writhed in the grass like a drunken turtle. Their captain turned and yelled to the sideline. "Hey, we need the vodka!" Then he pointed at Havelock Ben. "And keep it away from number 23!"

Ben threw up his hands in the middle of the field. "I seriously thought you were offering me the whole flask! I'm sorry!"

About three minutes later, the dude managed to sit up with an ice pack on his nuts and a half empty bottle of vodka in his hand. I helped him to his feet and patted him on the back as he pretended like he was going to give me the worst sack tap of my life.

"Sorry, buddy," I said.

He just nodded and lifted the bottle. All was cool.

They scored on the next point to finish the game 13-5, but all in all, we'd represented Flagler pretty well and showed ourselves that even against incredibly superior competition, we could come out of it with a respectable score. At that point, we had no idea the game we'd be reliving until the last of us dies was up next.

Flagler College vs. The University of Minnesota.

Now from what I remember that day, the guys on Club Sota (Now Grey Duck) were really cool. They had one ridiculously athletic 6'3"beast that got matched up against me a majority of the game, and though they had a short bench like us, the rest of their guys were pretty solid. Also, their team disc had the big red face of Animal from the Muppets printed on it, which gave them like nineteen extra awesome points.

Like normal, we came out playing like ass, but somehow managed to hang in there on hucks and defense. Three games into the day, our role players were starting to gain confidence and now weren't complete liabilities. They were only partial liabilities, which was apparently all we needed them to be. Minnesota took the first point after halftime to go up 8-4 before we came charging back.

I had two straight assists to close it to 8-6. On the next point, we got a quick turn. I picked up the disc and ducked the mark to rifle a flick toward Dustin that ended up sailing off toward the next parish. As I watched it fly out of bounds, I was sure I'd blown a great chance to pull us within one. That was until Dustin laid out with a dive I'd only seen in comic books. In a full sprint toward the right sideline, he left his feet, snagged the laser I'd gunned toward the neighboring field and somehow dragged both of his toes inside the line. He was the hypotenuse to a perfect right triangle. I swear when I remember that catch now, I see it in black and white ink with a giant lightning bolt behind him.

The Minnesota dude guarding him just hung his head. "He was in," he said with a stunned sigh before trudging back to the line.

Dustin got up laughing. He'd heard everyone on the field and the sidelines yell like they'd just seen unexpected fireworks. He flipped me the disc. "To answer the question you're about to ask, I have no idea."

"That disc was a good eight feet out of bounds," I said.

"Yeah, I know."

"You're only five foot ten."

"I don't know what to tell you, man."

From that point forward, we traded goals until the soft cap went on with them up 12-11. We'd need to somehow run off three straight goals to pull the upset. Really, at that point we were just happy to be so close, thrilled to be able to tell people back at school, *"Yeah, we gave Minnesota a hell of a game."*

We pulled to them and they worked it about halfway down the field. They got it to the guy I was covering, who panicked on stall eight and tried to break my mark with a high release backhand. I threw my arm up and got a thumb on it. It went fluttering to the ground. Turnover. We had a chance to tie.

I got the disc to Jerry Gloves who saw Dustin sprinting toward the end zone. I watched as he threw a bladey flick that was rapidly dying and falling to the left over the goal line. Dustin, who was in the middle of absolutely taking over the game, laid out, got his hands on either side of it and pancaked it a foot in front of the end zone. He popped to his feet and surveyed his options as we all sprinted toward him.

"Time out!"

It was a great call at the exact right time. Lord knows all we were going to do was end up clustering around him like hungry birds waiting to be fed. At least now we could set up a play. We huddled in the end zone, collectively giddy that we were so close to tying it up.

"All right," I said. "Here's the play. Jerry you're the dump. The rest of us are lining up vertical stack. As soon as it's tapped in, everyone digs in and sprints to the left. Except me. I'm faking left and cutting break side right."

Dustin nodded. "I'll break him for the goal."

"Everyone cuts left except me. Got it?"

The team nodded. We broke the huddle and lined up. Minnesota matched up, covering us hard to the flick side. There was nobody at all to the backhand side. Dustin wouldn't even need a great break toss to complete it. He picked up the disc. His mark tapped it in.

"Disc in!"

All five of us in the stack broke left, the four other guys continuing their cuts into the teeth of the defense while I stuck my left foot in the ground and broke back right. Dustin went low flick around the mark. I was wide open. The disc hit me straight in the chest for the....

"Pick!"

It had almost worked to perfection. Unfortunately, my defender got hung up on Big Bryan somewhere in the stack. We'd been so close to tying it.

As we walked back to the stack to replay the point, I was close enough to Chickamauga Jeff to whisper to him. "Same play but we'll isolate you this time."

"So I'm the one that goes right?"

"You go right. No matter what I say next."

As we filed back into the stack, the other guys looked back to me for advice on what to do.

"Same," I said, lining up in the back of the stack.

"Same?" Ben said incredulously from the front. "You realize you just told them what we're running, right?"

"They didn't stop it last time."

Ben nodded. "Ok. Same it is then."

Based on what they'd seen the play before, Minnesota was obviously looking for me to make the break cut - which was why Chickamauga Jeff was so wide open that nobody could've touched him with a deep sea fishing pole. Dustin faked his low flick and broke the guy backhand.

Jeff was all alone for the would-be score as the disc sailed through his hands.

He stopped and looked down at his fingers like a disappointed father, collapsing to one knee and looking to the sky, wanting to dig himself a grave right there in the end zone. He thought he'd just blown the game.

"Sorry, Cramer," he managed to mumble as I hustled up beside him.

"Hey, hey, Jeffy, play defense now. We're going to need you," I said swatting him on the back and trying to shake him out of his funk. "You're going to be the hero, baby. You're going to be the hero of this game."

He just nodded at my bullshit. The sullen look in his eyes told me he did not have a lot of faith in my version of future events.

So there we were, a single point from defeat once again. But the defense none of us could muster in the first half suddenly turned suffocating. Vegan Dan was all over their top handler. Their stud couldn't shake Big Bryan. Havelock Ben was flat out punishing the guy he was guarding. It was incredible. It felt like we had an eighth guy out there as we clamped down once again and forced a turn. I ended up with the disc about thirty yards out of the end zone. By this point, Minnesota was dropping two guys on Dustin. I figured those were actually pretty good odds so

I lobbed up a backhand. None of us were surprised when he leapt in between both of them to grab it for the goal. Tie game.

As we lined up, I could tell Chickamauga Jeff was still down about his whiff. He was hunched over, grabbing at his shorts and staring at the ground. I punched him in the shoulder. "I'm telling you, buddy. You're going to be the hero of this game."

He didn't say anything. He just nodded and pointed across the field toward his man. "I got number five."

Amped now that a victory was actually in sight, we flew down to cover the pull. They worked it to midfield where Jeff stuck with his defense and undercut his man. He reached up in front of his face and intercepted the disc a yard or so from the sideline. I immediately turned and bolted for the end zone. Seeing me release, Jeff put up a curving lefty backhand that hovered near the front cone. As I went up, my defender was so close that my right arm got pinned between his shoulder and my own stomach. It was an awkward but effective leap. I picked it lefty over his head and landed just over the line. Goal. 13-12.

Chickamauga Jeff was trying like hell to hide a smile as he jogged toward me after not only assisting on the go ahead goal, but having made the defense that led to it.

"What'd I tell you?" I said to him.

"I got number five again," he answered.

In my life, I've found that dramatic finishes in any sport don't often come without a little luck. And we didn't get a little luck. A little luck would've had us smacking our hands together at just how close we'd come to victory. We didn't even get a lot of luck. On the next point, we got an army of magic leprechauns.

Vegan Dan took a break and suddenly the suffocating defense of the last three points completely disappeared. We were barely speed bumps in their way as they weaved it straight down the field. Twenty yards out of the end zone, I had my guy covered on an in cut when Big Bryan's guy blew right past my shoulder. I planted and turned to switch, but it was too late. By the time I spun around, he was running free across the back of the end zone. I trailed five yards behind him anyway just in case something weird happened. Their handler flicked one out to space. I slowed up. There was no way I was getting to it. I stared at the guy's back, already mentally preparing for universe point.

And then I watched the disc keep going. And going. And going. Until it hit the grass about ten yards out the back of the end zone. It wasn't even close. He'd led his receiver by fifteen unnecessary feet. It was a pure and simple fuck up - the equalizer to Chickamauga Jeff's blunder. As I walked over to pick up the disc, I glanced back to see the dude who threw it practically pulling his scalp through his hat.

What happened next was beautiful in its pure ugliness. It was the ultimate equivalent of all furniture made in 1973. I walked the disc to the line. Dustin broke deep. By now they had most of Minneapolis surrounding him. I tried to get it to him anyway, but the mark slid over to block my attempt at a backhand huck so that option wasn't available. Havelock Ben was covered on his in cut. At stall seven the only guy open was Big Bryan out near midfield because his defender had also dropped to cover Dustin. He was my very last read before I got stalled on the goal line, so I put up a high release flick toward him, hoping to Zeus the thing didn't boff off his granite palms.

And for one glorious moment, Big Bryan's hands were soft as cotton. He hauled it in near the right sideline. In one pass, we were halfway toward the winning score. I was ecstatic until I realized, *"Oh shit, Big Bryan has it at midfield."*

He started into the jitterbug mini seizure that rookie deep receivers get when they're forced to throw. Everyone's seen it. On the wrong pivot foot, one arm absolutely locked in place while the other arm vibrates like a plucked guitar string as they try to aim at fourteen things at once. By stall six, Bryan had basically turned himself into a cubist Picasso.

Instead of sprinting toward him, I actually stepped back, figuring my defensive presence would soon be needed. At least we hadn't turned it over on the goal line. Dustin was cutting back in toward the stack after terminating his deep cut. Every Minnesotan who'd ever lived was now halfway in his shorts. Bryan decided to launch it to him anyway.

It was a disgusting throw. Stuff has come out of my lungs during bouts with bronchitis that looked better. It was the very definition of a hospital pass. (Basically a pass that hangs in the air so long that everyone on the field clumps up in a rugby scrum underneath it.) It's called a hospital pass because by the time it lands, someone's usually on their way to the ER.

Five yards from the end zone, both teams smashed together underneath the disc. Minnesota's whole team caved in toward Dustin, who of course leapt a full head above everybody…and came nowhere near it.

Just to the left of the jumble, Cherry Hill Ryan was standing there all alone waiting to see who would come down with it. He was ridiculously surprised when it ended up being him. The disc caught a slight breeze, flew over the nine guys in the cluster and nailed Ryan straight in the chest. He juggled it with a surprised cuss word and turned toward the end zone. Once again, the guy who'd barely touched the disc all day was in exactly the right place when we needed him.

Unfortunately, just like Big Bryan, Cherry Hill Ryan was not the ideal guy to have the disc in that situation. From sixty yards away I could read the panic in his shoulders. He wanted to get rid of it as quickly as possible. So without really looking, he wound up a backhand toward the end zone.

When I was in 8th grade, my middle school all-star team played the central PA city of Altoona in a basketball tournament. They had a kid named Danny Fortson who later went on to play for the Denver Nuggets and Golden State Warriors among other teams. I took a pass at the foul line and spun to attempt a turnaround jumper. For a second I could see the basket. Then it completely disappeared. Danny Fortson's arm swung down into the ball. It only bounced once before it went out of bounds the entire way underneath the other basket. Yes, the entire way underneath the *other* basket.

I only relay that story to give you a better picture of what their 6'3" beast did to Cherry Hill Ryan's throw. It was about a foot out of his hand when the dude descended on him like he'd been dropped out of a plane. He literally cast a shadow that completely consumed Ryan as he two hand spiked the disc toward the ground. It's still the most emphatic block I've ever seen in an ultimate game.

I still don't know why Havelock Brother was on the ground. I think he'd gotten knocked over in the original scrum. I couldn't see through the mass of bodies, but he told me later that as he was trying to get up, the disc suddenly ended up pinned in his armpit. All the emphatic rejection had done was give us a new stall count.

I wasn't kidding about the magic leprechauns.

A yard from the goal line, Havelock Brother stood up with the worst shakes of them all. Here he was, a fifteen-year-old high school sophomore in possession of the disc with a college game on the line. If he'd been a bird, he'd have shit right where he stood.

The guys from the clump scattered into the end zone as Havelock Brother stepped on a live wire. It looked like 4000 volts were going through him as his right foot danced around completely out of sync with his arms. I knew the stall count was getting high. We were so damn close. Why, oh God why couldn't it have been me with the disc? A yard from a win, we were about to get stalled.

I have to admit I didn't really see it. I was still down by the other goal line trying to make sure that no one went deep off Havelock Brother's inevitable turnover.

On stall nine, Havelock Brother, having no options and no real throws to begin with, reached in between the mark's arm and body to flip a two-yard backhand blade into the end zone. This is a pass that has been completed only once in history- the time when Havelock Brother's two-yard prayer was answered by Chickamauga Jeff's forearms. Jeff practically rolled up into the mark's calves as he dove, the disc landing in the crook of his elbows instead of his hands. When he stopped skidding, he was laying on top of the disc, which was pinned between his arms and his chest. Somehow it never touched the ground.

From downfield I saw Havelock Brother jump in the air. Followed by Havelock Ben. And Cherry Hill Ryan. And Dustin. Vegan Dan and Jerry Gloves came tearing off the sideline. Everyone was rushing to mob Chickamauga Jeff. And if they were all celebrating, that meant…..

"Holy shit, he caught it!" I yelled, taking off bounding down the field.

Flagler 14

Minnesota 12

At about midfield, I jumped as high as I ever had. To this day, the moment just before I hit the ground is the best moment I've ever had in sports. I've had bigger, more important wins at other times, but that one was by far the most special. The little team we'd put together out of a bullshit pickup game at a college with only 400 male students had just beaten a team from the Big Ten. We weren't just going to have stories of playing them close. We were going to have stories about coming back to beat them. Our three worst throwers had somehow managed to get the disc forty yards downfield and into the end zone on the ugliest series of consecutive completions anyone has ever witnessed. None of us cared how it looked. We'd won.

They were still going crazy when I finally got to the celebration. I grabbed Jeff by the neck and bear hugged him. "What did I tell you, huh? What did I tell you? Hero of the game. Hero of the fucking game!"

Jeff didn't say anything. He just beamed a smile. His whole body exuded the happiness that can only come from sharing the best damn moment of your sports life with a close-knit group of friends. It's the kind of moment that ultimate springs on you when you least expect it. The kind of moment you never think is coming in the hours after being cut from the baseball team.

And now that Minnesota won the 2016 national title, we can all say with pride that we beat the future national champions – conveniently neglecting to answer if anyone thinks to ask how far into the future.

We were riding high off the win as we lined up to face Haverford College in the next game. And weirdly, we came out smoking. The Havelock Brothers combined for four goals, I caught a big huck from Jerry Gloves, and we played pretty damn good defense. In an absolute rarity, we took half 7-5. At halftime, we were pumped. We couldn't believe the roll we were on.

This was about the time the magic leprechauns clocked out for the night. Three and a half games of running around had finally caught up to Dustin and I. Neither of us had taken a sub all day. Guys were getting behind us. They started to score easier and easier goals as our legs simply gave out. We didn't know it at the time, but the goal we scored to take half would be our final one of the game. Haverford beat us 13-7.

But the most memorable part of this game by far was a dude we'd come to refer to as "The Chicken God." We have no idea where he came from, only that as we were stretching on the sideline after the game, some random dude walked up to us with a giant bucket of fried chicken. None of us saw him walk up. It was like he appeared from the mist. Most likely the chicken came from one of the tournament sponsors, but I'd prefer to think of it as a gift from a warm and loving deity.

The Chicken God set it down beside us. "Hey, you guys look hungry. Want a bucket of chicken?"

Havelock Ben's head about popped off his neck with excitement. "Wait a minute, you're just *giving* us a bucket of chicken?"

"We had some extra. Don't want it to go to waste."

"Hell yeah we want a bucket of chicken!" Ben said, tearing off the lid.

I can not describe to you how delicious this chicken smelled and how amazing it tasted after seven hours of sprinting around on nothing but some Gatorade and a few bananas. The smell began to waft over toward the Haverford guys. One by one, their heads, like a pack of wolves, began to rotate toward us.

"Holy shit, they have chicken."

"Where the hell'd you guys get chicken?"

"The Chicken God brought it. Come on over!" I waved, looking around so I could point out who'd delivered our savory surprise. But I couldn't find him. Like an apparition, he'd disappeared into the twilight.

Next thing we knew, Flagler and Haverford were at an impromptu backyard barbecue, downing chicken wings, laughing, and swapping stories about the day. That moment right there is everything ultimate is supposed to be.

Now on the neighboring field, Wisconsin and Georgia were playing an epic game between the two best teams in Pool B. I'm not sure what the score was, or who was winning, but I know it was close. Just after Haverford came over to join us, Wisconsin scored and began to prep their defense. They were counting off when the guy at the end of the line started sniffing the air. It was obvious that the smell of chicken had reached the end zone. He turned and looked at us, spying the bucket.

"Ah, shit," he yelled. "Put the lid back on that! You're killing me!"

"Not our fault we had the good sense to lose quickly!" I yelled back.

Wisconsin's captain implored his guy to get his head back in the game. The hungry guy licked his lips and sighed, reluctantly turning his sights back on Georgia.

As we relaxed and filled our bellies, the two teams beside us battled it out, digging hard, fighting for space on every cut. Georgia put up a bomb. It hung just enough for the Wisconsin defender to recover and knock it out of bounds. Wisconsin picked it up and set their offense. Two passes later their hungry guy made a cut toward our sideline. He caught it right in front of us and looked upfield. Then suddenly, inexplicably....

"Time out!"

They had enough flow off that cut to work it a good thirty yards - hell, maybe the entire way to the end zone. Upon hearing the baffling timeout, the guy who I'm assuming was Wisconsin's captain threw his hands in the air. "Time out? What the hell are you doing?"

"That chicken smells *way* too good!" the hungry guy yelled back, dropping the disc and running over to join us.

"Are you fuckin'....that was our last time out!"

"I was going to turn it over thinking about this chicken," he yelled back, digging through the bucket. "Oh shit, can I grab a drumstick? Please, I'm begging here. You guys mind?"

"Well your hands are already in the bucket, so I guess go ahead," I laughed.

He found a drumstick and tore into it like a caveman. "Oh Jesus Christ that's good."

Their captain strode toward our sideline. "You're gonna fuckin'....get chicken grease all over the disc!"

"I do not care," he said chowing down. While both teams stood on the field watching, he devoured his drumstick in less than thirty seconds and tossed the bone aside. The hungry dude wiped his hands in the grass, patted Chickamauga Jeff on the shoulder and returned to his game. "You guys rock."

Twenty seconds later when the disc was put back in play, he completed an up-line break and took off. And that's how one of the best games of 1998 was interrupted by a bucket of fried chicken. I don't believe I've ever seen a better utilized time out. .

So our day was done. We'd gone 1-3, but showed that we at least deserved to be on the field with much bigger schools. Dustin and I realized we were personally as good as anybody out there, *and* we were bringing home stories that would last a lifetime. All in all, it was a pretty damn good day.

When I got back to the hotel room, I took a shower and flopped down on the bed while the rest of the guys cleaned up to head to Mardis Gras. I passed the hell out. Apparently they tried to wake me as they headed for New Orleans, but I wouldn't budge. Eighty-three straight points of ultimate had all but paralyzed me. I wasn't going anywhere.

They were pretty rowdy when they came back at 3:00AM. I barely moved. Because we'd crammed seven guys into one hotel room, Havelock Brother was forced to sleep underneath the sink beside the bathroom. In the middle of the night, I got up to piss. Unbeknownst to me, someone had managed to clog the toilet with paper towels before they went to sleep. I just left the door cracked without turning the light on, relieved myself in the dark and flushed. I returned to my spot on the floor and went to pass out again.

Next thing I knew, Havelock Brother bolts up, smacking his head off the underside of the sink.

"I'm wet. I'm getting wet. Why am I getting wet?"

From across the pitch-black room, I hear Havelock Ben. "Oh shit, did someone flush the fucking toilet?"

"Yeah I flushed the fucking toilet. That's traditionally what I do after I piss, Ben."

Havelock Brother flipped the light on. Water was pouring out from underneath the bathroom door. Half asleep, he splashed in there to turn off the valve, after which he crawled back under the sink and laid down. Right in the same puddle that woke him up.

"Dude, you realize you're sleeping in….." He was already out. "Nevermind."

We probably had a game the next day. I tried to get the guys up, but they were about as responsive as I was the night before. So we ended up forfeiting to some random team we probably would've lost to anyway. I still feel bad about that, but Sunday at Mardis Gras does sort of lend itself to forfeits.

Somewhere outside of Pensacola, some girls in a Mazda saw Havelock Ben's Mardis Gras beads on the rearview mirror and decided to lift their shirts. Or to be exact, they decided to lift their shirts after imploring me to do something that I now realize was kind of weird in a van full of dudes. I did it anyway, and the girls gave us a show. Vegan Dan was in the passenger's seat and took the beads off the mirror. Going 90 MPH down I-10, we had no real way to transfer ownership of the beads. That was until Vegan Dan decided to throw his first backhand of the weekend. Damn things went through the Mazda's open window and smacked the driver right in the face. Horrified, they sped up and took off. Incredibly enough Havelock Mom's 1993 Dodge Caravan didn't have the acceleration to catch them.

Havelock Ben was incredulous. "Dan, what the hell was that?"

"Man, they deserved beads. What'd you want me to do?"

"Flirt with them until we find a rest stop. Get out, hand them the beads."

"Oh," Dan said. "Yeah, that was a much better idea."

"Whatever," Ben laughed. "They were probably bitches."

Six hours later our epic road trip ended. When we got to town, we sought out all the lame excuse guys just to tell them a few stories.

NINE

The best thing to come out of the Mardis Gras trip was a simple comeback to any of the basketball or baseball players who happened to jack us about playing Frisbee.

"Shit, man, Frisbee ain't nothing. Play a real sport like the one I'm involved in which makes me cooler than you."

"Wait, wait. Who'd you beat last Saturday?"

"Stomped on Florida Christian, yo."

"Yeah, we beat Minne-fuckin'-sota. So how about you pipe down."

Two weeks later, we found ourselves caravanning to Gainesville for Frostbreaker '98. Our little team was now an actual participant in the tournament that had smacked Ben and I straight across the face only twelve months earlier. We'd come a long way in a year. Because of an article in the school newspaper about our modest success in Louisiana, everyone now wanted to be part of the traveling team. Suffice it to say, we didn't have to worry about lame excuse guys anymore. It also didn't hurt that Gainesville was only ninety minutes away. Fourteen guys made the trip west on state road 207. The tired legs that bogged us down against Haverford weren't going to be a problem. We could make a freaking wholesale change.

Anyway, just like Mardis Gras, the events preceding the games were almost as interesting as the games themselves. Somewhere outside of Hastings, Florida, as we drove down the wet two-lane highway, we got stuck behind of all things...circus folk. And they were not in a hurry. After a few miles of trailing them going about 38 miles per hour in Havelock Ben's Mustang of Death, I could tell he was getting anxious. Suddenly, he jerked out into the other lane. The two cars behind us decided to follow. Simply to get to the tournament on time, we had to zip in and out of a fourteen-car train of rolling animal cages, clown trailers, and the flatbed hauling the big top itself. You name it, we had to hydroplane past it. We almost lost half the team to deadly accidents because of…..

"Dude, lions. Slow down. That is a whole trailer full of goddamn lions."

"I can't slow down. Eventually there's going to be oncoming traffic."

"You have to see these fucking lions."

"I'm keeping my eyes on the road. You really want me to crash into a rolling, cheaply built box of predators?"

A pause. "Yeah, keep your eyes on the road."

A few of our guys would've missed a significant portion of the first game because of that traveling carnival if we weren't miraculously saved by another healthy dose of insanity.

When we got there, Ben and I attended the captains meeting only to find that our pool was banished to some elementary school across town from the main fields. This wouldn't have been a problem except for the giant fence that prevented us from gaining access to said fields. After being stuck behind the circus folk, we figured we'd be the last team to show up. Luckily all the other teams were on ultimate time, (think of a clock that's always running a half hour behind the rest of life) so when we pulled up to the locked fence, nobody was there yet. We all got out of our cars, walked up to the gate and looked mournfully out at the lonely patch of damp grass where we were supposed to be playing.

Not thirty seconds into our confusion, a voice bellowed from behind us. "Hey, don't be pulling on that gate! Get away from that gate!"

We turned to see a giant 45-year-old black man clomping down the wooden ramp that led to one of the classroom trailers behind the school. He was in a windbreaker that had the name "Coach Hayes" embroidered into it. And um….not much else.

I turned around just as bewildered as all the other guys. "We're here for the ultimate tournament. We're supposed to be playing on…."

"Tournament? There's no tournament here. Who authorized you to be here?"

"Um, the…University of Florida? I guess would be who…."

"Who are you?"

"The ultimate team from Flagler College. Over in St. Augustine. Who are you?"

"I'm Coach Hayes," he said, astonished at the fact we hadn't recognized him on sight. "Nobody gets in that gate without my permission. And you don't have my permission. So you best get on out of here."

There were a lot of baffled looks as we checked the six-page tournament packet that we were given at the check-in tent. According to the map, we were exactly where we needed to be. The last thing we expected when we showed up was a large man in his underwear acting like the bridge-keeping troll in an old nursery rhyme.

"We can show you the tournament packet," I said, handing it to Coach Hayes. "It has directions to this field like right in it."

Ben looked around at the back of the school and all the auxiliary classroom trailers. "I'm sorry, did we wake you up?"

"Yes you did," Coach Hayes said as he took the packet and examined it. After about a minute of flipping through pages, he handed it back to me. "You should've cleared this with me first. Everybody knows that if you want to play soccer on this field, you gotta come see Coach Hayes."

"And I'm sure we would've had we known you existed or had anything to do with setting up this tournament," I said. "I think we mentioned we're from St. Augustine."

Ben continued to search the grounds. "So is there like a little hut or cottage you live in somewhere behind these classrooms or...."

Before he could answer, the Swarthmore guys started to roll in. Coach Hayes about had an aneurysm as like eighteen dudes in yellow jerseys got out and started putzing around. "Ah, hell. Where are all of you boys from now?"

One surprised dude waited for his teammates to answer, and when none of them did, he grunted, "Philadelphia."

"Phila....ok.....somebody best tell me what's going on here."

I held up the packet. "Seriously, if you read this, it will tell you everything you need to know."

"Well, I didn't authorize any games on this field. So I don't care how many of you show up."

Just then North Carolina and Miami of Ohio pulled in. This only made Coach Hayes more defiant. Truth be told, there were enough of us milling about that if we organized, we could've just overrun him. We didn't, mainly because we were all aware that two or three of us would likely perish in the attempt, so all four teams simply decided to continue pissing around on the hoods of our respective vehicles.

We actually had to send a car back over to the main fields to track down the tournament director, this little dude with scraggly facial hair named Skool. Eventually, Skool rode up on his bike to show Coach Hayes a written note from the principal of the elementary school or something. Only then, nearly a half hour after our games were supposed to begin did Coach Hayes finally unlock the gate. He'd basically eaten our bye. There'd be no rest the remainder of the day.

So on a damp, cloudy day in Gainesville, the fourteen of us gathered together before the first game. Along with the familiar faces, we brought along Savannah Ron, Screeching Jon, Tampa Todd, Transfer Brad, Jam Band Todd and a couple others. We actually had a full huddle as we leaned in for the cheer we'd perfected at Mardis Gras.

"Amish…..Amish…..Amish…..FIGHT!"

Our first game against Swarthmore was surprisingly competitive considering that at the time the Swarmin' Earthworms were one of the better teams in the Metro East. They stayed about two goals ahead of us the entire game and the outcome was never really in question, although I did pull off a rare feat that I haven't duplicated since. I was marking one of their handlers at midfield and it was obvious he wanted to go deep. Our defense shut that down, so at stall eight, he tried to flip a backhand break over my right shoulder. I threw my hand up. And caught it. About a finger's length out of his hand, I just snared it out of the air. I'd never flat out caught a point block before. I was surprised. I was excited. I thought it would surely start a quick fast break that ended in an uncontested goal.

It didn't.

Unfortunately, it happened so quickly that none of my teammates saw it happen. They continued to play defense as the thrower switched from mortified to opportunistic in about a half second. He started to stall me.

I turned and started waving the disc around. "Hey! Hey! Turnover!

Run! Go!"

Every one of the Flagler guys on the field slowed to the same confused jog as I frantically pointed toward the opposite end zone and screamed again.

"We have the disc! Run the other way!"

The dude was on stall seven before any of my teammates even got close to me. I ended up with like five crappy dump options and Transfer Brad streaking down the center of the field being covered by two much taller guys. After one of the cooler defensive plays I've ever made, I ended up just chucking it out the back of the end zone ensuring that they'd at least have to work it the whole way upfield again. Which they did. We fell 15-9 setting up a Mardis Gras rematch with Miami of Ohio.

The best thing about this game was that my dad had taken a long weekend to come down to Florida to visit his good friend Dalton, a retired high school teacher who was well versed in fishing and philosophy. In the midst of their meandering bar tour of central Florida, they found their way to that Gainesville elementary school and plopped down a couple lawn chairs to watch us play. When I'd started school, I'd hoped my dad would someday be in the bleachers to watch me pitch in the NAIA College World Series. Instead he was in a folding chair on an empty sideline at some sleepy elementary school watching a sport he barely understood. And it was awesome.

Now our initial meeting with Miami of Ohio had gone smoothly. We'd lost by seven, but they seemed like ok guys who just happened to be marginally better than us at ultimate so we harbored no ill will toward them. That all changed as soon as their captain, a balding grad student type with a ponytail came over to flip for pull. I guess with that haircut, we should've anticipated his turdishness, but somehow it still caught us off guard.

"Who wants to flip?" he said, walking over to our sideline.

"Miami of Ohio again, huh? How'd you guys end up doing at Mardis Gras?"

"I wasn't there," he said. "These games are running late, so let's go."

Ben shrugged. "Fine. You flip. I'll call it."

The disc fluttered into the air.

"Tails," Ben said.

It came up heads.

"Ok," the Miami guy said, looking directly into our huddle and the white uniforms we were all wearing. "I guess we'll go lights so....you'll have to change."

"What?" Ben said.

"We'll go lights. You go darks. That was the flip for color."

"I thought we were flipping for pull."

At this point, I nudged my way in. "Hey man, all we really have are these lights, so why don't you just decide if you want to pull or receive."

"All you have is lights?"

"Yeah, we're new. And poor. We'll get red ones next year."

With his entire team warming up in pine green uniforms behind him, the turd looks at me and says, "Well, I guess you'll just have to go skins."

It was 52 degrees and drizzling. "Yeah, buddy, you clearly have a green uniform option. This really shouldn't be an issue."

"You lost the flip, so either go darks or skins."

I just laughed. "No."

"Fine. We'll take a forfeit."

Again I chuckled. "Look, is there someone over there who isn't a dickhead that we could talk to?"

"Dark, skins, or forfeit. Those are your choices."

"Know what?" I said, watching the rest of his team run an end zone drill about thirty yards away as we all lounged around. "Nobody on your team can verify the results of that flip. Ben, you called heads, didn't you?"

Ben nodded. "I definitely called heads, yes."

"Nice call, man," I said, patting him on the shoulder. "We'll go lights."

Seeing as he had no recourse, the turdbucket bitched his way back to his sideline, presumably with instructions to follow his turdbucket lead the entire game. I'm pretty sure their cheer before the game was....

"1....2.....3....BE TURDBUCKETS!"

Everything was basically fine as they raced out to a 7-2 lead, calling a few more fouls than we were accustomed to, but nothing completely out of the ordinary. Things changed once we started coming back. I hit

Transfer Brad on a 25-yard backhand for a score. Then Savannah Ron stole a goal right out of Ben's hands to cut it to 7-4. After I boxed out my guy and tiptoed the sideline to make it 7-5, they started getting really fidgety. Out of nowhere, our defense was shutting the door on them. At that point, we had no idea what horrors had been lurking just beneath the surface. Like Godzilla rising from the ocean, the suddenly close game had spawned the worst kind of creature imaginable - the rules monster.

Destined to destroy any great and free-flowing ultimate game, the rules monster gestates inside mediocre players with less than mediocre personalities. And it waits until critical moments to crawl from the slime of their mediocre mouths.

We forced another turn. Jerry Gloves launched a huck that I had to readjust for with a face up layout, catching it behind my head and landing on my back.

I flipped over as I saw Dustin sprinting by. No one was within twenty yards of me except the guy that I'd burned, and some poor schlub trying to catch up with Dustin. I got to one knee, then stood and hit Dustin with a ten yard backhand flip to cut it to….

"Travel!"

"What?" I exclaimed.

"Travel," shouted their assistant captain. He was the kind of smarmy preppy type you just wanted to smack with a shovel. "You established a pivot foot when you were on the ground."

"How can I establish a pivot foot when I'm on my back? I don't know about you, but I don't have feet in my back."

"When you got to your knees you established a pivot foot."

"Again, knees are not feet. You should really take an anatomy class."

"Travel. No goal."

"If I fall down, I'm allowed to get up."

"Not if you establish a pivot foot while on the ground."

No matter what logical arguments I used, the dude was convinced that I'd "established a pivot foot" while getting up from the ground. And to my dismay, I realized that no matter how bogus it was, within the bounds of the current rules, there was literally nothing I could do. No goal. The rules monster growled. He'd devoured another exciting play.

Luckily for us, after we put the disc back in play, Dustin easily juked past his guy. I flipped a forehand to him for the....

"Travel!"

"Whoa, whoa. Whoa. I didn't move my pivot foot at all."

"You were standing up. You established the original pivot foot on your knees. So any pass you attempt from a standing position will be a travel."

"Yeah, that's not even a rule. I'm not getting back down on one fucking knee."

"Any throw you attempt from a standing position...."

I really should've just gone down to one knee and fired the goal to Dustin through the jagoff's legs. But his clownish turdbucketry had me all flustered and pissed off so I just dropped the disc at his feet.

"Fine, asswipe. Take the fuckin' disc. I'll shut your ass down and score anyway."

The smarmy jackass and the monster inside him were clearly fine with this series of events and gladly took the disc. They worked it to midfield where our defense clamped down again. Jerry Gloves picked up the turnover. I hauled ass toward the goal line. My whole waist was above my defender's head as I caught the thing chest high and landed with a back strut into the end zone. 7-6.

Now they were really pissed. We had two defenses and subsequent breaks nullified by ticky tack or nonexistent fouls. To say we were kind of frustrated at this point would be like saying a tornado is kind of windy. On what was actually the fourth Miami turnover of the point, Dustin went racing downfield as I ran to the disc and put up a 35-yard backhand. Havelock Ben followed the pass toward the end zone. As Dustin sprang up from behind his defender to reach for the disc, the guy who'd been guarding Ben hustled over to leap for it as well.

In a spectacular collision, the two Miami guys took each other out in the air in front of Dustin, who got hit in the thigh and flipped forward just as he was about to catch the disc in full flight above them. He ended up punching the disc back toward the goal line.

Now I've jacked Ben a lot in this book about not being the most graceful human on the planet, so with that in mind, the catch I'm about to describe becomes practically mystical. Having stopped just over the goal line to watch the collision in front of him, Ben saw the disc fly past his left shoulder. From a complete standstill, the big galoot left his feet to twist back low and behind him, picking it an inch off the grass to tie the game. It was a catch none of us in our right minds thought he could make without ending up in an ambulance. And yet he did. It was fucking beautiful. Ben jumped up with the energy of a locomotive and thumped his chest. Even with all their bullshit, we'd run off five goals in a row to tie it at....

"Foul!"

Their smarmy preppy assistant captain sat there on the ground gesturing for the disc like the smarmy preppy jackass he was.

"What?" Ben exclaimed. "Foul on who?"

"You. You interfered with my play on the disc."

"I wasn't anywhere near you."

"I got fouled. Do you contest or not?"

Ben took a step toward him. "That was your own fucking guy! Your own fucking guy ran into you. He is on the ground right beside you. I'm clear over here."

"I didn't get a chance to make a play on the disc. You can contest or not."

"No," Ben yelled. "It's a goal. You can't call a foul on me when it was *your own fucking guy!*"

Their turdbucket ponytail captain yelled from the sideline. "He called a foul. Your only option is to contest or not."

By this time, I was pretty sure Ben was about to lean in and decapitate the dude with the disc. I did nothing to diffuse the situation as I came running downfield screaming my head off with a string of expletives I'm sure my dad was incredibly proud to witness. During the whole ordeal, the dude just stood there in his smarmy *"I now realize what actually happened, but instead of capitulating to the truth, I'm going to stick by my bullshit call and you can't do anything about it,"* glory.

There's a tenant of ultimate called "spirit of the game" that is supposed to oversee every match that's ever played. Basically, since the players are responsible for calling their own fouls, there's what comes down to a gentleman's agreement not to use the lack of officials as a way to gain an advantage. Call a foul if it's a foul, but otherwise respect the other team and more than anything, respect the game. Clearly Miami was not a big proponent of the social contract built into the sport.

There was nothing we could do. We'd scored, but simply because one guy didn't want the game to be tied, we lost our goal. It wasn't the only thing we lost. After that, we lost our composure. When it was put back into play at the spot I'd hucked it from, I was so pissed that I muscled up on the damn thing and put it out the back of the end zone. They got it back and took half 8-6.

At 10-7, I intercepted a pass and saw Ben break wide open down the field with nobody on him. All I had to do was put a 55-yard huck somewhere in the end zone and we were back within two. One of their guys saw what was happening. As I was winding up, he ran by and intentionally punched the disc straight out of my hands. It went flying out of bounds. He didn't contest the foul, but of course he got to set up his mark, thus eliminating our fast break.

Everything kind of boiled over a few points later. After they'd punched the disc out of my hands, Ben and I effectively told them, *"You want to play dirty, fine. We'll turn this into a street fight."* Every chance he could, Ben gave one of them a hard forearm to the back. One time when I got the disc near the sideline, their mark got uncomfortably close while he was stalling. Instead of calling for the disc space I was entitled to, I just put my palm under the guy's chin and shoved his head back. Twice. Then Transfer Brad manifested our frustration in one amazing and completely unspirited attempt at a defense.

They had a dude named Tyrone who was a high-school lineman type who'd been talking shit all game. At about midfield, he made an in cut and caught the disc. Transfer Brad dropped off his guy and a full step late absolutely clotheslined him across the jaw. Transfer Brad made sure to land on him and shove his head into the dirt as he stood up.

Had I been Tyrone, I probably would've reacted the same way. He leapt up and popped Brad in the chest. "C'mon motherfucker!"

Dustin and Cherry Hill Ryan swept in to grab Transfer Brad as both teams converged like two baseball teams running from their respective dugouts.

Out of all the people on the team that we thought might give them an over the top cheap shot, Transfer Brad was about the last guy on the list - ya know, considering he was the head of the Flagler College Bible Study and all. Apparently even Jesus couldn't take Miami's crap.

As we spilled onto the field, Ben shouted from beside me. "You wanted a rugby game. You got it!"

I followed it up with what I thought was a clever line at the time. "If you can't take the contact, go ice dance!"

Both of us were actively looking around for someone to punch.

I don't exactly know how cooler heads prevailed. I think it was a combination of Dustin's inherent calm and their realization that sans Tyrone, we as a whole were much bigger and a lot hungrier for a fight.

Fortunately, that incident seemed to pop the balloon. We traded goals the rest of the way and ended up falling 15-11, the whole time feeling like we'd been gypped out of a victory. They'd called back seven goals on questionable calls. We'd lost by four. Needless to say, we didn't shake hands after the game. And just like that we had an enemy. We had a rival. We didn't know it at the time, but we'd just set the stage for the most epic match of the following year.

My dad and Dalton left after that game, but not before asserting that we probably would've kicked Miami's ass in a fight. I'm not sure they realized that unlike hockey, fights weren't necessarily commonplace or encouraged in ultimate. Either way, they seemed to have a good time, and my father actually got to watch me play a collegiate sport. Even in defeat the game wasn't a total loss.

We got absolutely killed by North Carolina in the next game. It ended up 15-3 although Transfer Brad had an insane layout in the back of the end zone for our final goal.

Our last game of the day came at the main fields against Georgia Tech. They had three guys over 6'4" who clamped down on our hucks and were really the first team to effectively shut down me and Dustin. I had a couple assists, but got shut out in goals for the first time all season as we dropped the game 15-5 to go winless on the day.

In the end though, it was a successful first season. Counting the parking lot game, we ended up 3-8, but put our foot in the door nationally, beat a huge school, and came out of the whole thing with some incredible stories. It was about all a bunch of jackasses from a tiny school on the beach could ask for.

Dustin was graduating, so that was going to be a huge loss, but the rest of the team was coming back. I was confident we were going to be even better for my senior year as I headed back home for the summer.

I returned to the warehouse where I'd packed Swedish flooring displays the previous summer. On my second day of work, I ended up at the end of the assembly line, stacking 240-pound boxes of refrigerator parts onto a skid that the forklifts would eventually deliver to the loading bay. With about five minutes left before the whistle, the dude across from me tripped over an air hose as we were placing a box on the skid. He pushed the whole thing toward me, pinning my right leg against the six other boxes we'd already stacked. With 240 pounds on my groin, I tried to spin away, but my leg didn't move. My hip flexor, groin, and inguinal ligament ripped like a paper bag. It would be almost eight months before I took the field again.

TEN

It was a long eight months. The first four were spent rehabbing from the accident and subsequent hernia surgery. The shredded ligament in my hip was the one that allowed me to lift my right leg in the air. From May until September, if I was downstairs at my parents' house and needed to get up to the kitchen, I had to put my hand underneath the back of my knee and physically lift my right leg into position fourteen times until I reached the second floor.

Twice a week I'd drive out to Forbes Hospital in Monroeville, PA where the physical therapist would have me do various painful things in between the heat pack at the beginning of the session and the ice pack at the end. At first, I was simply trying to ride a stationary bike for ninety seconds without screaming. For a twenty year old who was used to sprinting past and jumping over people, it was a depressing situation. There were times I needed a cane just to make it down the hall. I'm pretty sure the World War II vets and car accident victims that surrounded me in the rehab center could've taken me deep.

My surgery wasn't until August, only three weeks before I was set to return to school for my senior year. Considering I'd be laid up in bed unable to move for one of those weeks, I decided it would be best to stay in Pennsylvania an extra four months to rehab. I wouldn't return to Florida until the spring semester. The only thing that kept me going was a mental picture of a disc in the air as it sailed over the turrets of the fort. Every time my leg caught fire halfway through some resistance exercise, I floated away into a warm Sunday morning, laughing with that stupid group of guys as we ran around like idiots. I didn't realize how much I missed it until it was gone.

Being twenty, I actually healed pretty quickly. By mid September, the stairs problem had gone away and I was actually able to lie on my back and lift my leg straight up with a five-pound ankle weight strapped to it. Considering where I'd started from, it was pretty momentous. At the beginning of October, the doctor cleared me for all physical activity.

So I ran. Everywhere. I was so happy to be able to run that I just sprinted around the neighborhood. I sprinted up the stairs. I sprinted to my truck. I hit the gym in the basement of my chiropractor's office two hours a day five times a week. All I could see ahead of me was a disc. I wanted to be back. I wanted to be better than I was before my hip got pinned by 240 pounds of Frigidaire parts.

I can't tell you how long that eight months trapped at home seemed. I love my city, but Pittsburgh winters are dismal. The morning I hopped into my truck and headed south was about the most liberated I'd ever felt. Two Sundays later, I was so excited for pickup that I got there a half hour before everyone else, virtually attacking Havelock Ben when he showed up.

"Let's throw!"

"Can you let me put on my shoes?"

"No. Go deep."

Ben had done a hell of a job recruiting. We had over twenty guys out there, including some dudes my absence hadn't yet allowed me to meet. We now had a short handler named Corey who'd played in high school in Harrisburg, a tall, long-haired snowboarder from Colorado named Ryan, a lanky congressman type from Columbus, Ohio who we'd later go on to call Goose, a big Jersey redhead we nicknamed Opie, a kid from Baltimore I'll call Rocky because he looked exactly like Sylvester Stallone, and a mountain of a guy from Orlando whose last name was actually Beer. Every one of them was good. I could barely believe it.

I didn't dominate the pickup game that day like I normally did. Having not played in months, I got winded and I was still a little timid to lay out or accelerate. My leg was tight, and as we got into the second game it definitely got sore. I was going to need the ice pack later. But I didn't care. I was back out where I belonged, flinging the disc around next to the bay.

After the game, I went and sat alone on the seawall, staring out over the glistening water, recalling my battles with the sand weights and Cybex machines under the hard florescent lights of the rehab center. And now there I was, in the future that I'd envisioned, flipping my disc into the air as pelicans glided over a tour boat. I was back home. I must've sat there for two hours. All the pain and agony had been worth it.

From back in Pittsburgh, I'd helped Ben arrange our second trip to Mardis Gras. We didn't have to worry about lame excuse guys this time. We had a full team going. In fact the only guy we were concerned about was the best player on the team now that Dustin had graduated. That player was Tall Andy, who we'd first met tossing bricks into the courtyard palm tree.

Tall Andy could charm you out of the keys to your car. Because of this skill, he never paid rent....anywhere. After the abandoned motel he was living in out at the beach finally got condemned, he was notorious for bouncing from couch to couch around St. Augustine. With a smile, he'd drink your milk, watch your cable, and pet your dog until you got sick of a guy on your couch - after which, he'd smile at someone new, pack up his stuff and go drink their milk, watch their cable, and pet their dog. But that was just Andy. Nobody ever really got mad at him. After a while they just said, "Hey Andy, it's about time I got some rent or you found somewhere else to crash."

And so he'd find somewhere else to crash.

Tall Andy was always at pickup. Always. And twice a week, he'd show up at my door with a disc, knock like a madman and yell, "Let's hit the beeeeach!" I'd drop whatever I was doing and we'd go spend hours throwing 80-yard hucks to each other over the ocean, showing off our kick tips, cartwheel catches, and 360 between the legs grabs for the bikini clad women of St. Augustine Beach. I'd complete every difficult catch imaginable while chubby old Italian guys were watching, but as soon as a good looking blonde walking her dog happened by, I'd overcompensate and the disc would smack me square in the ass - or the neck - or the junk - whatever would make me look the stupidest. Inevitably as she got closer to Andy, he'd jump over the disc, back heel it up to himself and pin it against his head like a hat. The girl would comment on how awesome it was. Andy would end up petting her dog. And for a week he'd be drinking her milk and watching her cable.

The year before, we thought he was coming to Mardis Gras. And he just didn't show up that day. Then we thought he was coming with us to Gainesville. And he just didn't show up that day.

The night before we were going to leave, I was lying in bed with April, the little hippie girl from Long Island I'd just started dating. We were about ready to fall asleep when suddenly it occurred to me, I better go made sure Andy's going to show up tomorrow like he said he would.

Anyway, April, being a cool hippie chick who was also quite aware of Tall Andy's tendency to vanish, agreed to help me find him. The only problem was that it was almost midnight. And I only sort of knew where he was crashing at the time because of a brief stop we'd made one Sunday between pickup and the beach. All I knew was he presently lived in the backwoods near I-95 somewhere. And that the driveway made a semicircle around a fire pit.

So there I was with a girl I'd been dating all of a week, wandering the trailer parks off state road 207 looking for the house where Andy may or may not currently be residing. After about forty-five minutes, we came upon a white doublewide with a similar driveway to the one I remembered. It was like 12:24 AM and we were a good three miles out of town. Outside was the color of a Goodyear Tire.

April looked at me. "This is the place?"

"I think. Probably. It might be."

"You have to be sure. It's after midnight. If you're wrong, we'll be shot by rednecks."

"I'm pretty sure. Yeah. This is….uh…." I wasn't sure at all. "definitely it," I said stepping out of the truck.

April ducked down into the seat. "Oh my God, don't leave me alone."

"You can come with me."

"Are you crazy? I'm not leaving the truck."

It really was the type of scene the police clean up in the morning. I was approaching a strange trailer in the dead of night, about to just rap on the door. That situation alone should tell you how good Tall Andy was at ultimate. Luckily, the screen door was open and the guy who lived there was still up watching Letterman. The television was making the living room flicker as I approached. As April reclined the passenger's seat to avoid detection, I tried to calculate the probability of ending up with a shotgun in my face. I took a deep breath....and knocked.

The guy in the recliner bolted up. I tried to reassure him through the screen. "Hi there. Hey, don't mean to scare you. Sorry. Sorry."

Luckily, he was more of a free love sort of redneck than a shoot first and figure it out later sort of redneck. He did not look like he was reaching for a shotgun.

"Yeah?"

"I'm looking for a guy named Andy. I think this is where he was staying."

He slowly walked over and opened the door. This was the moment of truth.

"Oh. You're one of Andy's friends? Yeah, he's staying here a while. Don't know where he went. You want to wait for him, come on in and grab a beer."

I breathed a sigh of relief as I stepped inside. While I was still voluntarily walking into a stranger's trailer, I hadn't yet had my brains splattered against the screen door, so things were looking up. "Oh, no. Don't need a beer. Thanks. Just need to leave him a note is all."

I probably spent five minutes inside while April panicked in the truck. When Andy came back, this note was left on the couch for him.

Andy,
I know where to find you. Show up tomorrow.
Cramer

At noon, we all waited, wondering if Tall Andy would be joining us. I hoped the note had worked, but you never knew if he'd even come back "home" that night. Then, to our delighted surprise at 11:58, he came striding up to my truck and threw his bag in the back with a smile.

"Let's get on the road, boys!"

To accurately picture what happened as we were driving into an elongated dusk somewhere west of Tallahassee, you need to know the design of my 1993 Chevy S-10. There were three of us in the cab of my truck on the road to Baton Rouge that day. Two of us were sitting very comfortably. One was not. There was a bucket seat that actually folded out of the side wall of my cab, designed to provide an extra seat for a tiny human being on a very short trip. Whoever sat there had to face sideways instead of forward. April was like 5'2" and 100 pounds. She sat back there on a few trips to Wal-Mart and didn't have a problem. It was definitely not designed for a wide-bodied guy like Cherry Hill Ryan to be crammed in behind the 6'7" Tall Andy on a ten-hour trip to Louisiana.

Somewhere in the nothing between Tallahassee and Pensacola, I got into the left lane to pass a minivan sporting a Florida State decal. Turned out, the van was filled with what I'm assuming were FSU sorority girls on their way to Mardis Gras for the weekend. As we passed them, Tall Andy smiled and waved. That was all it took. Andy had charmed them at eighty-five miles per hour.

I didn't realize what he'd done until about a mile later when they came roaring up on the left. I was in the middle of telling Andy about all the shit that happened the year before when his eyes lit up. His mouth dropped. He started blinking rapidly.

"What?" I said.

"Um….that girl just flashed us."

"Are you kidding?" I said.

By now the van had pulled directly in front of us. "Girl in the passenger's seat. Boom, pulled up her shirt."

"No she…."

And then from about five yards ahead, I-10 became a rolling Bourbon Street. Three hot brunettes smushed themselves together against the back windshield and in one perfect moment that jackknifed an eastbound tractor trailer, simultaneously pulled up their tank tops. Behind them, a couple unicorns slid down a rainbow.

"Holy shit!" I exclaimed.

"Wow," Andy said, nodding. "I like it."

From the bucket seat, Cherry Hill Ryan was straining his neck to see anything. "What's happening?"

"Three hot brunettes are dancing topless for us in the back of this van," I said, slack jawed.

"What? Fuck! I can't see!" he yelled, dislocating his axis vertebrae in an attempt to peer around Tall Andy. "I can't see anything! At least describe it for me."

"This is amazing."

Andy echoed my sentiment. "This is truly amazing."

"That's not a description! That doesn't help me in any way!"

After a good thirty seconds, the brunettes put their shirts down and moved away from the back windshield. "Shit, Ryan. It's over. You missed it. Wait....wait, no, oh Jesus, now there's two blondes and...."

"Oh yes," Andy said. "These girls are beautiful, Ryan, it is really a shame you're missing this."

"Andy, move the seat up! Move the seat up!"

"The one girl is, oh....Ryan, she's slipping off her jeans...."

"Damn it, this fucking seat's in the way....Andy, c'mon...can you angle the mirror somehow? Shit!"

This went on for a good three miles. It was like being at a moving strip club as all seven girls in that van warmed up for Mardis Gras. All because Andy waved at them. I swerved the truck all over the interstate, honking my appreciation. We passed them again and even the driver flashed us. Ryan pinched a nerve and yet the only rack he saw was attached to the roof of the van. Once again, Mardis Gras was epic and we hadn't yet played a point.

ELEVEN

APPARENTLY SOMEWHERE IN THE COUNTRY, LARGE YELLOW ROAD SIGNS ARE needed to warn motorists to be on the lookout for men on horseback. These men are depicted by a featureless black stick figure riding a featureless black horse. We came into possession of one such sign through means that I'm sure were completely legal on all fronts. An art major we knew added features like a hat and an Amish beard to the stick figure and stenciled the words "Flagler College Fightin' Amish" in the reflective yellow paint. As Havelock Ben and Goose were bringing it up the stairs of the Motel 6, a few guys from Notre Dame saw it and immediately adopted them as brothers - the adoption process involving a few cases of Miller Light. This, combined with the fact that one of our cars took a detour to New Orleans on the way into town made Saturday morning at Mardis Gras feel a lot more like Sunday morning. Before we'd put one foot on the field, more than half our guys were already wearing shades and chugging Pedialyte.

It was brilliantly sunny but brisk that morning, and luckily we got a first round bye, allowing everyone to recover. When Ben and I got there, we headed to the captain's meeting, picked up our information packet and looked at our pool.

Flagler College, University of Toronto, Washington University and…. are you freaking kidding me…..Miami of Ohio.

Ben dropped the packet and smacked his hands together. The beers from the night before had barely phased him. "Oh, it's on now. I don't care what else happens today as long as we stomp those fuckers into the ground."

It had been nine months since we'd last seen them and the mere thought of occupying the same field again was turning his face the color of molten steel.

Unfortunately during the bye we almost lost a guy. Because we'd been adopted by Notre Dame, we figured we'd head over and lend our loud and unabashed support as they battled Wisconsin. You wouldn't think cheering from the sidelines would be particularly dangerous - but this was Flagler Ultimate and weird shit followed us around like a puppy. One of the new guys, Beer, was sitting in a folding chair enjoying a thermos full of coffee, trying to rebound from the previous night when a pass went up toward the sideline.

The right wing in Wisconsin's smothering zone came flying over and laid out like he should've been sporting a cape. Just in front of the Notre Dame receiver, he swatted the disc out of bounds for an amazing D - and flew like a missile straight into Beer's chest. Coffee went everywhere as Beer's thermos spiraled off toward Arkansas. His folding chair snapped in half, bits of metal and plastic exploding as the two of them crashed to the ground in an epic collision not often seen outside of gladiator movies. We thought Beer was dead.

The two of them just lay there for a few seconds like worms after a rainstorm until to our absolute amazement, Beer cracked his neck and stood up.

"Anyone see my coffee?"

Behind him, a few of us were trying to help the Wisconsin guy off the ground as Beer picked up his demolished chair.

"Oh man, this is completely busted," he said glancing back to the punch-drunk Wisconsin guy. "That was a nice play. You all right?"

The dude stumbled forward and leaned on Beer a moment while he caught his breath. "What the hell are you made of?"

Havelock Ben laughed. "Beer. You just hit two hundred forty pounds of Beer."

Wisconsin chuckled. "Guess I gotta drink more," he said, shuffling back onto the field. "I'm gonna need a sub."

Already, the tournament was starting to develop eerie similarities to the year before. Not only were we matched up against Miami of Ohio, but we'd once again managed to bring a Wisconsin game to a grinding halt. And as everyone knows, weird crap like that comes in threes.

We were down 12-3 to the University of Toronto in our first game when I broke toward the end zone. Ben put up an outside-in backhand that curved over my head. My defender was trailing me as we both leapt. It was over the wrong shoulder, so I had to whip my body around in the air to two-hand grab it just in front of my face. As I did, my left heel swung back and….for the second year in a row, I sent a guy to the sidelines with an ice pack on his nuts. Dude dropped out of the air like a sack of flour.

Ben ran down to see what happened as the guy rolled around in agony beside us. "Again?" he said.

"Again," I answered.

"I am never guarding you in Louisiana."

Anyway, after a 15-5 loss that let all our rookies get accustomed to the speed of a tournament game, we were now ready to stare down the devil. As we circled up before the Miami game, I was going to launch into a biting tirade about what turdbuckets they were for all the guys who hadn't been there for the near brawl the year before. Then I thought better of it. We didn't need the game to be chippy. We didn't need to ramp up the animosity. Maybe Miami would be ok this year. There was always a chance it would be a fun and spirited game.

"Ok, so last year we had some problems with these guys. But…"

As I was talking, a few of them jogged by our huddle. Their smarmy captain laughed to a couple of his teammates. "Just treat this game like practice. We're going to roll these guys," he said like the preppy villain in pretty much every 80's teen movie.

Hearing this, Havelock Ben almost caught fire. "Practice? Are you freaking kidding me? That's the same….that's the same fucker who stole my goal! Fuck the game, I'm just going to go over and beat that kid."

"As you can see, there's some underlying hostility because they kind of screwed us last year, so…"

By this point, Ben had combusted. "Kind of screwed us? They kind of screwed us in the way that Germany kind of screwed Poland! These guys are evil fascists whose only purpose in life is to destroy the very foundation of civilization. They must be stopped in any way possible, preferably by stomping them into the ground and spitting on their corpses."

I nodded. "Yeah, that about sums it up." It was going to be chippy.

We rallied around our road sign, holding it up and banging on it with our fists, making one hell of a racket.

"Amish, Amish, Amish….fight!"

From the beginning, it was a stilted game with an odd wind that would just sort of show up out of nowhere every couple minutes. Our throws weren't great, but our defense was. Tall Andy put every pull into the back of the end zone. They'd work it to midfield before one of their throws would hang just enough for Goose, Beer, or Opie to get there and swat it. We took a 1-0 lead. They tied it. We went up 2-1. They tied it. Then I cut in front of my guy at the goal line to smack down a pass to the corner. Seeing nothing but green ahead of me, I took off. Andy picked it up. I wasn't even to midfield yet when he let it go.

Now the Toronto game had been a real test for my leg. A month of playing at the fort was a decent warm up, but it could in no way duplicate being on the field against a top-level opponent. (Torontula would win the Canadian University Championship the following year.) And I'd done ok. Not great, but ok. I had two goals and an assist, but I'd still been scared to accelerate, feeling like my ligament might just tear in half if I pushed it too hard. But this was different. This was Miami of Ohio. There was no such thing as pushing too hard. I was going to get there if I had to leave my leg in the end zone.

I swear I was still thirty yards away when the disc crossed the goal line. And it hung. It hung long enough for me to think that maybe – just maybe if I kept sprinting, I'd be able to lay out for it. It hung a little longer. It hung just long enough that if I really hit the turbo, I might even be able to baseball slide underneath it. I crossed the goal line. It hung a little longer. I wasn't even going to have to dive. It hung like it was on a string until I pancaked it in front of my chest on a dead sprint two steps inside the back line to take a 3-2 lead. When I turned back to look, there was no one within fifty yards of me. Heaving, I dropped the disc and thanked everyone at Forbes Hospital for pushing me through the pain. I was back. I was fast again. And now I knew it.

At 5-5, we forced a turn and I peeled deep again. Three of their guys saw me go and dropped. Tall Andy launched it anyway. It was one of the most perfect throws I've ever seen. I'd gotten a step behind all of them and with two guys on my back and another guy coming in from the left, Andy's 60 yard backhand bomb dropped in over all of them. I leapt and spun to shield the disc from the triangle of defenders, grabbing it in front my no longer busted right hip for the goal. 6-5.

Now they were down. Now they were getting nervous. So….

"Pick! Travel! Foul! Pick! Travel! Foul! Foul! Pick! Travel!"

So much for practice.

Luckily we'd brought along a secret weapon in the form of two little Italian guys named Tony and Sheppy. I still have no why they were there. I think they were Rocky's suitemates who decided to come to Mardis Gras because he had some extra room in his Jeep and they had nothing to do for the weekend. Honestly, both of them sort of resembled ventriloquist dummies from South Jersey come to life. And neither of them were playing, so they were free to dip into the cooler, get drunk and heckle. And heckle they did.

"Hey, that call sucked you preppy jerk!"

"Hey, that call sucked…almost as much as your sister!"

"Hey, that call sucked. Ohio sucks. Everything about you sucks!"

I didn't say they were great heckles. But knowing their calls were going to get roasted by our sideline allowed all of us on the field to concentrate on actually playing the game.

Because of their plethora of calls, a few arguments, the wind, some time outs, and a couple injuries, the soft cap actually went on before halftime with the game tied 7-7. First team to nine goals won. I lost my guy in the back of the end zone and caught my fifth goal of the game to make it 8-7. We were on defense, one point from an immensely satisfying victory when they put up a flick toward the guy I was guarding. I leapt over him and swatted it lefty out the back of the end zone to give us a great chance at….

"Foul!"

"Are you freaking kidding me? I didn't touch you."

"When you came down, you landed on me."

"After I leapt over your head and owned you, I bumped you when I landed, yes. That had no bearing on the play."

"You're not allowed to contact me. It's a foul."

I just shook my head. It didn't even pay to be angry at this point. "Contest."

From the sideline came, "Hey, that call sucked you piece of suck!"

Tony and Sheppy were somewhat intoxicated.

After that awful call, they got the disc back and punched it in, setting up the ultimate grudge universe point. A single point to exact revenge. A single point to prove we were more than just practice.

Havelock Ben got us together on the line. "I don't care what they call. What they say. What they do. We're going to take that disc, ram it down their throats and win this fucking game!"

I just nodded. "Again, that pretty much sums it up, yeah. Thanks, Ben."

Their pull was terrible and went out of bounds ten yards past midfield. Tall Andy brought it to the center of the field where we put it into play and meticulously worked it to a within a few yards of the goal line. I dumped it to Andy. His long spider legs allowed him to step around the mark and fire one to Opie cutting across the front of the end zone.

We'd done it! We'd slayed the....

"Pick!"

Of course there was. We didn't expect it to be easy. We all caught our collective breath and set up. Off the reset, Andy dumped it to me. Opie cut to the front cone. I zipped a forehand that hit him right in the chest for the.....

"Pick!"

And that was two winning goals disallowed. Instead of getting pissed, we actually got more determined. Off the reset, I flipped it back to Andy and made a scooter cut into the end zone. He and his ridiculous legs stepped around the mark. I caught a backhand flip just across the line for a...

"Travel!"

I dropped my head with a disgusted chuckle and flipped the disc back, now seriously wondering whether they'd ever let us score to end this godforsaken game. As I reset, I got right up in the ear of the guy who'd made the call. "He's six foot seven. Trust me, he doesn't need to travel to get around your scrawny ass."

The kid didn't even look at me. "It was a travel."

And so on our fourth try at victory, Andy tapped the disc back in play. I came off the goal line to try and give him a dump option, but he looked me off and flipped it three yards upfield to Opie. I took off on a big swing around the back of the stack hoping for a continuation cut. While I was circling, Colorado Ryan and his camouflaged bandana shook free and cut to the center of the end zone. Opie saw him. He put a flick about a foot off the ground. Colorado Ryan went to his knees just across the goal line to haul it in.

Our whole team paused for a moment waiting for the inevitable call. All we heard was glorious silence. And then we erupted. Our sideline screamed with such unanticipated fury during a 2nd round pool play game that it actually caused a turnover in the Winona State vs. Iowa game next to us. I'm not kidding, every field stopped and turned to watch, trying to figure out what the hell had just happened.

Havelock Ben bolted in and tackled Colorado Ryan. So did Opie. What followed was the only time I've ever experienced the jubilant pile of bodies that happens at the end of every World Series. The tension that we'd carried from the year before right through all their calls to end the game came roaring out in one incredible moment of unrestrained celebration. We may as well have won the whole damn tournament right there.

Ben started yelling at them as they sulked away. "How do you like practice now? How do you like practice now?"

At this point I may or may not have flipped them the bird. "Call a foul on that," I may or may not have yelled. I may or may not have had a lot to learn about winning with class.

Inspired by our theatrics, Beer and Goose ran to the middle of the field and slammed our Amish road sign into the grass like they were claiming the field for their clan. Ben was yelling like a madman as he tore off toward the tent that housed the tournament bracket.

I euphorically chased him. About all I could think to muster was,

"Hell yeah! Hell yeah!"

"Someone get me a marker!" Ben shouted toward the volunteer behind the tent. The dude somewhat hesitantly handed one over. Under
Pool E, he wrote our score on the white poster board and circled it about
ninety times.

Flagler 9

Miami of Ohio 8

I really wish we'd have thought to take that damn thing home. I'd have
framed it.

Anyway, after the elation of that victory, most of the team couldn't
help but pop open the cooler and throw back a well-earned beer or five.
The only problem was we still had a game left. I'm pretty sure that me
and Cherry Hill Ryan were the only sober guys on the field as we fell to
Washington 12-2. Cherry Hill Ryan dropped a couple wide-open hammers in the end zone, so perhaps sobriety wouldn't have helped much
anyway. It got so ridiculous that in the 2nd half, Tony and Sheppy actually
got into the game. I'd have been a bit more pissed at our effort had we
not already earned the victory to end all victories. In the end, I guessed
1-2 wasn't a bad day's work. Then on the way to my truck, Andy smiled
at the Wisconsin women's team. We didn't get out of there for an hour
and a half.

Now I figured since I'd missed Mardis Gras the year before, it was
my obligation to go check it out. While lying in bed after surgery, I told
myself that I'd never again find an excuse not to do something. With that
philosophy in mind, after a meal and a shower, I found myself crammed
into the back of Rocky's Grand Cherokee on the way to the tournament
party at some casino along the river in downtown Baton Rouge.

Excited at the prospect of free beer, we were the first ones there. In
fact, we were so early that the LSU guys sponsoring the party asked us to
help set up. Next thing we knew, we were hauling kegs of Abita Beer into
the back of the casino. Then Oklahoma showed up. And Louisiana-La-
fayette. They started helping with the kegs as well. And as often happens
at ultimate tournaments, we had new and immediate drinking buddies.

Now other than the Wisconsin girls that clustered around me because
I happened to be standing near Tall Andy, the best thing about this par-

ty was the entertainment. Krystal Dragon was the absolute worst local metal band these ears have ever heard. And I'm from the eastern suburbs of Pittsburgh where crappy local metal bands outnumber weeds. Normally ultimate parties have a great funk or jam band whose music takes over your body and all but forces your hips to shake and your face to grin. This one had four guys who all looked like dirty porn stars doing Black Sabbath covers. The music fit the atmosphere about as well as a mattress fits into your car. We sat there with Oklahoma, Lafayette, and the Wisconsin girls just fascinated at their abject awfulness. They were so bad we couldn't leave. In fact, they were so bad we had no choice but to rock with them.

I have to admit, their covers weren't all that terrible. It was when they resorted to their original material that our ears were stunned with jolts of music so bad that it somehow turned into Mozart.

Their lead singer brushed the dirt out of his mustache and grunted into the microphone. "This one's a little song we wrote about fire. The kind of fire that you get in your belly and you just can't put out. It's called Constant Burning."

What followed was four minutes of them wailing on their guitars as they belted out every word in the English language that rhymed with "burning."

"We are yearning, stomach churning, wheels are turning, kids are learning, gifts returning, CONSTANT BURNING!" the lead singer yelled into the night.

(Note: Those lyrics aren't verbatim, but they aren't off by much.)

We sipped our drinks and stared forward in awe. It took balls to get up in front of a crowd and suck that bad. And yet if I found Constant Burning on ITunes tomorrow, I doubt I'd listen to another song for months. Little did they know that they'd soon become a rallying cry.

It was midnight when we finally pried ourselves away from the music and hit I-10 toward New Orleans. One car left an hour earlier and got down there ahead of us. Somewhere in the vicinity of the Superdome we found a spot behind a parked New Orleans police cruiser, pulled the Jeep over and got out. I'm not sure when or where, but somehow Tony and Sheppy had gotten their hands on a can of silly string. We hadn't been there forty-five seconds when they approached the empty cop car and aimed it at the windshield.

"Oh yeah, good idea," I said, wandering as far away as possible. "I've heard New Orleans cops are pretty forgiving. They'll probably just laugh that off."

Havelock Ben hustled across the street and shouted from the opposite sidewalk. "Nobody's coming back here to get you!"

Luckily all the cops were tied up elsewhere. Although that move was so ungodly stupid that none of us would've had any qualms about waving goodbye to Tony and Sheppy as they got hauled off for a couple of days. "Have fun getting home guys!"

Without cell phones, we had one major hurdle to overcome. We had zero idea how we were going to meet up with the first car. Our best guess was that Bourbon Street was going to be somewhat crowded on the Saturday night before Fat Tuesday. In fact as we wound down the side streets, the sound of the revelry began to intensify, oozing around the buildings before we could see a thing.

Somewhere on St. Louis Street, we stopped. Ben looked at the rest of us. "It sounds insane up there. How in the hell are we going to find them?"

"I have no idea," I said as a drunk redheaded dude came around the corner, unzipped his pants and leaned against the wall to urinate. "Actually, isn't that Opie peeing on a door?"

Ben turned. "That is in fact Opie peeing on a door."

It was amazing. Not only did we randomly stumble upon one of our teammates, but we'd gotten there at the exact perfect moment to prank the hell out of him.

We quietly snuck up behind him. As he finished, Ben yelled in his most authoritarian cop voice, "Hey you! No peeing on the buildings!"

I covered my mouth like I was speaking into a walkie. "Yeah, we got a three-eleven in progress. Corner of St. Louis and Dauphine."

Opie about sprained his wrist as he fumbled for his zipper. Fortunately for him, he'd just urinated, sparing him the embarrassment of pissing his pants. He slowly turned from the door, unsure whether to put his hands up or not – and found half his teammates cracking the hell up.

"Eh, fuck you guys," he said, waving us onward. "Come on. Everyone's just up here."

And so we followed Opie into the belly of the beast. It was even more insane than I'd pictured. The whole thing was like being crammed into America's small intestine as the crowd pulsed, swayed, puked, drank, and cheered. Occasionally you were lucky enough to catch four or five notes of jazz saxophone floating out of some bar, penetrating the din of the crowd, but otherwise it was a constant low roar. Up on the balconies, ridiculously hot women and middle-aged banker types stood high above the drooling masses down in the filth. The girls would pull up their shirts. Beads would fly. Green, purple, silver, and yellow would fill the sky. Everywhere, people were dressed in weird costumes. It was a carnival mixed with Dante's Inferno.

Somewhere along the line, a dude with a dildo strapped over his nose tried to toss beads to the balcony above him but had such a candy arm, they kept falling back to Earth and plunking me and Goose in the head.

"Hey Dicknose," I said. "How about you point out what girl you're aiming for and we'll do the tossing for you."

"Stupendous!" he said in the exact voice you'd expect from a guy wearing a hollowed out dildo over his nose.

So for about a half hour, me, Goose, and Dicknose saw a lot of glorious breasts. For a while it was a dream. But then like silt drifting to the bottom of a river, a thought started to settle in my brain. It was a thought so foreign I thought I must've been drugged. After an hour of nonstop breast watching, I turned to Goose. "You're gonna think I'm insane, but…"

"Is seeing boobs actually starting to bore you?"

"Yes! The whole thing is really losing its luster."

"They're all so damn….far away."

We gave Dicknose his beads back and slithered through the crowd.

The rest of the night was spent trying to make sure Tony and Sheppy didn't get killed. Tony grabbed the ass of every girl he walked by. Each girl would inevitably turn around just in time to see Sheppy, who was trailing behind him. Sheppy was drunk enough to have zero idea what Tony was up to, so he'd see the girl making eye contact and stop in front of her with a drunken grin. Then before he could even get a word out.....

BAM! Slapped across the face.

This happened a minimum of six times. The best part was Sheppy had no idea why it was happening. As far as he knew, he was simply getting slapped for being alive.

Three hours and many slaps later we reached the very end of the party. The mosh pit cleared and we finally had room to breathe. One by one, the thirteen of us emerged from the bowels of Bourbon Street. Right next to us was a little stand selling pink margaritas for like $3.00. This excited the hell out of a bunch of drunk and nearly broke college guys, so we all gathered around in a big circle. Thirteen guys. This is important to note on a couple levels.

As the other guys started drinking their margaritas and debating how many tits they'd seen, I started looking around. There were a lot less boobs in the immediate vicinity. In fact as I scanned the street, there didn't seem to be many women at all. Directly across the street was an open-air bar. Their televisions seemed to be playing some sort of sports highlights.

Cool, maybe if I squint I can see who won the Penguin game. No, wait a minute, that's just a video of dudes rollerblading in spandex. Hold on a second…

Just as that thought was entering my mind, Rocky looked up from his drink with a gigantic grin on his face. To really picture this next part, all you have to do is envision Sylvester Stallone uttering the phrase….

"Oh yeah, someone just grabbed my ass."

By his smile alone, you could read his mind. It was filled with all the girls he'd seen on balconies throughout the night. In his head, he was already in some back alley pinning her up against a wall. Ready to see what hot blonde had found his backside hard enough to squeeze, he turned. From a few yards away, a creepy dude wearing nothing but a diaper waved back. Half of Rich's margarita spilled to the street.

"Nooooo….."

Prompted by Rocky's goosing, one by one all the other guys began to notice the rollerblading video. Cherry Hill Ryan finally brought into the world what we were all thinking. "So it seems there's a gay section of Mardis Gras we weren't aware of."

"It seems that way, yeah."

Ben held up his drink. "That explains the cheap pink margaritas."

At that point we really should've skedaddled. But then we realized there was affordable alcohol and virtually no line for it. The street itself was a lot less crowded. It smelled a hell of a lot better. Also for a few glorious moments we didn't have to worry about Tony and Sheppy getting murdered for being perverts. There were much worse places to hang out for a while even if we did have to fend off the occasional advance.

As we stood there laughing at our situation, I started to realize that something else was amiss. I started counting the guys in the circle. I kept coming up with thirteen. I checked and rechecked. Thirteen.

"Hey guys, didn't we start out with fourteen?"

Ben nodded, now on his second margarita. "Yeah, why? That's how many we have now."

"Really? Go ahead and count."

Ben counted. Squinted. Counted again. Squinted. Asked Tall Andy to count.

"Thirteen."

"Yeah, that's what I got."

The worst part was that for a good three minutes we couldn't figure out who was missing. We'd actually convinced ourselves that we'd miscounted originally until Goose's eyebrows shot up to his hairline.

"Oh shit. Wait a minute. Where the hell's Colorado Ryan?"

"I don't know. I haven't seen him in like two hours."

And that was the problem. Nobody had seen him in two hours. And worse yet, in all the insanity, nobody had noticed the kid who'd just scored the biggest goal in Flagler history was missing.

Slightly panicked, everyone downed their margaritas and hustled back into the crowd. The rest of the night turned into a desperate and incredibly futile search. We walked the back alleys hoping we'd randomly find him peeing on a door. No sign of him. Finally at about 4:00AM, Goose and I, cold and sober, volunteered to head back to the Jeep. We figured that's where he'd be if in fact he had any recollection of where we'd parked.

Trouble was, we'd forgotten to ask Rocky for his keys. It was 4AM in mid-February and the temperature had fallen to near freezing there next to the river. So for nearly two hours we shivered by the Jeep watching tiny bits of silly string float off a cop car while the other guys spread out around the French Quarter. We were all more than a little panicked at what the hell we were going to do if we didn't find him.

Finally after just about all hope was lost and Goose and I were half asleep and frozen to the side of the Jeep, Colorado comes strolling up with his hands in his pockets. "Hey guys, what's up?"

Goose sprung up and hugged him like a father who'd lost his kid at an amusement park. "Oh Jesus Christ, we thought we'd never see you again. What the hell happened?"

"I was looking at this one chick on a balcony. I turned around and you guys were all gone."

"Shit, man. We're sorry. It's hard to keep track of…."

He laughed. "Eh, I found a bar. Had a couple beers. Saw a lot of boobs. Good time."

Turned out he'd wandered Mardis Gras alone most of the night and didn't mind one bit. He was one rookie that was fitting this sport just fine.

The rest of the guys came by in a disheveled mob about fifteen minutes later. Colorado Ryan got like six more bear hugs as we all crammed in the Jeep, turned on the heater and got the hell out of there. It was nearing 6:00 AM.

It was fully light out by the time we got back to the Motel 6. Our first game of Sunday was at 9:00. We slept for a whole twenty minutes before getting up and heading to McDonald's for breakfast.

Now getting breakfast before a tournament isn't usually an adventure in waiting. Most times, you walk over to the McDonald's, eat, walk back, pack the car and go.

Oh wait, you've read that sentence before. Remember when I said that this tournament was developing eerie similarities to the previous year? As we're crossing Siegen Lane, we hear the squealing of tires. Just behind us, a blue Saturn decided it would be a good idea to jerk across three lanes of traffic to try and slide into the Race-Trac gas station. It made it across two. A Ford Taurus T-boned the hell out of it, driving it into the curb with a glass-shattering jolt. I still have no idea how the damn thing didn't go careening into the Days Inn parking lot. Both cars were destroyed. Traffic ground to a halt.

I just stood there in the median blinking. "Jesus Christ, this is a dangerous intersection."

Goose nudged me. "Should we go help?"

I just shook my head. People much closer to the accident were already on the scene. "Eh, I'm still waiting on my medal from last year. Let's go."

"Medal? What medal?"

"I'll tell you on the way to the fields."

We got there at 9:00 to find our first opponent absent. We were supposed to get a rematch with Haverford in the first round but only two of their guys showed up. (Because ya know, Sunday at Mardis Gras) This was totally fine with a majority of our team who spent our unexpected bye either passed out or popping aspirin tablets.

Simply by showing up, we'd evened our record at 2-2.

Incredibly enough, this actually put us in the round of 16 against Indiana. As we went to warm up, we realized we had eight guys at best who were in any shape to play. Beer, Rocky, and Opie were corpses on the sideline. The two Haverford guys were still at the fields waiting around, so Ben and I approached them. We'd shared chicken with them a year ago, so they were practically teammates anyway.

"If you guys want to play, we could sure use two more."

They nodded. They weren't there to just sit around. So a few minutes later the first and only Flaglerford hybrid team took the field against Indiana Hoosiermama.

Like normal we were down 10-3 before we could blink. We were just going through the motions. We needed a spark. And then it hit us. We needed a fire in our belly that we just couldn't put out.

I looked to Goose. "What would Krystal Dragon do here?"

"They'd belt out the most epic song that has ever been sung. And it would inspire them to victory."

"That they would my friend. That they would."

He threw devil horns in the air to let Indiana know we were ready to receive. "Constant!" he yelled.

"Burning!" I replied.

"Constant!"

"Burning!"

"Constant!"

"BURNING!" our entire line yelled back.

The Haverford guys were slightly confused but bought into it. The rest of the game, we yelled the chorus to that inspired piece of genius every time we pulled or were pulled to. It ignited a comeback of epic proportions.

While I still credit Krystal Dragon for the comeback, their inspiration also happened to coincide with us finally realizing that Indiana had absolutely no answer for Tall Andy. Because he was one of our best handlers, Tall Andy had mainly stayed back and chucked the disc all weekend. But now with the addition of the two Haverford guys, he was free to head downfield. One of us would lob it up. Tall Andy would easily go over the Indiana defenders for the goal. Who'd have guessed a 6'7" guy with a thirty inch vertical would make an amazing deep receiver? Seriously, it took us three and a half games to figure this out.

Hucking to Andy, we went on a 6-2 run to close it to 12-9 before they got two in a row to get within one point of the victory. Then I bombed one to Andy from midfield. He went up over two guys to rip it out of the air in the back left corner to make it 14-10.

They called a timeout. Their captain started yelling at them. "Come on! You know all they're going to do is go long!"

I laughed as I walked by. "That's pretty much our entire strategy right there, yeah."

"See. They're even admitting it!"

Off of the next pull, they worked it the entire way downfield when out of freaking nowhere Goose became defensive player of the year. Only yards from victory, their handler tried to stick a forehand into a guy digging hard for the cone. Goose came from behind him for the layout D. Threat averted. On the first pass out of our end zone, I put one into the grass behind Ben. They picked it up and tried to hit the same guy to the same corner. Goose came across the goal line, laid out and tipped it out of bounds. Second threat averted. Two passes later, the Haverford guys miscommunicated on a dump. Turnover. Indiana set up a stack in the end zone. They tried to hit that same pass to the same corner with the same result. Goose flew in from behind the guy, dove and spiked it to the goal line. Three layout D's by the same guy on three consecutive passes to deny a team the winning goal. I may have seen that again somewhere in my career, but if I have, I can't remember.

Off Goose's D, I took off. Tall Andy picked it up. He bombed it the length of the field. I ran it down just across the goal line. Suddenly it was 14-11. Now even the drunk tank on the sidelines was getting into it, summoning the energy to clap on occasion.

On the next pull, I switched from guarding one of their deeps onto one of their squirrely handlers who'd been destroying us all game. We thought my size might give him some trouble. So far, his passes had been right on the money every damn time. He was as shifty as he was cool and collected…until some epic metal descended upon him.

All sorts of fired up, we sprinted to the line.

"Constant!" Goose shouted.

"Burning!" we all yelled back.

Tall Andy launched an amazing pull into the back of the end zone. The squirrely guy picked it up. With the energy of the comeback inside me, I burned down to cover him, charging straight at him until he raised the disc to throw. Suddenly, the idea hit me to surprise him by leaping over to jump the lane between him and his outlet receiver. (To this day I call this move The Krystal Dragon) I timed it perfectly just before his release. To my utter shock and surprise, it worked. If he hadn't turfed the throw, I'd have gotten a first pass Callahan. We picked it up at the goal line and punched it in. 14-12.

"Constant!"

"Burning!"

Andy launched the ensuing pull into virtually the same spot at the other end of the field. I sprinted my ass off to get down there and figured, 'hell, the Krystal Dragon worked last time. Why not try it again?' I bull rushed the handler, then in a full sprint, I planted and jumped toward the receiver. The throw sailed behind the guy and out the side of the end zone. I couldn't believe it. The Krystal Dragon had worked twice in a row. One of the Haverford guys ran over to grab it. He brought it to the front cone and lobbed it up to Tall Andy in the end zone. 14-13. We'd come virtually the entire way back. One more point and we'd tie it up. At that point anything could happen. We could accidentally find ourselves in the freaking quarterfinals at Mardis Gras.

Amped up and ready to play some killer defense, we yelled like hounds ready to be released on their prey.

"Constant!"

"Burning!"

We were ready to pounce. We were so amped up that Andy's pull went out of bounds at midfield and never came back into play. The sounds of our amped up shouts were still echoing off the trees when Indiana scored two quick passes later to win the game 15-13. Sometimes ultimate really doesn't understand drama.

In the end though, it was probably the best result we could've hoped for. In the next round we'd have had to play a ridiculous team like Kansas or Wisconsin or NC State with half our guys still doing zombie impressions on the sidelines. Plus we had amazing stories about an incredible comeback versus another Big Ten school all while still getting on the road at a reasonable time.

Somewhere after Pensacola, I gave Andy the keys and crawled inside my truck cap to form a bed out of all of our gear. It's pretty cool to watch the stars roll by while your mattress is going 85 MPH. My leg was working again, the team was tighter than ever and we'd taken down our biggest rival. That was a hell of a good ride home.

TWELVE

THE FRONT PAGE OF THE FEBRUARY 27TH, 1999 EDITION OF THE ST. AUGUS-tine Record tells us that the St. John's County Commissioners approved a new resolution on billboards, there were 307 days left until the millennium, and two different women named Peggy had passed away the day before. But the main article in big bold letters proclaimed:

College Frisbee Team Flies

Like the video two years before, the article mainly focused on the rules but did mention that we'd beaten Miami, a fact that greatly pleased Havelock Ben. In fact, I'm pretty sure if he knew any of their names, he'd have looked up their addresses, driven straight up to Ohio and nailed the article to their doors like a modern day Martin Luther.

Conveniently enough, we saw the article at about 6AM on our way up to Statesboro, Georgia for a small tournament at Georgia Southern University. We were at a Chevron just off I-95 when Goose came tearing around a shelf full of powdered donuts to show me.

He was excited because 60% of the front page was a color photo of him skying a surprisingly frightened-looking Harrisburg Corey as Cherry Hill Ryan lumbered in to observe.

Goose smacked the paper. "Whole county is waking up to my sweet vertical. I'm buying like nine of these."

It was a pretty cool picture I'll admit. For a few moments it overshadowed the article and the two little insert photos that flanked it. But not for long.

The photo in the lower left was of me about to release a flick. But the real gold was the picture in the upper right hand corner. In it, Havelock

Ben is slightly bent over with the Frisbee out in front of him looking back for a dump toss. Just behind him, Opie is obviously trying to decelerate from a hard sprint. His arms are spread wide like a pterodactyl - his crotch thrust forward. The front of Opie's shorts were probably an inch or two from actually touching Ben's ass, but the angle of the photo gets your mind to wondering. It looks less like they're playing ultimate and more like the warden turned his back in the prison shower.

We took the paper up to the counter where Ben was in the middle of paying for a Gatorade. In front of the woman at the register, we spread the paper out to show him. For a moment, he was pretty excited.

"No way! Our article is on the front page!" he yelled. "Hell yeah! There's a picture of...hell yeah, I made the front page!"

I chuckled. "Ya know if you and Opie need a little special time together, we're all cool with it. You don't have to pretend to be playing ultimate."

"What are you...?"

It took him a second.

"Aaaaah! It looks like I'm taking it in the butt from Opie!"

"Don't worry, man. It's only circulated to like ten thousand households. In the majority of the country, your secret is safe."

Ben picked up the paper and stared at it. "Are you kidding me?"

Goose smiled. "I wouldn't worry about it. They'll all be so impressed by my awesome catch that they'll barely notice the love nest you two created."

"I had all kind of awesome plays in that game," Ben shouted to Goose. "You had *one!*"

"And yet mine's on the front page," Goose said, pointing to the woman behind the counter. "Yes, I'm going to buy these Pop Tarts and ten newspapers."

Anyway, the tournament in Statesboro popped up at the last minute, so we didn't have many guys. In fact when Beer got up at 4AM and stumbled downstairs just to let us know he'd somehow managed to hurt his knee while he was asleep (because that happens to people all the time) we were left with only six guys making the trip. And yet we were just dumb and adventurous enough to decide, *"screw it, let's drive up to Georgia and see what happens."*

We got to campus about an hour before the first game and figured we'd better hatch a plan pretty quick. That plan ended up being to wander around campus and offer a case of beer to anyone who looked athletic enough to play. We figured it was a slam dunk. College kids will do anything for beer. Goose and I split off to hit the campus gym while the rest of the guys hustled over toward some athletic fields across the parking lot.

Unfortunately Goose and I ended up spending twenty minutes flirting with the cute blondes at the counter and never even made it into the gym. Ben and Colorado Ryan spent the same amount of time chatting up the Coastal Carolina softball team. When we rendezvoused back at the parking lot, Ben came striding up scratching his head.

"Nobody?" he said.

"To tell you the truth we got distracted by girls. How about you?"

"Distracted by girls."

"So I guess we're playing with six?"

"I guess we're playing with six. Women are evil. Why do we talk to them?"

"Because we're idiots, Ben. Because we're idiots."

Anyway, we got our stuff out of the cars and walked over to the fields only to see two guys in white shirts tossing disc. They were pretty good. As we sat down on the bleachers to cleat up, I yelled out to them.

"What team are you guys from?"

The one guy caught the disc and walked over. "Oh, we're not playing in the tournament. We go to South Carolina. We just came down from Columbia to watch."

All of us quit tying our shoes at the same moment. *Well, that's convenient.*

Ben stood up to shake the guy's hand. "Know what's even better than watching?"

And so much like Flaglerford earlier in the year, South Flaglerina was born.

Ultimate is amazing like that. Somehow our decision to say *'screw it, let's drive to Georgia and see what happens'* actually worked. It's the ultimate magic that never happens in real life. Most times if you decide to head to another state with no real plan, you end up getting mugged outside a crappy motel and have to beg your uncle to wire you a hundred bucks so you don't starve to death. But in my experience, ultimate tends to randomly give you what you need right when you need it.

So we had eight guys that day. We had me, Ben, Goose, Colorado Ryan, the two Carolina guys and two dudes that I haven't mentioned yet. I only haven't mentioned them because they are worthy of a few paragraphs of introduction. These are the brothers that I will henceforth refer to as "The Swiss."

The Swiss were two tiny but fast European guys who spent their teen-age years in a remote part of Hawaii where they didn't get much in the way of human contact. As far as I can tell, they spent a majority of their time surfing and learning how to be awesome. Dionys, the older of the two (they were born in the same year but weren't twins) was good look-ing, stoic, calm, and forthright. He was a poet and a philosopher, the type of guy who sips on scotch and jots in leather notebooks as he stares off at the sea.

His brother Hermi on the other hand was a wild man with thick black glasses, hair that stuck up all over the place and a squeaky cartoon voice that could be heard for miles. He shuffled around campus in a T-shirt that said "I Feel Good," looking like a mix between a puppy and a mad scientist. We swore he was the inevitable result of what would happen if humans bred with Muppets.

I got a taste of their genius when we accidentally turned the wrong way off of I-16 and got lost in the tiny little town of Pembroke, Georgia.

"I don't think we're going the right way," I said as we plunged into the depths of Pembroke looking for a place to turn around.

Dionys opened the map. "Yes. Indeed. We went south when we should have gone north."

Then from the bucket seat came a squeaky voice. "Wow, look at all the rednecks! Can we get out? I want to talk to a redneck!"

Dionys dropped the map. "We're not stopping so you can talk to a redneck."

"I've never seen rednecks before."

"We're not stopping, Hermi."

"What do rednecks eat?"

Dionys turned around. If not for the seatbelt holding him back, I swear he'd have slapped his brother upside the head. "What kind of question is that? They eat food like the rest of us."

"Really? I thought they ate each other."

"That's cannibals, Hermi."

"Oh right. I always get them mixed up."

Ladies and gentlemen - The Swiss.

So with those two goofballs in tow, we lined up to face Georgia Southern. As we went to pull, I looked down the field toward their biggest, most athletic dude. I immediately shifted down to line up on him.

"I have the big dude," I said nonchalantly. In every other college game I'd played, I'd lined up on the other team's biggest, fastest guy and made sure he wasn't an option. Nobody scored on me. Guys barely ever got open. I figured it would be more of the same. I was wrong.

The guy's name was Tuba and he was a 6'2" African dude just out of the military whose biceps were so big, it looked like he had truck tires strapped to his arms. His calves were bigger than Hermi. In fact as I remember him now, I'm pretty sure I'm not recalling Tuba so much as I'm picturing former NFL receiver Terrell Owens. He was that kind of a beast.

Until that game, the 21-year old egotistical dumbass in me honestly thought I might be the best athlete playing ultimate in the entire country. Then Tuba ran right the hell by me. Then he did it again. And again. He scored three goals on me in the first five points. I'd only given up three goals to that point in my entire college career. I didn't know what hit me. I was not used to being the other guy in the poster. My head was spinning. We went down 7-1.

Ben shrugged at me. "What the hell's going on? That guy is eating you alive."

"Dude is freaking Superman. You want to guard him?"

Ben looked down the field. He sized up Tuba. "No. I'm fine on the little pudgy guy."

Somewhere just before halftime, I was playing defense on Tuba near the goal line and he trucked straight at me, stopped and cut to the right. They lobbed a high backhand. I stayed with him, boxed him out in the air and tipped it away. When we landed, I couldn't believe what I'd done. I'd made a D on Superman.

It was the spark of confidence I needed. The rest of the game was actually pretty evenly matched, a battle I'm sure he doesn't remember but I sure do. I'd never had to work that hard to get open - never had to work that hard to deny someone the disc. In the end he scored four goals on me and I somehow managed to get three on him in a 17-10 loss.

After the game I exhaustedly stumbled over to seek him out on the sideline. "I'm not usually this tired after one game, man."

He laughed and smiled. "Neither am I," he said.

Now he was a really cool guy so he might've just said that to make me feel better about getting turned into burnt toast, but I'll take it. To this day, he was one of the best players I've ever had to guard and yet what I remember about him was how humble he was about his super powers. He was everything ultimate is supposed to be. Personally gracious and athletically redonkulous. He patted me on the back as I turned to leave. "Great game. Good luck."

"I'd wish you luck but trust me, you don't need it," I laughed.

A crazy wind kicked up just before our next game against Auburn. They took advantage of a couple of awful turnovers to beat us 13-7, pushing us to 0-2 as we headed into our last game of the day against Savannah State.

And if not for a stupid sweatshirt, we'd have come out of that game with a win.

I twisted back to catch a disc that had glanced off Colorado Ryan's hands for a goal that tied the game 9-9. On the ensuing Savannah possession, we forced a turn. Dionys made a speedy sliding catch in the center of the end zone to put us up 10-9 late in the game. South Flaglerina was in control. We were playing crisp offense and smothering defense. It was looking like our trip to Georgia wouldn't end with an oh-fer after all.

Our only problem at this point was Hermi's apparel choice for the day. Since the Swiss had just transferred to Flagler a couple weeks prior, neither of them had a uniform. We'd informed them that our colors were red and white assuming that information would encourage them to bring red *and* white shirts. And Dionys did. Unfortunately, Hermi only brought one shirt, a bright red one that advertised one of St. Augustine's various surf shops. This didn't end up being a problem versus Georgia Southern who wore green and Auburn who wore blue. Since we all knew what players constituted our separate teams, Hermi spent the first two games running around out there like the spot on a 7UP can and nobody thought much of it.

But Savannah's uniforms were red. Hermi would have to change in order to avoid confusion out on the field. Unfortunately, his only option was the heavy zip-up hoodie he'd been wearing in the parking lot when it was 49 degrees at 4AM back in St. Augustine. It was no longer 49 degrees. A few points into the Savannah game, the wind died down and the previously overcast skies parted. It got oppressive in about three breaths as Georgia suddenly remembered it was freaking Georgia.

After Dionys scored to put us up by one, we excitedly high fived and fist bumped before turning around to see Hermi stumbling around in the middle of the field with the same general look as a patient who'd accidentally wandered out of a hospital. After a moment, he turned and followed Savannah back toward their goal line.

"Hermi!" I shouted. "Where you going?"

He stopped. Looked at us - looked back at Savannah - looked at us. I swear he was actually melting. "Why am I going with them? I don't know any of those guys."

"No, no you don't," I yelled back. "Maybe you should take a break and get some water, buddy."

He paused. "You know I should probably get some water."

As we lined up to play defense, Hermi made a dizzy parabola toward the water jugs. Still, we figured with time winding down in the 90-minute game, we could fight our way to a win even though our only sub had lost about eleven percent of his body weight in less than an hour. And then of all things, we got screwed by our own incredible defense.

On the next point, Savannah worked it up with a bunch of short, quick, contested passes until Goose's guy faked in and cut toward the end zone. Goose planted and turned to catch up. Savannah's guy broke on a diagonal toward the cone as the handler wound up and fired a flat backhand break that sailed behind the both of them.

"Up! Up! Goose! Goose!" we shouted.

Being as the cutter was headed toward the front right cone, Goose turned over his right shoulder to find the disc just as the receiver realized he was going to have to reverse course. He slipped back behind Goose ready to catch the tying goal.

All of Goose's momentum was headed toward the sideline. The disc was about to hit the receiver behind him at about chest level. There was no way Goose was going to make the D unless he turned into a ninja.

And wouldn't you know it, Goose turned into a ninja.

Having no way to reach the disc with either of his arms, he left the ground and sliced his right leg through the air. I'm positive the last thing the receiver expected to see was a foot kicking the disc away just in front of his fingers. As Goose landed, the ghost of Bruce Lee materialized out of nowhere simply to bow his acceptance and applaud.

The play was so amazing, Goose's groin popped with excitement. We barely had time to get out a "holy shit," before we realized he was crawling off the field. So, ok, maybe he didn't turn into a ninja. I've never heard of a ninja groin pull. But whatever is like a step or two below ninja, that's what Goose morphed into for a second.

We called out to him. "Goose, are you ok?"

"No. No, I'm not," he said, shaking his head.

Bruce Lee disappeared into a fine mist before we could ask him if he wanted to play, so in came Hermi and his sweatshirt of doom.

"Hermi!" I shouted. "C'mon, man, we need you to play again."

"Ok," he said as he cautiously peered over the water jug and started poking at the air in front of his face. "What are all these dots?"

I turned to his brother. "Dude, he's seeing dots."

"For him, that's not terribly uncommon. He'll…be fine."

So with Hermi out there stammering around like a mix between Marlboro Ed and a busted gyroscope, we desperately tried to hold onto our one point lead.

We didn't. We turned it. They scored. 10-10.

On the next possession they threw a zone. I was waiting for the swing when Ben went to throw a hammer downfield to one of the Carolina guys. The closest defender would've had to hop in a Ferrari to get there in time to make the D. Unfortunately, the humidity had turned the disc into a bar of soap.

Until that moment I didn't know that it was possible to throw the disc off your own ass. But it is. All the guys on the field that day can attest to it. It slipped right out of Ben's hand, rolled down his spine, glanced off his butt and hit the ground between his legs. It looked as if he'd laid a very awkward egg.

Ben kept his arm over his head in hammer toss position as he slowly glanced down at the disc on the ground. "Aaaah! Are you kidding? How the hell does that even happen?"

I yelled at him as I picked up on defense. "Were you afraid Opie was coming up behind you?"

"Shut up, Cramer!"

"Cause he's back in Florida. You really didn't have to protect your ass with the disc."

As I was jacking him we gave up goal number eleven. The soft cap went on.

Goals number twelve and thirteen can be summed up thusly:

"Hermi, we turned the disc. We're on defense now! Find a guy! Hermi, we're not on offense anymore! Hermi…we're on…."

Goal.

"Nevermind, we're back on offense."

Goal.

"Nevermind, the game's over."

Savannah State 13

Flagler 10

So our trip was another loser. We were really struggling to recapture the magic we'd found against Minnesota and Miami. But I did trade one of my uniforms to a Carolina guy for a really nice hoodie, so all was not lost. I like to think he has it in a climate-controlled frame in his game room. Anyway, somewhere on I-95, Hermi decided to fill me in on the circumstances that led to our epic four-point collapse. Still chugging water in the bucket seat, he tapped me on the shoulder.

"So, I was running and then all the sudden I was like, '*wow, I can't see.*' Which I didn't want to say anything about. Cause I thought you know... the other team might try to take advantage of a blind guy. So I just pretended that I could see for a while."

His brother turned around. "What do you mean, you pretended to see?"

"I just told myself things like, '*hey look at that cool bird.*' or '*hey, look at that hot babe.*' I thought maybe my eyes would get excited and work again."

"I told you to bring a white shirt," Dionys exclaimed.

Hermi tapped me on the shoulder again. "Cramer, do you know how many T-shirts I own?"

His brother almost slapped the water out of his hand. "Why would he know how many T-shirts you own?"

I laughed. It may have been the oddest question someone who wasn't drunk had ever asked me. "No, Hermi. I have no idea how many T-shirts you own."

"Fifteen. I have fifteen T-shirts."

"How is this relevant to anything?" his brother said, hand to his forehead.

Hermi continued. "Do you know how many of them are white?"

"We've established that he doesn't know the contents of your closet, Hermi!"

"Again, Hermi," I said. "I have no idea. Six?"

He practically pulled out his hair. "Fourteen!" he shouted. "Fourteen of my fifteen T-shirts are white and I wear the fucking red one today!"

I'm not kidding, when I'm depressed about something all I have to do is remember Hermi exclaiming the number fourteen and all seems right with the world again. At the time, I almost steered the truck into a ditch. Speaking of which.....

When we left Statesboro, Ben and I decided to fill up on opposite sides of Route 301 and then race home. The big prize for whoever won? We got to call the guys in the other car stupid idiotheads. We didn't even bet a cheeseburger or some sort of public humiliation. That's how tired we were. We just said, "Hey, last ones home are stupid idiotheads," and peeled out for Florida.

As we hit St. Augustine and pulled into the lot, the Swiss and I were relieved that Ben's Mustang was nowhere to be found. We weren't going to be branded stupid idiotheads for life. That would suck to have to put on a resume. After a couple minutes, we got bored waiting to gloat and crashed out for the night.

When Ben and Goose wandered into the cafeteria the next afternoon before pickup, I sprinted up to them. "Hey, there's the stupid idiotheads," I said, happily using the insult I'd waited to spring on them for going on twelve hours.

"Ok, that's not fair," Ben exclaimed. "There was a major incident that prevented us from getting home first."

"A major incident," Goose reiterated.

Ben socked Goose in the shoulder. "This assjacket tried to kill us."

"I didn't try to kill us," Goose replied sheepishly. "Not actively."

Ben shook his head. "I was tired, so I let Goose drive. Which as it turns out was a fairly egregious mistake on my part."

"As it turned out, yes," Goose said. "But I'm an excellent driver, last night notwithstanding, so I hardly think you can call it egregious."

"So I'm asleep in the passenger's seat and I don't know what woke me up, but I yawn and stretch and open my eyes," Ben said. "And you know that bend right as you're about to cross the bridge into Florida?"

"Over the river?" I asked.

"Yeah. Exactly. That's where I woke up. And off ahead I see some traffic. And brake lights. At this point, I'm unconcerned. Then the brake lights start getting closer. And closer. And we're still going the same speed. I'm thinking Goose is about to brake at any second. Any second now. But he doesn't. And we're careening…"

"We weren't careening."

"How the hell would you know?" Ben exclaimed. "Trust me, we were careening. At this point alarms are going off in my head, so I look over at Goose to see what the hell he's doing. And he's out freaking cold. Like he's nuzzled in his fucking bed."

"Holy shit," I said.

"So I shout at him, '*Goose, wake the fuck up!*' And I shake him. By this time, we're actually glowing in the brake lights of a tractor trailer."

Goose drew in a deep breath. "I woke up, saw the traffic ahead of us and jerked the wheel to the right."

Ben was shaking just telling the story. "I thought I was dead. Just dirt and trees and dirt and trees and dirt and spinning and then....we stopped. We just stopped. It's a miracle we're still alive."

I'd just found out a couple of my best buddies had legitimately stared down the reaper and instead of embracing them and telling them just how much their friendship meant or taking a moment to contemplate my own mortality, I did what any warm-blooded twenty-one year old guy would do. I made fun of them.

"You fell asleep at the wheel? That *is* something a stupid idiothead would do."

Amazingly enough, the story gets more incredible from there. Not only had Ben woken up just in time to save them from crashing into a bridge abutment at eighty miles per hour, but they'd also stopped mere feet from plunging into the St. Mary's River. When they got out of the car to examine what happened, they counted seven full revolutions in the shoulder and yet the car hadn't flipped over. The only damage to Ben's Mustang was a hefty blanket of dirt and mud that covered the windshield and roof. Otherwise not a single dent or scratch.

BUT WAIT, THERE'S MORE! Goose had no idea how long he'd been asleep as they flew down I-95, but apparently when he woke up there was a substantial puddle of drool on his shoulder and a totally different song was on the radio. Which means that at minimum they were shooting down a major interstate for almost a minute (probably longer) without a driver and not only lived to tell the tale, but came out of it completely unscathed. Lucky bastards. I joke about it now, but Flagler Ultimate almost ended right there. And who knows, something like that may have been traumatic enough that I'd have quit playing altogether. Fifteen years later, Carleton College couldn't avoid tragedy as three promising young athletes lost their lives driving to a tournament on an icy Minnesota highway. It's the nightmare scenario that ultimate had been dancing with for years as indestructible young men and women piled themselves into cars to drive for hours to play the game they loved. It hit the ultimate community hard because we'd all been in that car. Laughing, carefree, and cramped, joking of hammer dumps and wiping granola bar crumbs to the floor mats. We all saw ourselves in them. Even those of us who didn't know them felt like we did. We all mourned.

I'm just glad Ben woke up when he did.

Ben put his hand to his head as if realizing just how close their call had been. "Once we realized we were ok, we brushed off the windshield, waited for traffic to clear and pulled back on the road."

I guess when it's not your time, it's not your time.

So with those guys miraculously still corporeal and the Swiss now on board, we plowed our way toward Frostbreaker again.

By now you're probably asking yourself, *"Jesus Christ, is this guy going to write about every freaking tournament he's ever played in?"* The answer (incredibly) is no. A lot of my wackiest stories just happen to be packed into the Flagler years. So here's a very quick recap of Frostbreaker before we move on.

We were tossed into a bracket that contained the host team, Florida, and the teams that at the time were ranked #3 (Georgia), #8 (William & Mary), and #9 (Rochester) according to the UPA. We got beat that day by a combined score of 56-13 and seriously considered changing our name from The Fightin' Amish to Sacrificial Lamb.

After playing Florida semi-close and losing 15-7, we met William & Mary on a field that we affectionately named "The Sarlac Pit." (If you don't get that reference, put this book down immediately and go watch Return of the Jedi.) I don't know what the hell kind of construction they were doing on it, but I've played in beach tournaments where I ran in less sand. It was honestly like they'd planned on putting in a volleyball court but ran out of money halfway through the project, leaving a cross between a soccer field and the inside of a used Shop Vac. Anyway, I hit Dionys for the first two scores of the game to go up on William & Mary 2-0. We were feeling pretty good right up until they scored fifteen uncontested goals to win 15-2. What made it all the more impressive was that they rattled off those fifteen goals *after* one of their guys fell into the pit to be slowly digested over a period of a thousand years. And that is a true story.

While W&M and Georgia went off to get some food, Rochester came over to meet us on the Sarlac Pit. They plopped their gear down.

"What the hell is this shit?" they said. All together. In unison.

"We're still wondering that ourselves," Goose joked before pointing across the way. "Ya know, right over there is a field made of grass and niceness."

The Rochester guys looked. "That is a way better field," they said.

I nodded. "Ya know, if we start right now, we'll be six points in by the time the other two teams get back. At which point I doubt they'll bother to check which field they're supposed to..."

"Let's go," they said, quickly scooping up their gear and hustling over.

End result? We got crushed on a much nicer field.

A couple of our better players had to work at night meaning they had to head out right before the Georgia game, leaving us to play a nationals-caliber team with ten guys who were exhausted from a full day of getting our brains beat in. I swear Georgia had about forty guys. They substituted entire lines. On every pull, we'd look down the field and realize we were screwed.

"Oh look, seven fresh new guys. Awesome."

"Some of these dudes don't even smell bad yet. How is this fair?"

If you've never been on the field during a complete skunking, let me tell you, it's a pretty helpless feeling. You know that moment when you're sitting there on the commode, look over and realize you're out of toilet paper? It's kind of like that.

It was 10-0 before we discovered a couple sheets under the sink.

Ben made a D and swung it to Harrisburg Corey, who bombed one that Colorado Ryan caught two yards from the goal line. Goose and I, filled with the desire to avoid complete annihilation, sprinted downfield ahead of everyone and split the lone defender. In a panic, Colorado turned backward and dumped it to me as I was running by. With a full head of steam and absolutely no trust that we could complete another pass against their defense, I leapt just before catching the disc.

I found myself sailing toward the goal line. It was going to be really close. I pulled my knees into my chest. In cannonball mode, I soared past the Georgia defender and hit the ground, my cleats about the height of this sentence inside the end zone. We'd done it. We'd scored our goal.

Our ass was clean. Somehow we'd avoided the shutout on a pass that had actually traveled backwards. I gave the disc to Goose, who danced the entire way across the end zone as the whole team came screaming down the field to mob me. We made such a big production out of our solitary goal that it could've spent weeks on Broadway. Luckily the Georgia guys realized we were just goofballs and weren't in any way trying to show them up. Still, they were kind of ticked they didn't get the shutout and scored the next three goals on crossfield hammers to win 13-1.

And so ended our 2nd season - a season that saw us achieve a monumental 2-10 record. But one of those wins was against Miami of Ohio dammit so all in all, the season was a major success. Or at least a minor success. Ok, it wasn't a complete embarrassment. In fact, we somehow managed to finish above thirty-five other teams in the final 1999 UPA rankings including Alabama, Iowa State, NYU, Toledo, Fordham, and Northern Illinois, which I find quite remarkable seeing as it means a full 20% of the officially registered college teams in the country finished behind us. But it's right there in the records. You can look it up and find us tied for 144th place with Johns Hopkins.

Heading into the summer, I thought I might be going a few months without playing. Little did I know I'd not only be playing almost every day, but I'd also be helping pass the game to the next generation.

THIRTEEN

I'D PLANNED ON STAYING IN ST. AUGUSTINE THAT SUMMER, LIVING ON THE beach with a couple of my soccer buddies and generally living the sweet life of a 21 year old with nothing better to do. Opie got me a job selling crappy Indian artifacts to tourists at a marginally racist store called Tepee Town, so I had enough money for rent, utilities, and occasionally even some food. There was a tiki bar on the water about a block away. My girlfriend lived four streets over, so I was getting laid damn near every night. It was shaping up to be an amazing couple of months. Everything changed though when Havelock Ben got a call from Colorado Ryan.

We hadn't seen or heard from Colorado in the month and a half since school had ended. We knew he was spending his break in the mountains of West Virginia as a counselor at a sleep away camp for kids, but that was about as much attention as we'd given his stories on the subject. None of it seemed relevant until a couple returning male counselors ended up injured or pregnant or abducted by sharks or something. In their mad scramble to find suitable replacements at the last minute, Colorado made a phone call to Havelock Ben. Havelock Ben then called me.

While I was chilling on the beach, Colorado Ryan was deep in hillbilly country, sleeping on a mattress that had been pooped on by woodpeckers. What he proposed in his phone call was a summer full of bug bites and babysitting. And yet when he said, "I talked to them. They'd let you guys run an ultimate program for the kids," I decided to drop everything and go. Next thing I knew, Ben and I were driving all night for West Virginia, keeping ourselves awake by tossing disc at random gas stations up I-95.

Camp was an interesting experience. Trying to get an entire cabin of sixth graders to sleep is an exhausting task if you have to do it once, let alone every night for eight weeks. It was fun at times, but we were up at 6:45AM each day and didn't get off duty until midnight. I later calculated my salary at 38 cents an hour and quickly wished I hadn't done something as dumb as attempt to calculate my hourly wage. On average, I was more tired at the end of each day than I was after playing every point of every game at Mardis Gras. When it was all over, I returned to Pittsburgh and slept for three straight days.

If you're ever asked to run an ultimate program at a summer camp for kids, be prepared for one thing - the summer camp will be absolutely certain they have enough Frisbees to run the camp. And they will. Unfortunately, every Frisbee will be a completely useless bank giveaway with the aerodynamic properties of a welcome mat and will split right in half if you do something silly like...try to catch it. Luckily like every ultimate player in the country, I had fourteen discs chilling in my vehicle. So we had a program.

Days in the camp were divided into hour-long activity periods in the morning and afternoon, which were broken up by lunch and swim time. During each activity period, kids had about ten different choices, which usually included various sports, arts & crafts, nature hikes, fishing, and lessons on how to tease farm animals. Ultimate was up against tennis, soccer, and goat slapping in the very first session after breakfast. The first day we had a grand total of six kids - which truthfully was about four more than we were expecting, so Ben and I were elated.

After a brief demonstration on how to throw backhands and forehands, we let the kids toss for a while before briefly explaining the rules and breaking up into a small 4 on 4 game with Ben and I captaining each team.

There truly is something incredible about watching kids experience ultimate for the first time. It wasn't long until they started to get the hang of it, running to space to get open (most often as Ben and I pointed where to go) throwing wild 20 yard hucks straight out of bounds, and diving all over the place. If there's one thing ten year olds are not afraid of, it's laying out. They will lay out for a toss that hits them in the chest. They will lay out two full seconds after the disc hits the ground eighteen yards away. They will lay out reaching for a juice box. They don't care.

We played for about fifteen minutes with neither team managing to score a goal, but what I'll always remember about that first game was how the kids lit up when they made a catch, completed a throw, or swatted a D. It was new. It was exciting. It wasn't basketball or gymnastics or a sport they'd been dragged to by their parents. No, this sport was all their own and as they played, the smiles on their faces suggested they just unlocked a secret that none of the other kids knew about yet.

Just as the activities buzzer was about to ring out through the loudspeakers, I lobbed a forehand into the end zone for a freckled sixth-grader named Zach. He was in my cabin and was a cool but somewhat awkward kid who lacked the confidence of most of his bunkmates. He jumped and made the catch in the end zone, hitting the ground and staring at the disc in his hands with a look of complete wonder. It was the first goal of camp. Our team won 1-0. He was so happy, he might as well have just ended youth nationals as I rushed in to high five him.

"Yeah, buddy! Great catch. You know we control the universe now, right?"

"We control the universe? This game is great!"

He carried that disc around for the next two hours. I'm pretty sure he took it with him to chicken punting next period. The following morning, Ben and I called him up to the flagpole in front of the rest of the campers and told the story of his winning goal. The kid all but floated up there to be recognized. I don't think he'd ever been singled out for an athletic achievement in his life. The other kids high-fived him. He told everyone about how fun it was. And just like that, the secret was out of the bag.

The next session we went from six to twelve. Then from twelve to twenty-four. Next thing we knew, it was the most popular activity at camp. Sometimes almost a third of all the kids on the premises were out there running around on our field in a massive ten-on-ten game with five subs each. Ben and I could barely handle it. It was amazing.

I'd like to think that Ben and I had something to do with ultimate being so popular amongst the campers that summer, but I think it had much more to do with the sport itself. In a world where youth sports often single out the best players early on, many of those kids had already been told they weren't good at football, softball, or soccer. No one had yet put them down about their ultimate skills, so they were free to unearth hidden talents all on their own. I'd like to think that a few of those kids (who are now in their mid to late 20's) are still playing, looking back on their camp days and saying "I'm glad I showed up to ultimate with Ben and Cramer that summer. I already knew how to throw marbles at sheep." Hopefully the sport has enhanced their lives along the way as it's enhanced mine.

Things changed a hell of a lot when Ben and I got back for our super senior years.

Getting kicked off of the fort grounds pissed me off like crazy when it happened, but ended up being a blessing in disguise. The field we moved to wasn't only flat, square, and devoid of trees and tourists - it had lights. And since the ultimate team had been one of the major volunteer groups to help build that very community park, we kind of had our run of the place. Which meant we could do totally insane things like practice.

Those Wednesday practices were some of the best times of my life. One of the greatest moments I can recall was one night as we were all tossing before practice, Goose was humming to himself just loud enough for the guys around him to hear. And they joined in the humming, which was just loud enough for a couple guys around *them* to hear. They joined in as well. As the humming got louder, suddenly Goose sang out....

"WHY DO YOU build me up....build me up, Buttercup baby...."

And instinctively, all sixteen of us joined in, tossing flicks and belting out the song at the top of our lungs in a chorus that could be heard for blocks. It was just one of those collective waves of awesome you ride with your teammates on rare occasions. Two minutes later when the song ended, I looked around at the team.

"All right. Let's run."

I played a lot of ultimate that semester. Our new Wednesday night practices accompanied the regular Sunday pickup. The physical therapy school in town had a game at a different park out by the interstate on Saturdays, which a bunch of us hit up on a regular basis. On Thursday nights, I'd drive up to Jacksonville to play with the guys from UNF. Oh, and I was running cross-country on top of all of it. Which meant that in a typical week, I was playing eight games of ultimate, lifting weights three or four nights, and running forty miles. I have no idea how my heart didn't explode. Just remembering it makes me tired now.

With all the playing time we were getting, things were looking up on the field as well. Additionally, we got a couple great recruits. Our freshman crop included a super fast Irish kid named Murph, a surprisingly agile 6'4" defensive lineman we nicknamed, "The Keg," a rail thin handler we called Jeremy the Stick, and another dude I'll simply call Intense Joe. Added to me, Ben, Goose, Colorado Ryan, Harrisburg Corey, Opie, and the Swiss, we had the makings of a team that actually wouldn't suck balls.

The new field wasn't near as quirky as the fort, but it did provide its share of memorable moments and interesting characters. And when I say characters, I mean one in particular. As we were scrimmaging one night, one of the guys on my team called for a sub. In ran this scruffy little dude who looked like he'd just crawled out of the bushes. This only confused the rest of us because no one had ever set eyes upon him before. And now he was on the line acting like he'd known us for years.

"Hi there," I said, squinting.

"Hey," he said with the enthusiasm usually reserved for aerobics instructors. "I'm Kenny. I've been watching. Cool if I play?"

"Do you know the rules?"

"Sort of."

"Uh. Ok. Welcome aboard, man. You got the guy on the end of the line."

Kenny slammed his hands together and started hopping around. "Yeah! Let's do this! Let's go!"

Turned out he was a local kid who dropped out of high school and now worked as an apprentice HVAC technician. We called him "The Weasel," not because he looked like a weasel, but because he had this shaky, twitchy energy and honestly looked like he slept in the marsh. And I have never in my life seen someone who outwardly enjoyed playing ultimate as much as Kenny the Weasel.

He jumped around. He raised his arms in the air and shouted, "Hey, I'm open! Cramer I'm open," which is only acceptable on the field if you're yelling it with the pure unadulterated joy of a four year old. He was 5'4" and always lined up to defend Tall Andy before we'd make him switch. He had more energy than any of the sixth graders in West Virginia, which to that point, I thought was impossible. And these next two stories about Kenny the Weasel are true on my grandma's grave.

We were a few points into one of our Wednesday night games when Kenny came sprinting across the baseball field and dropped his stuff on the sideline. This was odd because he was usually there and waiting for us when we showed up to practice. After the next pull, he came ambling into the game.

"Kenny, we were worried something happened to you," I said, waiting to pull.

"Yeah, sorry I was late guys," he said, totally out of breath. "My girlfriend is in the hospital."

"Oh shit," I said, worried. "Is she ok?"

"Yeah, she's fine. She's just having a baby. Who am I guarding?"

The entire line went silent as we processed what he'd just said.

I dropped the disc and turned to him. "Wait...your girlfriend is having a kid? Right now? *Your* kid?"

"Yeah. It's cool. She knows I play ultimate on Wednesdays. Is anyone guarding Andy? Cause I can take him if..."

"Kenny, get the fuck back to the hospital!"

"No, really, it's cool. They said it would be a couple hours, so..."

"I will not pull this disc until I see you running back in the direction of the maternity ward. I'm not letting you miss the birth of your child to play in a pickup ultimate game."

I honestly thought we were going to have to throw a bag over his head and drag him kicking and screaming into the back of my truck. But eventually he relented and went to witness the birth of his daughter – who I'm pretty sure he named Goose.

A month later, he showed up on crutches in a giant air cast that completely immobilized his right leg. We, like most people immediately assumed his girlfriend's dad had finally tracked him down.

"Jesus, Kenny. What the hell happened to you?"

"Air conditioner fell off a truck. Crushed my leg. I had to get a couple screws and a rod in it. But don't worry. I can still play." He flipped his crutches aside and started hopping on one leg. "Toss one to me!"

Clearly Kenny the Weasel did not live in the same plane of reality that the rest of us did. Ben and I looked at each other in complete disbelief. He was either insanely tough, insanely crazy, or insanely stupid - and probably a mix of all three.

"No!" Ben yelled. "You're not playing in an air cast!"

"I can still get around. Let me play one point and if you think it's too dangerous after that…."

"Trust me, Kenny, if they had to insert a titanium rod into your leg, you shouldn't be out here," I replied. "You can't play ultimate with a shattered fibula. Go home and rest."

"Aw, man!"

After that, he came out once or twice more trying to convince us that a week's rest had done a world of good for his destroyed leg. After we refused to let him into the game a few more times, we never saw him again. My guess? He's either dead or running a multi-million dollar air-conditioning business. And knowing a little about life, I'm leaning toward the latter.

Now the new field didn't have obstacles like the fort (most obstacle courses don't have as many obstacles as the fort) but halfway through the semester we were thrown one pretty awesome curveball by the city, thus providing us with one of the all time great bloopers in the history of ultimate.

Beginning just after Thanksgiving, St. Augustine hosts its annual "Nights of Lights." White lights span the bridge, line the seawall, cover the buildings, and suffocate most of the palm trees. Those lights remain for the entire holiday season turning the town into glowing tropical wonderland.

The city decided to spread some of the holiday cheer over beside our field, building a thirty-foot high Christmas tree that came within about a foot and a half of our sideline. The whole thing was hollow inside, basically about fifty strands of Christmas lights extending down from the top of a central pole making it more of a Christmas cone than a tree, but a beautiful structure nonetheless. Incidentally, it was rip roarin' sick to go underneath that thing at night, look straight up at the point where all the lights met and spin around real fast. You got a completely sober LSD trip into outer space that was so cool you ended up happy for days.

I only set this up to tell you about the day Tall Andy stole Christmas.

It was a Sunday afternoon, our last game before December break, and the last one before I officially graduated. Tall Andy was guarding Murph and saw a pass go up toward Cherry Hill Ryan on the sideline. Like the beast he was, Tall Andy peeled off of Murph in the center of the field, covered thirty yards in about two strides and launched himself toward the disc. He was like a freaking whooping crane, a 6'7" dude flying through the air as he punched the throw halfway back to campus.

We were so amazed at how far he'd managed to fly that we didn't pay much attention to his trajectory…until we heard a sound that I can only describe as the snapping of tiny bridge cables.

THWONG! THWONG…..THWONG!

Andy had torpedoed himself straight across a few strands of Christmas lights, his body weight popping their tension until about seven of the fifty strands burst out of the ground and started swinging around like tentacles. Three of the strands had Andy wrapped up as if the Christmas tree itself had set a trap and was thinking about storing him to devour later.

He just stood there on one leg, ready but unable to tip to the ground in the tangled mass of lights.

"What the hell, Andy…you fuckin' Grinch!" I yelled.

"Yeah, hilarious. Someone help me out of here," he yelled back.

It took two minutes to untangle him and about twenty to reattach most of the lights back to the ground. It was a decent enough repair job, but I'm pretty sure kids around St. Augustine were asking their parents, "Mommy, why does the tree look sick? It's got a hole in it," all the way through New Year's.

All the craziness aside, I can tell you that the best part about our new field was how it was bringing us together and making us a better ultimate team. In fact, legitimacy crept up and bit us in the ass right where we least expected it – on the field against good teams.

FOURTEEN

I ALWAYS THINK WE PLAYED HALF A DOZEN TOURNAMENTS THAT SEMESTER, but in reality we only played two, both paid for with the money we won entering Dionys in the Mr. Flagler competition. We got like $250 because he was handsome and broke a lot of 2x4's with his fists. It was the first time any of us found out that in addition to all the other shit he did, he was also a black belt in karate. I'm also relatively certain he can fly.

One of the two tournaments happened to fall the same weekend as cross-country sectionals, the one race my coach would absolutely not let me miss to go chase plastic. While I was finishing my customary fifth to last running around the St. Louis Cardinals spring training facility, Flagler was doing surprisingly well in a tiny six-team tournament up the coast in DeLand. Without me they got by Stetson, Stetson B, and a local club team, losing only to Central Florida and Florida State – and even then just barely. Of course this led to half the team making jokes about how much better they were without me and half the team refusing to talk to me for a week because Flagler could've done the unthinkable and *won* a tournament if I wasn't off pretending to be a decent runner.

Cherry Hill Ryan is now a big shot financial planner in Cleveland. Through his company, he scored great seats to an Indians vs. Red Sox game and recently invited me to come up from Pittsburgh for the night. Somewhere in the middle of the fifth inning he turns to me, covers the ears of his six-year old son and says….

"You're still a dickhead for not coming to Stetson."

"Here's the thing, man. I didn't know the overall mediocrity of the teams would let us be that competitive."

Ryan Jr. peeled some cotton candy from his chin. "Why did you cover my ears?"

"I didn't want you to have to hear me call Cramer a dickhead for not coming to Stetson."

"What's Stetson?"

Cherry Hill Ryan nodded mournfully as Dustin Pedroia struck out. "Our one chance to be champions, buddy. Our one chance to be champions."

Every player has those couple things they regret in their career. That one time you wished you'd laid out - that momentary lapse of concentration - that epic tournament you missed because some clown from work was getting married. Stetson is one of mine. It was a crappy tournament with six teams that were far from elite, but had I been there, we more than likely would've brought a dumb trophy back to St. Augustine. For a team that all along had been thrown together like a junkyard tractor, that would've been as good as winning Mardis Gras.

The one big tournament we did play in that semester was called Itchfest. It was hosted by Vanderbilt University up in Nashville. Once again, I hit the interstate with The Swiss, but this time I didn't drive. My truck stayed at home in favor of the brand new 1999 Ford Mustang they'd somehow picked up as a Christmas present from someone rich in Hawaii. Seriously, I don't know what the hell those guys were up to. They owned surfboards, just enough clothes to survive, and a sick ass car. And that was it. Thinking about it now, they may very well have been actual Greek gods who only came to Earth to do a little research on the mortals they ruled. That's the only sensible explanation.

It was dark as we wound toward Chattanooga on I-75 north of Atlanta. Hermi was driving when this souped-up bubba truck roared past us. Seeing the Mustang, they slowed down. We caught up. For about a half mile, they paralleled us as Hermi cluelessly headbanged to Guns N' Roses. The whole time, the inbred in the passenger's seat was imploring Hermi to roll down his window as they sped up and slowed down, revving the badass engine that gave their lives a tiny bit of purpose. Hermi had no idea it was even happening.

"What is up with this guy?" he said. "Go past me already."

I leaned over and waved. "I think he wants to race you, man."

"Well that's dumb," Hermi squeaked. "I don't want to race him."

"In that case I think you should tell him."

So at 70MPH on the interstate, Hermi casually turns off the radio, rolls down the window, looks at the chaw-stained north Georgia rebel and yells into the wind, "Hello, sir! How are you tonight?"

"Let's go, boy. See who here got the better Injun."

We were all pretty certain he meant engine, so with Dionys giggling his head off in the back, Hermi shouts, "Ok!" and steps on the gas. We shoot forward with a roar. The truck flies past us and off into the night as Hermi casually decelerates back down to 73 miles per hour. "Oh shit, looks like he won," he said, turning up his music.

"At least you finally got to talk to a redneck," Dionys laughed from the back.

Even after losing the epic drag race, the tournament ended up being pretty awesome. With our fresh crop of good rookies, we were no longer a joke that the elite teams could just roll over. Instead of getting crushed now, we actually got to lose in heartbreaking fashion.

In a game that showed how far we'd come in a couple years, we battled Georgia Tech hard. Just after halftime, I cut in front of a toss at midfield, intercepted it and bombed my third assist of the game to Murph, whose speed they had no answer for. It cut the score to 8-6, but we couldn't get any closer and dropped a tough defensive battle 11-6. A year and a half prior, the same team had stomped us by ten in a game that was never close. Now we'd given them a moderate scare.

We even had the lead for the majority of the next game against Vanderbilt. It was stunning. Cherry Hill Ryan had two goals for god's sake, boxing out defenders for flicks I lobbed to him along the sideline. While none of us were looking, he'd somehow gone and turned himself into a good player. His play helped us take the half 7-6.

In the 2nd half, we relinquished the lead until I went over their tallest dude at the front of the end zone to grab a hammer that Havelock Ben had tossed directly into the sun. Honestly, the damn thing left Ben's hand and rode a sunbeam 93 million miles directly into my fried retinas. I have no idea how I caught it, but I swear the tiny hovering circle that appears whenever I blink is because of that goal. It tied the game 10-10.

It was 11-11 when the soft cap horn sounded during a time out we'd called on the goal line. Game to thirteen. All we needed to do was move the disc three yards to be on the precipice of victory. Three freaking yards.

Off the timeout, Murph swung the disc to Opie in the center of the field. From the front of the stack, I faked break side, lost my guy and struck a diagonal cut toward the back corner. There was no one near me. Opie could've practically handed me the disc for the goal. Instead he floated a forehand to space. Outer fucking space.

There's nothing on an ultimate field quite as helpless as the feeling of sprinting toward a disc that's inevitably going to hit the ground. You run anyway, hoping that for a few glorious steps you're faster than history suggests. I turned on the jets. I laid out. A half-inch in front of my fingers, the disc hit the grass. Our chance to take the lead and ultimately the game was gone. We fell 13-11.

So at 0-2, we met a team we thought would be a pushover, considering they were a high school team in a college tournament. And in 1999, who the hell ever heard of a high school ultimate team? The trouble was they were the Paideia High School Ultimate team out of Atlanta and every kid who goes to that school came here from another planet.

There are certain high schools that are nationally known for ultimate. Amherst out of Massachusetts comes to mind. These are teams who somehow get athletes who should be playing football and turn them into sick ultimate players. Also, they take nerds who fart algebra and trip over their music stands and turn them into sick ultimate players. Paideia beat us 13-9 in a game where our main highlight was the first Callahan goal I'd ever seen.

Note: A Callahan goal is when a defensive player catches the disc in their opponent's end zone for a score, much like a defensive touchdown in football. It's named for Henry Callahan, the founder of the ultimate team at the University of Oregon - one of ultimate's first true stars whose life was tragically cut short when he was murdered during a street robbery in 1982.

We were down 10-6 and the guy I was guarding pulled me deep, then stopped and came back in. I'd just turned around when I saw The Keg slide off his man and step in front of a short pass out of the end zone. It hit him square in the keg and popped up in the air. He took a step and caught it outright just over the goal line. Everything stopped. He held the disc up.

"Uh, I'm in the end zone!" he yelled back in my direction. "Is that a goal? Cramer, what do I do here?"

That seemed to be a piece of information a captain should know. And yet I didn't.

"I think it's….hell, it *should* be a goal. Paideia, is that a goal?"

I'm sure they knew damn well it was a goal, but were amused by our confusion. None of them answered. I think they hoped the stupid novices they were playing would decide it wasn't, then walk it back to the line, tap it in and turn the damn thing over.

"Are they stalling you?"

The Keg looked around. "No."

"There's your answer," I said, jogging toward him.

It was a goal indeed. We all did keg bumps to celebrate the most awesome moment you can possibly have in a game where your college team loses to high school kids.

Luckily at 0-3, our next game was versus the new team at Middle Tennessee State. It was under the lights in late October and once the sun went down, it was goddamn freezing. I'm pretty sure it's the coldest ultimate game I've ever played in, especially since it was still 80 degrees down in St. Augustine and our bodies were in no way prepared for it. A transaction at halftime perfectly sums up just how frigid it was. Havelock Ben approached their huddle and tapped one of their guys on the shoulder. This dude was a freaking genius of preparation - the only one on either team who'd brought along winter gloves.

"I will trade you a beer for those gloves for the rest of the game," Ben said, his breath clearly visible. "We have beer in the trunk."

The kid looked at him with a toasty warm smile. "I'm not giving these up for less than a six pack."

"A whole six pack?" Ben shivered, grimacing at the thought. He shook his head and took a few steps back toward our sideline before he was stopped by an idea and yelled back over his shoulder. "What about three beers for one glove?"

"One glove?"

"Yeah, we switch left and right every point."

"Four beers and it's a deal."

So for four beers, Ben got a glove that he was able to use to warm one hand. When he had the right-handed glove, he had to waste three seconds of his allotted stall count tucking the disc in his armpit and taking the glove off so he could throw. I thought he was a moron until I swatted a D out of bounds and lost all feeling in my right arm. The disc was so cold it was like smacking a rotating dinner plate. I had to promise to buy him a beer at dinner later, and in return I could borrow his borrowed glove for a point until feeling returned to my hand. It was well worth the $4.50.

We won 13-5, just sort of dismantling a team that amazingly enough, we were flat out better than. Murph scored four goals, Jeremy the Stick had four assists and me, Ben, Opie, and the Swiss pretty much dominated them. Near the end of the game when we had it well in hand, we barely knew what to do. Three years of Flagler Ultimate and so far the few wins we'd scratched out had all come in spectacular fashion. We were so bad at coasting home that I accidentally crushed a guy along the sideline just before the final throw. He was groaning at my feet as I lofted a high release flick about 35 yards that Ben pancaked between gloved and nongloved hands to end the game. There were no high fives, no screams, no nothing. We just lined up and shook the hands of a team we'd trounced, got in the cars, turned up the heat and left. It was nice to be on the good side of the beating for once. Ya know, like a real team.

We were seeded 13th out of 16 teams the next day, which got us a matchup with the University of Tennessee, at the time ranked 10th in the country. Yet another school whose population in relation to Flagler would resemble one of those charts showing how many Earths could fit into Jupiter. The game itself was awesome, but the part I still laugh at came just before the pull. We had ten guys. They had like 24 and right before the game as we were still pissing around, they got all hyped up and announced their starting lineup. Like honestly, they had a guy with a booming voice shouting into a bullhorn...

"At handler, a five-foot-ten sophomore from Crackertown, Tennessee, number seven, Artie Poopshoes!"

And then Artie would yell his head off as he ran through a tunnel of his teammates, giving them low fives as he headed out to the line. We watched in awe as they made a giant spectacle out of the whole thing. As we walked onto the field, I decided we couldn't let them have *all* the pregame fun. So right before they were about ready to pull, I looked at the guys lined up beside me.

"Yeah, we gotta do something to answer that. Just follow my lead, ok?"

My teammates nodded, completely unsure as to what I was planning until I took off my hat and placed it over my heart. In the loudest singing voice I could muster, I began to belt out…..

"O-oooh say can you see…."

To which the rest of the line bellowed with me, "….by the dawn's early light. What so proudly we hailed…."

Tennessee had no idea what the hell to do. The guy ready to pull the disc abruptly put it down. They all took off their hats and stood at attention while we sang. But that wasn't the best part. The best part was that the two club teams on the adjacent field had already started their game. Hearing us sing the national anthem, they slowed to a jog - all of them looking at each other and wondering if they became communists for not standing at attention as some dorks on the neighboring field mangled "The Star Spangled Banner." The same exact thing happened on the fields behind us as well. The entire tournament came to a confused, patriotic halt.

"….and the home of the…..brave!"

When we'd belted out the entire thing, we got some polite applause and the tournament hummed back to life. And when it did, Flagler College played its best, most complete game of ultimate ever. They threw a zone on us. We sliced through it. They switched to man. We ran past them. We made real honest-to-god ultimate cuts, weaving our way up the field. We played force defense that was actually frustrating one of the better teams in the southeast. For one game against a solid team, we weren't just a bunch of goofy losers. We weren't winning based on the pure athleticism of two guys. We were a truly good ultimate team fighting and clawing for every inch against another good ultimate team. It was bizzaro world.

I lobbed one up for Dionys and the 5'7" beast roofed a much taller guy to bring it down for the goal to tie the game 3-3. Six points in, the game was already so intense that upon landing, he exploded with a guttural roar and spiked the disc. It was five-thousand percent more energy than we'd ever seen burst out of the kid. Seriously, imagine Gandhi celebrating like Hulk Hogan for a second and you'll begin to understand our shock.

The Tennessee guy didn't take too kindly to having the disc spiked at his feet, so he got in Dionys's face. Dionys just pointed back toward the other goal line, which pissed off the Tennessee dude even more. Next thing we knew, we were all sprinting down toward the end zone to break it up.

"Hey, hey....he's foreign. It's cool. He doesn't know!" Murph yelled.

Ben pushed between the two of them. "He's Swiss! He's Swiss!"

A couple of the Tennessee guys ran over to help pull their guy away as Hermi calmly walked over from the sideline, sipping on a Capri Sun. "Dionys, please don't kill him. I don't want to have to explain to mom why you're in a Nashville jail."

"Oh yeah," I said to the fuming Tennessee guy as he got pushed by me. "He's a black belt in karate, so you might wanna just cool it."

Once it all calmed down and we had Dionys corralled, we realized how stupid the whole thing was.

I nudged Ben and laughed. "He's Swiss! He's Swiss! You said that like they're known for their violent outbursts. They're isolation...."

"I know they're isolationists! It was all I could think of," Ben said, turning to shove Dionys. "Where the fuck did that come from?"

Dionys shrugged. "Perhaps I went a bit overboard in my excitement."

"Eh, next time just spike it again," Ben said.

"Except rip off your shirt and spike that too," Murph added.

"And your pants," I said. "Just fucking spike your pants and run naked into the woods."

Dionys tried to remain stone-faced and intense, but a smile was cracking through. "I was really in a zone here, you know."

"It's settled. Next goal, you're spiking your fucking pants."

Anyway, I've found there are two possible outcomes after an incident like that. Either the game gets stupidly chippy or it ends up more civil and friendly as the two teams share a good laugh. Luckily the second scenario played out. They took half at 7-5 as we locked into an intense defensive battle. Earlier in the game, they'd called out an offensive set in the end zone called "Yo-yo." A guy came out of the middle of the stack, wrapped around the back and made a fishhook cut to the front corner for the score. Just after halftime they called it again so I didn't even follow my guy around the back of the stack. I just stepped out, waited for him and laid out to make the D.

Near the end of the game, they called a timeout at the goal line and set up a vertical stack in the end zone. The handler called "Yo-yo."

I pointed to Dionys. "Hey, your guy is going to swing around the back of the stack and head for the corner."

The guy who was set to cut looked at me like I'd just levitated. "No. No. That's not what we're doing at all." He gestured to Dionys. "Ignore him."

"You guys only have one end zone play," I laughed. "You've run it three times now."

He tried to alert the handler. "Hey Josh….hey, they know what we're…." The disc was tapped in. "Shit," he said taking off on his futile cut. Dionys smothered him. Opie had the dump shut down. The handler had nowhere to go with the disc and ended up getting stalled.

We were right with them. Our defense was better. Our athleticism was better. Me, Ben, and Opie ran a slick weave out of which I zipped a crossfield backhand to The Keg that I only had in my hands for a half second at most. It was the most crisp and precise point Flagler had ever run. It was the first time we'd ever looked like a machine. That goal closed the gap to 9-7. It was as close as we'd get. The next two points were hard fought, but even our stifling defense couldn't mask the fact that in the end they had more guys with better, more accurate throws. The last two points must've taken fifteen minutes. But they were able to punch in the scores that we couldn't. The best game of ultimate that

Flagler ever played ended up being an 11-7 loss.

Ready to hit the road, we dropped our losers bracket game 11-8 to come out of the tournament with a junktastic 1-5 record. Still though, with a couple breaks here and there, we felt we could've been 5-1. Our goal differential for the tournament was only minus ten, which to that point was considered a pretty competitive game against most teams.

Of course, we can't get home without one or two more idiotic things happening on the road. We stopped for gas at a Chevron in the booming metropolis of Manchester, Tennessee and as I flexed my leg to get out of the low riding Mustang, my right hamstring curled into a ball like a scared armadillo. In pain, I reached back for it, trying not to topple over at the gas pumps. In doing so, I clenched my left quad - which also decided to do the frightened armadillo.

"Aaaah!" I yelled, now completely unable to stand. Trust me, a Chevron is not the best place for dual leg cramps. There was nothing I could do except look like a complete nutjob pretending to be Superman on a concrete riser at the end of the pumps waiting for either leg to loosen up. It was a situation that would've been pretty tough to explain to the old people filling up their motorhome beside us, so I didn't even bother.

"What in the hell are you doing?" Hermi asked with alarm. "Are you shot?"

"Nah, it's...frickin....cramps."

Hermi nodded. "We should probably get you something to drink."

I grunted and gave a thumb's up. "That would be fantastic."

It was sixty seconds of pure agony, but finally my quad let up. About a minute later, so did my hamstring. I spent the next five minutes trying to stretch before deciding that with the entire state of Georgia still ahead of us, I'd better go buy some muscle balm to help soothe my legs.

Across the street was a Piggly Wiggly grocery store. Yes, that's its name. There's no joke here. With Dionys and Hermi sitting in the car in the parking lot, I quickly ducked in, bought a small tub of Icy Hot and walked outside. There was only one problem I hadn't anticipated. The only place I had to apply the stuff was in the passenger's seat of a Ford Mustang. And that was not going to work.

Hmmm.

I looked around. Nothing but parking lot. So I made a decision that like most decisions I made at the time was a tick below well thought out. There was a small enclave behind the shopping carts. It looked secluded enough. There, I tried lathering my entire hamstring by pulling up my shorts, but that wasn't working. The fabric kept falling and getting in the way. I looked around. Nobody was paying attention. Nobody would mind if I…

I'd probably had my pants down in that shopping center about ten seconds when a nice family in a station wagon drove by. In the passenger's seat, the mother looked at me with a smile that quickly contorted into something that would reflect back from a funhouse mirror. The way I remember it now, the kids in the back all dropped their lollipops to the floor mats and stared horrified at the creepy kid rubbing goo on his ass off behind the shopping carts at the Piggly Wiggly - but in reality, they probably didn't even notice.

"It's cramps!" I yelled in vain as the car drove off. "I got a hamstring…son of a bitch!" I jerked my pants back up and ran as fast as I had all weekend toward the Mustang. "Go, go, go!" I shouted to Dionys.

"What?"

"I just exposed myself to a family in a station wagon."

"You *what?*"

"It was an accident. Just drive, man."

It was a good fifteen minutes on the interstate before I realized that the Manchester cops probably weren't tailing us. I wasn't going to get written up for indecent exposure in Tennessee. Which is good because I'm pretty sure they send you straight to the gas chamber for that.

I don't recall feeling any sense of nostalgia when we got home. As it turned out, those would be the last games I'd ever play for the stupid little team I started almost three years before. They would be the last games I'd play with Havelock Ben, my right hand man for all that time. Like a lot of good friends in college, we'd graduate and go our separate ways. And though we went something god awful like 5-24 during our college careers, I wouldn't have traded all those trips with guys like Chickamauga Jeff, Tall Andy, Cheerleader Dustin, Goose, and The Swiss for a trip to nationals. I'd get that later anyway. Sort of.

FIFTEEN

So the millennium had come and gone and as far as we could tell, no planes had fallen from the sky and computers hadn't accidentally launched all the world's nukes. (Seriously, we were incredibly worried about this at the time.) Ultimate was still being played all over the country, including in St. Augustine where I now found myself like most new graduates, sporting a degree and having no idea what in god's name to do with it. And St. Augustine is the type of place that's so beautiful it murders your ambition - literally impales it with a palm tree. The amount of people I knew that passed up great jobs in Ohio or New Jersey to wait tables at Applebee's in St. Augustine was kind of staggering. You just couldn't peel yourself away. I got a six-dollar an hour job at Barnes & Noble and was perfectly content stacking books all day. Such was life on the beach.

And so having graduated, I also found myself a man without a team. In bigger cities like Seattle, Boston, and San Francisco the top club teams are waiting to pounce on any and all talent coming out of college. And if you aren't quite good enough for the elite teams, there are numerous second-tier teams to keep your passion fueled. There are, however, many places where club ultimate just isn't an option. Northeast Florida in the year 2000 was one of those places. There was just this weird amalgam of pickup games up and down the coast that weren't feeding any central team.

But the pickup was really, really good. Some nights it was an outright show. It was sort of amazing how many great athletes descended on a mosquito-infested soccer field built into a wildlife preserve on the east side of Jacksonville, Florida.

I'd always find myself pitted against another former college pitcher named Clancy who wore knee high socks and played ultimate like a sarcastic bull. We had virtually the same game right down to our throws, which the baseball player in us tended to rocket toward our teammates as if we were trying to light up a radar gun.

Everyone else out there managed to have an evil ultimate twin as well. Tall Andy had Big Tim. Goose had a former soccer player named Wall. Dionys had a little muscular dude I'll call Speedy Kyle. One of the reasons those games were so good was that we all showed up and looked downfield into a mirror.

One of the new players who showed up that year was a guy I'll call Black Tide Matt. He was a handler who just moved to the east coast from Santa Barbara and had a college national championship under his belt, which in ultimate-starved Jacksonville earned him instant credibility.

For those unfamiliar, UC Santa Barbara had two of the most amazing and sustained runs of excellence ever seen in college ultimate, winning three straight titles from 1988-1990 and again from 1996-1998. Matt was part of their return to the top in '96. In ultimate circles, UCSB Black Tide is like Notre Dame football. Even when they're mediocre, the name and the jersey still radiate power.

Typical conversations with Black Tide Matt started like this:

"Well, back when I played for Black Tide…."

In other words, you'd ask him a question like "Hey Matt, do you know a good place get tacos around here?"

And he'd answer with something like, "Well back when I played for Black Tide and we won the national championship, the team loved a place called Pepe's."

"Matt, that has literally no bearing on my situation here in Jacksonville."

"Oh, doesn't it? Well I guess if it doesn't have anything to do with winning championships, then you're asking the wrong guy."

I absolutely, unequivocally drove him insane. This was mainly because a few times a game, I threw behind the backers, between the leggers, no-look scoobers, spin overheads, and random crap that I chucked on the run however the hell I'd caught the disc. For a guy used to a very methodical, possession-oriented game, it was like taking a cheese grater to his brain.

The first month he was in town he'd casually take me aside at least once a game and say, "Look, Cramer, you're a really good player. But I'm telling you that if you ever want to get serious, that shit isn't going to work in a tournament. Please knock it off. You're giving me an ulcer."

It was a part of my game that I could never quite resist, despite his protests. To be honest, I probably put up 20% more unnecessarily weird throws than I otherwise would've just because I thought it was funny to look over and see his eyelids twitching.

Anyway, guys like him were the reason our pickup games exploded into the once- a-week spectacle they became. For two hours under the lights, it was nothing but hucks, bullets, layouts, and leaps. The stall count barely ever got above five. Even watching from the sideline, the brand we played those nights was fast and exciting. It was a run and gun up-tempo style that perfectly fit our personnel. It wasn't long before we all looked at each other and said:

"Ya know I think if we all got together and played against other teams…."

"We'd be pretty damn good."

Jacksonville Bad Chicken.

Big Tim must've been at the shitty wing joint in the strip mall beside campus when he came up with the name. Otherwise, I have zero idea where it came from. I never asked because I figured the story would likely be high on vomit and low on interesting. So we weren't blessed with the most intimidating name, but I guess it beat Lousy Beef or Rancid Salmon, so all in all it could've been worse.

Sometime before our first tournament games, we figured we should probably play together as a team once or twice. Our first opportunity came through a couple of ex-military guys on the team that I haven't mentioned yet. I'll call them Marine Matt and Coast Guard Robbie. Both of them looked like they could be called on to parachute into North Korea at any second. Apparently they had some connections because one sunny Saturday morning we all woke up at 0700 to go scrimmage the ultimate team from the Marine Corps Unit at Blount Island.

Listen to this next part, because it's important. If you like playing ultimate because it's a nice casual game played between friends, do not, I repeat, *do not* challenge the US Marines. You honestly think you want to win - that you'll do absolutely anything in order to score a goal – that losing is not an option. Then you have a 6'4" Hispanic dude with a flat top yelling a stall count into your face like he's in some paramilitary exercise and you realize you have no idea what internal drive actually is. As ultimate players, when we lose, we shake it off and go have a beer. As Marines, they've been trained that when they lose, people die. And when you have a team made up entirely of guys with that particular mentality, you have a game of ultimate you've never, ever experienced.

This isn't to say they weren't great guys, because they were. It's just that well - you want to feel like the biggest douche canoe in America? Call a foul on a fucking Marine. See how that goes over.

One of our main handlers was a very religious Christian rocker we all called Shark. He was the type of guy whose music collection included metal bands with names like "Weapon of God" and "Naylz in the Kross." Anyway, sometime on the second point Shark got the disc, went to throw a backhand and got nudged in the back for his effort. It was a legitimate foul in ultimate, but not in say - an alley in Somalia. The dude just stared at him.

"What do you mean, foul?"

"You….uh….pushed me as I went to throw."

"Yeah. I didn't want you to complete it."

"That's kind of the reason it's a foul," Shark said.

Black Tide Matt butted in. "Ya know, back when I played for Black Tide…."

Clancy piped up. "That's not going to impress these guys Matt…. seeing as some of them have been to war and all. Just saying."

"Oh, ok. Well then I got nothing," Matt said. "Shark, that's probably a turnover."

Shark nodded, realizing that we'd stumbled into a totally different world. "Yup. Ok then. Turnover."

And so we played two brutally awesome games with rules that were half ultimate, half rugby. Personally, I loved it. You had to learn to get off accurate throws with a forearm in your ribs, an elbow in the back, or knuckles to the collarbone. You had to get leverage and battle through the line just to get out of the stack. We were on their fields, playing by their rules and they didn't mind if you gave them a little shove to get open or if you full on boxed them out to grab a throw. Miami of Ohio would've called nine thousand fouls on the first point alone. As it was, I think Shark's call was just about it.

It was like a Ferrari battling an M1A1 tank. We had slick, fast, agile guys with precise throws they could only dream of. They had an endless wave of what seemed like the same exact guy whose battle-tested boot camp lungs were outright laughing at us. The Marines came out and dominated as we got used to their style of play going up 5-2 out of the gate. The Ferrari was being crushed under the tracks of the tank. But then like any good opponent, with our backs to the wall, we abandoned the tactics that weren't working in favor of something new and surprising.

The main zone defense used at the time was called "the cup." Basically, three players form a half circle (or cup) around the person with the disc. Three more defenders sit behind the cup in what amounts to a straight line wall, while one guy sits back deep to cut off any hucks. It became pretty obvious that zone defense had not yet made its way into military circles, which is surprising because you'd assume the boys at the Pentagon would've sent out a memo somewhere along the line. Suddenly, the tank didn't know where to aim as the Ferraris sped around it.

We ended up forcing a lot of turns and coming back to win the first game 11-7. We took the second game as well 9-4, but not before the M1A1 got in one thunderous shot. Big Tim put one up along the sideline for me. I went over one of the Marines and tipped the disc, then spun in the air to reach for it as it floated out in front of me. All I remember next was a big red wall, the word MARINES and an anchor smashing into my face as one of them charged in from across the field and laid me out like a free safety. I must've flown three feet out of bounds.

He came over to help me up as I struggled to catch my breath.

"You alright?" he asked.

"I'll tell you as soon as I can breathe again," I said before exhaling and slowly making my way to one knee.

I instinctively reached out for the disc just sort of assuming he was going to hand it to me. It was about the most obvious foul you could possibly commit. But when I reached for the disc, he kept it, assuming it was a turnover and that I was about to tap it into play.

"So....you're keeping the disc then?" I said.

"Yeah. Isn't that a turnover? You didn't catch it."

"Well....yeah, but..."

"Was I not allowed to flatten you like that?"

"Technically no. That's about as against the rules as possible."

"Oh shit, I thought once it got tipped you could just lay people out."

"Know what? I wish that was the rule myself," I said. "Just take it. Nice hit."

As I tapped the disc into play, Shark yelled to me. "Cramer, that's not a foul?"

"Not today!" I shouted back.

Our odyssey into military rug-timate definitely helped both the tank and the Ferrari. We learned how to play a little tougher and more physical. They hung around as we taught them how to play and beat zone defense, something which I'm sure they couldn't wait to employ against the other bases when they got a chance. All in all, it was just a great day. I know it might be a long shot considering the events coming down the road, but I hope every single one of the guys we played that day came through the conflict of the following decade with their lives and their good health. I sincerely hope every one of them can run outside on a beautiful day and toss a disc around with their kids. Those guys are the reason we can do silly little things like drive to Gainesville and chase plastic. I can't possibly thank them enough for both their service and for giving me bruises that I'm pretty sure I still have.

So the Bad Chicken of Jacksonville felt as if we were now prepared to head out into the world of club ultimate. In the rainy and windy conditions of our first tournament, we hung tough with the likes of nationals-caliber teams like Vicious Cycle out of Gainesville and Knoxville Hitsquad. We beat the teams we should've beaten and lost to the teams that were a ring or two above us. The main problem was that we never really had all our guys on the field at once. We'd play one day without Tall Andy and Speedy Kyle and the next without Marine Matt and Coast Guard Robbie. Because we were always missing key guys, we had to fill out the roster with some dudes who were fun to have around but shouldn't in any way have been on the field with a serious club team. Such was the case with a guy I'm going to call Receding Eddie.

Receding Eddie was about 5'5", hideously uncoordinated, and almost completely bald at 23. Like most dudes who find their way onto the field during games they should in no way be allowed into, he was just too nice a guy for any of us to stricken with the truth. And he was too happy and excited to be out there to ever consider that he shouldn't have been.

One of the older guys on the team had a sweet high-speed camera. He used it to snap action photos during a game that he had to sit out with a bruised quad. What he ended up with was an amazing pictorial microcosm of our team. I still have it in an old photo album. In that album, there are great shots of:

1) Coast Guard Robbie winding up to throw a backhand huck.

2) Clancy coiled and ready to fire one of his ridiculous 60 yard hammers.

3) Black Tide Matt effortlessly releasing a flick.

4) Shark steering a backhand through the cup zone.

5) Me leaping in front of a guy to catch a run-through D and….

6) Receding Eddie in mid stumble with his arms awkwardly crossed - looking like he'd puked the disc onto his foot with absolutely no one around him.

Unfortunately against teams like Vicious Cycle and Hitsquad, you can't hide guys like Receding Eddie. So even with all our amazing athletes, we'd consistently fall 11-8 and 13-9 and 15-12. The thing is though, having guys like Receding Eddie on your team gives you moments that are almost worth going 2-3 at every tournament. For instance, I give you the time Clancy and I were warming up, trying to gauge the intricacies of a pretty stiff wind after arriving at a tournament one morning. As one of his hammers died in a wind gust, Clancy turned to me….

"Man, I'm glad I'm crashing on my sister's couch and not trying to camp this weekend."

Just then out of the corner of our eyes, we see a green Coleman tent somersault past us, flipping over like a boulder on the moon, heading for the woods.

We watched it tumble away for about five seconds before we hear the distinct shuffling of feet in the grass.

Receding Eddie sprinted past us. "Shit….shit….shit….."

When the wind died down, he managed to catch up to it, lugging his tent the entire way back across the field. Clancy and I just shook our heads and laughed as we watched him once again make an attempt to tie it down. Three minutes later there was another wind gust.

Five….four….three…two…

"Shit…..shit….shit….shit…..shit….."

At a later tournament, the Florida sun was absolutely beating down on us. Eddie, being a pale fellow like me had done the smart thing and lathered sunscreen on his arms, legs, neck and face. The dude was totally set, except that earlier in the tournament, he'd lost his hat. Remember I'm calling him Receding Eddie for a reason. At halftime of our noon game, we all gathered around for water, rest, and a strategy session. Eddie was sitting in a folding chair, chugging water on the outskirts of our circle when we hear a shriek from Clancy's girlfriend.

"Oh my God, Eddie! You need to get out of the sun right now!"

He peered up at her from behind his tiny circular sunglasses. "What?"

While we were on the field, none of us had come to notice that his head was now the color of a freaking fire truck. Honestly, bury him to his eyebrows in tomatoes and you couldn't have found him. He actually missed the rest of the tournament because no one would let him out of the shade. Our level of play increased dramatically. As did his melanoma risk.

Receding Eddie was the guy on your team who unintentionally made the waitress uncomfortable at dinner and unapologetically belted out 80's pop songs in the van right after committing more turnovers than the rest of the team combined. But he was also the guy that you remember fondly years later when you realize that the wins and losses count a lot less than the time you spent with the characters ultimate brought into your life for a few glorious moments.

Speaking of which, I've found that some people you meet through ultimate leave an indelible impression having only been in your life for a couple of minutes. Such was the case with a four-year old girl who happened to be sitting beside Clancy and I as we watched the open club final at Frostbreaker. Two rounds beforehand, we'd dropped another 11-8 game against a team called Miami Refugees, a game I only remember for the fact that during a timeout, someone's dog ran into our end zone, lowered its ass and did the inevitable. The entire sideline basically watched the dog start to squat and in unison yelled….

"No….no….no…..aaaaah……shit."

It took a minute as both teams debated how to effectively move the deuce from the scoring area. Then we realized that the sideline happened to be filled with objects that were incredibly well suited for such a task. Someone was going to get an unpleasant surprise when they got back to the sideline. That person was Shark.

"Hey, was that my disc? That was my disc!" he said, nudging it across the grass with his toe. "Aw, come on. You guys are real assholes sometimes."

Anyway, even with our loss in the quarterfinals, a few of us decided to stick around and watch some great ultimate for the rest of the day. Sometime during an intense final between Gainesville Vicious Cycle and New York Bombsquad, we started conversing with a woman in a bandana who'd obviously just gotten done playing. We're talking and joking for a few points until during a break in the action, she gestured to her adorable little daughter who was sitting beside us going to town on a coloring book.

"Hey, is there any chance you guys could watch her for a second while I run back to my car?" she asked.

"Sure," Clancy said before pointing toward Shark. "This guy is totally rehabilitated so everything should be fine."

"Prison was really good for him," I said.

Shark swatted Clancy across the chest. "You can't joke about that shit, man. That's not funny."

"Really?" Clancy said, thumbing over his shoulder to find the mom silently laughing. "Mom here chuckled."

"I'm not some kid criminal," Shark said. "Your daughter will be perfectly safe."

"As safe as she can possibly be with three total strangers," I said.

Incredibly enough, the woman just grinned and stood up. "I shouldn't be too long."

And so we found ourselves entrusted with the care of a daycare-aged child as we sat on the sidelines stretching our hamstrings and eating stale bagels. Watch a toddler for five minutes. We were three grown-ass men. How hard could that be?

New York worked the disc down the field whereupon one of their guys uncorked probably the best throw I've ever seen in my life. He faked a crossfield hammer toward the back left cone and somehow wrapped it around his head, throwing it behind his neck, hitting a cutter in stride to the back right corner. It was sheer wizardry. In fact, I'm pretty sure word of that throw crossed the pond and inspired J.K. Rowling to write the Harry Potter series.

"Holy shit!" I exclaimed. "Are you kidding? Are you kidding me?"

"That was sick!" Clancy said, collapsing to his back.

"Little girl, did you see that? Did you *see* that?"

We turned to see a lonely coloring book. Uh-oh. The three of us sprung to our feet with more urgency than any of us had shown all weekend. We spun 360 degrees - no sign of her. All we saw was a giant swarm of barefoot guys with beards, chicks in sarongs, tents, flying discs, and beer cans. Slowly all of the horrible, horrible things that could befall a child in such an area started to give us the shakes. There was a parking lot just across the way. Holy shit, she could be under a van. There was a Chevron just behind the parking lot. Vagrants hung out at gas stations. Son of a bitch, she could be *inside* a van. She could be crushed by some dude chasing a disc, eaten by a dog, tumble into a well....

"See, this is why you don't joke around that I'm a kid criminal!" Shark exclaimed.

"Nah, that was still funny despite the current circumstances," Clancy replied as we walked quickly and awkwardly around the fields doing all we could to make it seem like we hadn't just lost someone's child.

"She can't be that far. It was only two minutes. How far can a little girl get in two minutes?" I asked.

"Far enough to be out of sight."

"Call out her name, man." I said.

"Her mom never told us her name. Which is flat out irresponsible," Clancy said. "I'm totally deflecting blame here."

"Ah, crap," I said. "Sunshine! Flower!"

"What the hell are you doing?"

"Did you see her mom? The chances are pretty good the girl's name is Sunshine or Flower."

Clancy nodded. It was our last hope. "Sunshine! Flower!"

No answer.

"Rainbow!"

We turned back toward the parking lot just in time to notice that the mom was now on a return trip from her car. She was barefoot and gliding along, talking to her friends and teammates along the way, laughing and smiling - but to us, each step sounded like the thunderprint of a monster.

"Shit, she's on her way back," I said, now running in nine directions at once.

Clancy slapped Shark on the shoulder. "Shark, go distract her."

"What? How?"

"Tell her funny prison stories. I don't know, just give us another couple minutes."

"Seriously, quit telling people I've been to jail!"

"Would you rather tell her that her little girl is wandering aimlessly around Gainesville?" I said. "C'mon, Shark, take one for the team."

"Fine," he said, turning around and practically smacking into the mom.

The three of us turned eight shades of white as we realized we were standing there yards away from the spot where we were supposed to be watching her daughter - yet without the daughter we were supposed to be watching. The mom sized up our sheepish, nervous looks. We didn't have to explain. She knew.

"You lost her didn't you?"

"Yes," we said in ashamed unison. "Yes we did."

One lesson I learned from the whole ordeal is that if you're going to lose someone's child, lose the child of someone who may or may not have woken up with a skinny J or two that morning. "Don't worry," she said. "I think I know where she is."

Two minutes later, the mom and her little girl returned to fetch her coloring book and we breathed a sigh of relief.

Mom laughed as she watched the worry evaporate from our bodies. "My husband is grilling burgers over by the college final. She was safe the whole time."

"We are so sorry," Shark said.

"It's fine," she answered.

"Thank you for showing us that we're not yet cut out for fatherhood," Clancy said.

"Seriously, rubbers from now on. Every time," I said.

The mom laughed. The girl waved goodbye to her worst babysitters ever and they were off. Afterward, the three of us unsuccessfully lobbied to have the team's name changed to "Three Men and a Baby."

And so I'd taken my first foray into the world of club ultimate on a team that was the very definition of mediocre. But what I'll take away from Bad Chicken beyond the wins and losses was the fact that I was once again part of something at its very inception. By no means were we an elite club level team, but what we did do was help to lay the foundation for ultimate in a major city that had so far lacked representation on a national scale. And as it turned out, Jacksonville Ultimate had some pretty good days ahead of it.

SIXTEEN

SOMEWHERE ALONG THE LINE, I REALIZED THAT I DIDN'T PARTICULARLY want to ring up books for the rest of my life and started to research ways of furthering my education. Although my degree was in Communication, I wasn't really amped for a career doing uh, whatever a Communication degree allows you to do, so I decided to explore other options. What was I good at other than ultimate and being a bit of a wanker? Well, I was definitely immature enough to connect with kids on their level. In fact my time at camp had showed me that I was incredibly good with kids. (Let's forget that I'd managed to misplace a child here for a second and just go with it.) So I ended up heading in a direction I'd never even considered upon entering school as a freshman. I decided to my future would be as a school counselor. The problem was, I was woefully short on psychology, education, and statistics credits - some essential components for being admitted into the top counseling programs.

A lot of the guys who made up the Jacksonville club team were actually students at UNF. Clancy and Wall were super seniors. Big Tim, Shark, and Black Tide Matt were graduate students. Tall Andy was taking "online classes." Probably. Nobody ever bothered to check. Bothering to check might've cost us a 6'7" super stud so everyone just sort of put him in the category of "guys we see on campus so often it's reasonable to assume they're a student." Although it was also reasonable to assume he'd been gently nudged off of every couch in St. Johns County and was now simply working his way north. Whatever the hell he was actually doing, he ended up on the team.

Needing the credits, I decided to join them. I told my mom that UNF had one of the best education departments in Florida, but by now she knew exactly what I was up to. I was going there to play ultimate.

The first time I put on the blue uniform of the University of North Florida was once again at Frostbreaker in Gainesville. Our first opponent was wrenchingly familiar. Off in the opposing end zone, the red uniforms of the University of Georgia mocked me as if to say, "There's a reason we're the color of tomato juice, boy. Prepare for another skunking." As I watched them warm up, all I could think about was the helplessness of being down 10-0 as guys in those same uniforms laughed and chuckled their way to an outright obliteration of Flagler.

A giant state university versus a team that was playing in its first ever tournament game should've been an absolute beat down. I almost had myself talked into defeat before we even pulled. Then I looked at my line. This wasn't the hodgepodge of moderately athletic goofballs I was used to sharing the field with at college tournaments. Our offense was going to be absolutely fine even if I didn't touch the disc. Hell, I might even be able to head to the tent for some water on occasion without feeling guilty.

One stat will tell you why. The heights of our starting seven were.... 6'7" - 6"7 - 6"2"- 6"2" - 6"2 - 6"2" and 5"10".

I don't think we truly realized what colossuses we looked like until we walked to the line to pull and peered toward the tiny, skinny freshman and sophomores that Georgia trotted onto the field.

On the second point of the game, Clancy tossed one slightly behind me at the goal line. My defender was right on my hip, but I managed to jump back, box him out and rip the disc away to put us up 2-0. For me, it was nothing to get excited about. I'd been up 2-0 on that very same field before only to end up losing 15-2.

We forced a turn and went up 3-0. Then 4-0. And 5-1. It was too easy. This was Georgia for god's sake, the team that had come within a half inch of shutting me out the last time I'd played them. Surely our lead couldn't last. Up to that point, all I knew about college ultimate was how to pseudo-gracefully get my head beat in. I was still anticipating our inevitable collapse when Big Tim hit Wall along the sideline for the goal that cemented a 13-6 victory. The University of North effing Florida had just beaten Georgia. Scratch that- *buried* Georgia. What the hell was going on? I looked to the sky for the inevitable speeding asteroid. Nothing. No streak of fire. No thunderclap. No mass extinction. We'd done it. We'd actually done it. In the course of one game, I went from thinking we were about to get crushed to *"Holy shit, we might roll right through this tournament."*

Unfortunately, just before our second match versus a University of Florida alumni team, a cold front roared down out of Saskatchewan and played havoc with the entire game. Seriously, where the first game was only marginally breezy, the second game was played into a thousand giant oscillating fans blowing straight out of the west end zone.

Just prior to the game, we had to wait out a thunderstorm for about forty minutes. During the delay, Receding Eddie managed to begin a trip to Subway by backing straight into Swarthmore's school van. Clancy and I were eating on the tailgate of Shark's minivan right next to the incident and watched Eddie run out into the rain to examine the damage. Some dude from Swarthmore cracked the driver's side window.

"Did you just crash into us?" the dude said, flinching as raindrops splashed into his face.

"Um…yeah," Receding Eddie said. "I….didn't see you guys there."

Clancy put down his granola bar and yelled through the downpour. "Eddie, did you ram another team's van again?"

He turned, water streaming off his head. "What?"

"He thinks it's intimidating!" Clancy yelled at the driver.

"I just didn't see them," Eddie said in a panic. "It's raining really hard!"

"Oh, he saw you," Clancy said. "And he kept right on backing up!"

"I heard him rev his engine!" I shouted.

"That's how we operate in Jacksonville!"

"UNF will fuck you van *up*!" I screamed, pounding on the bumper.

Meanwhile, through all of this, Eddie is vociferously trying to apologize and the Swarthmore dude is debating whether it's even worth it to get out and look. I don't really remember how the incident resolved itself but I am pretty sure Eddie's car insurance rate tried to sky someone.

I nudged Clancy. "You think they knew we were kidding?"

"If they couldn't take one look at Eddie and know we were shitting around… besides, it's not like we play them anyway."

More on this later.

I think I've made it clear so far that I absolutely love ultimate. As far as I'm concerned, it's the most amazing sport in existence. But I will say this - it becomes dumb and practically unwatchable in the wind. In fact, I don't think there's been a sport created by man that changes so drastically because of one particular weather condition. Imagine trying to play tennis in six inches of snow and you'll understand what happens to ultimate when Tropical Depression #4 shows up.

Staring straight into a rainless hurricane, the UF alumni prepared to send us the disc to begin the game. One of their big guys warmed up his arm, doing windmills with the disc, punching the air and cracking his back in anticipation of launching it downfield. He started off near the back line of the end zone, slowly gaining speed as he sprinted toward the goal line. His hips rotated like a mousetrap, violently sending his arm past his torso. With a torque normally reserved for power tools, he released the disc toward the heavens.

It went about eight and a half yards.

At that point, it was like a magician waved his wand and commanded it to stop. The disc fell straight to the ground, popped in the air, shot straight back through their line and rocketed out the back of the end zone.

Clancy turned to me as we casually jogged down the field to retrieve it. "Well this game is shaping up to be pretty stupid."

I picked up the disc on their goal line and flipped a two-foot pass to Black Tide Matt. Somehow we were winning and I hadn't even had to run yet.

Every point was just about the same. Get off a 20 yard pull, force a turn, use 37 passes to get it to midfield at which point one would go astray and the other team would simply punt, forcing you to do it all over again until they mercifully scored to put you out of your misery.

It was 8-8 before either team came close to the upwind goal line. Then just after we'd punted them back to the end zone like we'd done twenty times already, the weather decided to become the cover of a resort pamphlet. It was like someone tripped over the cord and temporarily unplugged all the fans. As they worked it out of their end zone with one crisp, flat pass after another, we struggled to catch up, our minds lagging behind as we continued to play passive containment defense. They crashed right through our surprised zone and punched in a backbreaking upwind goal to go up 9-8.

As we walked back to the line, we took solace only in the fact that with the wind no longer a factor, we might just be able to….

A gust roared down the field and took Black Tide Matt's baseball cap with it.

I've never heard a seven-person jinx before, but as we watched Matt's hat skip across the grass, the whole team simultaneously looked skyward.

"Really? REALLY?"

Matt went to retrieve his hat, shouting at us the whole way, "Back when I played for Black Tide, we never let the wind dictate our strategy. We'd just go out and…..shit, my hat's on the other field!"

We were so pissed at the little prank from the sky that on the next point, we almost broke the jet stream. I slipped way behind my defender who obviously thought all I'd done was deliberately take myself out of the play. Then Tall Andy wound up from midfield and threw a bomb that caused a heat wave in Quebec. When it left his hand, I swore it was headed fifty yards out the back of the end zone. Then suddenly it wasn't. I slowed, slowed, slowed down as the disc hovered over my head. Two yards in front of the goal line, it dropped like a sand weight and I had to go to my knees to catch it with my back to the field, Willie Mays style. Being that their entire defense was pushed forward, Wall came sprinting up beside me with no one on him. With nothing between us but four yards of cyclone, I gunned a flick as hard as I could. It made it about three yards. Luckily his layout covered the rest and we managed to slay the weather and tie the game.

I'm not necessarily proud of what happened on the next point. This doesn't mean, however, that I wouldn't do it again with more force and better insults.

There was a dude on their team who was probably in his mid-thirties. He might've been good at one time, but now he basically looked like a cross between a greasy-haired porn star and an Idaho potato. Being generous, I might've given him 5'7". On the next point, they decided to try our strategy and bomb one into the wind for the tall, quick guy I happened to be covering. It didn't work. About ten yards from the goal line, the disc stopped and hovered at about the height of a basketball rim. The short guy who I'll now call the Potatoman had scuttled over from the back of the stack and was trying to run it down. I peeled off my guy at the end zone, ran in, leapt and grabbed it about four feet above his outstretched Potatoman hands without so much as brushing a single stupid greasy hair on his body. I landed, ready to launch a huck toward Big Tim.

"Violation," he said from behind me.

I ignored him because surely he was kidding.

"Violation!" he yelled again.

By now he had my attention.

"What now?"

"Law of Verticality," he said, reaching for the disc.

"Law of.....huh?"

"Law of Verticality. I'm entitled to the area directly above me. The disc was directly above me when you took it. It's a violation, not a foul. You can't contest. It's my disc right here."

"Dude, you couldn't have reached that disc with a ladder."

"That doesn't matter. It was above me. I'm entitled to it. My disc."

Clancy joined the argument. "So wait, you're claiming you have unlimited right to the disc the whole way up to the moon?"

"If that's where the throw goes, then yes."

Through my shades, I glared a hole straight into his forehead. "Technically I was above *you* and the disc was above *me*, so according to your own rule, I'm gonna go ahead and use the Law of Fuck Off."

Black Tide Matt came scurrying over trying to diffuse the situation, "Ok, ok, can I just say something here?"

Clancy interrupted. "Is it gonna be about Black Tide?"

"Yeah, but it has relevance to the current situation."

The tall dude I'd been guarding turned toward Matt with awe. "You played for Black Tide?"

With pride, Matt beamed. "Yes I did. And the whole time I played for them, I never saw the Law of Verticality used like that. Not even in our national championship year."

Clancy sighed. "So I guess we can safely assume that at UCSB they didn't teach you the definition of the word relevance."

"Titles are relevant to everything, Clancy," Matt smirked.

By now, Big Tim had tromped his way over, casting his giant shadow on the Potatoman. If he'd wanted to, I'm sure he could've just made hash browns out of the guy right there on the field, but Big Tim was like giant, religious superhero. Maybe it was because guys his size ended up on the wrong side of slingshots in the parables he taught to school kids, but Big Tim never really used his size to intimidate.

Being as he was the captain and steadfastly lived by the laws of Christ, there was something about turning the other cheek and embracing your enemies and crap like that that the whole team was supposed to abide by. Apparently the Bible has a bit about the Law of Verticality. I believe it's in the second letter of Paul to the Thessalonians, which is why Big Tim knew precisely how to handle the situation.

He stepped over as calmly as a goliath could, hovering over the small Potatoman in front of him. "That rule only applies when contact is made."

The Potatoman didn't even look up. He just stared off at the horizon and said, "Law of verticality. It's my disc right here."

The other guys on his team were all just grinning as if they'd seen it before, their amused, upturned lips saying, "Ah, there goes the Potatoman making one of his funny little calls again."

Finally after a minute or so of getting nowhere, I turned back around. "Call whatever you want. We're on offense. I'm not giving you the fucking disc."

"Cramer," Big Tim said in the calming voice of a deacon, "he called a violation. It's his disc. This team is not about conflict."

I swear he laid his giant hand on my shoulder and suddenly all rage and frustration melted away. A beam of sunlight consumed me and all I could feel was the goodness of the Earth and the heavens flowing through me like a warm internal bath.

I turned back around. Big Tim was right. It wasn't worth it.

"All right," I said, turning back toward the Potatoman.

I really was going to hand the damn thing back to him kindly and gently. Until I saw the smug look on his stupid, greasy face. Suddenly my veins turned cold and the beam of sunlight was swallowed by dark clouds.

"Take the disc," I said, absolutely whipping a flick straight into his sternum from about two feet away. It made a dull thud against his bloated man boobs. "You're lucky I didn't spike the fuckin' thing on your fat little head you piece of…."

I was sort of ushered from the game at that point.

After the law of verticality violation, they only had to go about fifteen yards to smash our hopes, getting the upwind goal that all but sealed their 12-10 victory. Somewhere off in the distance, I can still hear the Potatoman laughing.

Anyway, after that weird ass game, the wind died down completely and we went on to beat the College of Charleston 13-8 before losing the battle of Florida directional schools to South Florida 13-11. The problem with the final game was basically one of geography. Gainesville was close enough to home that guys like Tall Andy, Wall, and Marine Matt felt they still needed to meet their work and study group obligations. Short handed and tired, we fell to even on the day.

So after a pretty sweet party with some funk band in downtown Gainesville, we woke up the next morning and drove to the fields anxious to find out who we were playing in the elimination round. As we warmed up, a school van with a crumpled fender pulled into the parking lot. A bunch of guys in yellow jerseys got out.

I looked over at Clancy. "Are you kidding me?"

As they filed out of the van and started to drop their gear on the opposing sideline, Clancy yelled across the field to Receding Eddie. "No Eddie, you can *not* go slash their tires! That's overkill!"

"It really was an accident, Clancy!" Eddie shouted back.

I caught a flick and responded. "No, you can't go smash in their mirrors with a tire iron instead! Jesus!"

The driver from the day before laughed as he started stretching out his quads. "Oh shit, you guys are the ones who smashed up our van."

Clancy nodded confidently. "You bet your ass we're the ones who smashed up your van."

Anyway, once Wall arrived at the fields after running a 10K up in Jacksonville that morning, (yes, a 10K *in between* tournament games) we had our full contingent of players on a beautiful day absolutely made for ultimate.

Against a very good opponent who would go on to finish third in the Metro East Region that year, we came out smoking. Truth be told, they were better at ultimate than we were, but we were bigger and faster. We were everywhere. Me, Big Tim, and Tall Andy absolutely shut down their long game. Clancy and Wall smothered the middle. Black Tide Matt and Shark controlled the disc, making sure we didn't just huck something insane on every point.

I caught an absolute bullet from Tall Andy just under the outstretched hand of a diving defender to put us up 2-0. From there, we exchanged points until off a turn, I put up a thirty-yard backhand from the left sideline that Wall ran down in the back of the end zone to put us up 6-3.

Down by three and getting thoroughly dominated, Swarthmore decided to call a timeout. On the sideline as we gathered around chugging water, Clancy looked at Receding Eddie. "Ya know if we end up winning this game, you're going to have to crash into every team van you see, right?"

"It was an accident, Clancy," he said exasperated. "I wasn't trying to be a goon."

I winked at him. "Of course you weren't. You need plausible deniability. We got it. Totally on the same page here, buddy."

"It really was an accident!"

The next point went on to completely alter the fate of UNF Ultimate. Who knows what we might've done had we taken half like we should've. Swarthmore was one of the top teams in the tournament (they'd go to nationals the following year) and with them out of the way, anything was possible. Florida, Michigan State, NC State, and William & Mary were pretty good, but Georgia was having a down year and really, if we caught a few breaks, there was a halfway decent chance we could've outright won the very first tournament we ever played in.

After their time out, we pulled to them and forced a turnover. Somewhere along the line, the ever careful Black Tide Matt hit me on a four yard scooter cut toward the sideline. I turned and saw Wall sliding toward the cone about 25 yards away, firing a backhand at him before my mark could set up. The disc briefly glanced off Wall's hands, but he recovered, made sure his feet were in bounds and corralled it as his defender bumped into him and fell over. We took the half 7-3 and were now marching our way toward an almost certain victory.

Unlike most of the guys I've played against who've made atrocious calls, I don't remember anything about this dude. He's a complete ghost. All I know is he played for Swarthmore and was probably a generally cool guy on a generally cool team – although none of this changes the fact that what he did next was so noxious that the grass beneath his feet immediately died.

"Foul," he said, dusting himself off.

Wall was already jogging across the field toward our sideline. "No, it's fine. I caught it," he said, assuming the dude was making a call on himself.

"You fouled *me*," he said.

Now Wall had basically run the entire distance from Gainesville to Portugal in the last two days, so his tired, flummoxed reaction wasn't all that surprising. He just sort of exhaustedly threw his hands in the air and stuttered incoherently, "Wha….foul? Wait a….are you telling me… how...I…*you ran into my back*!"

What the dude said next will live in Jacksonville Ultimate infamy. "You stuck your butt out and didn't allow me to get around it."

Wall's hands tore at his own sideburns. "I fouled you with my butt?"

"Yes."

Near the goal line, Clancy spread his arms like an insulted eagle. "Wall runs a hundred miles a week! He doesn't have a butt to call a foul *on*!"

Seriously, Wall might've been 6'2" but his ass was the size of your cell phone.

Even their guys were skeptical. The dude guarding Clancy came over to talk to his teammate. "You're seriously going to call a foul on that guy's ass?"

The guy nodded. "I could've made a play on the disc."

His buddy had the face you'd make after eating bad cheese. "Just know that if you make that call, it makes us all look like dickheads."

Clancy agreed. "It will indeed make you all look like dickheads. Then again, one of our guys did crash into your van."

"It was an *accident*, Clancy!" Eddie yelled from the sideline.

The guy who'd called the foul was adamant. He pointed at Wall. "Do you contest or not?"

Wall just dropped his head. "Yes, I contest the butt foul."

Now a truly elite team would not have let that call become a turning point. But we weren't quite ready to join the ranks of the elite. Off the contested foul, we worked the disc the entire way down to the goal line where Wall made another spectacular catch....with his foot on the line. They subsequently marched it the entire way downfield against our spent defense to cut it to 6-4. After running all over them without substituting our starters for the first ten points, a bunch of our better players ended up in need of rest all at once. Next thing we knew it was 6-6.

We managed to finally score to take half, but only by a single goal and we were pulling to them to start the second half - which Swarthmore began with a three goal run to go up 9-7.

A few points later, I hauled in a short pass just in front of the goal line and had the rare experience of remaining upright as my defender flipped completely over my back. He hit out of bounds with an awful thud as I all but handed the disc to Shark to tie it 9-9. Unfortunately, it was our last goal of the game. Aided by the butt foul, Swarthmore charged back to claim an 11-9 victory and a birth in the quarterfinals.

After the disappointing loss, we headed into the loser's bracket and met up once again with Paideia, that insane high school out of Atlanta I'd faced with Flagler. With nothing much to play for, Wall finally collapsed and a couple guys left for work, but I don't want any of that to diminish what this team did to us. These kids were all like nineteen pounds and except for a furious second half rally, they pretty much stomped on our heads with very heavy shoes.

I wouldn't even mention this game except for one point that will indelibly be stuck in my mind forever. We had just scored to get within 3-2 and decided to surprise them by throwing a zone. Clancy launched the pull a few yards into the end zone. We hustled down and encircled them. They had no chance of moving forward, even on a windless day. Our cup was sealed. Nothing was getting through. Big Tim was hanging out deep, bigger than any two of their players combined, so they weren't risking a long toss. Me, Clancy, and Black Tide Matt had the middle absolutely shut down. They were going nowhere. In fact, our defense was so impenetrable that we forced them backwards twenty yards, literally to within inches of the back line.

I could smell it. All I was thinking was, "Try and float one near me and I'm picking it for a Callahan." We were salivating. A turnover and easy goal were one pass away. And one more pass away. And one more. As we ran around drooling, they calmly swung the disc along the very back line. Their cleats were practically making out with the chalk. When they found nothing open upfield, they'd calmly swing it back. Eight... nine...ten passes trapped as far from their objective as possible. Then slowly, they began pushing forward. I don't have an exact count, but I'd be floored if I found out they used less than thirty passes just to get it out of their own end zone.

Somewhere around pass forty-six, defensive boredom set in. Then we got tired. Next thing we knew, our backs were pushed up against our own goal line. Somehow they'd moved it the entire way downfield without any forward passes longer than five yards. They never broke through. We never scrambled back. We held our positions the entire time. We just couldn't get those damn robots to malfunction. It was the longest continuous point I've ever played that didn't involve a single turnover. After what seemed like eons, they finally punched it in on a two-yard backhand and "The Point of a Hundred Passes" mercifully ended. Our entire line had to sub out until almost halftime in order to fully recover.

"So um....that's a no on throwing zone the rest of the game," Clancy said, literally crawling toward the sideline.

Wall looked up from under a floppy hat. "What were they doing out there that you guys couldn't stop?"

"Nothing," I said, collapsing into a folding chair. "They're just freaking cyborgs with acne."

I say this with all sincerity - congrats to them and whoever the hell their coach was. I still haven't seen anything like the kind of discipline those kids displayed that day. Ok, maybe the Marines had them beat in the discipline department. But that's about it.

Once I recovered, I played one of the best individual halves of my career, bringing us from down 9-3 to tie it at 11-11 when I somehow managed to do a lay out front flip over a dude for a goal but Paideia rolled off the next two scores to send us packing. And for the most part, it boxed up my Florida career as well. On a whim while at UNF, I decided to apply to one of the top graduate schools for counselor education in the country. To my complete surprise, Penn State accepted me and once my year at UNF was done, I loaded up the S-10 and headed back home. On the way, I took a little detour to Huntsville, Alabama to play for Jacksonville's first ever co-ed team.

The tournament was called Huckfest and the greatest thing about it was there was a two-point line. Any opposite gender huck from behind the midfield line was worth two points. Male hucking to female or female hucking to male and you could quickly get yourself right back in the game no matter how far you were down. Basically it led to a lot of players thinking to themselves, *"Don't catch it yet, just another yard or two, don't catch it yet, just another….ah, shit, it got D'd."*

One of our women was a tiny brunette named Renee who was some sort of freestyle Frisbee champion as a kid. Seriously, she has like medals from national competitions and once appeared on the old Nickelodeon show "Figure it Out." The girl could do all kinds of remarkable shit like spin the disc on her elbow and throw with her feet and catch it with her ponytail. Unfortunately, none of those talents came into play on the field, so adding women to the mix only enhanced our inherent averageness. We beat teams from Mississippi, Nashville, and Memphis, only to lose to Huntsville, Birmingham, Chattanooga, and the Nashville team we'd beaten on universe point the day before. Three wins and four losses. It was all so very familiar.

After Nashville scored to seal our fate, we packed up the coolers, the chairs, the backpacks, and the empty sunscreen bottles and slogged toward the parking lot for the long drive home. There were hugs and handshakes. Then the Jacksonville caravan got on the road headed south while I turned my truck north toward Pennsylvania.

That summer, Clancy and Tall Andy were given the opportunity to play for Vicious Cycle - at the time the most elite club team in the Sunshine State. Had I stayed in Florida, I'm sure I'd have gone with them. Those guys would finish second in the southern region to Atlanta's Chain Lightning the next two years, earning back to back invites to club nationals. I always wonder what it would've been like to experience the pinnacle of the sport with two good friends who'd also gotten their start at the uneven, tourist-infested field outside the Castillo de San Marcos. It would've been really cool, but it wasn't the path I took. I've found that like a lot of players, my path in both ultimate and life has never been quite that easy.

As for Jacksonville Ultimate, their co-ed team Jack's on Jill ended up representing the southern region at nationals in 2012, eleven years after me, Clancy, Big Tim, Shark, Renee, and Coast Guard Robbie took that first team to Huntsville. To me, it's what's great about the sport. If you're patient, you can occasionally watch something you helped build evolve into something much, much bigger.

SEVENTEEN

In the annals of an ultimate wanderer's career, there are bound to be teams that you don't remember so fondly, teams that you barely remember at all, and a glorious handful of teams that immediately elicit a smile. For me, I blindly stumbled into one of the latter while back home visiting my parents in the summer of 2000.

Each year around the 4th of July, there are two giant co-ed ultimate tournaments - one at each end of the country. The one on the west coast is called Potlatch. Held in Redmond, Washington, it typically attracts teams from as far away as Colorado, California, and Texas. Luckily for me, the tournament on the east coast was held at the Turner Valley Soccer Complex in Irwin, PA, fifteen minutes from majestic Trafford. The Mars Tournament (at the time) landed teams from the entire Atlantic Coast and from as far west as Chicago and Minneapolis. When I showed up as a casual observer on the final day of the tournament in 2000, I had no idea it was about to become an annual tradition.

I got out of my truck and meandered around the parking lot, trying to discern the best games to park myself in front of, finally settling down into some bleachers near the lot. I slapped on some sunscreen and relaxed.

Just to my left was a team of kids in white shirts who were trying to run a simple pass and cut drill with um....intermittent success. As I sat there, the disc kept flying past the intended receivers and rolling into the weeds beneath me. After each errant pass, I'd duck down under the bleachers, pick up the disc and flick it back to them.

"Thanks," they'd say.

"No problem," I'd answer.

Thirty seconds later, the same kid would come hustling over.

"Thanks."

"No problem."

By the third or fourth time, it was getting sort of awkward so I decided to engage the kid in more elaborate conversation.

"What team are you guys?" I asked.

The dude was a wiry seventeen year old named Jordan who looked like he should be sitting in a cubicle designing video games instead of running around in the heat. "Pittsburgh Weasels," he said before hustling back to his team.

The next time he came ambling over, I flipped him a push pass. "How are you guys doing so far?"

"Lost all six games. But we're getting better. Last game we scored three."

"Oh, well….congrats," I said, laughing. Recalling my days at Flagler, I was already feeling a kindred spirit with this obviously overmatched team. They had one single drill, which they ran over and over with the same seven players. For fifteen minutes I kept waiting for a carload of reinforcements to show up but those mythical creatures never arrived. Finally on about the eighth throw I had to flip back to them I asked, "Do you guys need another player?"

Cubicle Jordan's eyes lit up underneath his computer geek glasses. "You're not on another team?"

"Nah, I'm just here to watch. At least I was. My cleats are in my truck."

"Let me go ask coach Sid," he said.

Coach Sid was a jolly, rotund English teacher with a black beard. He nodded and next thing I knew, I was lacing up my cleats.

I found out that the Pittsburgh Weasels were made up of overly ambitious kids from North Allegheny High School who were really good when they scrimmaged other high school teams. Unfortunately, they were completely unprepared to face players who'd been to nationals. Hell, they were unprepared to face players been to the merchandise tent. So far, their tournament looked like this:

Opponents: 90

Weasels: 9

Yes, they were at minus 81 for the tournament. I was so geeked to play that I didn't care about any of it. At 22, I was an old vet to them. It was a very odd feeling.

The way the Mars tournament worked, each team had six games over the first two days and then based on an algorithm designed by a team of Fulbright Scholars, the teams were ranked one through twenty-four. The top eight ended up in the A bracket, second eight ended up in the B bracket, and so on, ensuring that each team would face similar competition on the final day. The Weasels, for obvious reasons were the very last team in the C bracket, matched up against a team out of Washington DC ranked 17th. The way I looked at it, we were going to get our asses handed to us, but it was *way* better than sitting in the bleachers.

DC quickly went up 1-0. But then remarkable things happened. The Weasels were young. They were fast. They simply didn't know anything. With me out there directing traffic, they finally gained some semblance of an offense. On the ensuing point, I burned past my defender and to my surprise, Cubicle Jordan curved a pretty sweet flick that I ran down along the sideline. The geeky kid could throw. We'd tied the game 1-1. They went *insane*.

"We're tied! We're tied! We're not losing! Holy shit!"

We pulled. DC threw it away almost immediately. I picked it up and lobbed one into the end zone for a skinny 5'11" kid named Joey. It hung in the air. I'd rushed it. Two of their guys were dropping back to make the play. I was about ready to tap my chest for a "that one's on me," when Joey turned into a gazelle, effortlessly springing over the two defenders to grab the disc. When he landed, we had a 2-1 lead.

"We're winning! We're winning! We're actually winning!" they yelled, somehow managing to top their previous insanity.

I rushed in to high five Joey. "I was not expecting that."

Jumpin' Joey just grinned and nodded. From beside him, his buddy, a blonde-haired Viking type named Darren wore a knowing smile. "Well he *is* the state high jump champion."

"See, this is information you need to make public if you want to win," I said.

Cubicle Jordan adjusted his glasses. "Wow, Cramer just put us and winning in the same sentence!"

You know you're on a great team when the very suggestion of victory sends your teammates into a frenzy.

On the next two points I lobbed passes from midfield to Jumpin' Joey. His leaping ability was really coming in handy. The Weasels were soon up 4-1, already eclipsing their high score for the weekend. At that point their excitement could've powered most of Pennsylvania.

From there, the DC team figured out our strategy. They were made up of older folks who were having trouble keeping up athletically, but in the end were much smarter and better schooled in the game. They all but dropped off our women, who were playing savage (without substitutes) and resting on offense to conserve themselves for defense. The Weasel women were warriors that day, but without the ability to rest, they wore down early allowing DC to take advantage.

Before we knew it, the 4-1 lead was a distant memory and we were on the wrong side of 14-9, one point from defeat. We called our final timeout to regroup and get some much needed rest.

As Cubicle Jordan paced around chugging water, he tugged at his hair. "Ok, we're only one point from double digits! Just one point. We need some sort of spark. Some crazy play or something to get us pumped again. We're not pumped. We need to get pumped. Cramer, do you have any crazy plays?"

"To get us pumped?"

"To get us pumped."

Luckily for the Weasels, I had just such a play. It was Havelock Ben's brainchild and to this day might be the most creative thing he's ever come up with. It was called "West Coast Offense," and like every gimmick ultimate play, it had three distinct elements:

1) It completely caught the other team by surprise.

2) It had choreography that made everyone on our team look like a jackass.

3) It had about a four percent chance of actually working.

The play went as such. We would let the pull land at our feet, then wait for the entire defense to sprint down and set up, at which point everyone on our team would flop to the ground, dance-hump the grass and yell....

"AIN'T NO PARTY LIKE A WEST COAST PARTY CAUSE A WEST COAST PARTY DON'T STOP!"

(Cause we're gangsta as hell)

While the defense was confused, all seven players would leap up and sprint as hard as they could for the end zone. After five steps, one selected player would peel off and sprint back for the disc, picking it up and hucking it into the end zone for the other six, hoping that the superior numbers created by the insanity would lead to a goal.

We'd run it once at Flagler when we were down 10-2 against William & Mary. It worked to perfection except that Ben and Transfer Brad couldn't decide who was going to catch my huck and managed to cooperate on a drop.

I can still hear Ben shouting across the field. "Damn it! It was going to work! West Coast was actually going to work! I hate my hands!"

And so on the next point, the Weasels enthusiastically flopped to the ground and danced like sexy white kids. DC ran down and stopped with looks on their faces like they'd just come across a massive fish kill. While they collectively shrugged, we leapt to our feet and took off toward the end zone. After five steps, I stopped and spun back for the disc. With my defender completely confused, I put up an unobstructed huck.

And much to my complete surprise, that dumbass play actually worked. Sort of.

As Viking Darren got himself in position to catch the goal, he got hacked across the forearm. The defender didn't contest the foul so we ended up with the disc at the goal line. We punched it in. 14-10.

Then something miraculous happened. We just kept scoring. Given new life by our stupid gimmick play, we were everywhere. Our exhausted girls made like three D's in a row. I caught a tipped huck to make it 14-11, then threw two midfield backhands to Viking Darren to make it 14-13. At this point, the kids were so excited their voices were stripping bark from the surrounding trees. When DC called a timeout to assess what the hell was happening, Cubicle Jordan gave a totally nonsensical but completely impassioned speech that damn near melted his glasses. The kids were practically vibrating themselves right out of existence. I knew the feeling. The unexpected joy of being so close to victory when all you're familiar with is taking one beat down after another is one of the better feelings you can have in sports.

DC's timeout didn't help their cause. Off a turn, Jumpin' Joey caught another goal to tie the game 14-14. The team that had scored four goals the entire first day of the tournament had just rattled off five in a row on the brink of elimination. I couldn't help but get caught up in their excitement. I came running down the field yelling my head off.

"See, this is what you play for. *This* is what you play for! Let's go!"

DC broke our streak on the next point, but the kids didn't let it get them down. They calmly worked it to midfield where I put up another bomb to Viking Darren to tie the game 15-15. Unfortunately, it was about all the energy we had. Even with a great goal line stand near the end, DC finally outlasted the Pittsburgh Weasels 17-15. Even so, no one seemed to mind. For the first time at a real tournament, those kids got a taste of the highs the sport could bring.

As for me, I felt pretty damned amazing about the whole experience. On a day where I didn't even expect to break a sweat, I caught three goals, had seven assists and helped bring a group of overmatched and undermanned high school kids to the brink of victory against a team of savvy vets - becoming a short-lived legend at North Allegheny High School in the process. All in all, not a bad day.

I was in the computer lab at UNF the next spring when I got an email from Cubicle Jordan.

We're putting another Pittsburgh Weasels team together for Mars this year. We were really hoping you'd play on our team again. We all play in college now and we're going to be a lot better. I swear.

It was like February when he sent that. Mars wasn't even accepting bids until May. But I agreed anyway. There was no way I was passing on that opportunity.

And Jordan was right. They were a lot better. The team I stepped on the field with the next July was basically an all-star team of Pittsburgh high school players from the previous year. We had guys who now played for Carnegie-Mellon, Penn State, Duke, and George Washington and girls who played for CMU, Northwestern, and M.I.T.

For the Weasels, it was different right off the bat. Our first game was against a team from Columbus and it was obvious most of the kids had learned something in college. Against a good team, we were anything but a pushover, taking an early 4-3 lead before falling 15-8, setting up a matchup versus some team from Cincinnati.

There's a play in ultimate that's called "the greatest." Basically, it's any play where a player leaps from in bounds, catches a disc that was sailing out of bounds, and throws it back into play before landing. In order to be a true greatest, it must be caught by a teammate to keep possession, and the greatest of all greatests results in a goal. It's pretty much the most exhilarating play in all of ultimate because it happens so rarely. My guess is that I've played somewhere over a thousand games in my career. I can remember five completed greatests in that entire time. I personally have never completed one. Not even in pickup. And it's not from lack of trying, believe me.

I set this up to let you know about two excruciatingly different plays that happened in this particular game. Joining the team that year was a really athletic Asian kid named Chen who'd dyed his buzz cut bright red for the tournament. Somewhere in the first half, I put up a break backhand flip as he sprinted for the corner. He was a lot closer to the sideline than he thought, taking an awful jumping angle that took him sailing out of bounds as he caught it - so just before his feet touched the ground, he awkwardly shoved it back over his shoulder into the end zone. Because our spacing was terrible, one of our very surprised girls was right next to the cone and pretty much caught it to avoid being donked in the face. We had ourselves a greatest! One of the uglier ones of all time for sure, but it didn't stop the whole team from screaming our heads off and running down to mob Chen. The goal put us up 5-4.

How could anyone on our team possibly top that? Surely it would be impossible. That's what I thought until somewhere in the 2nd half with the Weasels actually on top 11-9, I bombed a backhand toward a flying squirrel of a kid named SeaBass. His layouts were legendary. At least once a game he'd spring from the ground with the same general trajectory as a dolphin breaking the surface of the ocean. I expected some similar acrobatics as the disc sailed toward him along the sideline. And he didn't disappoint. As the disc came down, SeaBass gracefully took off, caught the disc square in the chest and well before his feet hit the ground, dished it to the side like a scalding hot plate.

Unfortunately no one was within fifteen yards of him. The disc hit the ground and flopped over in a lonely patch of grass. No harm. It was going to be a turnover anyway seeing as the disc was so far out of…..

Wait a second.

SeaBass had landed a good three feet *in* bounds. Which meant he'd leapt from….

"SeaBass, what the hell was that?"

"I don't know!" he yelled back, smacking his head as he mentally triangulated himself with the sideline cones. "I swear I was at the sideline."

"You weren't! You still aren't!"

"Please tell me I didn't just…."

"You pulled a lamest!"

The opposite of the greatest, the lamest comes when a player who was clearly going to land in bounds completely unnecessarily flips the disc back into the playing surface he or she was already a part of. The worst of all lamests comes when that player gives up a sure goal for no apparent reason. It's the equivalent of a basketball player scoring in the wrong hoop. In all my years of playing ultimate, I've seen it happen once - right there on that play. In fact, I may have invented the term lamest simply to describe what I'd just seen.

SeaBass turned into a hell of a player. I'd later watch him play at nationals. But he will never, ever live that one down. Nor should he. Thankfully, SeaBass's shame didn't come back to haunt us. Up 14-12, I lobbed a flick to Viking Darren in the end zone. Game to 15. He boxed out his guy and caught it.

Total silence.

It wasn't the immediate mob scene you'd expect in the initial seconds following a young team's first win. It was as if everyone on the team had expected to go 0-6 then finally explode after a miraculous victory on the final day. We anticipated some sort of build up - some sort of slow burn as we gradually scratched and clawed our way to the top of an admittedly small mountain. Winning our second game just wasn't in the script. Viking Darren held up the disc in the end zone like a lonely tree. Nobody reacted until suddenly Jumpin' Joey snapped out of his haze and hopped onto Darren's back. Seeing that, Cubicle Jordan's voice pierced the valley.

"Holy shit, we just won!"

Two games into their second tournament, the Pittsburgh Weasels were no longer a pushover. We were (gasp) legitimate competitors.

After our victory, the rest of pool play fell in a similar fashion to the first game. Except for a 15-5 loss against a team from Virginia Beach, we fell by three to teams from Cleveland, Syracuse, and Indianapolis. The 1-5 record put us into the newly formed "D" bracket for a matchup against Morgantown, West Virginia on Sunday.

There were only four teams in the D bracket so a single victory would propel the Weasels to a semi-legitimate championship game. Sunday at Mars tends to create a marked disparity between teams who are ultra competitive, doing everything they can to win their bracket, and teams that are playing half assed so they can get an early jump on their trip home. Luckily Morgantown only had a two-hour drive. They came to play.

It was a game we knew we could win, which oddly enough, made us a little tight running our end zone drills. Overall, the Weasels looked more like the kids who kept firing it into the bleachers the year before than the almost competitive team we'd turned into. Luckily we had a chubby handler from Carnegie-Mellon named Ben who thought that Chen's bright red hair looked really cool. But of course he didn't want to be a complete copycat, so when he showed up that morning, his hair was flaming ass firework blue. And so were his ears. And the back of his neck. It was a good thing he was skilled at engineering because his future in cosmetology was bleak.

It was hot as hell that day. Ben started to sweat. Soon his entire forehead was blue. When the dye reached his eyebrows, he'd wipe the sweat with his forearms - which also turned blue. Next thing we knew, we had an honest to god Smurf on our team. Put a white hat and white shoes on the kid and Gargamel would've chased him all over the field. You could honestly see how many times he'd touched the disc during the first half by counting the blue fingerprints on the white disc. As the game began we all got on him.

"Hey, that's a Smurfy throw, Ben!"

"Shut up! It's not that bad!"

"Let's play some Smurfy defense now!"

"Seriously, shut up!"

And just like that, the Weasels forgot how nervously excited they were and simply went out and played.

Just after half with the Weasels down by one, I boxed out a guy on the goal line to catch an awful quadruple helix that Cubicle Jordan fired about a hundred feet in the air and three yards downfield. A forearm in the back knocked me to the ground where I promptly sat up and rifled a flick to Viking Darren from my ass, immediately looking around just to make sure that jerkweed from Miami wasn't there to call a travel. 10-10.

Pumped, I sprinted down on defense and point blocked a hammer, just barely unable to dance around the guy in time to catch the ricochet for the Callahan goal. I picked it up, raced back to the goal line and flipped it to Viking Darren's younger brother to take a lead we never relinquished.

I was on the sideline resting in case we went to universe point when Viking Darren hucked one up for Jumpin' Joey. By now, you know how this story ends. Joey split two guys with a ridiculous leap to grab the goal. 15-13. We win. The Pittsburgh Weasels were going to play one of the four championship games that day. Yes, it was the D bracket, but we couldn't have cared less. We were in a final.

As we waited for some of the other games to finish, we looked over the hill and noticed an ominous death cloud rolling in from the west. A minute later, the previously calm, dead air stirred to life. After that the sky fell. Everyone in the entire tournament ran for the wooden pavilion next to the parking lot as lightning struck all around the valley.

When the tournament finally resumed forty-five minutes later, we trotted out to the field to begin our warm-ups. We were matched up against the same Cincinnati team we'd beaten on the first day, so we were confident. The Pittsburgh Weasels might actually take home a trophy.

And we waited. And waited. Ran a few drills. And waited. Cincinnati never showed up. Finally, ten minutes after the game was supposed to begin, Viking Darren and I headed back to the pavilion to find the tournament director - where he told us what every single tournament director in history has said multiple times on the final day of a tournament that's known for partying and drinking.

"Oh that team? I'm pretty sure they left."

Darren looked at me. "I guess we're the champs then."

"I guess we're the champs then."

We shared a high five next to a giant pile of discarded pizza boxes - just like we always envisioned our first championship. Laughing, we hustled back over to tell the team as they lounged in the shade of a row of pine trees.

"Alright guys, listen up because this is important, " I said. "Darren, you want to tell them?"

"They left. We win."

"Pittsburgh Weasels," I said. "D bracket champions."

SeaBass took a sip of water and nodded. "That's the Smurfiest thing I've ever heard."

"Shut up, SeaBass! It's not that bad!"

"You're only saying that because you don't have a mirror."

It was the first time I'd ever walked away from a tournament having won my last game. Even if we'd done it by forfeit, it still felt pretty awesome.

Summer League Snippets – Silver Naked Child

I can't with good conscience ignore my favorite teams ever, despite the fact that it's a complete pain in the ass to fit them into what I'm attempting to pass off as a narrative. This book would have holes in it like *The Hungry Caterpillar* if I didn't figure out a way to mention them. So they're going to get weird little bite-sized chapters I'm going to call "Summer League Snippets."

For a good long while as ultimate was developing, citywide co-ed summer leagues were where some of the best competition in the country took place. The Philadelphia Area Disc Association, (PADA) has like 48 teams. Other large cities like Washington DC, Seattle, Denver, and

San Francisco have similarly gigantic leagues that blend rookies with seasoned vets for twelve or so competitive weeks until a champion is crowned.

For years, the Pittsburgh Summer League was no different. When I first started as a nineteen year old on TOFU (See Chapter 8), the league had 16 teams. Nine years later at its very height, the league had 24. From the early 90's through the mid 2000's, everyone who was anyone in Pittsburgh Ultimate played summer league, and the championship was a coveted commodity. For over a decade, there was no bigger deal in the city.

In 1998, I got drafted onto a team called The Pimp Tank right before I got my hip crushed by all the refrigerator parts. I was profoundly disappointed because ya know, I never got to play a single point for a team called The Pimp Tank. Two years later, the same captains spent a low round draft choice on a 22-year-old kid who everyone in the city forgot about. We lost on universe point in the first round of the playoffs, but it was a great summer learning the game from a couple guys who played for New Jersey Pike at nationals. That year was the first time I got to stick around and watch the championship game. Seeing virtually the entire league lining the field, heckling, laughing, and cheering made me desperately want to experience the feeling of playing in front of an actual crowd.

Which brings me to the following year and a team called Silver Naked Child.

I figured I'd once again be drafted by the Pimp Tank crew, but instead I got a call from some kid I'd never heard of. He was a dude named Langstaff, a native of Pittsburgh who'd just spent four years as one of the main handlers for Syracuse. Langstaff had put more effort and thought into his draft than any captain in the history of summer league, doing the amount of research normally reserved for NFL general managers.

"Captain at Flagler College, right?" he said to me on the phone.

"Yeah. How the hell do you know that?"

"I have my sources. See you at practice."

Langstaff was a tiny, bug-eyed Jewish kid who sort of reminded everyone of a caffeine-wired squirrel. He'd thrown the entire league into hysterics because he'd bucked the gentleman's agreement that certain players would always get drafted on certain teams. His first round draft choice was one of the best players in the city, a super athletic do-everything handler everyone called Marky Mark. Until that point, Marky was always ticketed to play with a bunch of his club buddies on teams that tended to dominate the league. At the exact time Lang made his pick, the seismograph just down the road at the Carnegie Museum started to go nuts. Geologists will say it was from an actual 5.7 earthquake in El Salvador, but for me that explanation is just a little too easy. Suddenly anything was possible. Dogs could be governor. Candy was filled with nutrients. India and Pakistan made out with tongue. Summer league just got real.

Langstaff's research paid off. His second-round pick was a guy named Jason, who was virtually my twin. We were the same height and build - and both had glasses and beards. He just happened to be an actor and much, much better looking. Also, he was a black guy, which mostly kept people from confusing us. Hollywood Jason as I'll call him is actually the very first person you see on screen in the award winning movie "Michael Clayton" starring George Clooney, which also makes him by far the most famous guy I've ever played with. Lang's third-round pick was another lean, athletic 6'2" guy named Karl. His fourth rounder was me. His obsessive draft preparation had paid off. In addition to stealing Marky Mark, he'd managed to land three of the top athletes in the whole league.

Langstaff's female draft was just as good. His first round pick was Yale's captain, a quick, stocky, Indian girl named Divya. In subsequent rounds, he got two best friends from Pitt named Michelle and Dana. Michelle provided what every summer league team needs – a team mom. She brought snacks, meticulously worked on cheers, and pretty much did everything but change us into our jammies.

Her friend Dana was a lefty handler with curly black hair who may have been the most elegantly clumsy woman alive. She worked at an art gallery where I'd watch her glide from painting to painting in a little black cocktail dress with a glass of chardonnay, smiling and looking radiant as she flawlessly discussed the rust belt's contemporary art marketplace. Then afterwards, we'd go out to dinner and she'd end up with a beer soaked lap and nacho cheese in her ear.

We were out on a date one night when this happened…

"No," I said. "I'm serious. Off the field, you have this grace about you. Like you should be leading heads of state into a ballroom or something. I'm terrified that my mill trash ass is bringing you down a peg when I show up at the gallery."

"Dignified and graceful? I like this picture of me you're painting," she said.

I'm not kidding, we were at this *exact* point in the conversation when she leaned forward for more information. The weight shift caused the stool she was sitting on to rocket out from under her. With a giant crash, it careened away about ten feet and smacked into some people up at the bar. The sudden lack of support deposited her square on her ass, which of course, everyone at the restaurant witnessed because they'd been so startled by the tumbling chair.

She calmly stood up, plopped her elbows on the table, blew the hair out of her face and said, "So you were describing my grace? Go on."

She'd do the same thing on the field, making a precise cut to get the disc and getting off a sweet lefty flick through traffic only to subsequently trip and face plant into a mud puddle with no one around her a few seconds later. We never jacked her about it at all. Not a once.

Michelle and Dana lived together in the Oakland section of Pittsburgh in a place we all called "The Muppet House." Seriously, there were posters of Kermit and Fozzie everywhere and "Muppets Take Manhattan" was pretty much on permanent rotation in the DVD player. It was the go-to party house for the younger players in the league that year. There weren't many weekends that I didn't wake up on their couch wondering where the hell I was - until I rolled over and stared into the blurry face of Gonzo.

The Muppets were the reason the original name of the team was "Electric Mayhem." Any Jim Henson fan knows this is the name of Dr. Teeth and Animal's acid-jazz band. None of us quite remember how or when the name of the team changed - it just did. It changed because our Sunday night ritual was going to see Langstaff wow the audience at Ryan's Pub with thrilling karaoke renditions of early 90's rap songs. It was like the soul of MC Hammer got mistakenly crammed into the body of a little Jewish dude. At the time, it was the best three minutes of entertainment in Pittsburgh.

On a related note, sometime in the early 1980's, sophomores at the UCLA film school were apparently given a few credits in exchange for shooting background movies for all the current karaoke hits. I'm pretty sure these students were told that they wouldn't receive credit for the assignment unless their project included a guy on a motorcycle or the tide coming in. And as anyone who's ever been subject to an entire night of karaoke knows, there's one song that you can't avoid hearing at least once.

Ok, other than "Pianoman."

Yup, it's the Neil Diamond classic "Sweet Caroline." For no reason at all, the stupid karaoke video for that particular song features an eight-year-old kid carrying a blue kickball. This wouldn't be all that weird except he's also wearing a diaper and painted silver. He looks like a cross between a cherub and some junked aluminum siding. There's no reason at all for him to be there. Neil Diamond mentions Caroline quite a bit, but he never once says….

"Sweet Caroline….bah, bah, bah, random silver naked kid…."

Every Sunday we'd debate what the hell the kid had to do with the song until the sheer lunacy of the image wound its way into everything we did as a team.

Drop a pass….

"The silver naked kid would've caught that!"

Turf a throw…

"You're making the silver naked child cry!"

We talked about it so much that the other teams thought it was our name. So it just stuck.

In the end, Silver Naked Child was probably the most fun team I've ever played for. The core of the team was 25 or younger. For the first time in the league, I wasn't just an immature afterthought on a team full of young professionals. Most of my teammates were just like me, either in their first crappy job out of college or pissing around in preparation for grad school. We had an absolute blast.

And we were good too. Marky Mark got over the initial disappointment of not playing with his usual clique and reluctantly started to have a good time. We finished as the number five seed heading into the playoffs. Back then, the championship tournament was held all in one day with an accompanying party and cookout. Every year, four hundred people gathered together on a beautiful mid-August day in a valley that smelled like charcoal and burgers. For an ultimate player, it was damn near heaven.

As for Silver Naked Child, we won our first two games in close fashion to put our young, fun team just one game away from playing for the championship. It's a game Langstaff brings up every time I see him. After the bro hugs and the inevitable slap on the back, he'll hold out his hands and shake his head.

"I still don't know how I missed it!" he'll laugh with just the right mix of humor and self-loathing.

Against the number one seed, a stacked team of club and college players named Eye Candy, we came out rolling. We attributed all our success to a tiny plastic doll that Team Mom Michelle had painted silver and brought to the playoffs. We had a real silver naked child to answer to if we failed. And none of us wanted to let it down.

Eye Candy had a tall and fast guy named Dave who was one of the best players in the city. He matched up against me throughout the first half and despite his tough defense, I was firing on all cylinders. I caught three ridiculous goals, skying, shredding, and turboing past him as half the league ate their food and murmured to each other...

"Who the hell is this kid making Dave look stupid?"

It felt like my coming out party as one of the top players in Pittsburgh. Partially because I was having the game of my life, we were on the verge of taking the half. At 7-5, I was on the sideline getting my first rest of the game. On the field, Eye Candy tried a 20-foot pass up the opposite sideline. Langstaff was like an electron out there, so little and shifty, no one could ever pinpoint just where he was going to be. He used that quickness to cut directly front of that pass. Seeing the play develop, Marky Mark broke deep, already three steps behind everyone. Lang stuck out his hands to intercept it. The result was so inevitable that our fists were already pumped in celebration.

It was like watching a moth fly through a hole in a screen door. The disc snuck right through his wrists. The underside of Langstaff's arm actually gave the pass the skip it needed to reach its intended receiver. Eye Candy worked it down to make the score 7-6.

We didn't know it, but the disc sneaking through Langstaff's arms was the beginning of the end. While we had seven really talented guys, that was all we had. Eye Candy had multitudes of male subs. After two and a half tough games, our legs started to give out. Silver Naked Child's season ended with a 15-12 loss. We did, however, tire out Eye Candy so much that everyone's surefire pick to win the league that year got beaten in the final.

Even so, there wasn't a thing on or off the ultimate field that summer that Silver Naked Child didn't provide.

Except a championship. Which I'll get to later.

EIGHTEEN

Unfortunately on the cusp of respectability, the Weasels were done in by of all things, the intelligence of our core players. (You'd be surprised how often this happens in ultimate.) A few were off in foreign countries studying foreign things. Others were interning on the west coast. Because of this, the team that Viking Darren ended up scraping together looked a lot different than the previous two.

In addition to our academic absences, a freak accident cost us one of our best players. A few weeks before the tournament, Jumpin' Joey and Viking Darren decided to go skydiving. (Don't panic. Their parachutes opened. This isn't a snuff paragraph.) But Joey did blow out his knee upon hitting the ground. It all but ended the playing career of a kid who any good club team could've molded into an absolute monster. He was there in a giant leg immobilizer rooting us on from the sideline the entire tournament. What we were left with was a lot of high school kids. They were some of the best high school kids in Pittsburgh, but high school kids nonetheless.

Our women were as solid as ever but for me, the outright coolest thing about that year's female contingent was the inclusion of a girl who to that point had never played a real game of ultimate in her life. That girl was my little sister, Kelly.

When I first started playing down at Flagler, I didn't have anyone to throw with when I came home for the summer. Enter my thirteen-year old sister who I would drag to the back yard by saying things like….

"Hey, you're coming out to the backyard to toss disc with me."

"But I'm reading this book abou…."

(This is where I'd snap the book shut and toss it across the room.)

"What? What are you reading? I don't see you reading anything. Let's go."

She would just sigh and reluctantly trudge outside. Her reluctance waned however when she went to summer camp and all the high school boys started asking her for tutorials on how to throw flicks and hammers. The next three years she did not miss an opportunity to sling plastic.

By the time she was sixteen, Kelly was firing 60-yard flicks to me in the baseball outfield at Penn-Trafford High School. Her hammers were better than mine. She was 5'9" and caught anything that came near her. She also had three years of track and cross-country under her belt. Wherever the hell she went to college, she was going to be a force.

Then came a birthday party in a friend's backyard the summer after her junior year. She momentarily abandoned her seat. In that moment, someone tried to steal it from her. The only way to retain her spot was to leap the blanket they were all sitting on. When she landed, her feet slipped in the wet grass. Her knee buckled. Her ACL snapped.

The doctor performing the surgery didn't let us know that he'd "invented" a new and completely experimental way of repairing an ACL. We're not quite sure what he did but I think it involved submerging her knee in jellybeans and fixing himself a gin and tonic. She needed two more surgeries just to fix what that dickhead messed up the first time. Athletically, she was never quite the same - which was why it was cool that four years after the blanket incident, she took the field for the first time - hustling around in a giant knee brace, nowhere near as fast as she could've been but out there playing just the same.

She didn't play a lot - maybe two points or so each half. Her throws may have been awesome, but she didn't really know where to cut. In our first game, she got on the field but wasn't all that involved. Then about halfway through our second game against a team from Ann Arbor, Michigan, she lost the girl that was covering her and ended up wide open. I floated a 20-yard forehand, which she caught near midfield. With no one around her, she turned and threw a perfect flick five yards upfield to one of our other women. Hundreds of hours of tossing in the backyard had led to that throw. It was the only time my sister would ever touch the disc in a tournament game. After that point, her knee was sore enough that she decided not to risk playing on it any more - which while disappointing, was probably incredibly smart.

She left the sport having completed every pass she ever attempted.

As for the tournament itself, it was obvious we'd regressed from the previous year. We got smoked by a team from Edinboro, PA in our first game and then lost a hard fought 14-8 decision to Ann Arbor. In that game, Viking Darren popped his hamstring jumping over a guy for a goal. This put us in some bad shape for our third game against a Pittsburgh/New Jersey squad called Max Power. Max Power included a bunch of guys from a club team named Pike that went on to finish 10th at nationals that year. (Just ahead of Tall Andy, Clancy and Vicious Cycle) And their women all played for nationals-bound Pittsburgh Pounce.

We were well aware we were about to get killed. Max Power was just as aware they were going to athletically murder us. We needed an objective. Unfortunately, most things we suggested just didn't seem realistic.

"I mean our goal should be to win, right?"

Laughter.

"Ok, how about get to double digits?"

Laughter.

"Ok, what about scare them just a teenie bit."

Laughter.

Then in the huddle just before the game, the injured Viking Darren asked a great question. "Think we can make this game last a whole hour?"

Laughter. Then contemplation. And nodding. We had ourselves an objective.

Jumpin' Joey had a stopwatch. As soon as Max Power launched the disc toward us to begin the game, his thumb hit the button.

0:00:01

I do not remember much about this game other than ya know....them scoring rather easily on most possessions. We did, however, manage to score once or twice and putz around enough to send us into the half well within reach of our target.

0:30:34

In the second half, instead of counting goals, we started counting seconds. It wasn't too far into the second half before Max Power figured out what we were doing, mainly because Jumpin' Joey kept yelling out the time.

"Thirty-seven minutes!"

We'd turn it over then play some hard defense that wasn't quite hard enough. They'd score.

"Thirty-eight!"

Once they uncovered the subplot, Max Power ended up trying to finish the game in under an hour with the same veracity as we were using to try and push it over. It lead to a great competition between two teams with a huge talent disparity, creating what became a very fun, spirited, and competitive lopsided game.

As the clock neared an hour, we just kept bombing it deep like hockey players trying to kill a penalty. On one of those bombs, I managed to rip a sweet forehand to this fast ginger kid named Hurray. He burned straight through two Pike guys and dove. All we saw were the bottoms of his cleats as he snagged it and skidded about fifteen feet on his stomach. It was an amazing catch. Highlight reel material. The whole team ran down the field to mob him. We enthusiastically rubbed his head, punched him in the ribs, shook him and tore at his jersey, basically doing all the crap that only a young and overly excitable team would do when they're down 13-4.

In the middle of the scrum, Hurray smiled. "Thanks guys. But I was way out the back of the end zone. So you might want to calm down."

All thirteen of us turned around. He was right. We were mobbing him a full ten yards behind the back line. It was such a great catch that none of us bothered to check whether he was in bounds or not.

"Ah, shit," I said, staring back at the cones. "Man, that wasn't even close."

Our misplaced celebration did waste a bunch of time though.

0:55:51

Off the turnover, Max Power worked it down and scored in a little over two minutes.

"58:11!" Joey shouted.

Now every second mattered. They lined up and pulled to us immediately, sprinting down to try and force a turnover that would all but end the game. By this point, Joey was shouting out every ten seconds.

"58:40!"

We flipped it around between our handlers.

"58:50!"

I caught a scooter cut up the line.

"59:00!"

With a minute left, I got all kind of suggestions from the sideline.

"Call a timeout!"

"Chuck it into the woods!"

"Roll an ankle!"

"I'm not cheating!" I yelled back. Finally with everyone covered on Stall 9, I launched one downfield for no one in particular. It landed just out of bounds a few yards into the end zone. One of Max Power's guys sprinted harder than he had all day to retrieve it.

"59:15!"

All we had to do was play defense for forty-six seconds and we'd win the battle. Not the game, mind you, but the battle we chose to wage. We dropped back. They rushed it up field with absolute precision. Five passes and they were ten yards from our goal line. We were scrambling. We knew it was close. All we had to do was force them back. For one throw, interrupt their momentum. Get them to sputter just a little bit.

And we did. Ten yards outside the line, I caught up to my guy and threw on a tight mark, blocking him from hitting a wide-open cutter in the end zone. He had to dump it back to a trailing player. I thought that had done it - until the other guy immediately shuffled a twelve-yard backhand to one of their women for a wide-open goal.

On the field, the necks of both teams swung toward Joey and his stopwatch. The game was over. They'd won 15-3 - an absolute drubbing, but the hearts of everyone on the field were beating double time as if the tournament championship was on the line.

Joey held up the stopwatch and dropped his head. That wasn't a good sign.

"59:49!" he yelled.

Max Power celebrated as we dropped to our knees. Eleven. Friggin.

Seconds. But even though we'd barely missed our goal, we were incredibly proud of the fact that we'd managed to infuse a jolt of spirit into what could've otherwise been a dead game. And that was Weasels ultimate in a nutshell.

We got better the next day falling to a pretty good team out of Chicago 15-8 and 15-5 to team that was mainly old Pittsburgh players who now lived in San Francisco. At that point, we were 0-5, dead last out of 32 teams and set to play a middle of the pack Baltimore team. It was hot. We were all exhausted. But we knew we couldn't come out of pool play without a win. Going oh-fer would only kick the Weasels right back where they came from two years ago.

We found ourselves down 12-9 when the soft cap went on. We'd have to string together five straight goals against a better team in order to scratch out that first victory. It didn't look good, especially playing without Viking Darren due to his hamstring.

So it came down to me and our teenagers. One of those teenagers was just young and stupid enough to consistently take the field without shoes - because protecting his feet would I don't know, be sucking from the corporate teat of consumerism or something. The kid I'll call Barefoot Ben was one of those guys who was genuinely upset that there wasn't some startup company in Portland that utilized underemployed Nez Perce women to make quality, handmade hemp cleats. No mass-produced sweatshop apparel for him. Plantar Fasciitis be damned.

Barefoot Ben was also well prepared for the tournament. Before the games, he'd done a bunch of Internet research and printed out his favorite impassioned speeches from historical figures. After Baltimore scored goal number twelve, he deemed the moment pivotal, worthy of inspiration, unfolded his printouts and invited us to gather around.

"This is a speech that Queen Elizabeth gave to the English Navy in 1588 the night before they - against overwhelming odds, defeated the mighty Spanish Armada," he said, clearing his throat. "I have come amongst you in the midst and heat of battle to live or die amongst you all. To lay down for my people, my honor and my blood in the dust!" he exclaimed. "I may have the body of a weak and feeble old woman…."

"You sure do, Ben."

The whole circle busted out laughing as Barefoot Ben scratched his head. He shuffled his papers. "I forgot that part was in there. But hold on, this really is inspiring."

"Tell us more about how you're an old woman."

"Can you guys let me…finish?" he said, flustered. "Ok….I may have the body of a weak and feeble old woman, BUT…." he paused for effect. "…I have the heart and stomach of a king. Huh? See? Inspirational. And think foul that Parma or Spain…"

"Dude, seriously, we really need to get back out on the field."

"Hold on there's more. There's uh, judgment, virtue…uh….damn, where is it….ah, here. Here it is," Ben said clearing his throat again. "We shall shortly have victory over those enemies of my God, my kingdom and my people!"

Barefoot Ben stood there with his papers raised in the air waiting for us to holler our approval. It uh, didn't happen.

"So can we get back on the field now or…."

"Yes, that was it." He pumped his fist. "Go Weasels."

Weirdly enough, the Queen Elizabeth speech did actually light a fire under us. I put up a backhand huck that Barefoot Ben managed to tip into the hands of Hurray to make it 12-10. We then forced a turn and I hit good ol' Smurfy Ben (who'd quit resembling a blueberry roundabout the previous Christmas) with a long forehand to cut it to 12-11. One of our women, a girl I'll call Fast Jess made a D on the next point. I picked it up, threw a hard flick fake and drilled a backhand into Barefoot Ben's stomach as three defenders swarmed on his back like zombies. 12-12.

Even with the adrenaline of the comeback pulsing through me, I could tell I only had about one more good point left. In video game terms, my energy bar was used up and blinking. Fast Jess once again stuck with her girl, stretched out and tipped one away. Barefoot Ben ran over to pick it up. I took off toward the end zone knowing it was the very last run I had in me.

I remember the Argentinian guy guarding me being like 6'5", but I think most of that was actually stylish pompadour. He may have just been 5"11" with a half foot of brilliant South American hair.

Barefoot Ben put up a backhand. Me and the Argentinian were stride for stride tracking the disc into the end zone. At full speed, we both leapt. I managed to reach across his haircut and pick it two-handed just off the tips of his fingers. As we fell, I knew we were nearing the back line. I stretched my feet toward the end zone. My heels thumped the grass. My hip smashed the ground. The South American guy crashed down on my left quad and tumbled away. It was the type of landing you spring right up from in the first game of the tournament. At the end of the sixth, however, you think there's a very real possibility you're lying right where your teammates will soon be scattering your ashes.

In agony, I rolled over. The Argentinian slowly got to his knees. "You in?" he asked with a slight Spanish accent.

"That's an excellent question."

In the absence of officials or video replay, we did what any ultimate players do when faced with that situation. We became amateur forensic experts.

I sat up. "I think those two divots are where my heels hit."

He pointed to another smeared track just out the back. "Then what's this?"

"I think that might've been your knee."

The Argentinian checked. His knee was indeed now covered in fresh dirt. "Hmmm," he said, caressing his hair back into place.

I pointed to a larger depression in the grass just in front of me. "Ok, so this is where my ass hit, so realistically those could be my heel marks in bounds."

"Let's see," he said, standing up and examining the divots. He really should've had a magnifying glass and a checkered hat.

I skidded up to sit where the indentation was. I stretched my legs out. Perfect fit.

He nodded and reached down to help me up. We both raised our hands above our heads. Weasels 13 Baltimore 12.

I desperately wanted to stay in the game at that point, but my body was screaming for water and rest. I stumbled off the field knowing I'd be needed for the impending universe point should Baltimore come back to tie the game, which I figured was all but inevitable with mostly high school kids on the field.

I was chugging water when Barefoot Ben laid out to catch a midfield chuck from Smurfy Ben to give us the 14-12 win. Five uncontested goals on the brink of defeat had brought us our first win. It was a hell of a game that would give the young team a lot of confidence going into the next day's defense of the D bracket championship.

Special shout out to Queen Elizabeth and the English Navy on that one.

Our first opponent in our title defense was the Edinboro team who'd spanked us in the very first game. They had some incredibly athletic players including a club player from Cleveland named Tim who due to our athletic similarities, I'd find myself matched up against for years. After draining myself completely the day before, I did not feel particularly well. At 24, you just sort of ignore your body, tell yourself to quit being a pansy and go out and play. I figured it would probably only be for a single game anyway, seeing as Edinboro had trounced us only forty-eight hours before.

Edinboro had a really gangly 6'6" redheaded hippie. Early in the game, I went over him to pick a goal that tied it 4-4. Maybe I was feeling better than I thought. Down 10-9, I laid out over a guy and dragged my toe just inside the line, catching a goal that tied the game 10-10. We could tell they were getting frustrated. I'm pretty sure a few of them had too much to drink at the party the night before figuring they'd have at least one easy game to recover. Their sluggishness combined with our young, fresh, underage legs was producing a stunning result. Even with how lousy I felt, I was still managing to make some pretty good plays to keep us in the game.

That was all about to change. On the next point, we forced a turn near our own goal line. I got the disc three or four times as we scrambled to midfield where somehow Edinboro lost our only true veteran, a guy I'll call Professor Geoff. By veteran, I of course mean that Professor Geoff was all of 26. With a full beard and creaky knees though, he sort of looked like one of our dads had decided to join us on the field. Noticing Edinboro's defensive miscue, he crept downfield until Smurfy Ben saw him uncovered and launched a backhand huck. Cleveland Tim was guarding me near the sideline at midfield and saw it go up. He took off like a dog after food. I figured I better take off with him.

I'd been guarding Cleveland Tim all game and I have to admit, the dude was wearing me out. He was good. Really good. I couldn't rest when he was out there. Not even for a second. As the disc descended toward a wide-open Professor Geoff in the end zone, Cleveland Tim and I sprinted side by side toward him as hard as we could.

Luckily Smurfy Ben's pass wasn't quite perfect. It took an unexpected little flop toward the sideline that was just enough to throw off Cleveland Tim's angle. It allowed me to dart in front of him, temporarily slowing his momentum, allowing Professor Geoff to catch the disc at the front cone. It was a move that some would call "savvy" and others may call "straddling the border of legal."

Weasels 11 Edinboro 10.

Down for the first time in the game, Edinboro called time out.

As I tried to catch my breath from the all out sprint, I turned back to congratulate Geoff on the goal. "Loving the sneaky deep cut," I said, patting him on the shoulder as the team celebrated our newfound lead.

"Well, if there's one thing I'm blessed with, it's the ability to capitalize when the other team has completely forgotten I'm playing."

As Geoff and I walked back to the sideline, I remember the world getting a bit blurry, but I thought it was just sweat dripping onto the inside of my shades. The team huddled up. I was on the outside of the circle as Barefoot Ben once again shifted through his papers, ready to deliver another rousingly inspirational speech. Suddenly it felt like I was a little too close to a propane grill. My skin felt hot and clammy all at once.

What the….

And then the world disappeared.

When I came to, I was on the ground with Viking Darren and Jumpin' Joey slapping me in the face. Their voices were distant and muddled.

"Giddim somwater….water……hey…."

My worried and helpful teammates practically drowned me in their attempt to bring me back. It may have been the world's first case of someone contracting swimmer's ear on a soccer field. But it worked. As consciousness once again smiled upon me, I could feel the fire on my skin gradually extinguishing.

"Wha….the…..fu…..happ….." I mumbled to Viking Darren.

"You were standing there and you just…..fell over."

Jumpin' Joey nodded. "You fell over. Like….a shitty old tree."

I never really knew what heat exhaustion was until that particular moment. That sprint had capped three days of running the liquids right out of my body. I'd been playing 90% of the points on the assumption that if I wasn't on the field, we were done for. That assumption damn near killed me. But now the young kids of the Pittsburgh Weasels were about to see what they could do all on their own. My delirious overheated ass sat out the rest of the game and yet the Weasels never relinquished the lead, coming out on top 15-13. Maybe I wasn't as critical as I thought.

I hydrated like crazy and got on the field for a few points in the next round against a Harvard alumni team called Suckwagon. Drained of all nutrients, I was not especially effective in the first half. Then in the second half, I went deep and leapt for a disc at the goal line. The big guy trailing me socked me in the back of the head, knocking me straight into another defender, who brought his shoulder up into my jaw. My shades went flying one way as my visor sailed the other. When I hit the ground, the big guy managed to spike me in the elbow. I just remember being on all fours at the goal line, my forehead pressed to the ground, doing everything I could to stay conscious.

Hurray came over to check on me. "Cramer….you ok?"

"No," I whispered into my armpit. "Not ok. Not….ok."

And that was the end of that game. For me at least. Once again I watched from the sideline as our young guns made play after play to send us to the D bracket final.

Our opponent in the final was a group of old Pittsburgh players named "Jews in Space" who were once the beasts of Pittsburgh but were now mostly on the wrong side of 40. (And yet still looked much younger than Professor Geoff.) There were guys on that team who were damn near triple the age of some of our high school kids.

This year, we were going to have to win it outright. No thunderstorms were massing over the hill. And we'd have to do it against a very experienced team who'd know exactly how to exploit our youth.

I was severely dehydrated, sporting a badly swollen right elbow and most likely had a mild concussion, so when Viking Darren asked me before the game if I was ready to go, I obviously told him....

"Yeah, I'm good."

I wasn't of course. On the field, I ended up with a goal and an assist in limited time. But as it became obvious I was in no shape to finish the game, I decided my job would be to inspire the troops. On a normal day, Jews in Space would've systematically taken apart the Pittsburgh Weasels. But it was the ninth game in three days for a team whose average age was probably somewhere around 42. Our average age was more like 19. It was a big factor. Late in the game with it tied 13-13, I gathered the team around on a timeout.

"All right. Some of these guys are our friends. Our mentors. Old teammates. But you know what they are right now? In the fucking way! Don't let them knock us off the D bracket pedestal! We will not abdicate the throne. We own this bracket. We're the defending champs, damn it! Go out and take what's ours!"

Man, they erupted. I think they may have been too young to pick up on my blatant sarcasm. But hell, maybe I wasn't being as tongue in cheek as I thought. We were one of only eight teams remaining on the field at that point and damn it, why not go home winners?

Two points later, I mustered all the energy I could to jump for joy when we took the game 15-13. The Pittsburgh Weasels were back-to-back D bracket champions.

We were one of a handful of teams to stick around for the awards ceremony where we received I don't know, a popsicle stick or something with our team name written on it in Sharpie. It didn't matter. We were one of four champions that day. It felt good.

To top it all off, due to things like the Max Power Hour, the other teams had voted us winners of the Spirit Award as the team that was the most enthusiastic and fun to play. That award meant the most of all. Because what is ultimate if you're not having a good time and passing that good time along to others?

The following year, everyone ended up so scattered that fielding a team just wasn't possible - which meant that the Pittsburgh Weasels of all teams, the team of overambitious high schoolers who got completely dismantled in their initial foray into tournament play, ended their history on a four game winning streak.

And nobody's gone back-to-back in the D bracket since.

Weasels represent.

NINETEEN

IN THE FALL OF 2001, I LOADED ALL ELEVEN THINGS I OWNED INTO THE BACK of my truck and drove them two and a half hours to an idyllic little town in the middle of the Pennsylvania mountains. The town of State College, aptly enough, is home to Penn State University where I was beginning my graduate work in counselor education. I moved into a cheap apartment west of town with my sister's boyfriend because he was one of the only people I knew up there. This was a bad idea on many levels, but like all bad ideas, it "seemed to make sense at the time." But I digress.

Classes began in late August and ultimate practice soon after. The team practiced on the HUB Lawn, a giant field smack dab in the middle of campus. There were like eighty guys out there that first day and they ran the gamut from hardened veterans to clueless freshman who'd played once or twice at Camp Wimpapuss and had no idea how intense the game could actually be. It was amazing how many guys suddenly remembered about an evening class right in the middle of wind sprints.

"Twenty full field sprints? Oh shit, I totally forgot....I have Intro to Something in like ten minutes so...."

We ran *a lot* that first week. But with good reason. By Friday we'd thinned the herd to around forty or so.

I have to admit, I showed up with an ego. I was going to be the best player on that field and I knew it. I didn't care that it was a huge school, a Big Ten program with 20,000 guys to choose from. (Compare that to Flagler's 200) I was going to walk onto that field and be a star right away. Everyone would see my skills and immediately defer to my knowledge and experience.

It um...didn't turn out that way exactly.

The captains were two junior handlers who'd just moved into the captain position after a group of seniors graduated. They were polar opposites. Ian was a ridiculously quick and ridiculously quiet math-teacher type with a 50's crew cut and every break throw imaginable. Diggs was a short, muscular, boulder of a kid who did not mind loudly telling you when he thought you fucked up. It was a very odd feeling not being one of the guys in charge. I'm not sure I adapted well to it. Still though, it was amazing to be out there running around doing actual drills on an actual field with a team that had an actual shot at winning.

Penn State's club team was named SPANK. Our jerseys featured a single handprint over the left nipple, to this day the only logo in history that actively invites strangers to grope you at a bar. Why the team was called SPANK, none of us had any idea - which was fitting because the rumor was that back in 1981 when the team was formed it was an acronym for "State Penn And No one Knows." But hell, for all we knew it stood for "Some People Are Not Krispy" or "Scott Pooped Across Northern Kentucky." Either way it was just as dumb as it was mysterious.

One of very first things I was asked to do for the team was to help raise funds. On the surface it seemed like a great trade off. We'd earn a couple thousand bucks to help pay for our travel, tournament fees, and uniforms and in turn the university got cheap labor in their attempt to clean up the 113,000 seat football stadium. The Sunday after the first game of the season, I woke up at 5:00AM, figuring I'd be spending a couple hours sweeping and be out of there by noon. That was before I understood just how much garbage 113,000 drunk people can produce.

The night prior, I was at the game with SeaBass from the Weasels (who was now a sophomore at Penn State) when I got the first inkling that my plan for a lazy Sunday afternoon might not materialize. It was the opening game of the season against the #1 ranked Miami Hurricanes so the place was absolutely packed. Also, it was an emotional night because a kid named Adam Taliaferro walked the team out onto the field eleven months after he'd been paralyzed while making a tackle at Ohio State. It's still the loudest and most stirring thing I've ever seen in sports - a guy who was told he probably wouldn't stand on his own again leading his teammates out of the tunnel. For a moment, it seemed like anything was possible.

Unfortunately after all the build up, Penn State didn't play much better than the smell rolling in off the freshly manured fields north of town. It was 33-0 before we completed a pass, which caused more than a few students in the south end zone to start hurling random crap all over the place just for something to get excited about.

As SeaBass and I watched the nachos, soft drink cups, hot dog wrappers and burning couches fly through the air, we cheered right along with the chaos. Then SeaBass had a terrible realization.

"Dude,…you realize we're gonna have to pick all this shit up tomorrow?"

Wide-eyed, I turned and yelled to the crowd behind me. "Hey, how about we show our displeasure by throwing stuff into designated receptacles!"

The crowd was not particularly receptive to that idea. And so the next morning, we showed up in the fog with the men's lacrosse and women's water polo teams to clear out a structure that ten hours prior held the entire population of Green Bay, Wisconsin.

We did get to toss disc for a couple minutes on the field, diving on the Nittany Lion logo in the end zone, toeing a real sideline and attempting to bomb hucks from goal line to goal line. I tried to imagine the stadium full of blue and white fanatics roaring with every throw and layout D as we battled Iowa or Michigan State or Purdue. I knew it was a pipe dream but I could almost see it as I blinked, a fuzzy intrusion from some alternate reality. Then before I knew it, I was knee deep in garbage.

And I do mean knee deep. One of the maintenance guys singled me out to accompany him and a hearty freckled girl named Sarah from our women's team on a special assignment. And ya know what I found out really suck?

Special assignments.

While the rest of the team was sweeping the stands, Sarah and I rode around with this old hillbilly dude in a white pickup truck pulling the garbage bags from every single trashcan in the stadium's lower ring. I swear there were bodies in some of them. Then we got to ride a half mile to a dumpster city and heave them out the back of the truck. Every fifth bag or so, we'd get slimed with a mystery liquid that seemed to be equal parts Pepsi, Mountain Dew, mustard, and other liquids Sarah and I tried to convince ourselves were Pepsi, Mountain Dew and mustard.

I got through about a hundred of those godforsaken bags before I felt a shooting pain in my lower back. It was a pain that would finally go away somewhere around the following May. So my Penn State career hadn't started off on the most positive note. I'd managed to injure myself fundraising.

Nine days later I woke up late and prepared to head to my afternoon classes. I grabbed myself some breakfast and flipped on the 13-inch television that sat atop the lone dresser in my tiny little bedroom. I expected to hear the music from "The Price is Right." What I got instead was a live shot of a smoldering dust cloud at the southern tip of Manhattan Island.

It affected us there in central Pennsylvania in a lot of different ways. Flight 93 slammed into a field about eighty miles down the ridge from us. For a while that semester it seemed like the whole campus and subsequently the entire country squeamishly looked into a mirror and wondered who the hell we were. What was really important in our gaudy and seemingly superficial American lives? My girlfriend, my parents, and my professors all had to talk me out of dropping out of school to join the army. I wasn't the only guy on the ultimate team who had to be convinced to stay either.

Things were very, very unsettled that entire September. Anyone who says they didn't feel a bit rattled and unsafe once or twice a day in the immediate aftermath is lying to you. Trucks backfiring, abandoned backpacks, police sirens, low flying airplanes - it took the majority of that fall and winter for our collective mental darkness to fade.

What I do know though is that at a time when a fringe sport like ultimate should've barked its insignificance in our faces, the opposite ended up being true. Coming together and playing our wacky little game was the best thing any of us could've done. I'm betting that was true for just about every single ultimate player who was lucky enough to be actively playing the sport in September of 2001.

My first tournament with Penn State came at the very end of that month. The rookies and a few selected veterans left State College for

Salisbury, Maryland before dark on what turned into a beautiful late fall day - in Pennsylvania. Unfortunately as we headed over the Bay Bridge across the Chesapeake, we could see the dark clouds of some coastal storm that had parked itself directly over Maryland's Eastern Shore. What was a sunny day in the mid-60's back home was 42 with horizontal rain when we stepped out of our cars.

My first goal with Penn State was the only one we'd score against Navy. It was a sliding layout on a pass that dropped like a stone as it crossed the goal line. We fell 13-1 but I'd now managed to score a goal for my third college team. Some of the other veterans were pretty angry at the lopsided result. Luckily, I was used to it.

We figured a few things out in a close 12-8 loss to Salisbury State before matching up against William & Mary. By this time, we were all soaked, shivering, and quite frankly as miserable as you can be playing ultimate. Things didn't get any better when William & Mary went up 7-1. All we wanted to do was jump into our cars, blast the heat and head back to PA. But then ultimate did what it does and turned a forgettable game into something memorable.

There was no shame in getting beaten down by William & Mary that year. They'd go on to reach the final four at nationals, ending up tied for third in the country. But the best thing about them was not only were they sick at ultimate, they were cool enough to win the spirit award at nationals as well. You don't often find teams that are really good *and* really fun. Most fun teams are awful because fun is all they have going for them. I've had a lot of fun playing ultimate.

Anyway, you could recognize William & Mary immediately on any adjoining field by their dark green jerseys - all sporting the exact same number. And quite frankly if any college ultimate team comes together and decides to all wear the same number it's going to be one of these three...

a) 69

b) 420

c) 666

William & Mary went with option b. The 420 boys also had great nicknames on the back of their jerseys as well. Thank God they did because otherwise it would've been impossible to play transition defense against them.

"Hey, Cramer - switch. I got number 420. I got 420!"

"They're *all* number 420!"

Their captain was named Garbage Dick. As far as we could tell, it was his given name. I think his middle name was Edward. Garbage Edward Dick.

Near the end of the game with them slaughtering us 12-2, they threw a roller pull into the wind.

Garbage Dick yelled to his line. "Braveheart Defense!"

They all locked arms at the goal line and stared us down as we effortlessly brought the disc toward them uncontested. *What the hell were they doing?*

Garbage Dick shouted toward his teammates. "Hold!"

We came closer.

"Hold!"

We worked it to within twenty yards.

"HOOOOOOLLLLLDDDDD!"

As we neared the goal line, he raised his arm.

"Now!"

And they ran at us with the fury of 12th century Scottish Highlanders. It was a full on battle to get the disc those last ten yards but we managed to slam our way into the end zone, laughing the whole time.

After that point, we figured we couldn't let them have all the fun. Since they'd pulled a stupid defense that all but let us score, we'd be complete jagoffs if we didn't return the favor. As we went to pull to them, our captain for the day, a lanky handler named Herschel shouted "Cuposaurus!"

The cuposaurus was a simple zone defense with one major caveat - your wrists were forbidden to lose contact with your ribs, thus turning your arms into the useless forelimbs of a T-Rex. Needless to say, it's pretty impossible to make a play. We were in our cars with the heat on within six minutes.

And thus speaks to what is amazing about ultimate. In a matchup of teams that would become serious competitors on the national stage that year, the game ended with complete clownishness. Try as I might, I just can't imagine some SEC football team stomping on an outmanned foe and deciding to run around like dinosaurs once the game was safely in hand.

As the country crawled its way back toward normalcy, we practiced three times a week on the lacrosse fields and prepped for the spring season with a few local tournaments. For me, the most memorable was a trip we made down to the University of Maryland to play in an eight team round robin.

The life of an ultimate player is littered with 4AM wakeups. Such was the case that day when a carload of guys showed up outside my apartment long before sunrise. The driver was a skinny senior named Bobes who kind of looked like he'd just woken up from a yearlong coma, took the IV out of his arm, slammed a Red Bull and was ready to roll. The passenger was a skater freshman I'll call Slacker Sam who slept about twenty hours a day and as far as we could tell only woke up for ultimate practice. The third dude was a blue collar Pittsburgh yinzer named Duffy who could charm the skirt off a girl at three hundred yards.

Somewhere around sunrise, we stopped at a Hardee's on I-83 outside of York, PA where me, Bobes, and Duffy got a true taste of Slacker Sam's inner world. After ordering his breakfast, the three of us watched in amazement as Sam reached into his jacket pocket, whipped out a tube sock full of quarters and dumped them on the counter. Honestly, he could've pulled a .44 and robbed the place and we'd have reacted about the same.

"What the hell are you doing?" Bobes asked.

"What?" Sam said. "I gotta pay. They don't just let you take their food."

"Is that your wallet?"

"Nah, man. It's a sock."

"When was the last time you *wore* that sock?" I asked.

"I don't know, man. I don't have like a notebook of what socks I wore on what day. You guys are fuckin' weird."

The grossed out dude at the register counted the change as Sam scooped all the excess coins back into the sock, rolled it up and jammed it back in his pocket.

We turned to leave only to get to the door and realize Duffy wasn't with us. He was at the soft drink machine flirting with the girl restocking the cups.

"Duffy!" Bobes yelled.

"One second. I'm chatting with Becky here."

"It's six in the morning! We're in York. C'mon."

Duffy smiled and nodded. And I'm probably making this part up, but I swear they hugged before he sipped on his lemonade, turned around with the grin of a prowling tiger and followed us out the door.

We arrived in College Park on a beautiful and sunny mid October day. It was an incredible setting for ultimate, right on the main green in the center of campus. Carloads of people stuck in homecoming football traffic gave us a pretty decent audience. The Penn State team that took the field in our first game against Delaware was a much different group than the one that had traveled to Salisbury. A majority of our starters were able to make it. The difference was noticeable. With Captain Ian and Bobes leading the offense, things ran much, much smoother.

As for me, I felt amazing, stepping on the field and proving I belonged. With the game still close in the first half, I absolutely smothered their top handler on a mark at the goal line, forcing a terrible dump to no one. It felt great to have the entire team mob me for the effort when we capitalized to go up 5-3. I ended up with a goal, an assist, and four D's and we never looked back, crushing Delaware 15-6.

In the next game against Carnegie-Mellon, I leapt to snag a long forehand from Duffy, circling the disc around my back in the air so the defender in front of me couldn't swat it. It was the final goal of the game, ending our 15-4 victory with a flourish. It made us 2-0 going into a battle with UPenn, another nationals contender from the Metro East. We switched fields and ended up right next to the five busy lanes of suburban traffic called US 1. (If you've ever played Frisbee right next to a highway, you already know where this story is headed.) Somewhere in the first half, one of the teams yanked a pull to the right. And we all helplessly watched as the disc kept going and going - out of bounds - over the wall - past the trees and…

As we sprinted down on defense, we all slowed up and clenched our collective teeth waiting for the disc to bash into the windshield of a

Dodge Neon and instigate a forty car pileup. Luckily it just skipped off the asphalt in between cars, ending up in the northbound lanes just sitting there waiting to be destroyed. That disc needed a hero.

One of the deep guys on our team was a big burly wrestler we all called Hands. It must've been his disc because even before it landed, he was hopping the fence. The human Atari game that happened next was one of the most exciting parts of the entire day.

Our whole team rushed over to line the stone wall as Hands readied himself, rocking back and forth, judging the speed of traffic with the rest of us cheering him on.

"Go!" we'd shout at a break in the cars before realizing some dick in a BMW was coming much faster than we thought. "No, no….ok go now! No wait. Ok go!"

"Shut up!" he yelled. "I can see the cars. You guys are fucking me up!"

Hands sprinted across the southbound lanes, dodged a Mazda that had meandered into the turn lane and grabbed the disc just before a speeding Greyhound Bus - ok, I'm lying - I don't think there was a speeding Greyhound involved, but it was indeed pretty exhilarating to watch him retrieve the disc from the highway before either of them got steamrolled. He hopped the wall with a pristine disc to much applause from both sides. Later on in the game a UPenn guy laid out and landed on it, folding the disc nearly in half. Fate is a cruel mistress.

As for the game itself, it was a hard fought match between two good teams. I caught a huck from Captain Ian to get us within 10-9, but it was as close as we'd get, falling 15-11.

The most satisfying game of the day came in our final bout against Princeton. They were another solid team and yet again I came out on fire, making a big D in the end zone, catching two hucks for goals and ending the game by outsprinting my guy to the corner to catch a five foot backhand flip at the cone. I dragged my toe just inside the line to give us a 15-12 win and a 3-1 record on the day.

As we packed up and headed out, I felt amazing. I was a beast all day, playing dominant both ways and even ending two of our victories with goals. As my chemistry with my teammates grew, I knew there'd be no stopping me. My goal was to be Penn State's Callahan nominee. (The

Callahan Award is ultimate's Heisman Trophy, awarded to the top collegiate player in the game.) And yet as good as I felt about how I played,
the best part was getting to know the guys, joking around and doing all
the goofy shit that happens outside the lines.

We got stuck in traffic on US 1 a few blocks from the Maryland campus on our way home. While we sat there going nowhere, Slacker Sam
fell in love with some girl in a Honda Civic in the next lane.

"That girl is gorgeous," he said. "I want to talk to her. Is that creepy?
That seems like a creep thing to do. Hit on a girl in a traffic jam. Duffy
is that creepy?"

"Depends on how you present yourself."

"How do I not present myself as a creep?"

Duffy thought for a moment. "Write your number down on a little
piece of paper. When we pull up next to her, smile and hand it to her
without saying anything. It's an adorable story. Girls love an adorable
story."

"Show her your sock full of quarters, Sugar Daddy," I said. "You
might get laid before we reach the next light."

"I'm just nervous."

Duffy grinned. "Want me to hand her the number for you?"

"No. Fuck no. I don't want her to be disappointed that the number
isn't yours."

So Slacker Sam wrote down his number. Unfortunately as he did so,
her lane of traffic moved substantially. His solution? Make an airplane
out of the paper and attempt a miraculous fifteen-yard car-to-car toss. It
uh….didn't work.

"Shit," he said, despondent.

"Dude," I said. "You realize that your phone number is just laying
in the middle of the road now, right? You could get a call from anyone.
Chain smoking grandma….. hobo on a pay phone…"

"Aaah!" he said, throwing open the door to go retrieve it. In the middle of traffic, he looked back at us for advice.

Bobes hung out the driver's window. "At this point, just go hand it to
her!"

Sam nodded and ran down the center line until about six cars away, he surprised the hell out of the girl by knocking on her driver's door. We watched him nervously hand her the paper through her open window, give her a big goofy smile, then turn and immediately sprint back for the car.

"Bobes, roll up the window and lock the doors," I said, cracking up.

A few seconds later, Slacker Sam pulled up on the door handle and realized he was stuck in the street. "Ah, fuck you guys. Seriously, c'mon, let me in," he said as the girl peeked at him in the side mirror. Sam gave her a sheepish wave. "You're making me look like a shithead. C'mon." Finally we let him in and he sunk down in the passenger's seat covering his eyes with his hand. "I fuckin' hate you guys. That was awesome."

Try as we might, we couldn't catch up to her. Fortunately, we had these CB type things that we were using to talk to the other two cars in our Penn State caravan. Bobes turned the thing on and flipped it to the correct channel.

"Hands….can you hear me?"

"Yeah, Bobes."

"Do you see a cute girl in a Honda Civic anywhere up there?"

"Uh yeah….cute girl in a Honda Civic right beside us."

"Tell her Sam says hi."

Sam sunk even further into his seat. "Bobes, seriously, that's embarrassing. Is he talking to her? What's she saying? You guys are such assholes."

The thing beeped. "She said he was adorable and she wants to meet him for sex later," Hands said.

Duffy smiled. "I told you."

Sam perked up. "Really?"

Bobes responded. "Really?"

"No, her window's up and the light just changed," Hands responded. "She's gone."

I have no idea if the girl ever called him or not. But considering he never mentioned it again, my guess is no. Apparently the story wasn't as adorable as it needed to be.

As we rode through the mountains that night, we listened to a benefit show for the victims of September 11th. And as the four of us laughed and sang and talked nonsense with the other cars on the connect phones, I realized that we were all doing exactly what we needed to be doing. We were living our uniquely American lives. We were fighting back simply by driving down to Maryland, playing ultimate and dicking around. Things were going to be ok. For the first time in a month, I truly let myself relax.

Of course my moment of reflection was quickly snuffed out when one of the other cars flew up beside us honking like a flock of geese. Another of our freshman, this poofy-haired kid named Putz had his bare ass pressed to the window. The rest of them laughed like morons as they flew up the mountain.

I tapped Bobes on the shoulder. "Give me the walkie," I said, pressing the button. "Putz, why did you have your face all pressed to the window like that?"

It was a great, great night. Ultimate, of all things, let us all exhale.

TWENTY

The day after the Maryland tournament, I woke up and could barely move. I thought it was just regular post-tournament soreness until it didn't go away. Whatever I'd done to my back cleaning up the stadium was now resonating through my right hip and hamstring. This was not good because our biggest tournament of the year was coming up in two weeks – College Easterns, an invite only tournament featuring sixteen of the top teams east of the Mississippi. And I wasn't going to miss that for anything.

As the weather in central PA turned crisp at night, my hamstring would tighten up during practice to the point where I'd get a nice gentle stab in the back of my leg every time I accelerated. On a particularly cold Wednesday night practice the week before we were supposed to head out, my hamstring clenched so tight I couldn't run at all. I told the captains I just needed a day or so to rest so they wouldn't give away my roster spot. Then I spent the better part of Thursday with ice underneath my ass hoping for a miracle.

The coolest part about Easterns was that I got an honest to god athletic excuse to get out of my Friday classes. As was to be expected, my professors all stared at me with nine pounds of skepticism.

"You're missing class to head to North Carolina to play Frisbee?"

"Um….yes."

"*Frisbee?*"

"Yup."

"Are there…."

"No, there aren't any dogs."

At that point they'd just give a confused nod and tell me to make sure

I read chapters nine through forty-six (it was grad school after all) for discussion on Monday.

So that Friday morning, we rented a couple of fifteen passenger vans and our men's and women's teams hit the road for Wilmington, North Carolina. One of our guys was a short, quick Asian handler named Ray who insisted on driving the entire way. I was in the passenger's seat controlling the music when I noticed the speedometer approaching the century mark on I-99 north of Bedford.

"Shit, Ray. We're pushing a hundred, man."

Ray looked down at the gauges. "Oh sorry. I didn't realize I slowed down."

It should take like ten hours to make that trip. I think we were actually on the road for about forty-five minutes. A little while later as we flew past endless tobacco fields on I-40, one of the pure goofballs on our team, a pale Brazilian dude named Felipe kept leaning up and poking Ray in the shoulder.

"Ray, how long? Can you please speed up?"

I turned around. "Felipe, he's going a hundred and six."

"I ate way too much at Shoney's," Felipe said, squirming. "And it wants to come out."

So that's how we ended up at a McDonald's in the thriving metropolis of Burgaw, North Carolina. And at that McDonald's at 10:00 on a Friday night, some shit that had nothing to do with Felipe's bowels was about to go down.

We parked the van and Felipe quickly leapt out the side door, shuffling past a large group of black guys who were practically guarding the entrance to the restaurant. None of us thought it was a big deal. They sort of grunted and let him past, eyeing our van curiously.

Just after Felipe got in the door, three backwoods Bubba trucks came peeling into the lot doing burn outs. I was standing outside the van stretching my hamstring when the insults started between both groups.

"Hey fuck you (racial epithet)."

"Yeah well fuck you (opposite racial epithet)."

And next thing we knew, venom was flying back and forth between the gang of black kids in the parking lot and the gang of white kids in the trucks.

One of the girls on our team, a mild mannered blonde named Heather peeked out the door at all the commotion. "Cramer, what's going on?"

"Not much...except it seems we've stumbled into a good ol' southern race riot."

Her face turned whiter than the outside of the van as she stared out at the scene with this newfound information. "Oh....oh great. A race..... Ray, can we please go somewhere else?"

"Heather, we can't abandon Felipe in Burgess.... "

"Burgaw," I interjected.

"Burgaw, North Carolina."

"The good of the many, Ray," Heather pleaded. "It outweighs the good of the.... Felipe."

I laughed. "Heather, they're not going to jump a van full of people. I mean they might jump Felipe when he comes out of the....oh shit, they might jump Felipe when he comes out of the bathroom."

Ray adjusted the rearview mirror. "Yeah, this isn't good. He really looks like a white guy."

"He's Brazilian."

"I doubt they're going to ask what country he's from before they start throwing haymakers."

Heather tapped Ray on the shoulder. "Maybe you should go talk to them."

Ray turned around. "Why me?"

I laughed and leaned in the van. "Well you *are* Asian."

"Oh yeah cause black guys and rednecks love Asians. I'm sure they'll just work out their differences and go share a milkshake."

"I guess a couple of us could go in there and fetch him. Maybe if the whole team...."

As we were developing a master plan for Felipe's extraction from the restaurant, Felipe hopped into the van. "Man, that feels better. I seriously almost shit myself. What are all those guys yelling about?"

He'd cluelessly walked right through the pending brawl as we were diagramming an escape route like a SWAT team going after a hostage.

Ray turned. "Shut the door!"

Heather reached over and slammed the door shut. I leapt into the passenger's seat. Ray threw the van into reverse and we peeled the hell out of there leaving a fun filled Burgaw Friday night in our wake.

We got to the Comfort Inn, met up with our teammates and passed the hell out. For me, this was twistedly unfortunate because my girlfriend, April, now lived in Athens, Georgia. I hadn't seen her since August and we'd made plans to have a nice weekend together, sharing a room at the hotel, going to dinner after the games and doing the things that 24 year olds do when they've got a hotel room to themselves. It was a great plan until both of us ran out of money at about the same time and she wasn't able to get a bus ticket. Instead of spending the night with the girl I loved, I got to share a bed with Felipe. The snuggling was nowhere near as intimate.

Anyway, we got up the next morning, decimated the continental breakfast and headed to the fields. I was pretty nervous about my hamstring until I stepped outside and realized it was 75 degrees. The more I ran around, the better it felt. I couldn't believe it. I was going to get to play.

When we lined up for that first game of the day, I looked at the opposing end zone and couldn't help but laugh. Standing there at the other end of the field was Georgia- a university I was now facing with my third different college team.

I'd quickly come to learn that before big games, Penn State's cheers were legendary. We'd all smash ourselves into a circle and put our thumbs on the disc while Bobes stomped around us yelling like an insane middle school basketball coach. He'd scream and we'd answer.

"What's the longest river in the world?"

"DENIAL!"

"What keeps the dog in the yard?"

"DEFENSE!"

"Where do you fuck in the woods?"

"INTENSE!"

"What's a little messed up vegetable that grows in the ground and sort of looks like a pumpkin?"

"SQUASH!"

And we'd go berserk.

For this game, however, Bobes had props. He produced a box of animal crackers and dumped them in the center of the disc.

"You know the drill. Everyone grab one," he said.

I didn't know the drill. But everyone snatched an animal cracker from the disc so I followed suit. I think I got a lion. It was some sort of vaguely predator-shaped blob. Maybe it was a hyena. Who the hell knows.

Bobes started out low, but intense. "Bite the heads off animal crackers, bite the heads off first…."

After the first round, we all joined in. The lyrics weren't hard to learn. "Bite the heads off animal crackers, bite the heads off first. Bite the heads off animal crackers, bite the heads off first. Bite the heads off animal crackers, *bite the heads off first!*

At this point the entire circle was throbbing like a human bass drum.

"Bite the heads off animal crackers, bite the heads off first! BITE THE HEADS OFF ANIMAL CRACKERS, BITE THE HEADS OFF FIRST!"

In unison everyone took their animal cracker, bit off the head and spiked the rest to the ground, which granted, wasted the yummy torso of each cracker, but I'm not sure I've been so fired up at the beginning of a game in my entire life.

I got put on the D-line and my main job was to be the first one down on the disc to harass the Georgia handlers coming out of the end zone. It was my first big tournament with Penn State so I didn't mind being a bit of a role player. I figured I could be a star later. We needed fast defensive guys and damn it, that's what I was going to provide. So every D point, I sprinted my ass off and got in their face as they were picking up the disc. No easy first throws. No controlled breaks out of the end zone. And the whole time I was so warm I didn't feel so much as a prick from my hamstring. I did my job, helping bog them down coming out of their end, forcing a couple bad throws that led to turnovers and we rolled them 13-6 to start the tournament 1-0.

In a bit of personal vindication, I did the math and realized that after nearly getting shut out with Flagler, my three teams combined were now ahead of the boys from Athens 27-25.

Our next game was vs. the 420 gang from William & Mary. When we came out flying and went up 6-2, we thought there was no stopping us. Then we realized what "Elite Invite Only" meant as we watched W&M claw their way back. We went up 12-11 just after the cap went on. First to 13 won. I was on my guy trailing a huck into the end zone when Hands went up against Garbage Dick a few yards in front of me. Hands was one of our better defensive players and like usual boxed out perfectly, tipping the disc as Garbage Dick got some serious air behind him, practically rolling up Hands's back. It ricocheted off Hands's wrist, then Garbage Dick's forehead as he fell to the ground. Just before he hit the grass, Garbage Dick reached down and grabbed it. It was a ridiculous catch.

Fortunately for us, it bounced first. For the briefest of seconds, it impacted the ground before it hopped up straight into Garbage Dick's descending hands. He fell on top of it and cradled it to his stomach.

Unfortunately for us, Garbage Dick jumped in the air and started celebrating wildly about tying the game. His teammates mobbed him. They were rightfully going nuts after such a sick catch had seemingly tied the game. All our guys hung their heads and headed back to the line to prepare for universe point. Except me. I let their celebration die down a little bit as I slowly walked toward their mob scene.

"Hey man, that was a freaking awesome play. But it hit the ground."

"Nah, no way, man. I got it. I know I got it."

I looked around at my teammates who had already resigned themselves to being tied. I was the lone Penn State guy still in the end zone as our O line took the field. I was also apparently the only one who had the right angle on the play. That thing only brushed the ground for a millisecond before he'd grabbed it, but I was sure of what I'd seen. I can still visualize it perfectly to this day.

"I'm really not trying to be an asshole here," I said. "If you caught it clean, I'd be the first to say so. But I swear to you, it hit the ground."

He looked at the disc in his hands. "I know I had it, bro."

I looked to my sideline. No one else had seen it. I was alone. I had no one to confer with. Without observers or other tangible evidence, I was going to lose. I put my head down and shrugged.

"All right," I conceded.

In the heat of what was now a 12-12 game, we shook hands, patted each other on the back and wished each other luck on the coming universe point. And really nothing describes what's at the heart of ultimate like that type of exchange. Near the end of an intense game, two competitors were able to resolve their differences of opinion in a spirited way. We'd let universe point decide. And it was such a spectacularly athletic play that it was halfway impossible to be angry at the result anyway. A half-inch here or there, what's it really matter in the overall scheme of things?

Our offense got the jitters and turned it over almost immediately on the final point. A game we should've won turned into a heartbreaking 13-12 defeat to a team that would go 5-0 on the day and eventually win the tournament.

After that bitter defeat, we came out flat as old soda against NC State before fighting our way back to make it close. I had a chance to cut their lead to 10-9 after we forced a turn. Captain Ian put up a huck to Felipe. I trailed the play and when their guy leapt across Felipe and smashed the disc toward the ground, I nearly made a miraculous catch, throwing out my left leg and pinning the disc to the inside of my shin. I desperately tried to keep it off the turf as I tumbled over twice, keeping it pressed to my leg with my forearm. I ended up sprawled out next to the sideline with the disc balancing just below my knee and my left wrist on top of it. I wasn't sure I had possession, but I was hopeful as I held up the disc and turned to Felipe. Our conversation needed only four words.

Felipe shook his head. "Nope."

"Really?"

"Yup."

"Damn."

All I got from the effort was a bloody leg. We dropped the game 13-9. At that point, the tournament split with the top two teams in each pool making the A bracket and the bottom two teams sliding into the B bracket. Downtrodden after letting our early success slip away, we figured we'd lost our shot at making the top eight. But weirdly enough, we beat Georgia, who beat NC State, who beat us, and we'd all lost to W&M. With our +2 goal differential, we somehow managed to sneak into the A pool. After all that, we still had a shot to win the tournament.

In our first A pool game, we met perennial powerhouse UNC-Wilmington. They'd been to nationals the year before and would go on to finish 5th in the country in 2002. They were without question a great team. They were also without question a bunch of irredeemable dickheads. I don't say that lightly either. They went out of their way to earn that reputation and I doubt any of them would try to deny it. I have to admit it was slightly unnerving. Most ultimate games have at least some semblance of civility and an underlying joy at the very competition. This one....did not.

I don't remember any of their players except for these two short, quick handlers who ran everything. One dude had long black hair and one dude had long blonde hair. Somehow they managed to look like fun, laid-back surfers all while acting like asshole state troopers.

I've never had less fun on an ultimate field than I did in that game. It was an endless cycle of fouls, violations, and arguments. It all came to a head when we tied the game 11-11 on a pass from Captain Ian to Herschel along the sideline. Herschel reached out to grab it, his feet coming down either just inside the line or with his toe barely touching it. He called himself in - to which Wilmington acted like we'd just infected the world with smallpox.

"In? Are you fucking kidding me?" yelled one of the jerk surfers. "Fuck you. You're kidding me, right?"

"Nope. Not kidding," Herschel said. "That's a score. So head on down the other way."

"No. You're not making that call," the other jerk surfer shouted, running up to the line and gesturing angrily. "You are *not* making that call."

"Yeah I am. I don't know what to tell you."

Seriously, at this point the guy whipped his hair back and stomped around with his hands on his hips like an angry drag queen. "Unbelievable. That's fuckin' bullshit, man. Fuckin' bullshit! Fuckin' unbelievable!"

Inevitably all the hotheads on both teams started to circle up and cuss at each other, all gesturing to the same spot as Herschel held the disc and shrugged. And in the middle of it all, one of their alumni, some fat, long-haired dude in board shorts and sandals got out of his folding chair and ambled down the sideline to insert himself in the discussion.

"Terrrrrible call! Terrrrible call!" he shouted. (Note: I've drastically cut the number of "r's" the dude actually inserted into the word terrible or they'd have taken up most of the page.) "You weren't in," he continued. "Give us the disc back and let's go!"

Captain Diggs turned around. "Who the hell are you? You're some guy in a chair. Get the fuck out of here."

"Hey," he yelled. "No one knows who you are. You're nobody. Your team is nothing. Penn State? What have you ever done?"

"Well, at the moment we're tied with *you*," Duffy answered to much laughter from our sideline.

"Terrrrrrible call!" he yelled. "Your program sucks. You've never done anything. Know your damn place. That's a terrrrrible call!"

At this point, he was standing right next to me on the sideline so I walked in front of him. "Dude, guys I know are getting shot at in Afghanistan right now. We're playing Frisbee. You realize in the end this doesn't really matter. You see that, right?" I said extending my hand to shake.

I don't know what I was thinking. Somehow I thought logic would win out and the dude might shut up. But I forgot one key component. Pompous pricks aren't swayed by logic. Or sense. Or the extension of goodwill. He slapped my hand away.

"No, man, I don't see. I don't fucking see," he shouted in my face.

I laughed at him. "So I'm actually a counselor. I can help you work through those anger issues. You not get hugged enough? This whole fucking town needs a hug."

"Fat, old, and pissed off is no way to go through life!" Duffy yelled.

Behind me, Hands was shouting, "Get a haircut! The 80's are over!"

I really don't know how the whole thing got resolved. The smug dude finally walked off and pissed on a few babies or something before coming back and continuing to be an abrasive moron. After five minutes of arguing, Herschel's goal eventually counted but it made the last few points insanely contentious. The game went to universe point. They made some asshole calls and we responded with a couple asshole calls of our own. Somehow they ended up coming out on top 13-12. We walked off the field angry and once again the victim of a close, hard fought loss.

Luckily the final game of the day was much more spirited. Under the lights, we played a really tough Illinois team at the exact same time our schools were meeting on the gridiron in Champaign. One of the dudes on their sideline had a portable radio that was getting the Wake Forest game. Our sidelines mixed together as we all huddled around it waiting for them to announce the out of town scores. Six years later and someone would've undoubtedly had Internet on their phone, but that technology hadn't quite materialized yet so that static-muddled radio was all we had. Because of that radio, the game became the exact spiritual opposite of the previous one against UNCW. The two teams basically made one giant sideline as we collectively listened to a broadcast none of us actually cared about, laughing and joking in the middle of what turned out to be another close and competitive game.

My first point of the tournament came early in the game when I ran down a huck from Captain Ian on the goal line then waited for Asian Ray to catch up. With a relatively uncontested three-yard flick, we went up 4-2.

Sadly, both Penn State teams would end up blowing second half leads. The football team would lose 33-28 and we'd fall 14-12 ending the day 1-4 with a goal differential of only minus one, finding out that indeed we were a good team but cursed with a pesky case of the late game yips.

We woke up the next morning and promptly lost 13-10 in our final pool play game versus a very good George Washington team. Of course, every time we'd mention it upon returning to campus, some genius would make a variation of the same joke.

"You lost to ONE guy?"

"Man, that dude must've been pretty good!"

"How'd he beat you at Frisbee? He's been dead for years. HAHAHAHA!"

*Note: College ultimate players should prepare for this joke every time they play James Madison, John Carroll, George Mason and Stephen F. Austin as well. Surprisingly, people aren't as adept at making the same joke about William & Mary. They don't know how to incorporate both genders and it just ends up bombing.

So we went into the elimination round as the number eight seed coming out to battle top-ranked Ohio State who'd rolled through the tournament undefeated so far. Even though we were at opposite ends of the seeding, we knew it was going to be a big game. After all our close losses, we could still put our stamp on the tournament and announce ourselves as a nationals caliber team if we just figured out how to keep a damn lead. I hadn't played a lot in the GW game, so I was just hoping to get on the field for a couple points. And then before the game, we huddled up and called starters.

Bobes led a rousing pregame cheer to an old Beastie Boys song, then Captain Ian called the lines.

"We're going with me….Diggs…..Bobes….Pete…..Hands….Duffy and…..Cramer."

I tried not to smile too wide. I was going to start our biggest game so far. At that point I was so pumped I could've picked up a car. A very small car. Like maybe a Fiat.

We took the opening pull and sliced it straight down the field to score the first goal. Then we forced a turn and put up a midfield huck to stun them by going up 2-0. I headed to the sideline to a madhouse of high fives.

A few points later, I reentered the game and was playing left wing in the zone when a wind gust took an easy dump toss way over the head of its intended target. Across the field, Bobes saw it floating and sprinted in from the opposite wing, running it down uncontested in the end zone for a Callahan goal to put us up 5-1. Upon pancaking the disc, he spun and did an excited cross between an Irish jig and terrible aerobics as the team swarmed him. The eight seed wasn't rolling over. Ohio State was in an unexpected battle.

And cue the yips.

Before we knew it, we were down 9-6. In the time it takes the average human to yawn, they'd gone on an 8-1 run to put our title hopes in serious jeopardy. We were absolutely reeling until Captain Ian took over the next two points, making a D and throwing pinpoint scores to close the gap back to one. At that point, I got called onto the field to play defense. Almost immediately, they tried to regain their comfortable lead with a big huck that one of our deeps swatted out the back of the end zone. We took it back down the field methodically, using great flow out of our vertical stack and were on the verge of tying the game when Captain Ian got stifled just outside the goal line. With no options on stall eight, he called time out.

In the huddle, we knew it was a big moment. After seemingly being down and out, we were right back in the game. The nerves and excitement radiated from our huddle. No one managed to stand still. Everyone was rocking on their heels or pounding their hands together. All of us could hear our heartbeats in our ears.

"Ok," Captain Ian said with quiet confidence. "It's coming in on stall eight so I don't have much time. I need options. Duffy, start out behind me as the dump and cut force side toward the goal line. I don't have time to turn and look for you so I'll just put it to space. Hands, stand at the front of the stack as a lob option if Duffy's not open. And Cramer.... let's have you come from the middle of the stack and cut hard break side as my third read."

We all nodded in agreement.

"Ok," he said way more meekly than the situation warranted. "Let's tie it up."

As I took my place in the stack, I watched Ohio State set up on defense. They had one guy covering Duffy and a second guy poaching the lane at the goal line. If Duffy made the cut he wanted to make, there was a guy right there. Even his best cut wasn't getting him open. OSU's biggest guy was fronting Hands at the front of the stack so that option was shut down as well. Ian surveyed the defense. He saw exactly what I did. I was now option A in our attempt to tie the biggest collegiate match I'd ever played in.

Ian's counterpart steadied himself, digging in his cleats and squatting down to seal off the right side of the field.

"Ready?" he said, hovering his palm over the disc in Ian's hands. Their defense nodded. "Disc in!" he yelled, reaching out to smack it back into play.

Seeing this, I threw a quick jab step to the middle and exploded from the stack. My defender recovered, but I had a step on him. Ian was magician, shaking his hips to get the mark off balance, then firing a low, flat laser from around his ankles, his knuckles scraping the grass just under the mark's forearm. The disc was out. He'd broken him.

It was up to me now. It had been absolutely gunned from about four yards away, low, quick, and out in front of me. At full speed, I dropped into a baseball slide and held out my hands.

THWACK.

I scooped it off the top of my thigh and popped to my feet with the disc in my hands. Tie game. Our sideline roared. I got absolutely mobbed by everyone on the field. I can clearly remember every guy on the team running toward me, their faces strained with elation as they rolled forward in one giant wave. They knocked my hat sideways, pounded my chest and practically tore off my beard with excitement. With four points to go, we were tied with the number one seed. Hope was very much alive. Things were going as expected. I'd scored a huge goal in a big game. The first of many, I was certain.

I had no idea it would be the high water mark of my Penn State career.

I stayed in the game on defense and we surprised them with a zone. I shut down the right wing as we frustrated them into a drop. Our subsequent goal put us in the most dangerous position possible - leading with the finish line clearly in sight. By now you can guess the outcome. Send in the yips.

Ohio State 13

Penn State 10

For the tournament, we'd gone 1-6, never losing by more than four and blowing second half leads in every loss but one. We were so frustratingly close to being elite.

The loss knocked us out of the tournament. Fortunately or unfortunately depending on how you looked at it, we couldn't leave because our women's team, ISIS was steamrolling their way to the final. Our women that year were incredibly good, captained by a girl named Nico, who was the hot sarcastic tomboy that all straight guys are both attracted to and marginally afraid of. Her co-captain was a lanky Asian girl named Shelly who wore her baseball cap backwards and never seemed to have clothes that fit quite right.

And wouldn't you know it, they lined up in that final game against the fun and gracious hosts of the tournament, UNC-Wilmington. I think the game would've been intense anyway, but what really raised the bar for better or worse was the ring of testosterone that lined the field. The battle from the previous day was still raw. We wanted revenge and if we had to get it vicariously through our women, then by god, we were going to get it vicariously through our women.

As the sun went down and the pull went up, we shouted our faces off. I honestly think it was a bit disconcerting at first for the girls who weren't used to being squarely in the middle of a very loud and very contentious verbal war between the sidelines. Every defense, every layout, every goal was met with a roar. Every call was met with derision.

Their alumni dude in board shorts was sitting across the way in his folding chair being a moron again. We outright hated him, so every time the UNCW women called a foul, pick, or travel, even if it was legitimate, the sixteen guys on our sideline would bellow....

"Terrrrrrible call! Terrrrrrible call!"

Of course, they'd loudly remind us of our loss the previous day so we had to come back with more and more outlandish stuff.

After a particularly egregious call, I shouted. "How is it that your women are even bigger pricks than your men?"

"It's cause the women *have* bigger pricks than the men!" Duffy replied.

"Ooooh! Ooooh!" And we shouted and stomped around like we were at a pickup basketball game in Harlem. We may - I repeat *may* have been a tad over the top.

A few points into the game, Nico and Heather (from the van) started glaring at us.

"Guys, knock it the hell off," Nico said. "You're making us nervous."

Heather gave us all the stink eye. "Could you just cheer for us without being assholes? How about trying that?"

"But they're…" we all stuttered.

Evil death glares prevented the rest of our words.

And so we shut up. Me, Hands, or Duffy would think of some awesome zinger and would have to pocket it, whispering it to the other guys instead of shouting it across the field. Then just after halftime, Nico wound up for a backhand and got shoved in the back and run over. As she went to get up, the UNCW girl used Nico's head as leverage, pressing her face into the grass.

"Whoa!" she shouted. "Foul! Jesus!"

The UNCW girl said something back to her and they started chirping back and forth and next thing you know, the scene was a carbon copy of our game except with a lot more boobs.

When Nico came to the sideline to get water after the point, the look in her eyes could've melted rubber. She took a sip and stared off at the field, glaring at their sideline. "Heckle as much as you want," she growled toward us. "Fuck these bitches." She slammed her water bottle to the ground and stormed off.

And the ceasefire ended. By the end of the game, our collective voices were nearly gone. At 12-12, Shelly got behind the defense and caught a huck from Nico, executing a sweet toe drag to keep herself in bounds. She went tumbling into their sideline and flipped over one of their empty beach chairs, snapping it clean in half. This led to the heckle of the night from Hands.

"Oh shit! She's been breaking your women all night, now she's breaking your furniture!"

The girls got a huge lift from the well timed and well executed burn and punched it in to go up 13-12 in a game that was almost destined from the beginning to go to universe point. At 14-14, with our voices knocking the tide back out to sea, ISIS worked it down toward the goal line and with a simple swing pass from Nico to Shelly, won the game and the title 15-14. We stormed the field as if they'd just won the national title. I think confetti and streamers randomly fell from the night sky. The Wilmington guys running the tournament ground their teeth and reluctantly handed over the trophy. It was an awesome moment.

Unfortunately, the girls wanted no part of a sweaty ten hour drive, so they decided to shower. They'd earned the right, but it meant we didn't even get out of there until 8:00PM. Fortunately, Asian Ray cut a good 90 minutes off the drive by going 140MPH on the way home. Even so, I showed up completely delirious for class on Monday – with a hamstring that was in no way happy with me.

TWENTY-ONE

ONE OF THE REASONS MY HAMSTRING WAS SO UNHAPPY WAS THAT WHEN I should've been resting, I was off playing more ultimate. That year a few of my friends from back home decided to reawaken the defunct Pittsburgh co-ed team and rename it Double Entendre. (Because at that point every co-ed team was either named using a clever sex pun or some sort of weird inside joke.) We had stylish V-neck T-shirts featuring the silhouette of a naked dude skying for a disc as a naked woman laid out directly in front of him. The silhouettes intersected at the crotch. It was class all the way.

The team we threw together managed to do just well enough at sectionals to squeak into regionals as the number thirteen seed. So in early October, we packed our cars and made the six-hour drive to Richmond, Virginia to try and earn a trip to nationals. Try being the operative word. We were pretty sure we weren't going to nationals. At this point, we were a fun team and by now you know what that means. Our whole goal was to win one game at regionals. Baby steps. Baby steps.

I was stretching on the field before the first game vs. the #4 seed, a team out of Durham called Elvis Loves Boats (this has to be an inside joke cause if it's a sex pun, I'm totally lost) when the sky let loose in a downpour of Biblical proportions. Rain was blowing sideways, managing to soak both the inside of my ears and the inside of my nose, which realistically should've been impossible. As far as the game went, we threw a zone on them, forcing enough turnovers to keep it close for a while before eventually falling 15-8. This is where things got funny.

Between games, the rain was still coming down in tropical fashion and at best it was fifty degrees. Our captain was a friend of mine named

Bram, a short, poochy guy who was never quite as good at ultimate as he was at political activism. Ten years later, he headed up the Pittsburgh version of the Occupy Wall Street protests, spending most of his time in a tent outside of BNY Mellon, shouting into a bullhorn and aggravating hedge fund managers. The other co-captain was Langstaff, the crazy Jewish squirrel.

Anyway, while we all huddled in the tent to get warm, the two of them somehow got a bug in their asses about doing a box drill to prepare for the next game.

Hollywood Jason was on the team and like all pampered movie stars did not want to do a box drill in the cold rain. "I think I'll just stay here in the warm, dry tent," he said.

Channeling my inner diva, I agreed. "I'm gonna have to side with Jason here."

Bram and Lang stood next to each other pumping their fists like wet, delirious Hobbits. "We're hearty souls! This is nothing!" Bram shouted, blinking incessantly as the water pelted his face.

"It's just rain!" Lang yelled. "It's water - like the number one thing we need for our very survival! C'mon now. Box drill on three. One….two…"

No one moved.

"Ok, on three we all run out to the end zone. One….two…."

Two of our women ran out to join them.

"Like I said on three….."

Lang had to count to three about nine more times just to annoy enough people onto the field. What followed was me, Hollywood Jason, Fast Jess, and a few others staying in the dry tent, feeding each other grapes like Greek royalty - boldly mocking our shivering teammates as they ran the most sloppy and unproductive box drill in history. They may as well have been out there practicing beekeeping for all the good it did them.

Bram came in from the drill mildly annoyed at how comfy and well fed we all looked. His teeth were chattering as he brought us all together. "Ok, so this is basically an elimination game. (Chatter….chatter….blow into hands…shiver) Our goal coming down here was to win (chatter) one game and break seed. This is our opportunity." He then proceeded to glare in my direction. "*Most* of us are warmed up and ready to go. Some of us still need to get our blood pumping." A sadistic grin crossed his face. "Seven of you stayed in the tent. It's raining even harder now. You got the first two points. Enjoy!"

Damn it. There was no way we could just refuse to take the field. To be honest, it was a pretty good burn by Bram. Never mind that in his quest for revenge, all the warm people sat down and got cold, completely nullifying any advantage they may have gotten from doing the drill in the first place. The seven of us who'd stayed in the tent reluctantly trudged out to the line and stared out at a team from D.C. named Sabotage. (Somehow a sex pun. I'm sure of it.) As we stood there waiting for the game to start, my whole body felt like I'd been thrown into wet snow. Our uniforms were stuck to us. I looked over at Jason as we prepared to pull.

"Let's score quick and get the hell back in the tent."

"Yeah," he said just before launching the pull down to their goal line.

In the rain, their first pass slipped right through the receiver's hands. I picked it up and saw Hollywood Jason slogging his way toward the back of the end zone. I fired a wet hammer over three people that he bobbled and caught to put us up 1-0. We were halfway back to the tent.

On the line, we arranged our defense and Jason once again prepared to pull. "You realize how pissed off Bram's going to be if we walk off the field with a 2-0 lead?"

"I love that our captain is going to be furious that we're winning."

It was true. In Bram's ideal scenario, we'd go down 2-0 and sulk back to the tent, begging for forgiveness just before he and the others triumphantly used their newfound skills to work their way downfield in a box-like pattern three times to take the lead. Then upon throwing the third goal, he'd gallantly stride over, place his hands upon our sinning heads and say, "You are forgiven my children. Take the field and use what you've learned."

Wanting to avoid *that* embarrassment, I ran my ass off to cover the pull, forcing a bad throw that Fast Jess swatted to the ground. Hollywood Jason retrieved it. At the goal line I turned and pointed in the air. He nodded and threw a hammer that half slipped out of his hand. I barely had to move, boxing out three players that the wobbly toss had allowed to surround me. I came down with it for the goal. We'd been on the field a whopping three and a half minutes and were now jogging back to the tent with a 2-0 lead.

Bram passed us on the way out to the field, mumbling. "You sons of bitches."

When the warmed-up players came back into the tent, we were down 3-2.

"Don't say anything!" Bram yelled. "Don't say....*anything!*"

During the second half, the rain tapered off to a steady drizzle. We were up 12-11 and one single point from victory when I made a defensive play I'll remember for my entire life - for all the wrong reasons. I was playing the deep in our zone, a position I always dominated. I never let much past me so after the first few points, our opponents would typically abandon their deep game all together. This game was no different.

After being lulled to sleep for most of the game, I'd pinched up the field trying to cut off the little flips they were throwing over our wings. On this point, I must've pinched too far because a guy got behind me. Their handler wound up and sent a huge curving backhand over the tents a good five yards out of bounds. I turned to track it, but it was so far OB that I'm sure I wasn't sprinting as hard as I could. That changed when it caught the wind and started to slice back into play.

I had it lined up the entire way. I was going to have to lay out, but I wasn't concerned. I had it tracked. Just before the sideline, I launched myself into the air to punch it out of play.

I went skidding out of bounds, flipping over and landing inside one of Sabotage's tents, my leg coming to rest on top of a Coleman cooler. As I crawled to my feet, I was stunned to see them celebrating like mad. I stumbled toward the field, confused, turning to one of the women on the periphery of the celebration.

"Don't tell me he caught that."

"Don't ask me how, but....yeah. He caught it."

From what I was told later, I'd laid out completely over top of the disc as it sliced down out of the fog. I swear the thing physically passed through my body. The Sabotage dude behind me had slipped in the wet grass and was sitting on his ass by the front cone. Disc landed right in his lap. I stared at my hands the entire way back to the tent.

"I don't know how I missed it," I said.

Bram smiled. "Well maybe if you'd have done the box drill…"

Sabotage forced a turn and scored on universe point to win 13-12 making us 0-2 going into our pity game versus some team from Charlotte. They were up 9-8 when one of our women, a doctor named Suzie shattered her ankle catching the tying goal. Players from both teams helped load her into the back of a cold, wet van, causing a twenty minute delay that none of us really wanted to return from. So we decided to call it a day and tie for 13th place. Double Entendre may not have won a game at regionals like we'd planned but at least we could say we played in a game we didn't lose. And we held seed.

Concerned for the health and well being of our teammate, we decided there was only one thing we could do for Doctor Suzie - pick up a case of beer, head back to the hotel and get buzzed. Before we could relax completely though, there was one vital matter at hand. In the tent just prior to getting hurt, Doctor Suzie had called dibs on first shower. And now she was at the ER and not at the hotel to cash in.

"This is a dilemma," Lang said. "She called dibs. I mean, realistically we have to wait for her to get back or go find her at the hospital and have her officially rescind her dibs."

Bram cracked open a Miller Lite. "None of it matters. You guys may not have heard because she said it so softly, but as she was lying there fighting back tears in the back of the van, being so brave, I asked her, 'Suzie, what can I do to help?' She took my hand and gently whispered. 'Bram, if I don't make it back, I want you to have my first dibs in the shower. It would mean so much.'"

"Yeah, I could see that being the first thing on her mind as her ankle was ballooning up."

Bram nodded. "Can't go against a fallen teammate's wishes so…."

"You realize if that story isn't true and you break dibs, you're cursed for years, right?" Hollywood Jason said.

"There's no curse associated with breaking dibs," Bram said confidently before thinking about it for a moment. "Is there?"

I cracked open a beer of my own. "I wouldn't risk it."

Ultimately we sat there damp and smelly watching football for a half hour, cautiously eyeing each other, waiting for someone else to get fed up with their own griminess enough to risk angering the gods.

Finally Bram couldn't take it anymore. "Ok, it's been over an hour since she called it. There's gotta be some statute that says…."

"I don't think there's a time limit on dibs," Lang interrupted.

"Nobody gets infinite dibs. You have to act upon your dibs in a timely fashion or else it's nullified," he said popping off the bed and fumbling in his bag for clean clothes.

"Dude, you're gonna slip in there and crack your head open," I said.

"Ok, I lied before," he said. "Suzie didn't vocalize it but she passed her dibs to me. We shared a look. It was unspoken. But unmistakable."

"Yeah, be careful in there, " Hollywood Jason said.

I sipped my beer. "I'm not hauling your dead naked ass out of the bathtub."

"I'm gonna be fine!"

A few moments later a loud crash emanated from the bathroom.

"My deodorant fell off the sink! That's all. I remain unconcerned. I forge ahead!" The toilet lid fell with a bang. "Oh Jesus…."

So Bram took the most nervous post tournament shower ever and somehow managed to come out of it unscathed. Out in the hotel room, while one guy showered, the other three would down a few beers and talk politics. Next thing we knew, the four of us were feeling pretty good. Eventually after about ninety minutes, one of our sober teammates knocked on the door to find us much cleaner and much drunker.

"I was thinking about heading to the hospital to check on Suzie," said random teammate. "Anyone want to come along?"

"You bet. Drunk hospital trip. Let's do it."

So we enthusiastically piled into his car and soon found ourselves wandering through downtown Richmond trying to find the entrance to the ER - which was harder than it seemed, especially after four or five beers. Every entrance seemed to have a sign that said EMPLOYEES ONLY. And bars on the window. And stone-faced Russian guys with machine guns. We must've circled the VCU Medical Center three full times.

"How the hell do you get into this place?" we yelled, banging on random doors.

"It's like a fortress."

"She's never coming out. The hospital has her now. We just need to let her go."

We were in the middle of giving Doctor Suzie an impromptu sidewalk eulogy when we finally realized that the ER entrance was actually in an adjacent building. We were euphoric until we realized that finding the entrance was going to lead to a lot of waiting. And sitting. And sobering up. Two hours later, tired of old Newsweeks and Wheel of Fortune reruns, we decided the best thing we could do for Doctor Suzie was to head to dinner where we could get more beers. Stupidly, we also vowed not to order any food until she showed up. Now the VCU Medical Center in downtown Richmond is both incredibly slow and ungodly slammed on your typical Saturday night - which meant in our attempt at chivalry and solidarity we put a lot more beer into our empty stomachs than we'd originally planned. Let's just say things got uh….a bit blurry.

It didn't take long for Bram to start reassessing our plan. "Ok, we won't eat dinner until she gets here but it's totally cool to order appetizers. We wouldn't be assholes if we ordered a sampler platter."

Lang disagreed. "We've held out this long."

"I really don't think appetizers count," Bram responded. "They're a completely separate entity. Otherwise they'd be listed under entrees. This logic holds."

I laughed. "Dude, why do you hate Suzie so much?"

"I don't hate Suzie. I'm just hungry!"

"Steal her shower dibs, eat before she gets here - I'm just following the evidence."

"I don't…." Bram said, frustrated. "I'm getting a sampler platter. There's no hatred involved. I don't have to justify this."

So Bram ordered his appetizer platter, which I knew was going to be pure torture for the rest of us - because he was going to offer us some and then pounce on our moral failings as soon as we took a bite. Luckily it took the platter a while to arrive. It was well after 10PM when Doctor Suzie crutched her way into the restaurant to wild, Heineken-fueled applause from all of her half plowed teammates. It was the type of random outburst that causes other patrons to fumble their silverware.

We pounded our empties on the table. "Suzie's not dead! Suzie's not dead! Suzie's not dead!"

And now that we had confirmation that Doctor Suzie was indeed alive and well, Bram had pressing issues to deal with. "Suzie, I took first shower," he said. "I know you had dibs, and I apologize. But considering the circumstances - I just need you to give me your blessing."

"He wants to make sure he's not cursed," I said.

"I know I'm not cursed," Bram exclaimed. "It's simply a matter of principle."

"He wants to make sure he's not cursed."

Doctor Suzie leaned her crutches against the table. She pointed to the brand new, untouched appetizer platter that the waitress had just put down in front of Bram.

"That all looks really good."

"You want me to buy you an appetizer platter?"

"I think you already did. Unless you're fine with the curse."

"But I...waited so long."

"You could always order yourself another one."

Bram dropped his head and slid the platter across the table before raising his hand and turning around. "Waitress!"

"You're absolved," Suzie said, digging into a mozzarella stick.

We all laughed and drank and ate well into the night. It's amazing sometimes how little your success on the field has to do with your best memories of ultimate.

TWENTY-TWO

SOMETIME AFTER WE GOT BACK FROM EASTERNS, I GOT SLID INTO A GIANT space tube. And that giant space tube told the doctor I had a partially torn hamstring. Which meant that I'd been playing against top-level competition when realistically, I shouldn't have been able to run. In doing so, I'd most likely made it much, much worse. I, like many other ultimate players who play a relatively physical sport without the benefit of sideline medical experts tend to feel any non excruciating pain and go, *eh, this will go away…. eventually*. Incredibly, most times it does. The problem comes in those rare occasions when it doesn't.

One perk of being a pseudo college athlete at Penn State was that you got access to the "other sports" rehab center. "Other sports" of course meaning, *"You're not as important as the football players but since you apparently go to school here too, we're forced to take care of your silly ass."* (It says that on a gold plaque when you enter the facility.) So three times a week, I limped in there, had some middle aged woman smear goo on my ass, shoot me up with sound waves and lead me through a series of unpleasant exercises.

Because I was going to be out for the two most critical months of the spring season (mid February to mid April), I decided to make it easy on the captains. Instead of being rostered, I offered instead to coach the "B" team made up of our freshman and sophomores. (Most bigger schools have a "B" team that they use as a training ground for their players of the future.)

It was a motley collection of really weird dudes as any B team tends to be. We had SeaBass, Putz and Slacker Sam along with a slow, gangly 6'8" deep threat we called Lurch, a short but super athletic freshman who for reasons that will become evident later I'll call Kosher Josh, a completely insane Jeep of a kid we called "The General," and a fat badass troll with a mullet named Benji. And like ten kids named Lee.

There's one other kid on the team who I'll give his own paragraph simply because he managed to sustain the most improbably hilarious injury in the history of sports. The dude's name was Shawn and he was a crooked glasses kid. Everyone knows one. (That kid who weighs about thirty pounds and looks like he's been in a bunker working on his female robot twins for the last six months.) Anyway, I was slowly jogging with the team on their warm up lap when I noticed him hustle up beside me. He'd missed the last two weeks of practice.

"Shawn, where the hell have you been?" I asked.

"I've been injured."

"What? What happened?"

"Well," he said, adjusting his glasses. "I uh….had to get stitches."

"Stitches? Oh shit. Where?"

You could tell he didn't want to say, but couldn't think of anything but the truth. "My ass. I….sliced open my ass."

"You cut open your ass? You seriously cut open your…..how?"

If he wasn't starting to breathe heavily from the warm-up, he would've sighed. "Pop Tarts."

I had to quit running. My legs weren't going anywhere after that information. "Wait a minute, wait a minute," I said, grabbing him by the shoulders. "You cut your ass open on Pop Tarts? So badly that you had to miss two weeks of practice? Is this what you're telling me?"

"Yeah," he said, chuckling. "My mom bought me one of those big savings club boxes of Pop Tarts. It's heavy duty cardboard and I had it right next to my bed. I'm on the top bunk and I guess I wasn't really awake one morning…and I sort of fell out and landed on the corner of the box. Had to go to the hospital. I'm sorry for missing practice. They said not to run until a week after I got the stitches out."

"Dude, you lacerated your ass on Pop Tarts. There's no way to be mad about that. Absolutely no way."

And Pop Tart Shawn rounded out the team.

So I got to hold the clipboard as the B Team headed for Towson University. Instead of playing, I just got to watch and teach. It was the first time I realized I actually knew things about the game, showing guys where to cut, what was open, how to time their runs, set up their defense, etc. At one point Slacker Sam got the disc on the goal line against University of Maryland-Baltimore County. To that point he'd only been a deep receiver and wasn't comfortable at all with the disc in his hands. He called time out and came to the sideline.

"Cramer, we need to set up a play so I can get it to a handler."

"Why?"

"Cause ya know….if we don't, I'll throw it away."

"How are you going to learn to throw upfield if you don't throw upfield?"

"Yeah, but like….its a close game and…."

"Dude, you're not here to win this game. You're here to win big games two years from now." I looked at the huddle. "Nobody gives Sam a dump option. All six of you stack up in the end zone. We score on this pass or we turn it over. Anything else and you're all doing sprints."

"Ah, damn it, Cramer," Sam said, dropping his head, now with no choice.

I smacked him on the back and shoved him out to the field with a smile. "You got this. I'm not worried. Why are you?"

And wouldn't you know it on stall eight, Slacker Sam threw a beautiful curving backhand around the mark that damn near led to a score. Damn near. He squished his own face as he watched it hit the ground just beyond the fingertips of The General.

"Sam," I yelled from the sidelines. "That's a great throw. Next time it's a goal."

Amazingly enough, it was. He ended up with four or five assists in that tournament. It felt good. As much as it was killing me not being out there, I was finding that this coaching was agreeing with me.

Our final game of the day was a relatively easy victory against Franklin & Marshall College out of Lancaster, PA. (The Huckin' Amish) Unfortunately, due to that game, we lost our mulleted hero, Benji, for the rest of the year to an MCL sprain. Not during the game, mind you. We lost him after the game. We lost him because the two girls playing for F&M that day convinced him to strip down to his underwear and sumo wrestle one of their fat guys in a mud hole behind the end zone.

When you're an ultimate player, you're used to seeing your teammates do gross and disturbing things. Not much really fazes you. Unless it's two bare, jiggly, sweaty stomachs slamming into each other like giant ugly pancakes.

As both teams lined the pit, cheering like shady bettors around some basement cockfight, I laughed toward Lurch standing next to me. "Dude, what the hell are we doing with our lives?"

"Being young and carefree, Cramer. Being young and carefree."

I nodded. It was a fantastic answer. "C'mon, Benji, get some fuckin' leverage!"

I don't remember who won. In many ways, I wish I didn't remember the incident at all - mainly because I wouldn't be able to recall with unsettling clarity the image of Benji's mud streaked thighs running toward us for chest bumps.

"Yeahhhhh!" he yelled, his mullet swaying in the wind. "Give me some love, boys! Sumo! Sumo! Sum-oh....shit," he said suddenly limping. "My knee hurts."

So we lost one guy due to a freak Pop Tart accident and another sumo wrestling in a mud pit. Ladies and gentlemen, your 2002 Penn State B Team.

To be honest, I loved coaching but it was absolute hell watching from the sidelines - especially when I didn't have the clipboard and basically became a glorified cheerleader. The "A" team had a tournament in Philly just before Duffy and I headed south to Myrtle Beach for spring break. Duffy was playing and I needed a ride so I didn't have much of a choice. We played UMass, Swarthmore, Haverford, and Dartmouth - four games that I had to stand there and...witness. In terms of things that suck in an ultimate player's life, watching a game you're unable to participate in ranks somewhere in between having your apartment fumigated and the moment you realize you need to have your apartment fumigated.

I'll remember that tournament for two things. First, we had a deep receiver named Pete who was the size of most college tight ends. And sometime in the Dartmouth game, he leapt along the sideline to swat a D and landed on a stump. An honest to god stump - where there once was a tree. To tell you the truth, no one even noticed there was a goddamn stump that close to the field until Big Pete fractured his ankle on it.

Safety – the number one thing tournament directors are concerned about behind *"How many fields can we realistically cram into this space?"* and *"Do we have enough bagels?"*

Now the parking lot was a long, long way from the fields and Pete had no chance of walking. His ankle was swelling and we had to get him to the ER as quickly as possible. The resulting conversation basically went like this….

"Do we have anyone who isn't doing anything right now who's big enough to carry Pete? Like probably a guy who hits the gym all the time and might be sitting out with a pesky hamstring problem?"

Want a workout that will take days to recover from? Carry a 240 pound guy across five soccer fields in the rain. But it's what you do for your teammates. When you're a useless, injured sideline guy you'll do anything to remain relevant - anything to feel like you still belong. And trust me, after lugging Pete a fourth of a mile, my body felt like it had played every point that day.

The second thing I'll remember about that trip was Kosher Josh's house in suburban Philly. Until we showed up, we had no idea his family was loaded. I think his dad owned most of Delaware County, PA. It was really just the most amazing palace of a home that anyone has ever let a mill trash guy like me set foot in. And for good reason. Over the weekend, Duffy and I did our best to destroy it piece by piece.

It started off harmlessly enough. We decided to hold a ping-pong tournament in the basement after we arrived on Friday evening. There was a fine glass table in the corner of the room that was lined with mahogany. Here's a lesson for you - don't sit on glass tables. It was a lesson I wish someone had passed along before I plopped my ass down to watch some ping-pong that night. Yet somehow in the middle of the resulting glass shards, I managed to avoid the very thing that Pop Tart Shawn couldn't when confronted with a box of toaster pastries. No bloodshed.

Feeling bad about that, I followed the guys up into the living room to play video games. Wanting to make sure I didn't break anything else, I flopped down on the couch because in my experience, couches don't often shatter. Unfortunately, as I sat down, the couch shifted just enough that a large baseball trophy behind it tipped like a poorly engineered building. The top of the trophy hit the end table and things exploded. Literally exploded. Little trinkets from Italy, precious heirlooms, important archaeological finds, not to mention the trophy - all broken instantaneously.

"Jesus," Duffy said, tossing me the keys to his car.

I caught the keys. "You thinking I should sleep in the car so I don't annihilate the entire house?"

"No, I thought you might want to have some more fun and drive it through the dining room wall," he laughed.

Beside us, Kosher Josh was quickly attempting to sweep up his family's broken memories before his parents discovered the carnage and kicked us out to the backyard. Or New Jersey. My demeanor within the house the rest of the weekend can best be described as "cautious tiptoeing."

Seeing that Duffy was the one giving me the hardest time about the clutzy wrecking ball I'd unleashed, what happened around 2:00 Sunday afternoon was damn near hysterical. We'd gone to Chili's the night before and Duffy ordered pork chops. He couldn't quite finish them off so he got a to-go box, brought it back to Josh's place and put it in the fridge figuring he could have himself a good meal before we hit the road for South Carolina.

Fresh off getting eliminated from the tournament by Salisbury State, we rolled into Kosher Josh's kitchen and started eating our leftovers from the night before. Duffy asked Josh if it was cool to use a knife and cutting board to slice up his stuff. Josh said it was perfectly fine.

So Duffy's calmly slicing his pork chops and we're laughing and joking around when we hear a gasp I've only heard in movies when someone witnesses a murder.

We turn to see Kosher Josh's mom standing in the archway of the kitchen in serious need of a brown paper bag to breathe into. She points an appalled finger at Duffy.

"Is that…..*pork*?"

Duffy, now on the verge of trembling, drops the knife and steps away from the kitchen counter. "Um…yes."

"*Oh my God!*" she screamed before trying to collect herself. "Ok, ok, if we throw away the knife and the cutting board....did any of it hit the counter?" she asked on the verge of a total breakdown. "If none of it hit the counter, we won't have to remodel the kitchen."

I swear Duffy was about to put his hands up and surrender. "What'd I do?"

"Eh," Kosher Josh said. "We're not supposed to have pork in the kitchen."

(Ah, *there's* the reason I'm calling him Kosher Josh)

"You're Jewish?" I said.

Kosher Josh nodded. "I thought that was pretty obvious but I guess yeah, you're right, it's never actually come up."

"Josh!" his mom shouted. "Was it in the fridge?"

He rolled his eyes and sighed. "It was in a container, mom. None of it…"

"It doesn't matter, Joshua! It was in there. Contaminating everything. This fridge is only two years old and now we have to get rid of it. Not to mention the rest of the food! We will talk about this later. And this will be the *last* time any Frisbee players stay here!"

Then in a livid flash, she disintegrated. Duffy was left there practically frozen, not wanting to move a muscle. There's nothing like the awkward silence of six guys in a kitchen after they've been eviscerated by an irate mother. Especially after she'd been so nice and hospitable the entire weekend.

Finally after about a minute of staring at each other afraid we'd be struck dead for speaking, Kosher Josh turns to Duffy, who still hadn't moved. "Sorry about that, man. I should've warned you."

Duffy nodded. "So…can I have my sandwich or what?"

Kosher Josh laughed. "I guess since we're tearing down the whole kitchen anyway."

"Duff," I said. "Can I just say what a good friend you are for doing something so heinous that all the shit I broke on Friday night barely registers?"

Duffy took a bite of his pork sandwich. "You're welcome."

Kosher Josh would later transfer to Stanford where he'd lead Bloodthirsty to nationals and then go on to win the USA Ultimate Club Championship twice with San Francisco Revolver. (He caught the championship-ending goal in 2013.) Did he run to the west coast for the top-level education or simply to make absolutely certain that me and Duffy never ended up in his house again? We may never know. In my self-centered view of the world, I prefer to think Revolver was given an inevitable nudge toward the 2011 & 2013 titles because of a shattered table and some leftover pork.

So Duffy and I headed to Myrtle Beach, hit on most of the girls in the appropriately named Horry County and came back home to prepare for the rest of the season. Our home tournament "Spring Phling" was at one time one of the bigger tournaments east of the Mississippi. 32 men's teams and 24 women's teams from all over the country descended on State College in early April. For us, it was a big event. There's just something pretty damned amazing about heading to a tournament where your commute takes five minutes instead of five hours.

Coaching the B team made not actually playing just a little less crappy. Still though, there's an energy about a tournament, especially your home tournament, that you just don't feel when you've been pushed to the sidelines. I did everything I could. I filled my tiny living room with tournament packets, sorted bagels and water, managed the B team roster, shuttled injured players to the ER, and most importantly, drove all the beer to the party. But it just wasn't the same. I wasn't on the field when Penn State met Cornell for the tournament championship on a glorious Sunday afternoon.

The funny thing was though, as I stood there on the sidelines rooting on my teammates in that championship game, my perspective began to change. It really should've been the pinnacle of the tournament, a battle between two teams who'd fought through top-flight competition and were rewarded with the opportunity to showcase their talents for everyone to see. And it was everything it should've been – during the few moments when the guys on the field were actually playing ultimate.

There was a span in the game where four exciting hucks went up and everyone watching got that little heart-flutter of anticipation. Who was going to come down with the disc? It was pure ultimate - two guys sprinting their asses off as the disc bounces on the whims of the jet stream. They were the type of plays that make you rise up if you're sitting and inadvertently walk five steps downfield if you're standing.

And every one of them was nullified with a travel call.

Cornell's strategy seemed to be, "If they huck, call a travel whether it's legit or not. We'll get to set up and be ready on the restart."

And so after a few points of that crap, we started giving it back to them. And the whole game became a bullshit argument fest with little gems such as:

"Your pivot foot slid a bit."

"You weren't even looking at my feet!"

"I was too."

"You were not!"

It was about as exciting as watching middle school debate club. Sitting there on that sideline, a very foreign thought raced through my mind. It was a thought I wanted to dismiss, but couldn't.

Damn. I'm not positive I want to be a part of this next year.

I immediately shook it off. I was rehabbing and working my ass off so I could come back for my final year and be the best damn player in the country. I couldn't win the Callahan pissing around with the B team. If I wanted to be recognized, I'd just have to deal with the perverted way the game was being played at the top levels.

Despite all the fouls, Hands was a complete beast in that final game against Cornell. And there was a reason. He was in charge of making the trophies and in a spark of genius, had taken a regular Mr. Potatohead and turned him into a ninja. And let's be honest, if you have a heartbeat at all, you're going to end up emotionally attached to a Ninja Mr. Potatohead that you crafted with your own sweat and blood. Now Hands was just a single game from avoiding the heartbreak of seeing it leave State College. So he scored half the team's goals.

Unfortunately, he got so caught up in making the Ninja Potatohead that he forgot to make a women's trophy all together. Apparently, he realized during halftime of the championship and sprinted over to the tournament Winnebago that I'd been manning all afternoon.

"Cramer, you gotta help me. I forgot to make a women's trophy."

"What? How the hell do you forget to…."

"Once I made Mister Potatohead Ninja, it was such a masterpiece that I realized I couldn't have something totally lame for the women. And I couldn't think of anything. So I just kept putting it off and putting it off and then I just forgot."

"Why didn't you do a *Mrs.* Potatohead Ninja?"

"Wow that's….obvious," he said, knocking his head off the side of the Winnebago. "That would've been incredible. Damn it! Look, I just need you to find something we can pass off as legit."

Luckily ISIS won against Bucknell to bring home the Spring Phling women's title so it wasn't quite as embarrassing when Hands gave them a plastic goblet I found in the Winnebago filled with a couple tulips I'd picked from the side of the road. Even with the flowers, it still looked pretty empty, so as filler I used some old wiper blades from my truck. It was the best I could do on short notice.

"What the fuck is this?" Nico said as she accepted it. "Cornell gets a Ninja Potatohead and we get Cramer's fucking wiper blades?"

"There's a couple flowers in there," Hands said.

Nico and Shelly glared at him.

Hands hung his head. "I'll make a Mrs. Potatohead Ninja."

Nico shoved him. "You bet your ass you'll make a Mrs. Potatohead Ninja."

So my first year playing major college ultimate hadn't exactly gone as planned. I hadn't come in and dominated the region like I thought I would. Hell, I was basically an injured afterthought who wasn't even starting for my own team. But I still had one more year. I was going to train my ass off, get into pique physical condition, and nothing was going to stop me.

So I thought.

Summer League Snippets – Axis of Naughty

By the time June rolled around, my hamstring was no longer a concern. The rehab had worked and I was more or less back to 100% when I put in my name for the summer league draft.

After coming so close the year before, Langstaff reworked his draft strategy and somehow came out of it with a buzzsaw. His first round pick was a dude named Stan who had a crew cut, huge glasses, and was kind of built like a football. He was a fast guy in a slow guy's body, which pretty much got him wide open all the time as defenses continued to ignore him no matter how many goals he scored. The summer before, I'd put him out for the season by breaking his thumb as I swatted away a huck he was reaching for. Because of it, I got a somewhat deserved reputation as our team enforcer. I'd barely made it out of my truck before the first games of the summer when I heard Lang shouting across the fields.....

"Cramer, how about we try not to break Stan's thumb this year!"

"Well shit," I yelled. "Whose thumb can I break then?"

"I don't care! Just not Stan's!"

We ended up with a bunch of veteran handlers in their early to mid 30's including Iron Mike, the Sioux Warrior lookalike from chapter five who could get off a backhand huck against a charging moose. He was five years older than the last time I'd played with him but that monster huck was still the same. Lang's steal of the draft came on a tip from me. His seventh round pick was a solid handler named Tom who I'd played with at Penn State. I was proud of myself. I'd gotten to be one of Langstaff's "sources."

Our female captain was one of the top players for Pittsburgh Pounce, the city's women's team. She was a Jewish tomboy named Dara who took life very seriously. Trust me, she does *not* have time for your crap. For instance, one time she was selling Pounce visors at Sunday night karaoke. She pulled up a chair next to me.

"Cramer, do you want to buy a Pounce visor? They have a cat on them."

"Yeah, sure," I answered. "If you make out with me."

Her expression didn't change for about five seconds as her mind flipped through all possible reactions. The whole time, she just blankly stared into my eyes, finally settling on, "For how long?"

"Eight seconds. Like riding a bull."

Another ungodly length of time went by without a response. She had no idea how to react to the wrench I'd tossed in the transaction. "But they're only twelve dollars. Do you want one or not?"

I sighed. "Fine. You got change for a twenty?"

We were hanging out in Langstaff's kitchen the night after the first games as the three of us tried to think of an official team name. Lang and I were pretty set on *Weezy Jefferson* but Serious Dara hated it. So we spent about two hours just tossing stupid names back and forth.

"What about *Lush Puppie?*" I said.

"Oooh, yeah," Lang said, jotting it down in a little notebook. "That's on the short list. Or what about like...*The American Moustache and Beard Champions.*"

"But that leaves out half the team," Dara said. "Girls can't grow beards."

"Neither can Lang," I said. "And he's the one who came up with it."

"Hey, I can grow...." He paused. "Ok, so *that* one's out."

Serious Dara was leaning against the wall just sort of staring into space. "What about *The Refrigerator Magnets?*"

Langstaff squinted back at her. "I'd say we're looking for something slightly more creative. Like maybe something political. Like, I don't know, President Bush keeps referring to the Axis of Evil. How about that?"

"Yeah," I said excitedly. "But a play on it like - *Axis of Kinda Repugnant.*"

"*Axis of Irritating.*"

"*Axis of Off-putting.*"

"How about *The Spatulas?*" Serious Dara interrupted. "Or like, *Block of Cheese.*"

"What? No," Langstaff said. "I kind of like this *Axis of Whatever* thing so let's just keep....ya know....exploring that."

"Oooh, wait," Dara said with a jolt of excitement. "How about *Three Green Mugs?* Yeah. *Three Green Mugs.* C'mon guys, that's good. Seriously."

"*Three Green Mugs?*" I said, shaking my head. It was then that I followed her eye line. "Dara, are you just looking around the kitchen and naming everything that you see?"

She was taken aback. "No. No. Of course not. Why?"

Langstaff laughed. "Cause there are currently three green mugs occupying the sink directly in front of you."

"Guys, I'm more creative than that," she scoffed. "I'm not just looking around the kitchen."

"Ok. You gotta admit that's a hell of a coincidence though," I said.

"Guys, I'm not just looking around the kitchen."

A few moments of silence and the discussion ramped back up.

"So Axis of what?" Lang said. "We have something here. We just gotta hit the right beat."

Dara nodded. "What about *The Microwaves?*"

*To this day, Langstaff names his fantasy baseball team *Three Green Mugs*.

Eventually we settled on Axis of Naughty. AoN was so solid all around that we finished as the #2 seed headed into the playoffs where we barely broke a sweat in the first three games. When Serious Dara toed the line on a huck from Iron Mike for the goal to send us to the final, I could barely contain my excitement. I was going to be *on the field* in the season's feature game. I was going to get to play in front of an honest to god crowd.

And it was just as cool as I thought it would be. We played the #6 seed, a team called Botox Party. Most of the league stayed to watch the game. There was a small hill next to the field that was crowded with a couple hundred people all poised and ready to cheer and heckle the living shit out of us. I couldn't wait.

The feeling of having eyes upon you as you perform is one that's special in an ultimate player's career because let's face it, most of the time the only people paying any attention are your teammates and maybe the guy cutting the grass on the other side of the soccer complex. At least that's how it was back in 2002. Now with AUDL games and the college and club championships broadcast on ESPN and other internet channels, newer players are getting the chance to shine in front of an audience on a much more consistent basis. As for me, the summer league championship was what I got. I intended to take full advantage.

My best play of the afternoon was on defense when from the back of the stack, I saw them trying to execute a huck play. The guy I was guarding sprinted in on the force side but I saw the deep cut developing and dropped off him. I took three steps, got some sick air and swatted the disc from the center of the field the whole way over the sideline tents inciting an "Oooooh!" from the hill that I can still hear to this day.

It was awesome - significantly more awesome than a play later in the game where I was one-on-one with a much shorter guy in the end zone. For me, it was going to be an easy goal. Too easy. I didn't even bother to jump. I was anticipating a tip that never happened and the disc floated over him and donked me right between the eyes. The "Ooooh," from the crowd had a much different inflection.

I didn't really get to dominate the game like I'd hoped. I wanted to put an exclamation point on our season with at least one or two insane catches or layout D's. But in the end I didn't have to. We were so solid that I didn't have to do anything crazy to come away with the victory.

We were up 14-10 in a game to 15 when Serious Dara put up a long backhand to Penn State Tom - the kid I'd convinced Lang to draft. I sprinted by him with my defender on my hip and shot to the corner. Tom looked me off, so I stopped quickly and came back to the middle. I have no idea what happened to my defender. It wasn't *that* nasty of a cut, but somehow he fell into the void. I was wide open. Tommy lobbed a flick into the end zone. I caught it with no one around me. We were champions. And more than that, I'd been the one that ended up with our victory disc. At that point, less than 15 players could claim that they'd caught the final goal of summer league. Now I could add my name to the list. It was one of the physically easiest but most memorable goals I've ever scored.

Our team name got printed on a popsicle stick and glued to a lame plaque that listed all the past champions. But in that moment, the damn thing might as well have been the Stanley Cup. We hoisted it, posed for team pictures and finally, mercifully got to eat. Langstaff's endless nights of ultimate research had paid off. We now knew what it was like to win a championship.

TWENTY-THREE

It was a bitter cold January night in central Pennsylvania, but inside the Penn State Indoor Sports Complex, we were sweating like hell. Twenty sets of stairs followed by 200-yard sprints around the indoor track, plyos, lunges, and suicides all to prep us for the best chance SPANK had at making nationals in twenty years. And I was flying. My hamstring troubles were a distant memory. I was finishing first in every heat and sticking around a half hour after all the other guys had left to get in more plyos and sprints. I was going to be unstoppable.

The poster on my bedroom wall was so clear in my mind. In one of ultimate's most iconic images, Alex Nord of Carleton College is captured so far off the ground in the 2001 national championship game that his ribs are scraping across the top of his defender's head. He's almost totally horizontal, legs flailing behind him, his right arm thrust into the air practically crushing the disc in his fist. He looks like a pale, redheaded Superman. If you're unfamiliar, go Google "Alex Nord" right now. And make sure you pee first because once you see it you never know how your bladder is going to react.

And there was one thing I knew as I hopped on the bus and headed home on that ice cold January night - I was next.

The 2003 poster was going to feature Kevin Cramer laying out over top of some unfortunate soul for a ridiculous Callahan goal to win Penn State their first-ever national championship. Behind me, slightly out of focus, Duffy and Captain Ian would be in the first stages of realizing we'd just taken the title. I saw that image in my mind every time I thought I was too tired to do one more rep, one more sprint, or one extra jump. That image fueled me through a grueling fall and winter.

The team was loose during those indoor conditioning sessions. I hadn't seen them in action in a while and forgot about the sinking feeling I'd gotten watching the foul fest against Cornell. I was all in. I was having as much fun as you could possibly have in that zone just before you throw up or collapse. In fact, on that cold January night as we all struggled through round after round of wall squats, we even helped the world heal a bit.

We'd chosen that particular wall because the Penn State cheerleaders were out in the middle of the track doing their kicks and spins and flips and all that shit. It gave us something to focus on other than our quads slowly giving out. Anyway, in the middle of our first round, these two male cheerleaders decided they needed to loudly address the love triangle they were in with one of the little blonde girls they'd just been chucking toward the rafters. And this argument went on forever. Through one – two - three rounds of knee knocking wall squats, a muscular white guy and a muscular black guy loudly divulged the intimate details of their lives.

"I love her! You hear me? I fucking love her!!!"

"You don't love her, bro! How 'bout we let *her* decide who the real man is!"

"Don't be calling me bro! I'm not your bro! And we all know who the *real* man is here!"

Let me tell you, it's hard to silence an entire sports complex - especially with the women's soccer team, club baseball, and the rest of the cheerleaders all practicing in there as well. But these two dorks managed to do it. And like the temperature outside, the comfort level of everyone within earshot dropped well below zero.

The power of song is an amazing thing. And there's only one song you can possibly sing while watching a black guy and a white guy get ready to throw haymakers - a brilliant, Grammy winning duet by Stevie Wonder and Sir Paul McCartney.

My knees bouncing during an excruciating fourth round of squats, I began to bellow…

"Ebony and ivory……"

Next to me, Putz joined in.

"….live together in perfect…..harmony."

Struggling with their wall squats as well, Slacker Sam, SeaBass, Lurch, and Duffy picked up the melody.

"Side by side on my piano…."

And soon every guy on the wall squat line who knew the words was avoiding fatigue by belting out…

"…keyboard, oh lord why don't weeeeee!"

When we quit, there was an eerie silence as the other cheerleaders and the women's soccer team turned away and laughed into their hands. The two irate dudes turned and glared at us as our thirty seconds expired and we collapsed to the track.

"What?" I said pulling myself off the ground. "We always sing during wall squats."

They didn't know what to do. They were pissed at each other, they were annoyed at the blonde girl, and now they were pretty ticked off at us. It was too much. They just grunted and stomped off in opposite directions. I'm not kidding, I really think our harmony prevented a fist-fight. Also, I'm pretty sure Duffy swept in to comfort the little blonde cheerleader rendering their fight moot in the first place.

As for the upcoming season, I was pumped. I was fast. I was strong. I was ready to dominate. And I did - for three entire points. Early in the spring season, Swarthmore hosted a small tournament down in Philly and we sent the B team to get some work in. Seeing how much fun I'd had the year before, I decided to head down with them as a player/coach. I couldn't wait to get on the field again.

Our first game was against Villanova and they had no answer for me. On the first point, Sumo Benji put up a long huck that I grabbed high over my defender to open the scoring. Then I got a D, raced downfield and laid out for a hammer in the end zone to make it 2-0. At 2-1, the huck-happy Sumo Benji looked at me on the line.

"If I get it, just go. They can't stop you."

"I like the sound of that, fat man."

Three passes into the point, Benji caught a dump toss. I broke out of the stack and went streaking downfield. Benji launched a hanging 50-yard flick. I was stride for stride with my defender, but the disc was on the other side of him as we both leapt, tipping the disc at the same time. It popped into the air behind us. I stayed on my feet as we landed. He…did not.

I was about to reach back to make a layout catch off the double tip when he rolled through the back of my legs. Somehow I ended up getting whipped straight onto my back. It felt like I'd been taken to the top rope and suplexed. When I hit the ground, my left shoulder joint ripped out of socket for an excruciating second before settling back in its regular home. I hopped up to shake it off, but there was a knife under my scapula.

"Ooooh, I'm gonna….need a sub," I said jogging to the sideline.

I spent the tournament subbing in once or twice a game hoping that somehow a few points of rest had healed it. It hadn't. Every time I raised my arm past 90 degrees, it felt like I was being stabbed with a fork.

Back at practice, I tried to hide it. I was just as fast as ever and the injury was to my non-dominant shoulder, so I could still throw just fine. I just sort of hoped no one would notice that I couldn't reach for anything up and to the left. But it *was* noticeable. I couldn't lay out. I wasn't as strong in the air. My play dropped off considerably. It plunged to the point that in a couple weeks I'd gone from one of our starting seven to the bottom of the roster. In trying to grind through it, I was sinking myself further and further down the depth chart.

What really ended up derailing my season though was this fucker named Saddam Hussein. In early 2003, for reasons that in retrospect make less sense than they did at the time, we invaded Iraq again. My cousin Eric (from battle Frisbee) would spend most of the next year over there dodging IED's. I'd been interning at the junior high in an Appalachian dream town called Philipsburg just over the mountain from State College. The Dean of Students there was a helicopter pilot in the Army Reserves. One day he got a phone call that his unit was shipping out to the Middle East – within the week. For the school, there wasn't much time to prepare. So in a convoluted mess of a plan that was the educational equivalent of duct taping parts back onto your car, the regular guidance counselor assumed the role of Dean of Students until they could find a replacement and I became the full-time counselor on an emergency basis. Which meant that I was now working 40 hours a week all while trying to go to class and work on my thesis. It didn't leave much time for ultimate.

And that's the thing that often happens when you're playing a sport that doesn't pay for your education. Your real missions in life tend to get in the way. I missed practice. I missed tournaments. Other guys were stepping into my role. And there wasn't much I could do about it.

Luckily my new roommate, Duffy, was in charge of the roster. Just about every night when he was burnt out studying engineering and I was fried from analyzing case studies, he'd knock on my door with a disc. We'd head out to our tiny living room, push all the furniture out of the way and work on our break throws while talking about women and damn near destroying everything we owned.

"I'm keeping a spot on the roster open for you," he'd say, flipping a low backhand over the coffee table.

"I appreciate it, man," I'd answer, lobbing a flick that would inevitably come within inches of killing our goldfish.

The best thing about that semester was that Duffy was also the tournament director for Spring Phling. This led to all kinds of unanticipated hilarity. About a week before the tournament, he got an email from the team at Queens University in Kingston, Ontario. They'd forgotten to reserve hotel rooms and wondered if there was anywhere nearby they might be able to stay.

"Oh hey," Duffy told me the Monday before the tournament. "We're gonna have a bunch of Canadians crashing with us over the weekend."

"Canadians?" I said. "Damn. Apartment five just got exotic."

And when he said "a bunch," he wasn't kidding. There were seventeen of them. That Friday night, our living room looked like the site of a mass beaching. I swear one of the smaller dudes had to sleep in the fridge - which was fine because he was Canadian and found the temperature quite pleasant.

And the Canucks were hilarious. They had great Canadian names like Stu, Rick, and Mooney. I was helping them move some of their gear inside about ten minutes after they'd arrived when their captain, Rick, threw open the door to the parking lot. Outside, two of their skinny, long-haired freshman were obscured in smoke, halfway into a fatty.

"What the hell is this?" Rick said.

The half-baked freshman nodded and leaned back against the brick wall. "It was a long ride. I needed to relax."

"You were in the fuckin' back of the van sleeping the whole time, ya hoser! What the hell do you need to wind down from? And where'd you get that, eh?"

"I brought it."

"From home, eh? You brought drugs over the border?" Rick yelled, incredulous.

"Man…they're not gonna check …."

"…a van full of scruffy, long haired ultimate guys? No, never." Rick said, extending his hand. "Give me that."

"Man, this is really good shit…."

"I know. Which is why I don't want you to drop it when I smack you."

The freshman did as he was told. Ontario Rick took the joint, sighed and then gave him the greatest palm smack to the forehead I've ever seen. He turned to the other kid and did the same thing. It was top shelf Canadian slapstick.

Rick handed the joint back, shaking his head as we walked away. "Freshmen."

I knew what he meant. I was surrounded by them. Since my shoulder hadn't quite healed, I once again volunteered to coach and play with the B team. A lot of guys from the previous year's squad had moved up to the travel team so I had to reteach just about everything. And thus for the first day at Phling, we were mostly on the wrong side of competitive.

Our first game against Syracuse was played in an absolute downpour on a field that mirrored portions of the Everglades. Your entire cleat sank into mud up to your ankles with every step. Uncaught blades splatted to the ground and stuck out of the field like dorsal fins. One of the Syracuse guys laid out at midfield and never surfaced. A thousand years from now, scientists will find his body and proclaim it the best preserved human remains in history, all the while wondering why his hands look as if they're stretching for something just out of reach.

We actually went up 5-3 when I caught a flip just over the line on a sloggy, post-turnover fast break. From there though, they threw a zone, exploiting our lack of handlers. It didn't help that the disc was so heavy it was like trying to chuck a small birthday cake. They scored easy goal after easy goal eventually outlasting us 15-6.

After a semi-competitive 13-9 loss to Carnegie-Mellon, we got trounced in windy but drier conditions by Maryland and Case Western to finish the day 0-4. I couldn't stay disappointed for long, however. The tournament needed me.

Twelve kegs. That's how much beer I purchased and threw into the back of my truck. The tournament fund was going to pay me back, but for the moment I personally owned $573 worth of Pennsylvania's finest lagers and ales. Me, Duffy, and The General loaded it all up and caravanned to our party cabin in the middle of nowhere on a twisting mountain road six miles outside the thriving metropolis of Port Matilda, PA.

Each year, Phling brought something like 600 ultimate players to central Pennsylvania. And each year the cabin at the end of the universe allowed us to throw one of the sickest parties on the college tournament scene. This year was no different. As was tradition, we hired a funk band named Phat Albert, served a full buffet dinner and lined all twelve of my kegs up on the back porch. Then we waited for everyone to stream in. And stream in they did. It was one of the only times in my life I can honestly say I was at a party that resembled something dreamt up by Hollywood.

By 9:00, the cabin was jam packed with hundreds of people, ultimate players from all over the country dancing, drinking, stripping, and tripping – a crazy pulse of humanity that spilled from every entrance. Every fifteen minutes or so, I'd go cut the beer line – which meant every fifteen minutes or so, I was unable to resist the temptation to turn to the masses like a Roman Emperor and shout, "Enjoy my beer, people, for I bought it for *you*. I bought it for *you*."

Around 10:00 as the party throbbed and bounced around me, a group of girls from Delaware approached. Things were about to get interesting.

"Hey Beer Guy!" one of them said, yelling into my ear over the music.

"What's up?" I answered.

"Do you have a disc?"

Now it was loud in there so what I heard first sort of excited me. Then I realized we *were* at an ultimate party and the girl was probably asking for something else.

"Yeah, I have like forty in my truck."

They let out a simultaneous giggle. "Can we borrow one?"

Unable to say no to a cache of cute women, I met them outside, crawled into the truck, and flipped one out to them.

"Thanks," they said, taking off around the side of the cabin.

"Am I gonna get that back or….."

Five minutes later, I was back inside the party when I realized why they needed my disc.

Landshark: (n) Often seen at ultimate parties, the landshark occurs when one member of an ultimate team is carried face down through the crowd, buck-naked on the shoulders of their teammates while clenching a disc between their buttocks. The result looks moderately like a shark to drunk people in the dark.

A roar went up from the dance floor as five completely naked freshman girls from Delaware came bouncing into the crowd, one petite brunette flying above the others – my disc touching places I knew I never would.

"That's my disc!" I yelled to anyone that would listen.

Every female landshark can be summed up thusly - three girls hooting and hollering like they're having the time of their damn lives, one girl looking down, totally ashamed, and one girl looking disinterested and practically yawning as if it's the fifth time she's been naked in front of four hundred people this week. They plow their way through the crowd like a Mardis Gras float while everyone in the room simultaneously claps, cheers, and yells things like, "Now it's a party!"

Every male landshark can be summed up like this - it includes at least one obliterated chubby guy, begins with rolling yet slightly uncomfortable laughter and ends with people deciding it's about time to head out and rest up for tomorrow's games.

Anyway, I was standing by the front entrance when the slightly ashamed girl approached me, having not yet had the time to dress herself. She averted her eyes and held out the disc.

"I was told to say thank you."

Outside, I heard ridiculous giggling from the shadows.

I did everything my drunk ass could to not stare like a creep. "You're welcome," I said, taking back the disc. "This is a surprisingly awkward encounter."

"At least you know where your pants are!" she said, hustling away.

So it was one hell of a party. Able to cut in the beer line, I slowly made the world spin. Somewhere around 2:00AM, I ended up passed out on a balcony above the main floor with some random girl from Case Western. I woke up to Duffy slapping me awake.

"Cramer," he said, shaking me. "Ian's sober. He's taking people home. I'm going to have you go with him."

My eyelids barely moved. "What about this girl, man? And my truck?"

"I think we should leave both of them here."

"Ok," I said. "You coming with us?"

I asked before I realized there was a girl standing next to him. He gestured to one of the cabin's bedrooms. "Nah, I think I'm gonna stick around for a while."

My head fell back to the floor. "I am not at all surprised by this development."

So at 3AM, I got home, stumbled over seventeen Canadians and passed the hell out. Our first game was at 9:30, so I figured I could wake up at 8:45, grab something quick to eat and drive out to the fields in plenty of time to warm up.

The boys from Ontario were fairly serious about winning and managed to get themselves to the fields on time. I slept right through their exit. To my surprise, I woke up alone in the apartment. I stumbled to the kitchen and chugged a Gatorade before scarfing down a banana and some Pop Tarts and preparing to head out.

After three or ten beers the night before, I wasn't exactly raring to go. But I couldn't abandon the B team no matter how crappy I felt. Not at our home tournament. Not when I so vividly remembered manning the Winnebago instead of cleating up the year before. All of that fueled me as I grabbed my keys, threw open the door and walked out into the sunlight to get my truck. I'd be at the fields on the other end of town in like five minutes.

Just needed to find my truck and head off to the fields. Just had to remember where I parked my....

And then a blurry image of Duffy rolled into my brain. *"I think we should leave both of them here,"* said his cloudy face.

My keys dropped to the pavement. "Ah, shit."

Now normally I could make the mile and a half run in about ten minutes. But I was carrying my spikes, my water bottle, and a rather weighty hangover. I sweated out half a keg as I awkwardly shuffled and sprinted my way down Prospect Avenue. To my delight, however, as I reached the community fields I saw the team pissing around on the sideline. I hadn't missed a thing. I jogged down the hill toward our huddle and put my stuff down, quickly changing out of my running shoes.

Sumo Benji clomped over to meet me. "Cramer, where the hell have you been?"

"Funny story. I was all set to drive over here like twenty minutes ago."

"So what happened?"

"Turns out my truck is on top of a mountain sixteen miles away. Who are we playing?"

"Haverford."

"Damn. If I'd have known, I'd have brought some chicken."

"What?"

"Nevermind. We flip for pull yet or...."

Benji laughed. "Yeah. A half hour ago."

"And you still haven't started?"

Benji patted me on the back. "Dude, this is halftime. It did *not* take them long to put up seven goals on us."

The main problem was that our offense had absolutely no forward momentum. In ultimate, the phenomenon of quickly working the disc forward is called "flow." Great teams are like the Niagara River, an unstoppable force rushing downhill. Our offense was more like a clogged toilet. The reason was obvious. Most of the guys were freshmen who hadn't been taught what cuts to make at what times. Luckily the quick 13-3 beat down gave us time to hold an impromptu practice before our consolation game.

For a half hour, Sumo Benji and I swung the disc and simplified the game, putting the guys into a vertical stack and yelling at them when it was their turn to bust their ass.

"Danny, break side….go!"

"Shawn, force side….go!"

"Now Joe, that's your deep cut. Go!"

After a half hour, they started to get it. Most of them were engineers. It was amazing how quickly they picked up the pattern.

And so with a bit of newfound field awareness, we headed over to the main fields in the shadow of Beaver Stadium to play James Madison. (You only had to play *one* guy? HAHAHAHAHA!) And it was outright stunning how much that single practice did to improve our game. It was like a giant plunger for our offense. Guys suddenly had the confidence and the knowledge to run to the right places. We had genuine flow. Late in the game, JMU somehow lost Sumo Benji and let him run deep. Scarcely able to believe how open he was, I launched a 60 yard backhand. He looked like a humanoid peanut M&M as he caught it and rolled out the back of the end zone. It put us up 13-11.

"Never fails! Once a game, everyone forgets about the little fat guy!" Benji yelled, happily tossing the disc in the air.

By this time, the guys were electric at the possibility of a victory. At 14-11, we forced a turn and got the disc to Benji about ten yards from the end zone. He called time out. We circled the team.

"Alright guys," I said. "We've gotten our damn teeth kicked in all weekend. But ya know what? We score here, and none of that shit matters."

(I suddenly had déjà vu as if I'd given this exact same speech to Flagler and the Pittsburgh Weasels in previous tournaments.)

At the very end of our impromptu practice, we'd run a gimmick end zone play I'd learned from Langstaff. The play was called "Quotes." Basically, you set up five guys in a vertical stack in the end zone and a dump option three yards behind the disc on the break side. When the disc is tapped in, the last guy in the stack takes a step out of the back of the end zone while the other four guys all run to opposite corners. The objective is to clear the defense out of the center of the field so the dump can cut into open space all by himself. It was a stupidly ingenious play that

I'd never actually seen put into practice. Throughout the game, the guys begged us to run it, but I was saving it for the right time. Ten yards from the end zone a single goal from victory seemed like that time.

In the huddle, I looked at the all the amped up freshman in front of me. "All right, guys. We're running 'Quotes.' Let's win this damn thing right here."

After a sixteen-man techno beatbox cheer that would still be played at European dance clubs if anyone had thought to record it, we broke the huddle with some serious electricity. We set up. JMU matched us. I planted myself three yards behind Sumo Benji. I nodded. He nodded back and stuck out the disc. The mark tapped it in.

Here we go.

In the end zone, the freshmen made their cuts to perfection, completely abandoning the center of the field and confusing the shit out of the defense. I sprinted over behind Benji to the open side where he turned and faked a dump toss as I planted and quickly shot left between my defender and the mark. Benji faked a crossfield hammer to freeze the backside defenders as I ran straight off the mark's hip toward the end zone with my defender trailing behind. Benji floated an easy flick out to open space. It was a stroll in an alpine meadow. There was no one there – not a soul within ten yards as I easily hauled in the winning goal.

And here it came - that amazing few moments of jubilation as a bunch of guys who to that point had only known losing finally got to hop around, scream, and celebrate victory. We didn't give a crap that it was a consolation game against a below average opponent. I was suddenly glad my shoulder wasn't fully operational – because it gave me yet another amazing moment I may never have gotten had I been playing for the "A" team that day.

Over on the main fields, our neighbors to the north were doing very well. They ground their way to the championship game with a victory over Ohio State before falling to Michigan State 15-13 in an epic final. And perhaps more importantly when Duffy and I returned home that night, on top of the TV sat brand new bottles of Crown Royal and Absolut Vodka with a note that said:

"Thanks for the hospitality, ya hosers." – The Canadians

Also, the whiteboard by the door looked like this:

~~Shower list:~~ *Most likely to lick Rick's nuts list:*

1) Stu
2) Kid
3) Mooney
4) Jen
5) Ramsey
6) Rick

As far as I know, none of them got detained going back across the border. And every single one of them is now an upstanding member of Canadian Parliament.

There is one final story from Phling that for me ranks right up there in my favorite stories of all time. Sunday night after the tournament was done and all the teams had left, we had to head back to the party cabin to clean up in order to get our substantial security deposit back. Mainly we needed to clean the walls, empty the trash, and mop away the disgusting black layer of beer and mud that tends to cover the floor after every party that's worth remembering. (Or not remembering) I came along partially to help Duffy and partially because I needed to retrieve my damn truck. We're flying down the mountain seven miles out of town in Duffy's old white Toyota when his cell phone rings. Duffy answers, then starts nodding and looking perplexed.

"No. I don't have it. They never gave me anything," he said. "We'll figure something out. See you in a few minutes."

"What was that about?"

"That was Putz. A couple guys are already at the cabin. But apparently, this morning someone came by and locked the mop closet. Which they never gave me a key to. So we got buckets, water, and soap, but no mops."

"Think we should turn around and head back to Wal-Mart?"

"That'll set us back almost an hour. I still have three tests to study for."

"Well there's a gas station in Port Matilda. Maybe we'll find something there."

Know what gas stations don't have? Fuckin' mops for sale. And it was Sunday night. The town's little hardware store was closed. We were screwed. The cabin floor was huge. It was going to take all night to scrub it with sponges.

Duffy and I solemnly got back into his car. "What do you want to do?" I asked.

He let out a breath. "Head to the cabin and figure something out I guess. Fuck, this is gonna suck."

"Yup," I said, not looking forward to the labor that awaited our sore post-tournament legs and backs.

We were on a middle-of-nowhere, dirt and gravel mountain road debating our next step when the miracle happened.

"I guess we could try to bust the closet door open," I said.

Duffy shook his head. "We're only cleaning the cabin to make sure we get the security deposit back. I don't think breaking stuff fits into that objective."

"That's a good...." my words trailed off as we approached a large white farmhouse – the type that was built by someone's great, great grandfather in 1822. Something caught my eye. "Duff, slow down."

Leaning against the wood paneling at the front corner of the house was a junkyard jumble of wooden-handled objects. My eyes quickly scanned them as we approached.

Shovel, shovel, rake, hoe, shovel, axe.....

"Duff, holy shit is that...."

"That's a fucking mop!" he yelled, slamming on the brakes in the middle of the dirt road.

Before I could blink, he was out the door and sprinting across this random farmer's front yard. And suddenly we were in a heist movie. My heart was beating so hard the windshield nearly cracked.

Focused and determined, Duffy failed to see the giant black Doberman chained to a tree near the front porch. It started barking its head off and charged him. To this day I can still see the scene in slow motion, Duffy noticing out of the corner of his eye at the last second and shifting to the left just as the snarling dog snapped at his crotch. His face looked like a half melted clown for a moment until the Doberman hit the very end of its chain, choking itself no more than an inch from tearing Duffy wide open.

With that threat averted, Duffy nervously backpedaled toward the house. Unfortunately, the barking dog had alerted the family at the dinner table just above the jumble of wooden-handled objects. I watched from the car as the people inside curiously stood up. In backwoods Centre County, it wasn't a stretch to fear that they had their shotguns as accessible as their butter knives.

With the family now stirring in the window above him, Duffy hurriedly approached the tools, grabbing the mop and yanking it out from the pile as half the shovels and rakes fell over with a crash. He held it up like a lance and charged back through the yard, once again barely avoiding the Doberman.

Inside the car, I urged him to hustle. "C'mon, c'mon!" I said, leaning across the shifter and extending my hands toward the open driver's door.

In a full sprint, Duffy chucked the mop through the front of the car. I caught it and passed most of it through my open window as he skidded into the driver's seat and fired it into drive without closing the door. As I remember this now, the dirt beside the back tire kicked up after being hit with a hurriedly aimed bullet, but that might just be my mind exaggerating. I do know a guy in overalls was opening the front door as I shouted.....

"Go, go, go, go!"

Rocks and gravel shot backward and we peeled out of there over the hill like twin Dillingers. If there was a moment in my life that contained more nervous adrenaline, I'm having trouble recalling.

As we pulled up toward the cabin and realized we'd somehow gotten away with it, our nervous, labored breathing turned into gut wrenching laughter.

"Duff, did we just steal a goddamn mop from some backwoods farmhouse?"

His head hit the steering wheel sporting a grin bigger than the dashboard. "Yeah, we did. I almost got killed by a dog."

"I'm pretty sure we almost got shot."

"Over a mop."

"Over a motherfuckin' mop."

Lord knows what the farmers thought when they discovered what was missing. We walked into the cabin heroes. We weren't going to have to scrub the floor by hand until 2AM. On the way back home we clicked off the headlights, slowed down and chucked the mop into the farmer's front yard. So we didn't steal it so much as borrow it without permission it for a few hours. Which is totally legal in most states.

A week later we got our security deposit back. And it was a good thing too. Because we'd need the money later to rent a bus.

To head to Texas for nationals.

TWENTY-FOUR

WE WERE TIED 16-16 WITH CORNELL ON THE MOST INTENSE UNIVERSE POINT Penn State had seen in decades. UPenn had won the Metro East Region and this was the game for second place – the backdoor game to go to nationals. Whoever scored the next point was going to Austin, Texas in three weeks to battle for the national championship.

The pull landed in the back of the end zone and our defense came charging down at Cornell, immediately clamping on a tough, three-man cup zone. For a while, they swung it side to side, gaining inches at most. Then a popper cut behind Captain Ian. Their handler, getting sick of testing the outside, tried to force it through the cup. Captain Ian didn't even have to move. He simply reached out and grabbed it. Stunned, he looked down at his feet, which were clearly in the end zone. A Callahan goal on universe point was sending SPANK to Texas. Our sideline went insane.

I heard about it a few hours later when the team returned home.

As my teammates were celebrating their once-in-a-lifetime victory, I was into my fifth straight hour of typing my thesis on drama therapy for preteens of varying socioeconomic populations. I'm not going to lie, I had mixed feelings upon hearing the news. I was incredibly happy for my teammates and friends. All the hard work had paid off. I was sort of happy for myself, knowing that I'd made a small contribution on the field and a bigger contribution as a coach. With how close the Cornell game ended up, there was a good chance that something I'd taught one of the B team players the year before had nudged us over the top. But I wasn't in uniform when it happened. I wasn't there to mob Captain Ian. I didn't touch the disc a single time in that amazing, epic game. I couldn't help but be disappointed and slightly bitter. And I had no one else to blame but the guy in the mirror – and obviously Saddam Hussein.

I still remember the moment I made my decision. During Spring Phling, I was guarding Maryland's deep threat like I always did. I had him smothered as he went long, but they launched a big flick huck down the right sideline anyway. Stride for stride, I leaned into him to take away any space he had to explode into the air, launched myself off the ground, and boxed him out. I had the disc read like a children's book. But I couldn't lift my left arm. I had to stretch my right hand the whole way across the top of my head. It sailed an inch over my fingers and the guy grabbed it for a goal.

I landed knowing I was a liability.

Later that week, I came out of my bedroom to see Duffy sitting in our big recliner, staring at the roster. Most of it was filled out. "What do you think?" he asked.

I just shook my head. "Roster me with the B team."

"You sure?"

I saw my poster – the one with me laying out to win it all – the one that drove me through all the sprints and wall squats – gradually fade into an unrealized dream.

I tried to lift my arm one last time just to make sure. And like normal, I got stabbed with a fork. "Yup."

Now at the time I made my decision, I didn't know we'd be going to freaking nationals. I'd known that for sure and I might've given him a different answer. But sometimes you work your ass off for something that just isn't in the cards. Shit happens. You move on.

As it turned out, it was a good decision. Feeling slightly better a few weeks later, Sumo Benji and I devised a plan to lead the B team to regionals. We really thought we could pull it off too. Then in our second game of sectionals, I went up to make a lefty D on some swilly crap along the sideline. I was guarding a big, awkward guy from Susquehanna University who tried to bull past me and reach up for it. Our arms hit like crossed swords in the air. POP! I was clutching for my shoulder before my feet even hit the ground. Season over. Penn State career finished.

As it happened, I scored an interview for a guidance counselor position back in St. Augustine - a place I desperately wanted to return to. It was scheduled for the Wednesday before nationals. Knowing I was going to be in the south anyway got me to thinking. I'd busted my ass with that team for two years and I'd earned my way onto that sideline. I'd figure out how to be useful when I got there. Before I took off from State College, I shook Duffy's hand.

"See you in Texas," I said.

"No shit?" he said, stunned.

"No shit."

After a successful interview, I hauled ass west on I-10, decided against stopping at the most dangerous intersection in America, and made my way to Lafayette, Louisiana. The next morning I took off for the Lone Star State. It was the first time I'd been more than 300 yards west of the Mississippi in my life.

After four more hours on the road, I found the fields and stumbled into an ultimate player's dream. A giant tent featuring the Texas state flag sat at the center of field after field of championship caliber play. It was the same feeling I had when Havelock Ben and I first emerged from his Mustang at Frostbreaker six years beforehand. Ultimate surrounded you. Engulfed you. I walked by Texas vs. William & Mary just as one of the Texas guys went flying across the front of the end zone for a D. The hometown crowd lining the field roared. It really was a dream.

I found SPANK just before their second game of the day against Wisconsin. I snuck onto the sideline and started humping Duffy from behind. He turned and practically tackled me.

"Cramer, holy shit!"

"Told you I'd see you in Texas."

The cool thing about my arrival was the amount of guys who quit what they were doing to yell in elated surprise. Putz, Bobes, most of the guys named Lee…they all came sprinting over to jump on my back. After eleven hundred miles in the truck, I knew I'd made the right choice. Even though I wasn't playing, I was exactly where I needed to be.

SPANK went 0-3 on a brutally hot day losing competitive games to Brown and our old friends William & Mary while giving a respectable 15-7 showing to eventual champion Wisconsin. In the end, it was just cool to see my friends out on that field battling at the highest level.

As for me, I roamed the sidelines helping shout instructions to our defense and warming up guys who were about to go into the game. I felt like a bullpen catcher at the College World Series as guys who were antsy about going in would grab a disc and pat me on the back.

"Cramer, let's toss."

"You bet."

And so that was my nationals experience. In every huddle - participating in every cheer - throwing, coaching, catching, and strategizing - but never on the field. I'd have killed for one damn point.

My most athletic moment of nationals was actually in the pool at the Ramada Inn later in the day when I won us a brutal game of 21 that we played against some of the Oregon guys.

*21 is a game whereby throwers at one end of the field (or pool in this case) assign their forthcoming throw a certain number of points from 1-10, then lob the disc into a crowd. If you catch it, your team receives that amount of points. But if you drop it, you lose the same number. As the disc comes down, it's usually an all out war of forearms, shoves and other illegal tactics. First team to 21 wins.

On the winning point, I exploded out of the water and went in between three sets of arms to grab a hammer. I held the disc in the air triumphantly. I yelled back to Putz, Felipe, and the other guys on my team. "We are!"

"Penn State!" they hollered back.

Mildly annoyed at the loss, one of the Oregon dudes yelled, "Dunk him!"

"Ah, fuck." Next thing I know, three guys I met a whole twenty minutes earlier are taking turns trying to drown me.

Again, this was the national championship. In ultimate circles, it's a really big deal. And yet there were two of the teams battling for the title sharing a few beers and shoving each other around like kids at camp. Try as I might, I just can't see Kentucky and Kansas doing that at the Final Four.

And the dumb thing about my MVP performance in the pool was that in the gurgling silence of the dunking, I realized I'd caught the damn thing with my left hand. My shoulder, after three painful months - was fine. I popped to the surface and just stared at the sky. There I was at nationals, completely healthy, and yet unable to play. For a moment I wished I could just stay underwater.

The next day started the elimination round of the tournament. Felipe was so excited that he jumped out of bed and tramped directly on my ribs as I slept on the floor. It was an injury I'd feel for days afterward - my one battle scar from nationals. I took the team bus out to the fields and everyone debarked with fluttering stomachs. I could tell they were nervous. Hell, I was nervous for them.

A familiar opponent awaited. Warming up across the field was Ohio State, for all intents and purposes the same guys who outlasted us the year before at Easterns. It was going to be a tough match, especially considering they were the higher seed. But somehow it wasn't. I don't know what the hell happened. I don't know whether their top guys were hurt, whether they all went out and got bombed on moonshine, or whether they just didn't care. Whatever the cause, Ohio State didn't even put up a fight. We destroyed them 15-3.

It was so lopsided that at 12-2, Duffy and Putz were lobbying to get me into the game.

"Cramer, I'll give you my jersey," Putz said. "Just run in. What are they going to do?"

It was a tempting thought. A hell of a tempting thought. For a moment, I seriously considered it. I'd dreamt of playing in a game that big for so long and now all that separated me was an imaginary line between orange plastic cones. Ohio State was done for. They'd never even notice, let alone give a shit. Plus, I was on the B team roster anyway so it's not like I was some illegal ringer.

Putz started taking up his shirt. "One point, man," he said. "You need to get into this game."

It was such a good idea. And yet in the moment, I couldn't do it. I saw the tiniest possibility of some omniscient tournament volunteer blowing into a whistle as soon as the pull went up.

"Illegal participant! This game is forfeited!"

The last thing I could do to my teammates was somehow nullify this amazing win simply because of my own selfish dream.

"Keep your shirt on, Putz," I said, letting out a deep sigh.

And so I watched as we moved on to play another familiar opponent – Georgia. The boys from Athens were up 12-10 when Felipe snatched one of the top five goals of the tournament. It was a huck to nowhere, so far out in front of him that most people on the sideline shifted their eyes toward other fields. Then Felipe came roaring past us. The disc couldn't have been more than a foot from the ground a full twenty yards away and yet he kept chugging. It seemed like a completely futile sprint until a miracle gust of wind popped the disc off the tips of the grass just long enough for him to lay out and snag it in the very back of the end zone. It helped push the game to the brink. The hard cap went on at 13-13. Winner went ultimate's Elite Eight.

I don't remember how Georgia scored. I'm sure every aspect of the point would've been seared into my brain had I been playing. But I wasn't and it isn't. Just like that, Penn State's best season in 25 years was over. We finished tied for 11th in the country.

The rest of the day was spent watching great ultimate. SPANK headed over to cheer on ISIS as they battled Colorado in the women's quarters. Our ladies fought hard but lost, also finishing with their best season ever, tied for fifth in the country with UC-San Diego.

With nothing to do and the season over, Duffy and I found the best spot in history to watch ultimate. We plopped ourselves down next to the Arizona women's team on a set of bleachers in between both open semifinal matches. We were not only able to watch championship play on our left *and* right, but semi-successfully hit on cute girls from Tucson as well. It was a win, win, win for everyone involved.

And the ultimate was incredible. On our left, Wisconsin battled Colorado in a loud, emotion-filled huck fest. It seemed like every time we turned, someone was running down a 70-yard bomb and exploding with a guttural roar upon stopping rotation.

On our right, Oregon battled perennial ultimate powerhouse Carleton College in a more precise, more possession oriented contest. We'd heard rumors of a west coast stud named Ben Wiggins who played for Oregon and I couldn't wait to get a glimpse of him in action. 2003 was the first year that nationals would actually be covered on TV. (On a cable channel called College Sports Network, and trust me, people were flipping the hell out that there were real cameras aimed at the games.) Before that exposure, if you didn't get to play against certain guys, you only "heard rumor" of their prowess through hearsay or articles in the UPA magazine. I heard so many stories about how good this dude was that I was picturing some kind of plastic-slinging Paul Bunyan. Then just before the game, Duffy and I happened to walk past him.

"I think that's Wiggins," Duffy said, pointing to their sideline.

There was a large, sleek-looking bearded dude standing there in a white and green Oregon jersey who was just about what I'd pictured. I nodded. "Yeah, he looks pretty tough."

"No, no....not the big dude, the little guy next to him."

I adjusted my shades and squinted. Beside the big guy was a shorter, kind of paunchy looking dude with glasses and his hat on backwards. "The dude who looks like an IT guy warming up before a company softball game?"

"Yeah. That's him. Ian pointed him out to me yesterday."

As we walked toward the bleachers, I was skeptical. How could the best ultimate player in the country look so completely and totally unassuming? One glance and I knew I was twice if not three times the athlete he was.

And then I watched him play the game. I was indeed twice the athlete he was. And he was at minimum ten times the actual ultimate player. It all seemed so easy to him - like he had every move everyone on the field was going to make mapped out in his head three passes before it even happened. Carleton was an incredible team. They'd won the national championship only two years earlier. And Wiggins dissected them like a frog. At times he looked like he was out for a casual stroll, then he'd somehow end up with the disc and let fly a perfect crossfield hammer that looked like angels had personally delivered it into his receiver's hands. His game was saintly and unbelievably calm. I'd never seen anything like it. He took chaos and with one flick of his wrist, delivered order.

I turned to Duffy. "Ooooooh. I get it now."

That year Wiggins won the Callahan Trophy – ultimate's Heisman.

The actual Heisman Trophy is a big deal, announced in a gaudy room with a big stage encircled by fine oil paintings of past winners. In 2003, Oklahoma quarterback Jason White accepted the Heisman behind a fine maple podium in a suit and tie surrounded by thirty or so gallant looking gentlemen. In 2003, Wiggins accepted the Callahan on a large wooden porch surrounded by goofy drunks at a giant party somewhere in Texas Chainsaw Massacre country.

The party for nationals was a hell of a site to behold. Shuttle busses were constantly rolling into the parking lot and dropping off entire teams at a big old cabin much like the one where we'd hosted Spring Phling. Practically every elite college player in the country was there. The entire gathering was alive with all kind of crazy games – races to see who could build the quickest beer can pyramid and then knock it down with a disc from 30 yards away, games of flutter, milk, pokey, bear-ninja-cowboy, and even a stopwatch contest to see who had the most accurate stall count. People were crowding around to watch other people count to ten. And somehow it was riveting.

"Ooooh…..nine point nine four!" the timer would shout into the night and fifty people would dance and cheer. It was amazing.

I was sitting on the porch railing with a beer when the Callahan Trophy "ceremony" started. There was a guy with a microphone and the five men's and five women's finalists lined up behind him. And um, I'm not sure who the microphone guy was. He was either some dude from the UPA, a guy associated with Texas Ultimate, or someone who'd wandered over cause he smelled chicken wings. Whoever he was, he did not in any way have a plan other than to blather on like he had a bet with someone on how long he could speak without getting the microphone taken away.

"All right," he said. "It's time for the trophy presentation. But uh, first we have some sponsors to thank….well actually let's have a round of applause for Austin for hosting this great event first. It's an event that couldn't take place without some people I'd like to mention. Sarah….. where is Sarah? Anyone see Sarah? She was just here. I mean we have to thank Sarah…and Brian. What? He's in the beer line? Hey Brian, get me a beer! What's in the keg way over on the left? Anyone know? What? What is it? Miller Lite? Nah. Wait, ya know what, it's fine. Brian, just bring me whatever. It all gets you drunk right? Am I right? But ya know it's really hard to pinpoint just what ultimate means to me. It's a great sport. A great sport. And I mean when the disc goes up, wow, ya know. Like wow."

I've never seen a trophy presenter get heckled before. But this guy got up there and managed to say absolutely nothing for a full on fifteen minutes. And he was completely oblivious to how boring he was. I mean, he thought he was *on*. Which is why he kept going. For a while everyone was being respectful until....

"Fascinating! Tell us who won!"

"Someone toss him off the porch!"

"We're going to start throwing things at your head!"

"Please die!"

And those were just mine. The heckles from people who were really on pins and needles were way better. I can't imagine what it was like for the ten players waiting for him to shut up and say their name.

"Sarah? Have we found Sarah yet?"

Finally, well into the night, he turned and gave the trophy to Wiggins. It was the trophy I'd set my sights on winning at the beginning of the season. And it turned out I did get pretty close – about twenty feet or so. I told myself that if I hadn't gotten hurt, it could've been me up there. But even in the moment, I knew I was kidding myself. Wiggins was better than me. Significantly better. It's a lesson all athletes learn at some point. No matter how good you are there's always someone a step above.

And so that was nationals for me. The next day I got up, hopped in my truck and decided that since I was already in Texas, I wanted to see the Palo Duro Canyon. And I did. Then I decided that since I'd already gone that far, I might as well see the Rocky Mountains. So I drove to Colorado. And then I decided since I was in Colorado, I might as well go up and see Yellowstone.

A week later my thermostat fried on my way toward the South Dakota Badlands, so I decided it was about time to end the adventure and head home. By early June, I was back in Pittsburgh. The very day I got home, the St. John's County School District called. They wanted to know if I could be there on Thursday for a follow up interview. So after making a 6400-mile rectangle across the country, I rested up for an entire afternoon and prepared to head back on the road.

The best part of my unexpected trip back down south was that I got to return to the crazy pickup game under the lights at UNF. As I slipped out of my truck on the bluff above the fields, I looked down to see twenty or so familiar faces. My voice carried over the scrub brush.

"Tall Andy is the best lover I've ever had!"

(Again, the interview was for a guidance counselor position.)

Andy looked up, stunned. "Whoa! What's up, bitch?"

In life, there isn't much better than returning to friends you haven't seen in eons. I don't remember much about the game. I just remember it was amazing to be back there bathing in mosquito repellant and laying out in that itchy Florida grass. Hands down though, the best moment of the night came when Tall Andy and I were launching hucks before the game. He wound up and bombed one over my head that was sailing toward the fence that separated the soccer field from the wildlife preserve. An armadillo had somehow gotten through that fence and was now scampering along side of it. I only mention it because the Frisbee took the general trajectory of a hawk swooping down on prey and smacked the armadillo square in its armored little ass.

Unless you're a zoologist, you're going to think I'm exaggerating this next part. Upon getting nailed with the disc, the scared armadillo leapt straight in the air nearly three feet, did a full backflip and then sprinted off into the woods. I swear to god it shouted, "Holy Moses!"

"Did anyone see that?" I yelled across the fields. "Please tell me someone saw that!"

"Saw what?" Clancy yelled.

"An armadillo just did a three-foot backflip! I'm not kidding!"

"You saw an armadillo do a backflip?" Clancy said. "What has Pennsylvania done to you?"

"Pennsylvania hasn't done anyth….hell, Andy saw it."

Tall Andy smirked. "I thought it was more of a back handspring."

"Thank you, Andy." I said. "That helped tremendously."

It was good to be back.

As it turned out, Jacksonville had gotten a bit more organized after I'd left. Tall Andy and Clancy returned from two years with Vicious Cycle and brought back a lot of the newest strategies. Jacksonville was rising as a club power in the southeast and due to a great interview, I was planning on being part of Jacksonville Ultimate once again by the end of the summer. The principal at Murray Middle School liked me so much he actually welcomed me to the staff. I thought that was a pretty good sign that I might be on my way back to Florida.

Oddly enough, Jacksonville Ultimate was actually headed to North Carolina that very weekend to play in the Furniture City Shootout, a tournament featuring most of the top club teams in the southeast. Hell, for me that was halfway home. So the next day, I found myself driving to High Point, North Carolina to meet up with the team, which now even looked legitimate. We no longer had uniforms that Big Tim borrowed from Students for Christ. Jacksonville Bad Chicken was completely re-branded. We were now Jacksonville Hammerhead and had sleek, silver Nike Uniforms with a black hammerhead shark logo on the front. With my usual #28 unavailable, I took #16.

We all stayed at a Crestwood Suites where Tall Andy and I spent most of the night trying to launch hucks from one end of the 3rd floor to the other. Let me tell you, trying to throw a Frisbee perfectly straight down a narrow corridor is a maddening endeavor. You think it should be simple, but the angles are so odd you end up chucking it off the fire extinguisher no matter the throw or release point. It's why we ended up spending over an hour pissing off every family that had the unfortunate coincidence of needing a suite in High Point, North Carolina that night.

Nearing midnight, Andy tried a flick that nearly got to me before skipping off a door frame. "Damn it! Why can't I do this?"

"Cause you're six-foot-seven! You look like a giraffe stuck in a garage!" I yelled.

"Ten more throws. If neither of us get a clean one by then, we're done."

"Yup. Ten throws. Good idea. We need to get some sleep."

About a hundred fifteen throws later we called it a night.

Anyway, the tournament was incredible. All the top teams in the southeast were there and we were amped and ready to compete with all of them. The biggest game for us was probably our first game against a team out of Charleston, South Carolina called Helmar. As we got ready to pull, I looked down at the other line and saw a familiar face. Standing at the end was an African dude with biceps the size of manhole covers.

"Fuck....that's Tuba," I mumbled to myself. "I got the guy on the end." I knew I was in for one hell of a game.

I didn't even get to say hello before he started running my ass around. Somehow at midfield, I stuffed his cut. All that did is cause him to plant and go deep. Luckily, just as he took off, their handler went to swing it to the sideline and Clancy got a finger on it. I saw the disc wobble to the ground and took the hell off. I was a good twenty yards behind everybody when Wall hopped over a guy who'd laid out for the disc, picked it up and launched a hanging backhand for the end zone. With no one around me, I basically jogged beside it for fifteen yards trying to milk it for the goal.

Ten yards from the goal line, I took a peek back to make sure I was in the clear. That's when I saw Tuba come sprinting out of a blob of players at midfield. They tell you that bears and lions can close on you from fifty yards before you can raise a pistol from your hip and fire. Luckily I've never been in a position to confirm or deny that fact, but I imagine the feeling is similar to the one I had at that moment. One second Tuba was way off in the distance. I glanced up at the disc and when I turned back, he was double the size he'd been. Here came the lion.

"Crap," I muttered to myself, desperately waiting for the disc to glide itself over the goal line.

Five yards away from the end zone, I heard both sidelines take in a collective breath. Four yards away, Tuba's footsteps were like distant gunshots. Three yards away both sidelines started to roar in anticipation. Two yards away, his footsteps were bass drums. I was one yard away when he started to fly. Knowing I'd used up every available millisecond, I reached out and grabbed the disc, pulling it into my chest about an inch or so from his outstretched palm. It was like standing on the edge of the station platform as a freight train came roaring by.

I looked down. I was in by about three blades of grass. We were up 1-0. My heartbeat could be heard down in Charlotte.

Tuba got up and turned to see me standing there with the disc. He shook his head, gave a sly grin and patted me on the back. "I almost got you there," he said, smiling.

"Yes. Yes, you did. That was actually quite frightening," I laughed as he jogged to the Helmar sideline.

Wall came running downfield to congratulate me on the goal. "Ya know, you almost milked that right into your own death."

"I'm well aware. A little more zip on that would've been nice."

As it turned out, my anticipated battle with Tuba sort of fizzled the rest of the way. They kept throwing him out there whenever I needed a rest. I'm not sure if they did it on purpose or not, but it sure worked out for me. He was everywhere and all I could think was - *well at least I'm not the one getting roasted*. We both had amazing games with multiple goals, D's, and assists, but in the end I watched from the middle of the stack as they put a big curvy flick to the back of the end zone to beat us on universe point 11-10. Familiar faces – familiar results. Welcome back to Jacksonville.

We evened our record with a 13-10 victory over Tallahassee before lining up for our third game against one of the giants of ultimate - Raleigh-Durham Ring of Fire. The previous summer, the boys in black and orange had come within a breath of winning it all, dropping the championship game to Vancouver's Furious George. There was a poster of that game in the UPA magazine. I'd torn it out and taped above my desk back at Penn State. And now I was staring across the field at the guys on that poster.

I was amped. I was slightly intimidated. But overall I was ready to roll. They pulled to us. Seven fiery rings charged toward me. It was the most athletic collection of players I'd ever lined up against. A burly 6'2" dude with a scruffy five o'clock shadow thundered down to cover me.

Here went nothing.

I cut deep force side, planted quickly and turned, shaking the guy. I was wide open. I caught the disc and flipped a backhand up the center of the field. They had the deep cut shut down so I planted and came back. Wide open again. I shot a forehand up the line and bolted, making another catch a few yards from the end zone. I was fast. My cuts were

quick. The guy couldn't keep up. I'd astonished and completely flabbergasted myself before the point was even over.

Holy shit, you caught the disc three times against Ring of fuckin' Fire!

We shocked the living hell out of them by flowing straight down the
field and scoring to take an early lead. They were not prepared for some
new team from Jacksonville to shred them. Hell, to be honest, we weren't
prepared for that scenario either. The first half was close and hotly contested, much to the surprise of both squads. They kept putting different
guys on me and I kept getting open everywhere. I had two assists to
Tall Andy and somehow got four D's in the first half against some of
the most precision passers and cutters in the country. On one of them
I came the whole way from the other side of the field to catch block a
huck to a guy who thought he was all alone. I couldn't believe what I was
doing against the nation's top team.

After we tied it 3-3, their captain pushed through some of their de-
parting defenders at midfield. With an agitated snarl he grumbled…

"Would someone do something about number sixteen? He's goddamn killing us."

*Wait, I'm number sixteen. He's talking about me! The guy I have a poster of is
bitching about what a pain in the ass I am! This is great!*

Two months prior I'd been struggling with a bum shoulder and not
really distinguishing myself against teams like Dickinson College. Now I
was tearing up Ring of Fire. In fact as the first half neared an end, they'd
tried just about every defender they had and nothing worked. I felt damn
near invincible. Unfortunately we had a couple dumb turns near the goal
line and they broke us twice to go up 6-4. After their sixth goal, I looked
down the line to see who'd they were sending over to guard me now. And
what I saw made me wish I was playing a bit more under the radar.

At 6'11" Mickey Madzinski is most likely the tallest guy to ever play
ultimate on any field at any time. He was the star of some excellent
University of Colorado teams in the late 90's. Like Wiggins, he was one
of those guys you "heard rumor of" in articles and pictures and game
recaps. It didn't seem right that a guy that tall could have the agility and
speed for ultimate. But he did. The dude was a complete freak of nature.
Apparently he now lived somewhere near Raleigh. And his giant legs

were walking over to line up on me.

Are you goddamn kidding?

Luckily, I was fast and shifty enough to shake him. (There was no way I was even entertaining the notion of going deep.) Incredibly enough, I did the same thing to him that I'd been doing to everyone else. I got open, flipped the disc upfield, burned to another open spot, got the disc again and moved it. Things were going swimmingly well until one of our guys threw a floater over my head and out of bounds. It was a turnover. Which meant everyone on the field would just turn and guard the guy who'd been guarding them. Which meant....*oh, son of a bitch.*

I desperately looked around for Tall Andy as Madzinski loped over to pick up the disc. "Andy, a little help here?"

Andy waved off the idea. I'm pretty sure he wanted a break from guarding a dude who was four inches taller than *his* giant ass. "Eh, you'll be fine," he yelled back.

"How? How will I be fine, Andy? I see no scenario here where I will be fine!"

I was correct in my assessment. Madzinski picked up the disc along the right sideline. Honestly, it was like trying to play defense on the Washington Monument. I did the best I could. I sort of had his backhand huck cut off and by stall five, I thought maybe I had a chance to force something swilly that we could D. That idea faded quickly as I saw him cock his arm back behind his head.

Really? Is this monolith seriously going to let go a hammer?

I would've needed a twenty-yard running start to have any prayer of a point block. On his follow through, his index finger brushed a helicopter and sent it spiraling out of the sky. Three tourists died in the resulting crash, but no one noticed be cause the throw was so beautiful – a perfect 45 yard butterfly to the back corner for the goal. I've never felt so helpless on an ultimate field in all my years prior and all my years since. I might as well have been on the sideline for all the resistance I put up.

As the disc floated down into the hands of the Ring receiver, I turned back to Mickey. "That was gorgeous. And the very definition of unfair."

He just laughed and shrugged his shoulders like he was well aware there was no human being outside of Kareem Abdul-Jabbar who could've defended that throw. I turned and shuffled off to my own side-line suddenly feeling very, very small.

Despite being down 7-4, we came out scorching in the 2nd half. I made two more D's and kept getting open everywhere. Unfortunately Ring's defense clamped down as we neared the end zone. We turned it seven times on short or mid-range passes that would've scored had they been caught. But they weren't. When the field got smaller, the Ring defense got bigger. It was a learning experience for all of us as we found out the plays you can pull off against good teams you can't pull off against great ones. Realistically, we should've dropped the game by two or three. But we didn't. We only punched in two in the second half and lost a game that was much more competitive than the 13-6 final score.

In the end, we lost our final two games to Wilmington Warriors and Raleigh-Durham's Masters (Over 33) team. Both games we fell by two, the final one aided when my dumb ass tried to fight through a pick without making a call. It led to their go-ahead goal just after the soft cap. I was kicking myself the whole way home.

Despite my mental blunder in the final game, the tournament was a great thing for me in a lot of ways. After sitting on the sidelines at na-tionals, I'd been burning to play. And I got to. Not only did I get to play, I managed to succeed against the absolute best. I couldn't wait to return down south and help my good friends lead Jacksonville Ultimate to new heights. I had dreams of Hammerhead slipping in the back door to na-tionals. We had the personnel. We just needed more big game experience.

Unfortunately, good ol' southern nepotism prevented my hiring at the very last second and I entered the summer jobless. My dreams of taking Hammerhead to nationals popped like a balloon. I had no idea where I'd be playing ultimate next.

Summer League Snippets – Back in Black

At the time, the universally recognized best athlete in Pittsburgh Ulti-mate was a kid named Steve who played for New Jersey Pike. He was a former high school soccer champion who could jump up and place the star atop the Rockefeller Center Christmas Tree. Other than videos of Beau Kittredge and Alex Nord (and now dudes like Seattle's Matt Rehder), I've never seen a guy who could leap like he could. For me, when I leapt, I took off like a leopard and muscled past guys in the air. Steve was a damn pronghorn. It was effortless. Every time he left the ground, you swore you heard "POING!"

Anyway, I took pride in the fact that I was the only guy in the league that could halfway shut him down. For three years, we had fierce battles. For those same three years, I thought he was a complete prick because he never said a word to me. Turned out he was just incredibly quiet. My bad.

Anyway, with Langstaff sidelined with the hip flexor injury that would eventually end his career, Pronghorn Steve decided he'd had enough of our battles and drafted me. He also drafted Iron Mike, which gave us the best hucker and the two best deeps in the 24-team league. Unfortunately, due to weddings, injuries, and vacations, the three of us only played together twice before the playoffs. We ended up as the #13 seed.

Now the day before the championship tournament, I was back in State College helping a friend move and it prevented me from getting into town early. I had to wake up at 5AM and drive home that morning. Halfway there I got hungry, so I stopped at convenience store outside of Ebensburg. I ordered a sausage biscuit. What they gave me was a landmine.

By the time I arrived at the fields two hours later, my stomach was narrating an audio book. I somehow managed to get seasick on Route 22. Adding to the pleasantness of the whole experience, I stepped outside to find that it was already approaching ninety degrees. And uh, we were called "Back in Black" for a reason.

Our first game was against the number four seed. I played well, albeit sparingly. They had no defense for Iron Mike hucking to Pronghorn Steve so we just kept doing it. On the points I could manage, I played pretty solid defense - all the while feeling like a tiny backhoe was scooping out my guts. I made a big D on a crossfield hammer in the end zone, which Iron subsequently picked up and hucked to Steve to put us up 5-1.

As we lined up to pull, Iron Mike held up the disc. "We ready?" he asked.

It was a simple question. A question I'd simply nodded at a thousand times before. But this time was different. This time I was most assuredly *not* ready.

I held up my hand. "Hold on a second, Iron."

What I did next became instant legend – at least for the better part of that afternoon. I took five steps over into the weeds, doubled over, chucked my breakfast onto a carpenter bee, wiped my mouth and walked back.

"All right," I said to a line of stunned and kind of grossed out team-mates.

One of our women put her hand on my shoulder. "Maybe you should take a…"

Before she could finish the thought, Iron had launched the disc. I was in for that point whether I liked it or not. Without poisoned sausage in my body, however, I felt a hundred times lighter. I sprinted down and tipped away a pass, then went to the end zone and caught a hammer to put us up 6-1. We'd go on to easily upset the much higher seed and the legend of my vomit & score spread around the tournament.

We rolled through our next game to set up a semifinal matchup with the kings of the league that year, a team of super fast, super athletic kids in fabulous pink uniforms named "Big Gay Bourland's Big Gay Ultimate Team."

As a side note, Big Gay Bourland (who was actually a tiny ladies' man) blew away the competition at the Ryan's Pub Halloween bash that year by singing "Sweet Caroline" dressed *as* the silver naked child. He'd later meet Fast Jess from the Weasels in my parents' basement while they were waiting to use the shower after the Mars Tournament. The two of them would go on to get married, have a daughter, and move to Boulder when he got a job as one of the head honchos at USA Ultimate.

Anyway, there was no way we should've kept that game close. Except they just couldn't stop our hucks. They'd meticulously work the disc up with skill and speed, then as soon as anything went haywire, Iron Mike would pick it up and huck to Steve. And when Steve was tired, Iron would huck to me. And if we were both exhausted he'd huck to Steve's ridiculously fast sister Christie. In the best, most exciting game of summer league ultimate I'd ever played, we outlasted them 15-13, scoring at least twelve of those goals on long bombs, sending the #13 seed to the final.

We were big underdogs against the #2 seed, a team called Spin Doctors. Coming off our thrilling victory, we weren't quite ready to play and went down 3-0 out of the gate. On the next point, I finally got the opportunity that eluded me the year before. Pronghorn Steve got the disc on the right sideline and I made a continuation cut to the end zone. He lofted a flick that two defenders were just starting to settle under when I went sailing over the both of them to snag the goal that cut it to 3-1. It elicited an all out roar from the gallery. I'd finally done what I'd dreamt of doing since I first got drafted into the league. I'd skied someone in the final to huge applause.

It really could've been a close game, but by this time we were sweltering in the late afternoon heat. I didn't know it at the time, but running around in a black uniform all day was about to combine with my earlier bout of mild food poisoning to create a wacktastic scenario I could never have dreamed up.

We were down 7-5 when we forced a turn. I released deep and Iron Mike saw me in the end zone. He put up a long hammer that I outfought a taller, much better positioned defender for in the air. I was feeling pretty damn good when I landed. We'd cut the deficit to one and I'd just thrilled the crowd with my second spectacular air raid. I didn't know it, but I was about to find out that I'd reached the limit of what my body deemed were its contractual obligations.

Before I could even take a step to celebrate with my teammates, my left groin popped like a busted guitar string. As I was involuntarily falling to my knees, my right groin decided to join the fun. Next thing I knew, I was squirming around on the ground while the crowd heckled what they assumed was a wildly inappropriate goal celebration. Seriously, I was all but humping a gopher hole in front of the entire league. Until that point, I had absolutely no idea the human groin could cramp. I'm now *well* aware.

Pronghorn Steve's cleats moved over in front of my face. "Man, what are you doing?" he said, quietly.

"Praying I black out soon," I grunted into the sod.

"You look like you're trying to have sex with your imaginary girlfriend."

"She's real in my head, Steve," I said, writhing around.

It was the longest sixty seconds of my ultimate career. I could hear the murmuring from the crowd behind me until finally, mercifully, my groins released at practically the same time and I managed to slug myself over to the sideline so they could resume the game. Trouble was by that point, we only had seven healthy guys. I was desperately needed even if just as an extra body.

I chugged as much water as I could, but I knew I needed some food. A banana - a granola bar - some trail mix - anything. By that point in the day, all the team's solid food had had been consumed - which left one rather interesting option. I don't know how or why, but Steve's sister ended up with an extra can of incredibly yummy mushed peaches designed for easy ingestion by tiny humans with no teeth.

She handed it over with a hopeful smile. "Try this," she said.

"Christie, I'd be willing to bet that somewhere close by, a baby is in need of this."

"It's packed with nutrients. It says so right on the label. If I was having full body cramps, I don't think I'd pass up anything that says it's packed with nutrients."

I stared at the adorable infant on the jar. He stared back at me as if to say, "You're a grown man and you should find some grownup food." But I didn't have much of a choice. So I ignored him.

(By the way in a ridiculous aside that you'll never believe, the Gerber baby was actually eaten by cannibals. I swear to you this is absolutely true. He grew up to be a geologist and never came back from a remote region of Papua New Guinea. My father-in-law went to grad school with the guy and swears by the tale. Although Hermi's pretty convinced the dude was actually eaten by rednecks.)

So there I was in the biggest game of the year and instead of gunning flicks and laying out, I was on the sideline shoveling baby food down my throat with a tiny plastic spoon. The stuff tasted like peach wallpaper paste. And I got the *good* flavor. The peas must've redefined the word dreadful. Since that day, I'm stunned every time I learn an American child has made it to adulthood. All in all, it was not the best day for my digestive system.

In the end, the baby food *almost* worked. It got me to the point where I could at least shuffle around ineffectively for the second half. I got an assist on our 9th goal, but it was the last one we'd get as we fell 15-9.

And so the season was over. But we'd made an amazing run through the tournament as a very low seed. And at the awards ceremony afterward, I was nominated as one of three guys for Finals MVP. It went to Pronghorn Steve, who deserved it, but I still felt pretty damn proud of the accomplishment. And if there'd have been an award for best cramp dance, I'd have won in a landslide.

TWENTY-FIVE

YORK, PENNSYLVANIA ISN'T REALLY A DESTINATION SPOT. PRETTY MUCH ALL you need to know is that it's where some famous guys signed the Articles of Confederation. Shortly thereafter it became a crack den. And it's where I wound up. My first real adult job would come as a guidance counselor and baseball coach at Kennard-Dale High School, a rural district whose southern edge was the Mason-Dixon line. It was the type of place where families had feuds that went back to 1797. It was the type of place where teeth were optional.

Because of this, I was a bit nervous there might not be much ultimate in the area. York was a decent-sized city of 44,000 but without a major university, it wasn't quite large enough to support a healthy ultimate community. Luckily, as I'd find out, it didn't have to. About 20 miles north of York was Harrisburg, the state capital - which turned out to be the central meeting point for all the ultimate players in the surrounding counties. This included the cities of York, Hershey, Lebanon, Carlisle, Gettysburg, and Lancaster. Along with Harrisburg itself, the Susquehanna Valley had a population of over two million - more than enough to find a good game.

Every region's ultimate community has a unique feel to it. Jacksonville's was a sports car with bald tires - beautiful, sleek, and fast, but impossible to steer at high speeds. Pittsburgh's community felt like a new Toyota Camry, reliable and completely underrated. If I were to describe Harrisburg's ultimate scene, I'd have to go with a rusty old van with purple shag carpeting, a well-stocked minibar, and spare tire cover that featured an airbrushed scene of a topless woman riding a dragon.

Co-ed was the only game in town. And that changes a few things dramatically. In a co-ed town, everyone wants to win, but never at the expense of the overall social experience. And man, did we have an overall social experience.

Subscribing to the unwritten rule that co-ed teams must be named after stupid inside jokes or horrible sexual puns, the team had recently been renamed Harrisburg Adult Flicks. (After years of being called the G-Spot All-Stars.) Our uniforms were yellow and pink tie-dyes with the purple silhouette of a naked woman on the back. The mainstays of the community were a bunch of old stoners who all played for Penn State back in the mid 80's. The whole league pretty much had the feel of a blazed-out naked hot tub party - of which there were many.

My first tournament with Adult Flicks was sort of a microcosm of things to come, as if the world was telling me to quit taking the game so seriously. It was a great spring day in Carlisle, PA, an old 1700's-type town just on the eastern side of the Appalachians. Leading up to the small, ten-team tournament, I'd been sick for two weeks and hadn't felt like doing laundry. Because of this, at about 6:30AM on Saturday morning, I realized I had no clean gym shorts. I dug around in my closet and eventually found a pair of what used to be khaki work pants that I'd worn holes in the knees cleaning out rental cars the previous summer. I took a pair of scissors to them. Not optimal but they'd do.

Our first game was against Shippensburg University who at the time was fielding a pretty good college team. At the beginning of the game, their young legs ran right the hell past all of our old hippies to the tune of a 9-3 lead. I remember standing on the sideline next to one of Harrisburg's legends, this aging 6'3" guy with long, graying hair we all called Freak. He was the perfect personification of 80's ultimate culture. He was the anti-athlete's athlete, big and fast but only because he was born that way, not because he chose to be. He was the type of guy who sprinted after a disc less because he wanted to catch it and more because it let him better understand the thoughts of the wind.

"Man," Freak said. "They are young. And fast. And young."

"Freak, are you high already?" I asked.

"It's nine o'clock in the morning, man. No…no, man. I quit puffing this early months ago. Why? You wanna blaze one? I guess I could…it *is* a nice day."

"Nah, you're just repeating yourself."

"Cause it was a point that needed emphasis, man." He continued to stare out at the field. "Cause if they're young, logic would dictate that they're also inexperienced. Why are we not throwing a zone, man? Why do we not have our thinking caps on here?" He reached into an imaginary pocket and pulled out an object that only he could see – then placed the invisible object on his head. "Yeah, zone is gonna work."

"Is that your...."

"My thinking cap, man. Here, I got you one too," he said, flipping an invisible hat to me – which I'm not ashamed to admit I caught and placed on my head.

"It's a little tight," I said.

"You can adjust it. There's a thing in the back."

"Oh," I said, taking it off and contouring it to my head. I stared out at the field with a newfound clarity. "Yeah, we should definitely throw a zone."

And so we threw a zone. And very quickly the score went from 9-3 to 9-9. I even had a Beau Kittredge moment when they threw a floaty backhand into the center of the field for one of their poppers. I shot in from the deep position and jumped clear over the guy to grab it. Unlike Beau, however, I didn't have the privilege of landing on my feet. The dude's head caught me right under the knee. Somewhere in the resulting flip and violent reintroduction to the ground, my lungs disappeared. But apparently it looked pretty sick. Thanks to Freak's thinking caps, we ended up going on an 11-2 run and winning 14-11.

And man for that one weekend, my nineteen year old hops were back. The next team on the schedule was from Messiah College. Sometime in the middle of the game, they hung a hammer over our wall to the center of the field. I saw it coming and sprinted in. The receiver it was intended for was about three yards in front of me when he jumped for it. Still, I thought I could get there before him. I exploded off the ground.

In the air I felt something unexpected brush against my hip as I got knocked slightly off line. I still managed to get my arm over the guy's head and smack away the disc, but I hacked the hell out of his wrist in the process. I felt my chest hit the back of his head as I got punched sideways, clipping his left shoulder and plummeting to the ground. As I slowly stood up and collected my visor, which had been knocked off in the collision, I looked at the guy as he sat wide-eyed in the grass next to the disc.

"Foul," he said.

"Oh yeah," I said. "No contest from me," I responded, slowly realizing that everyone on the field was silently gaping in my direction.

It was then that I noticed the girl just behind the dude I'd hacked. She was standing perfectly still with her hands up at the side of her face, eyes bugged out, slightly hunched over with the same general look as someone who'd just survived a building collapse. Apparently she'd scrambled over to back up her teammate in case he missed the disc. And I'd gone sailing over her, buzzing her head like a low flying 747. I didn't see her at all. Then I landed on top of the guy who was already a foot off the ground leaping for the hammer. It may have been a bit much for a local co-ed tournament.

"Cramer, you're like a missile out there!" Freak yelled. "But this is ultimate, not war, man! Think about it."

I nodded in contemplation. Perhaps I should dial it back a bit.

I'm pretty sure that play was also the beginning of the end for my shorts. Sometime in the second half, I sat down on the sideline and realized that all the gravity-defying leaps weren't doing wonders for the integrity of my khakis. For instance, they no longer had a crotch. Also with every step, they were developing an evening-gown style slit up the left side. The final nail in the coffin came when I stood up to stretch. One of our women, a redhead named Jennie who looked and acted like every female movie cop in history tapped me on the shoulder with an amused smile.

"Cramer, you know the back pocket of those shorts is falling off? I can see your ass."

"I know. I know. It's like it's carved out of granite." I said. "You don't have to keep going on about it, I've heard it all before."

She gave me an even more amused smile and reached into her gym bag. Next thing I know, a gray lump of fabric hit me in the chest. It was small, pleated, and round.

I squinted. "Is this a skirt?"

"Put your money where your mouth is, champ," she said. "Your thighs could use a little color."

I was conflicted. On one hand I was one sprint away from my shorts becoming four random, unrelated pieces of fabric. I wasn't particularly keen on playing the last two games in my undies. On the other hand, I'd been taught at an early age that skirts weren't for boys. And on a third hand, guys who wore skirts at ultimate tournaments (this used to be a thing) were really, really good. It sounds dumb now but back then you kind of had to *earn* a skirt. Like if a dude was wearing one, he was probably the other team's best player. Either that or he was a complete poser who thought he was way better than he was - the type of guy who would throw it away and blame it on a gust of wind that no one else felt. That happened a lot too. Miami of Ohio had one of those guys.

Between games I went back to my truck and slipped it on. And to my complete shock and surprise, I liked it immediately. As a guy, you don't often get a chance to experience how incredible a cool spring breeze feels down there. On most days, it's pretty much just a place for sweat to collect. But this was loose - non-constrictive - freeing. I felt like a cross between my Scottish warrior ancestors and a West End transvestite.

I got a lot of whistles and catcalls as we warmed up for the next game but by then I didn't mind. In the skirt, I felt at minimum ten percent faster. As I returned to the sideline after making a particularly sweet defense that led to a score, Movie Cop Jennie looked up with that same amused smile.

"You like that don't you?" she said.

"I feel kind of pretty, yeah."

It'd be a solid eighteen months before I played a game in shorts again.

Later in the spring, there was a tournament back in Pittsburgh featuring a bunch of pretty good teams from the Northeast and Mid-Atlantic. Because my parents were visiting my aunt in South Carolina, we had an empty house that they nicely let a bunch of strangers into for the weekend. And it was the perfect place to house ultimate players because unlike Kosher Josh's house, we didn't have anything a sane person would consider "valuables."

Oh, you broke that Steelers Super Bowl mug? No worries, we have eighteen more.

Saturday was one of those perfect sunny and cool ultimate days. We came out rolling, beating teams from Johnstown, PA, and Morgantown, West Virginia, before falling to my old Pittsburgh team and a team out of Toronto called Bombin' Mad Fatties. No one was surprised when our old stoner crew easily pushed aside the loss and hung out in folding chairs the rest of the night smoking weed and trashing the Bush administration with the Canadians.

The funniest thing of the tournament, however, was that Movie Cop Jennie was getting married the very next weekend. And the girls on the team decided she needed a bachelorette party. They also decided that Jennie's bachelorette party was going to coincide with the tournament party that night at the fields.

They failed to inform the rest of us about their plan.

One of our women was a short, stocky little handler with curly black hair that we all called Peaches. Yes, that's right - Peaches. Therein lies all you need to know about her other than the fact that she was 40 and could still reasonably be described by the word "adorable."

I hadn't even gotten to snag a burger or a beer yet when Peaches grabbed me by the elbow. There was panic in her eyes.

"Cramer, oh shit. Oh no," she said. "I forgot the cake."

"What cake? What are you talking about?"

"The penis cake."

"Uh….what now?"

She smacked her palm to her forehead. "We're throwing Jennie a surprise bachelorette party. Ah, I'm so stupid."

"If you're asking me where to buy a penis cake around here, I swear to you I have no idea. It's not something that came up much during my youth."

"No, I already bought it," she said, exasperated. "It's in your fridge."

I paused. "So hold on a minute. What you're telling me is there's a penis cake in the fridge at my parents' house?"

"I'd go back and get it but I don't know how to get there. I followed you," she said. "Could you please, pretty please go back? Unless maybe you think we don't need it. Maybe we'll be fine without it."

"I'm not leaving a penis cake in the fridge at my parents' house. They think I'm weird enough already."

Peaches folded her hands together in prayer and sidled up against me. "So you'll go get it?"

"Fine," I said, pulling my keys from my pocket and slowly walking away.

"Don't take too long!" Peaches shouted at me. "You and Wyatt are the strippers!"

I didn't even look back.

Every co-ed team has a Wyatt. He's the dude with blue hair and facial piercings who is really, really suspect of the government's motives on pretty much everything. He's also the guy with no shame whatsoever, which is why upon my return I didn't feel too bad pushing the next embarrassing part of the plan onto him.

Before I even put the cake on the picnic table, Peaches had out a tuxedo thong. It was like a tuxedo T-shirt - except it was a freaking *thong*. She was already a bit tipsy and happily stretching it out and biting on it in anticipation.

"Unfortunately we only have one," she slurred towards us.

I looked at Wyatt. I looked at Peaches. I looked back at Wyatt. "Yeah, dude, I had to drive twenty minutes with a penis cake in the passenger's seat. I got stuck at a light next to a trucker who was giving me the stink eye."

Wyatt nodded. "All right. I'll make it work."

The results were frightening. "Bad to the Bone" or some other lame rock song blasted from the speakers as we came out from behind the pavilion and tore off our shirts. I hopped up on the picnic table behind Jennie, dancing shirtless in her own skirt, but fortunately no one noticed because Wyatt was piston-thrusting his tuxedo thong into Jennie's knee-caps. Peaches and the other girls filled Wyatt's thong up with dollar bills as we danced, silently weeping inside at being treated like the sexualized pieces of meat we were. In the end, it made the women happy and as anybody who plays co-ed knows, if the girls come out of the weekend smiling, the tournament was a rousing success.

And it wasn't all bad for me and Wyatt. When it was over we were rewarded with surprisingly delicious penis cake.

Like I said, Harrisburg was a co-ed town. We only tried to split up once in what probably would've been less of an unmitigated disaster had the weather been better. There was a tournament in Lancaster in early April, which in Pennsylvania is a complete crapshoot. You are basically firing guns at poop if that's when you schedule your tournament. You could get 67 degrees and brilliant sun or 40 degrees and pouring the hell down rain. We got option number two.

By the fourth game, we were simply counting down the minutes until we could take off our socks - so my frustration fuse was a bit shorter than normal. We were 2-1 on the day and in the middle of a semi-competitive game against Ithaca when I called on our defense to set a cup zone. On the line, I put three guys into the cup, then set the wings and the middle. I'd be playing deep.

"Everyone knows their positions, right?" I reiterated before I pulled.

"Oh yeah, you bet," they answered.

My pull was a pretty good one through the rain, landing the front corner of the end zone. We ran down to cover. And for some inexplicable reason two guys in our "cup" decided to play man defense while the other guy set up the zone alone. This, in turn confused the other three guys, two of which decided to abandon the zone and pick up the same guy. It was like watching a gang of preschool kids running from a bee. There was no rhyme or reason to it. Clusters were having intercourse. And it wasn't the first time it had happened that day.

Patrolling the back of the zone, I shook my head, mystified. "Jesus Christ, what the hell are we doing? Go man! Just go man!"

I'm not kidding, at this point the three guys who were playing man defense remembered they were supposed to be playing zone in the first place and hustled back where they should've originally been. This was at the same time the other guys listened to me and abandoned the zone. And these were pretty decent, experienced players, not a bunch of dumb rookies. Their brains were just wet.

As I watched Ithaca easily move the disc upriver, I just couldn't take it anymore. "Fuck it," I said, turning and walking toward the sideline.

One of the guys on the team had torn his MCL and was acting as our coach for the day. His name was Darin and he was wearing galoshes and a big floppy rain hat. Along with his soggy knee brace, he in no way resembled the top-notch player he was that day. He just looked like someone's dopey uncle. Anyway, Soggy Darin saw me walking off and did a double take.

"Cramer," he yelled. "Get the hell back in there! The point is still going on!"

As I neared the sideline, I answered him. "I can't guard five guys, dude. Look at this shit. We look like morons."

"We look like bigger morons if one of our guys walks off the field in the middle of a point!"

"What the hell's it matter where *I* am if no one else is covering anybody?" I said, waving my hands around. "I'm effectively doing the same thing they are. I'm just not expending as much energy."

"We'll discuss it *after* the point! Get back out there!"

"Goddammit," I muttered.

And I'm not kidding you with the timing on this. As I'm arguing, they swung the disc toward the sideline. My guy is wide the hell open in the center of the end zone. I mean no one was within twenty yards of him. I glare at Soggy Darin and turned to take a couple sulking, angry steps back into the field just waiting for them to score and put me out of my misery. I was actually walking at this point. Not running, jogging, shuffling, or anything else you should be doing on defense. No, I was thirty yards out of position and *walking*. I hadn't been paying attention *at all* for the last seven to ten seconds.

Yet when I lifted my eyes back toward the game, it was just in time to see the disc about to sail directly over my head to the wide-open guy. Without breaking stride, I hopped up and let out my frustration. I just windmill annihilated the thing, slapping it nearly the entire way to the other side of the field.

As pissed off as I was, I couldn't keep a sly grin from breaking through as I turned back to Soggy Darin, who had his rain hat pulled down over his eyes.

The great thing was that none of my teammates knew what I'd done.

They'd all been chasing the disc like old, arthritic dogs and had no idea I'd nearly walked off the field. They turned to see the D and cheered.

"Yeah, Cramer! Way to be there! Great play!"

I looked back at the sideline. "What can I say, the disc finds me."

"Just go play offense," Darin sighed. "Jackass."

I'd go on to have a lot more good times and great stories with Adult Flicks but I feel I have to break this section in a couple parts because of one particular tournament that I need to highlight. I have to highlight it because the tournament I'm about to speak of would change my life forever.

Because if it weren't for this particular tournament, I'd have never met my wife.

TWENTY-SIX

WILDWOOD.

Every ultimate player on the east coast knows what I'm talking about. It's cotton candy, carnival games, roller coasters, video arcades, and square after square of ultimate as far as you can see. The largest beach ultimate tournament in the world is a late July tradition every year at the southern Jersey shore. If it sounds like a giant party occasionally broken up by some running, you'd be right.

Beach ultimate is essentially the same as regular ultimate, except it's played on a much smaller field with only four players per side.

Advantages of Beach Ultimate

1) Laying out is the adult equivalent of diving into that ball pit at Chuck E Cheese.

2) You don't mind having to go skins.

3) Playing barefoot ensures your car won't smell like wet cleats all week.

4) You're at the goddamned beach and not some boring half-mowed soccer fields outside of Scranton.

Disadvantages of Beach Ultimate

1) Sand in your ears.

2) Sand in your nose.

3) Sand in your mouth.

4) Sand in your…uh, you get the idea.

The first time I went to Wildwood was an absolute blur of nonsense. While I was at Penn State, Duffy and I picked up on a team with two of his friends from Boston University and four girls from Bucknell. We had a pretty solid team. I think we did well. All I really remember is that during our final game, a storm blew through. By the time we were all done laying out in the wet sand, we resembled the unfortunate souls of Pompeii after the Vesuvius eruption.

We'd spent the previous night at a campground but now with the volcano ash stuck to our bodies, we realized we were in desperate need of indoor plumbing. So while the guys went and packed up the tents, the girls got a room at a local bed & breakfast. And thus began the most important mission of the weekend - sneaking the unregistered guests into the hotel room. The plan involved a fire escape door, code names, and complicated hand signals. In the end, our strategy and cunning defeated the elderly woman at the front desk and the eight of us successfully infiltrated the Doris Vernon Inn.

Later on that night, there was a huge tent party on the beach sponsored by Samuel Adams. There were also like fifty parties going on at the tournament hotel. We spent the night drinking and trying to fire hammers from the seventh floor balcony into a trashcan down in the parking lot. (No one put one in or the entire Beach Terrace Motor Inn would've collapsed in the ensuing celebration.) When we got tired of that, we started betting on the go-kart races going on across the street. Duffy was stupid good at it, winning ten times in a row as if he'd been scouting the New Jersey go-kart scene for years.

"I got the kid in the blue kart on the outside," I'd say confidently.

"Nah," Duffy would answer. "I got the dad. That's a Dale Earnhardt cap he's wearing. No way he's letting his kids beat him. He's not there to have fun. He's there to teach them a lesson."

It wouldn't even be close. His predictions were as stunning as they were accurate. And he'd already had a good day. In our second game, Duffy tweaked his knee and had to get carted to the medical tent. He spent the entire ride flirting up the cute blonde trainer.

When he jogged back for the third game with nary a hiccup in his speed or cutting ability, I tipped my shades down in his direction. "Were you really hurt or did you just see that girl over there and need an excuse?"

He just smiled a big Duffy smile. "Turns out my knee wasn't as bad as I thought."

Anyway, since I'd had such a good time in my previous Wildwood experience, I jumped at the chance to go back two years later. The team was put together by my friend Todd, a ridiculously skinny dude with a blonde beard who rode his bike 200 miles a week. He was one of those guys who wore the form-fitting neon bike suit and would just pedal to Maine and back for the hell of it. Todd grew up in rural Lancaster County training with Floyd Landis who'd win (and later be stripped of) the Tour de France title in 2006. Additionally, Todd was such a nice guy that we were all concerned he might be an Amish spy attempting to learn our ways so he could exploit our weaknesses and someday destroy us.

Anyway, the team he put together was called "Sunny Place, Shady People." The rest of us found this hilarious simply because Todd was the one who came up with it and he was the least shady person any of us knew. And he was very excited - so excited he made sunshine colored uniforms and designed an SPSP logo specifically for the weekend. And his excitement was justified. We had a pretty good team. Along with the two of us, we had Todd's big buddy Durrell, Movie Cop Jennie and her husband Greg, another Jennie, and an amazingly athletic lesbian couple I'll call K1 and K2.

K1 was super quick and always in the right spot. (She'd later go on to play at nationals in the women's division with BENT out of New York City.) K2 was a former college basketball player who was pushing six feet tall. The two of them pretty much dominated any woman they lined up against. The only problem was that once a game they'd have a very public spat over a dropped pass or throwaway that would result in one or the other walking off and threatening to quit. This would cause the other one to have to take a sub and give chase halfway down the boardwalk.

Right at the point when we thought we'd have no female subs for the rest of the tournament, the two of them would stroll hand in hand back to the sideline and start making out. This was a double-edged sword. It was good because we had our full contingent of women back, but now the guys were tossing flicks halfway to low tide because K1 & K2 were pretty hot and that shit was ultra distracting.

It wasn't necessarily the best beach weather. For late July it was kind of cloudy, windy, and cold. It felt more like summer in Scotland than the

Jersey Shore, which made our team name more than a bit ironic. As we hit the beach to warm up in the stinging drizzle, I looked down at my uniform and then over at Todd.

"Shady People still works, but I think you may have jumped the gun on the Sunny Place thing, dude."

"Yeah," he said glumly. "I printed the shirts before I checked the weather forecast."

The day was still pretty amazing even though there was a Nor'easter blowing straight down the beach that turned dumps into hucks. You had to absolutely gun everything as hard as you could just to get it a couple of feet up the beach. Every game was determined by a single big defense near the upwind end zone. One break and you controlled the game.

Our biggest goal of the day came on universe point in our second game against some team from Philly. The point started on our own goal line with me being forced to throw a bullet flick to K1 that stopped in midair like it had carbon fiber brakes. She laid out for it as it died, then dumped it to Tour de France Todd who tried to hit her with a low back-hand going up-line into the end zone. The wind was having none of that though and killed the throw a foot before the line. K1 dove and caught it, popping to her feet just as I sprinted past her into the end zone, chunks of sand spiraling from my heels. I threw a shoulder fake on my guy and stopped cold in the center of the end zone, wide open for an uncontest-ed backhand. Unfortunately, I pulled that maneuver about a millisecond after K1 decided to break the mark with a flick to the corner. The de-fender, trailing me by a step saw me stop and put on the skids. He fell to his knees, then turned to face guard me with no idea that due to the gale force wind, the disc was hovering like a tiny spaceship over his shoulder.

I did one of those roadrunner starts in the sand, my legs spinning and going nowhere as I tried to get traction in the uneven lump of coastal mush my feet were buried in. It hovered there so long that if K1's mark was paying any attention, she could've just taken a step back and made the D herself. Finally after what seemed like an entire stall count, my feet popped out of the hole I'd created and I laid out chest high to haul it in, eating a bowl full of Jersey shoreline in the process.

K1 often made this face that sort of resembled an irritated chipmunk. When you did something she wasn't expecting on the field, she just stared at you for eons as she contemplated how to best lambast you for it. I was greeted with her pissed chipmunk impression as I pulled my head out of the Earth.

"Why didn't you keep going to the corner?" she asked.

"Pfft….cough…..pfft," I said, spitting sand. "I went to the corner… pfft…..eventually."

Her chipmunk face faded as she stepped in to give me a bro-hug. "Nice catch. I mean if you don't fuck up the cut, it would've looked a lot prettier, but…."

I would've had a witty comeback but by this time K1 and K2 were making out and I was having some trouble talking.

That night after the annual Samuel Adams party, I found myself me-andering through town with K1 & K2 as they decided on their drink of choice for the night. The choice was vodka and once it was purchased, we headed back to the Beach Terrace looking for a good time. And man, did we find it.

The old Harrisburg stoner crew had put together a team in a separate division. They were called Creamsicle and most of them were my Adult Flicks teammates. Team Creamsicle had a hotel room about seven doors down from us on the fourth floor of the Beach Terrace. When we passed by their open door, it was like peering into a funhouse. Strange sounds, weirder smells, a yellowish haze, and crazy laughter – all the tell tale signs of a great hotel party. We ducked our heads in and the twenty people packed into the room exploded with cheers.

"Come on in Harrisburg brother and sisters!" they yelled. "Beer's cold, everything else is hot!"

I had no idea how wandering into that room would alter my life.

I grabbed myself a drink and circumnavigated the room, chatting with friends and friends of friends as I pounded a Yuengling Lager. Some-where along the line K1 & K2 produced the infamous Paris Hilton sex tape. Where they got it and why they had it, I have no idea - but next thing I knew everyone around me was getting high and watching a tal-entless debutante make herself famous. In night vision, Paris looked like an opossum curiously approaching a security camera.

As the "movie" started, I was apparently blocking the television. K1 smacked my hip. "Cramer, get out of the way," she shouted.

"What do you think you're going to miss?" I asked. "It's people with glowy eyes doing shit you can barely see."

K2 glared at me. "Out…..of…..the…..way."

The only unoccupied seat was on the arm of the couch, so I hopped over and sat down, laughing at the ridiculous debauchery that surrounded me.

"I'm watching a homemade porno in a room with like eighteen lit joints," I said to no one in particular. "I am a high school guidance counselor."

She was sitting just to my left in her own little optimally buzzed world, a skinny girl with a brown ponytail. She had on a white tank top and a red sarong with these really pissed off suns all over it.

"I wouldn't mention this to your administration," she said, smiling at me.

I smiled back. "I don't think I will," I said glancing at her skirt. "What the hell are those suns so angry about?"

"Could be any number of things."

"I bet it's sunspots. That's like star acne. I bet it's like right before prom so they're freaking out."

"Actually I think they're just constipated," she laughed.

"Stars poop? I didn't know this."

She laughed. "Uh,…yeah. What do you think comets are?"

Her name was Julie and she was a senior at Gettysburg College where everyone called her "Barnacle" for the ultra clingy hugs she'd dole out to anyone who happened to walk by. Seriously, she could latch onto you and not let go for hours. Creamsicle had picked her up for the tournament at the last minute when one of their women dropped out with an injury. She was the only person on their team I didn't know. So I decided to remedy the situation.

The party crackled and roared all around us. People got up, toppled over, darted in and out of the room, slammed the bathroom door, wrestled each other, and passed out, but the two of us barely noticed as we talked and drank.

Earlier in the day I ran into Duffy and told him to come find me at the Beach Terrace so we could go out on the town and stir up some trouble. As I'm sitting there with Julie, I see him peek his head in the door, smile and head straight for the couch. I leapt to my feet, picked a beer out of the mini fridge and flipped one to him.

"What's up, buddy?" I said.

"You tell me," Duffy answered. "Looks like you're the one that found the party."

He glanced down at Julie, who by this point was obviously smitten with my stunning wit and incredible good looks. (I'm sure her level of intoxication had nothing to do with this.) There were no instructions, no words exchanged, barely even a look. Duffy knew what to do. I'd been *his* wingman for damn near three years. It was finally, gloriously time for him to return the favor. He reached out to shake Julie's hand.

"Duffy," he said.

"Julie," she answered.

"I see you found the most interesting guy at the party. I mean, I don't want to interrupt but I haven't seen this guy in like six months and I know he has some crazy tales I've got to hear about." He patted the couch. "You want to have a good time, don't leave this spot all night."

Julie laughed, grabbing my wrist. "Wow, the pressure's on. Now I'm going to be disappointed if I'm not thoroughly entertained."

"What?" I said. "The dimly lit sex video isn't doing it for you?"

She laughed. She leaned into me. "Your friend Duffy's right. This *is* a good spot."

I owe you, buddy.

The three of us must've hung out there for an hour joking around and swapping stories as Duffy subtly and sometimes not so subtly pumped me up. In fact, he was so successful that it triggered an interruption from K1. She came over, sat on the coffee table facing us and put her hand on Duffy's knee.

"I don't know who you are," she said, just on the neutral side of hammered. "But it's obvious that you and Cramer know each other very well and you've done this many times before."

Duffy and I shared a smile across the top of Julie's head. "Done what?" he laughed.

K1 nodded and stood up. "Uh-huh. I've got my eye on you guys."

"In that case you might want to take notes," I chuckled.

She pointed at us before stumbling off. "You're good. You're very good."

The next morning we easily handled a team of college kids from Montclair State before losing 13-10 to a really good team out of DC. So our tournament was over but we'd gone a respectable 4-2 and even more importantly, had a hell of a rambunctious weekend. Barnacle Julie played so well at Wildwood that Adult Flicks decided the team could use her services. Her first tournament with us would be that upcoming September. By that time we'd been dating for over a month. Suffice it to say I was very happy with the result of the rainy, windy weekend in south Jersey.

Summer League Snippets – Thunderstruck

Pronghorn Steve really liked AC/DC. He'd go on a six-year streak of naming his teams after songs that Brian Johnson and the boys created. For some reason, the 2004 draft allowed Steve to snag Iron Mike and I for the second consecutive year. And that year, there were significantly less weddings and vacations. After starting 0-3, we rattled off seventeen consecutive victories to finish first overall in the league.

Iron Mike was now in his mid-thirties and starting to slow down a bit. It opened the door for Steve and I to lead the team. We were both right smack in the middle of our primes and no one in the league had an answer when we were both on the field.

What made our team incredibly unique though was one of our main handlers who was playing organized ultimate for the first time in his life. He was an incredibly small thirteen-year-old kid named Alex who was given a special exception to enter the league at such a young age because his father was a Pittsburgh legend and league board member. All of us who'd played against his dad all those years had watched Alex grow up. He would be off on the sidelines hucking thirty-yard flicks when the disc was half as big as he was. When I say Alex was tiny that summer, I mean I'm not positive he was five feet tall yet and I'd bet my savings that he wasn't a hundred pounds. I spent every game being simultaneously amazed at his precision throws and terrified that he'd be scooped up by a hungry eagle and taken off into the sky. And yet even though he was so young and small, he was arguably our fourth best player.

We'd be on the sidelines during games swapping stories about drunken one-night stands or terrible car sex when someone would inevitably realize that there was an eighth grader in the huddle.

"Alex…..earmuffs," we'd yell. "Cover 'em up, buddy."

He'd give us a sheepish, preadolescent grunt. "Guys, I know what you're talking about. I like….know stuff."

"And we want to make sure you don't find out more. So….earmuffs."

He'd always reluctantly sigh and cover his ears. That summer, he was everyone's little brother. At minimum, Tiny Alex averaged one noogie per minute of play. But he helped us flatten everyone in our way and return to the championship game.

As we lined up and looked out at the hill once again, I laughed toward Iron Mike. The two of us were in our third straight final. "Well, this is familiar."

In response, he smiled for what I'm assuming was the first time ever.

Pronghorn Steve and I totally controlled that game. At 14-8, a single goal from the championship, I caught a long swing to the right sideline. I was a yard from the cone, surveying my end zone options. The dump was covered and I thought about firing a high crossfield hammer until I saw Tiny Alex break out of the stack. Thinking it would be really cool for him to catch the final goal of summer league, I hung a push pass over the cone for him to run down.

Now my friend Mike was on the opposing team and he was blatantly poaching at the goal line. Mike is an incredible vocalist, known around Pittsburgh for absolutely stunning unaccompanied renditions of any song you can think of. He's opened for some of the top a-cappella acts in the country and in 2015, I was the official timer as he grooved for 26 straight hours to set the world beatboxing record. Part of the reason he's such an amazing singer is that well, he's got some girth through which his voice can resonate. The nightmare scenario we'd been trying to avoid for Tiny Alex the entire season was about to materialize right there on the very last point.

Beatbox Mike did a flying flop (I hesitate to use the term lay out) toward the disc. Beside him, Tiny Alex pancaked it. Imagine a basketball being thrown at a pencil and you'll get a clearer picture of the one-sided collision that happened next. The disc flew out of Alex's hands as he went tumbling out of bounds, through the weeds, and halfway *up* the hill.

"Oh shit," I said, running over, thinking I might not be congratulating him so much as being the first one to discover the body.

Beatbox Mike tromped over as well. Much to our relief, Tiny Alex wobbled to his knees, looking around with the same general expression as if he'd just been born. Mike and I each took an arm and got him to his feet as the sideline cheered.

"That's a strip," Mike called. He raised his hands. "He had it. Good goal and congratulations."

I picked up the woozy Tiny Alex and hoisted him into the air like Simba in the Lion King, then planted him on the ground so we could all give him noogies. I had my second summer league championship and now I'd not only caught the final goal of a season, I'd thrown one. Once again I was nominated for Finals MVP only to lose out to Pronghorn Steve. But I didn't mind. Another one of my teams was about to be immortalized on a popsicle stick. It was a good summer.

As for Tiny Alex, he grew (a little bit) and went on to lead the University of Pittsburgh to back-to-back national championships in 2012 &13, coming in second in the Callahan voting in 2012. That year, he ended the collegiate season by throwing a goal to his little brother Max to beat Wisconsin. He was one of the first ultimate players to ever sign an apparel sponsorship, and is arguably one of the top players in the world.

All because of the earmuffs.

TWENTY-SEVEN

It was dark as we drove over the Tappan Zee Bridge and into West Chester County, just north of New York City. Barnacle Julie and I were headed to a town called Elmsford where Adult Flicks had two rooms reserved at the Days Inn before a tournament the next morning. In the back of the car was Julie's friend from Gettysburg, a tiny computer mole of a kid we all called Whopper. He was a quick little dart with some pretty decent throws. With a bunch of our better players either injured or out of town, Whopper was certainly a welcome addition.

We were the last ones to cross the Hudson so when we got there, the entire team was already halfway through dinner at a classier place than any of us expected Adult Flicks to gather. It was a quiet Italian joint called Anthony's – the type of place with white tablecloths, wall mirrors, and a martini glass on the sign. The team had two tables pushed together and all of them seemed to be a bit loopy on wine already. Sitting with them was a regal looking Italian guy in his early 50's that none of us recognized. He had an amazing Italian guy mustache.

As we entered the crowded restaurant, K1 & K2 waved and urged us inside. The Italian guy stood up.

"Come in, come in. We've been waiting on you. Sit down, join the evening," he said, motioning to the waiter. "Joey, three more glasses and let's have another bottle of the Riesling." And without missing a beat, he turns to the others. "So you throw the Frisbee, and then what? What happens?"

Turned out the Italian guy was Anthony himself. And he was hands down one of the greatest people I've ever known for a single night. The guy was absolutely fascinated that we'd driven all the way from Harrisburg to play Frisbee. He wanted to know everything about it - all the details about who we were and what caused us all to cross his path that particular evening. He kept the wine coming and only had us pay for maybe half of it. When he realized that Barnacle Julie and I couldn't afford anything on the menu, he had the waiter bring us free appetizers. I can't stress this enough - on that particular night, the guy was a superstar of human beings.

As the patrons gradually left, Adult Flicks and Anthony were the only ones left in the restaurant. He motioned to the waiter once more. "Joey, close the bar. We're having a private party tonight."

And next thing we know, we're on the other side of the restaurant at a gorgeous wooden bar, just us, Anthony, the bartender and a couple regulars. We'd shown up in New York City without any real plan other than to find the hotel and somehow, some brilliant way, ended up with our own private party. It was incredible.

An hour or so into the gathering, I approached Anthony as he sat on one of his barstools. "We really appreciate you doing this for us. This is amazing."

He shook my hand and raised his wine glass. "I do this a few times a year when I meet interesting people with stories to tell. When I woke up this morning I knew nothing about Ultimate Frisbee. Now I do." He gestured around to all of my smiling, laughing teammates. "Thanks for sharing your night with me. This is life. Remember that."

Superstar of human beings. I will never in my life forget that night or that advice.

Anyway, the next morning was a bit eerie. We were in New York on September 11th, only three years after the attacks. Everything was more or less back to normal, but there were signs everywhere. As we drove down Route 1 through Rye, New York, we passed their fire station just as they were marking the anniversary of the first plane hitting the towers. With the windows down, we could hear them playing TAPS to honor their fallen comrades. Julie and I drove in silence the last four miles. It's one thing to see it on the news. It's quite another to see it in front of you.

The tournament itself was on the sound just north of the city in a town called Mamaroneck. It was the flat-out prettiest place I'd played since back at the Castillo in St. Augustine. The fields were on a little peninsula that jutted out into the water between two marinas. Throughout the day, sailboats drifted across the glistening water behind all the flying discs.

We came out on fire against a team called North Jersey All-Stars. I had an assist and a couple D's in the first few points, but from there we sputtered and fell apart losing 11-8. This all but made us 0-2 because our next match happened to be against arguably the most legendary team in ultimate history.

Boston's "Death or Glory" won the national club title six years in a row from 1994-1999. Six years in a freaking row. It's a streak of sustained excellence that will probably never be matched. DoG would later go on to win a Masters title and much further down the road, a Grand Masters title. The players who formed the team are absolute legends. Their captain and founder, Jim Parinella wrote the book on ultimate. (Literally, he wrote one of the first actual books ever published on ultimate skills and strategies.) Half of the offensive and defensive methods employed today were invented or improved upon by the guys and girls we were about to step on the field against. It was like sharing the court with the Celtics.

Anyway, that day Death or Glory brought their co-ed team down I-95 to play a game against a riffraff team of old stoners who'd been out partying way too late with an Italian restaurateur the night before. In the end, it was just awesome to run around on the same field as those guys – to have a legend guard you and occasionally do cool things anyway.

We were down 9-4 when Shameless Wyatt made a big D in the end zone. K1 picked it up and worked it around with a couple of our old vets. I faked deep and shot in to grab a five-yard flick then immediately dumped it back and made a scooter cut up the right sideline. They swung it to me. Fifty yards away, Barnacle Julie had gotten a half step on her woman. I caught the disc with momentum and my defender trailing so I figured "what the hell."

It was one of those throws that you just stand there and enjoy for the five seconds it's in the air because you already know the result. Sixty yards away, Julie caught it just in front of her hip as her defender stretched out and missed it by a foot. 9-5.

A few steps from the back of the end zone, Julie momentarily froze in shock. People in Connecticut could've seen her eyes light up. She dropped the disc and came sprinting up the sideline. The baseball outfield we were playing on may as well have been a wildflower-strewn Austrian meadow. At around midfield she jumped into my arms.

"Oh my God, I love you," she exclaimed, kissing my beard.

"You just caught a huck for a goal against Death or Glory," I said, beaming a smile off the sailboats.

"Why do you think I'm kissing you like this?" she exclaimed.

Later on, there'd be times in our relationship where I'm pretty sure that throw was the only thing keeping us together.

It was by far the best on-field moment of our day. We dropped that game 11-6 then fell in similar fashion to teams from NYC Metro and Long Island to go 0-4. But with the music blasting and dogs and burgers on the grill, a couple kegs, and the water in view, there was no complaining. Even without a victory, it was worth the trip.

And we didn't go home empty handed either. During the awards ceremony just after the championship game, it was announced that we'd tied with a NYC team named Sangria for the spirit award. And they only had one trophy so we'd need to decide a winner somehow.

The rules were simple. The members of your team could use any article of clothing they were currently wearing - first team to make a continuous chain the width of the field (40 yards) from sideline to sideline won.

They blew the whistle and with a large post-tournament gathering cheering us on, we started shedding clothes, firing off our cleats, sandals, and shoes as Barnacle Julie and K2 straightened them into a line. It was chaos as our uniforms started coming off, the guys soon shirtless and girls standing there in sports bras. Whopper tossed in the warm up pants he'd been wearing. I slammed down my visor. We were shedding clothes so fast that by the time any of us went to put another item on the ground, seven other items had appeared and you had to run twenty feet to drop what you just took off. We brashly flew past the center of the field with no nerves as Sangria muddled along behind us.

We were absolutely demolishing the contest until with about eight feet to go, we encountered a problem. We'd lost everything that wouldn't cause some blushing. The line came to a momentary halt. Surely someone had something more to give. Shameless Wyatt had tossed in his shorts and everything else at the very beginning. He'd been down to his boxers since the second the whistle blew. K1 & K2 were in undies and sports bras. I was down to Movie Cop Jennie's skirt and one sock, which I quickly took off and tossed on the field.

K2 and I had a panicked faceoff across the line of clothes. Sangria was slowly but surely catching up.

"Cramer," K2 yelled. "The skirt has to go."

"Your sports bra would cover way more ground."

"You have underwear on. We saw it every time you laid out," she said, crossing her arms. "All I have under my bra is boobies."

(She was the type of girl who'd say boobies)

I looked behind me to see Sangria methodically marching toward us. "Damn it," I said with a sigh, slipping it off, now down to my briefs facing the marina and all the good people enjoying a nice afternoon out on Long Island Sound.

I tossed the skirt in the line, stretching it out as far as possible. We were still about a foot and a half short even after Freak threw in his sweaty bandana.

"Your move," I said to K2.

She peered over her shoulder at Sangria, still yards away, putzing around and hoping we'd finish before any of them had to really show some skin. Still, they were closing on us. With a squinty, demoralized face, K2 reached up toward her back.

Just as she did, Whopper was struck with a brilliant and horrendously timed idea. He realized that technically his glasses counted and placed them on the ground next to my skirt. Seeing them, K2 quit reaching for her bra and instead took down her ponytail, throwing her hair tie into the fray. It was just enough to touch the other sideline.

The judge knelt down and verified the results. Our clothes indeed stretched the entire width of the field. He raised his arms in the air.

"We have a winner!"

Adult Flicks exploded in half naked triumph. Behind us, Shameless

Wyatt fumbled with the waistband on his boxers –which were down around his ankles.

"Looks like we didn't need me to….so I'll just pull these back up then," he mumbled, mooning a yacht.

K2 punched me in the shoulder. "You thought you were gonna get to see my boobs."

"Yes I did," I answered. "Damn it, Whopper," I said smacking his glasses back into his chest.

"What? I thought it was clever," he whined. "Wasn't it?"

"Yeah," I sighed. "It was clever. Really….fuckin'…..clever."

We got a big trophy and everything - and probably the biggest cheer of the entire day the moment we secured our victory. As the tournament director said when presenting us the trophy, "In a naked race, never bet against a team called Adult Flicks."

As it turned out, winning the naked race was the high water mark of the Harrisburg Pleasure Van. Over the winter, a couple of the more dedicated old stoners (that may be the first time that phrase has ever appeared in print) either got hurt or afflicted with some life event that ate up the time they'd otherwise been dedicating to ultimate. It left the younger, more competitive crowd in charge. This in turn, led to a complete rebranding of Adult Flicks.

On March 28th, 1979, reactor unit 2 at the Three Mile Island Nuclear Facility just southeast of downtown Harrisburg partially melted down. It was the worst nuclear accident in US history. 40,000 gallons of radioactive wastewater ended up in the Susquehanna River. Obviously the downside was nationwide panic and local soil samples dotted with distressing levels of cesium-137. On the upside though, twenty-five years later we got some cool uniforms out of it.

We renamed ourselves Harrisburg Fission and our logo was the three-eyed blinky fish from the Simpsons. Above him, Fission was spelled out with two reactors for the "I's" and an atom substituting for the "O." Our colors were white, orange, and radioactive green. It ended up being a radical and very abrupt switch in tone, but to tell you the truth, the van was due for a tune up.

Our first tournament with the new name was called White Nights, a tournament fully sponsored by the Ommegang Brewery in Cooperstown, New York. An ultimate tournament put on by a brewery? There was no way we were missing it. Just because we rebranded didn't mean we forgot our roots.

In the first game, we went down 5-0 against a team out of Massachusetts called Huckulees only to come back and win 15-12. The best goal and one of the best catches I've ever seen came when I stepped around my mark and gunned a flick as hard as possible toward my receiver who was chugging toward the right front cone about fifteen yards away. The pass was right on target. It wasn't a hard catch in any way - except for one minor detail I forgot as I let the thing go at 90 miles per hour.

The receiver was named Josh. He had kind of a scruffy black beard and dark oily hair. Other distinguishing characteristics, let's see….he was about 5'10" and oh yeah - he only had one arm. Needless to say, this wasn't the most optimum disability when it comes to catching rockets that your dickhead teammate just lasered toward your groin.

The catch he made defies belief. One-Armed Josh laid out straight into the disc, putting his hand up to save himself from getting pelted in the face. The disc popped into the air off his palm as he landed on his head, his neck bending at a poltergeist-like angle. His defender skipped to the side at full speed, swiping his arm just over the disc as he tumbled out of play. With his head and shoulders in bounds and upside down, Josh reached out and snagged the disc just before his back and his legs smacked down out of bounds. It tied the game 5-5. Our sideline popped like a confetti cannon. I ended up being the last one to pat him on the back.

"Someone's trying to get on Sportscenter tonight," I said.

He laughed. "Cramer, how long have we been playing together now?"

"I don't know. A year, year and a half?"

"So by now you must've figured out that I only have one arm, right?"

"I thought that was just an optical illusion."

"Maybe a little less mustard in the future…."

"You got it."

Most ultimate parties are pretty sick, but this one was in a giant tent set up directly outside the brewery with the obligatory funk band playing and fresh kegs that only had to be transported like 200 yards from where the beer itself was born. It doesn't get much better than that. It was like the first pass Callahan of ultimate parties.

Speaking of which......

In my faster days, my dream was always to complete the near impossible and intercept the other team's first pass for a Callahan goal. (It was the image that had gotten me through those brutal track workouts at Penn State.) I'd come within mere inches on a few occasions but never managed to actually grab the thing for the score. If I could just get one in my career, I could die happy. And that Sunday morning, I'd get my chance. On universe point no less.

We'd gone down 5-0 (again) to a speedy young team from Providence, Rhode Island before finally sweating out the microbrews from the night before and roaring back to tie it 10-10 just before the hard cap went on. On the ensuing pull, Soggy Darin pinned them deep in the center of the end zone. It was time for me to make the big play I knew I was destined to make.

I shot down there as fast as I've ever run in my life, a full twenty yards ahead of my teammates as their handler picked up the disc. As I sped forward, he threw a backhand toward the other handler up near the goal line. It wasn't crisp. It floated. Ten yards away, I smelled blood.

The handler at the goal line was going to have to jump for the hanging disc. I accelerated. The disc was mine. I left the ground three yards behind him and sliced through the air, bending my body to slide past his right shoulder, reaching a foot or so over his outstretched fingers. This was it. This was my first pass Callahan. And it was going to win us the game.

And for some inexplicable reason, the disc just stayed where it was, hovering there about ten feet in the air. Unlike footballs or volleyballs, Frisbees do that on occasion. They just sit there defying gravity. And when they do they can turn you from a hero into a total dope.

My fingernails brushed the underside of the disc as I flew past; my head twisting back to watch the rest of the play unfold before my feet even hit the ground. I'd blown it. I'd jumped too soon. All the dreaming about that first pass Callahan had made me too anxious when the situation actually presented itself. I'd probably covered six yards horizontally but didn't get enough lift. The disc sat down into the other guy's hands like a feather at the goal line. My one glorious unobstructed chance at my dream goal was gone.

That would've won us the game. Instead, they marched it down and scored on us to knock us into the loser's bracket. I'd love to say I was inconsolable but let's face it, we were at a tournament sponsored by a brewery. Winning was like fourth on the list in terms of my goals for the weekend. If that had been a chance to go to nationals, I may have walked off the field and straight into traffic, but it wasn't so it was more of a moderate annoyance – kind of like those slightly elevated cesium levels around southeast Harrisburg.

During my couple years in York County, I played a lot of ultimate. A lot. Pretty much every weekend, I was somewhere chucking around a disc. One of those weekends happened to be a tournament called Jive Fest over in Carlisle. It was the fall version of the tournament where my shorts had fallen apart six months earlier. The late October tournament featured all local college teams….with one exception – an alumni team from the host school, the traditionally awful Dickinson College. They were bad. Maybe the worst college team I'd ever seen. (Consequently they were often the most fun.) Flagler would've crushed them in less than an hour. The weird thing about their consistent awfulness though was that Dickinson always had one or two great players out there in the middle of a bunch of nerds who didn't know what they were doing.

Those great players included a bug-eyed Superman named Mike with an incredible white-guy afro, and another Mike with a crew cut and dirty blonde mustache who looked like a cross between a rugby player and a hillbilly mechanic. All of their top alumni were coming back for the tournament, but their numbers were still low. Desperate for a substitute or two, Rugby Mike pestered me during pickup the entire week leading up to the tourney.

"Cramer, we're going to be good, I swear," he said. "With you we could actually win the whole thing."

"That sounds great," I answered. "I only see one potential problem here."

"Yeah?"

"I didn't ya know....go to Dickinson. I was under the impression that's a critical factor in how they determine who qualifies as an alumni."

"Nobody's checking. Who's going to check?"

"I assume you'll be playing Gettysburg College. My girlfriend is on their team. She's pretty aware I didn't go to Dickinson."

"Just sweet talk her."

I bought her silence for some ice cream and a back rub. It didn't much matter anyway. When we played Gettysburg, everyone knew I was a blatant ringer.

I only mention this tournament at all because of two stories. The first is hands down the greatest throw I've ever made and the second is.... well, you'll see.

Because I was dating Barnacle Julie, I got to know the Gettysburg College team very well. I ate in their cafeteria damn near every weekend. I played pickup with them once a week just down the hill from the cannons that lined Confederate Avenue.

One guy in particular was always talking smack. He was a dude named Rambo, a lovably cocky guy with a permanent five o'clock shadow. At the time, not many folks would've disputed that I was the best player in the area. This was due to two factors...

1) I was at the absolute top of my game.

2) Though there was a pretty damn good scene, it's not like the Susquehanna Valley was an ultimate hub like Boston or Seattle or the Bay Area.

Even so, Rambo always talked shit about how he was as good as me if not better. I knew it was all in fun - kind of. In many ways, the brash 21 year old really believed it. He was a small college superstar just like I was at Flagler before Tuba ran the arrogance right out of me. (Which is why I tolerated his crap. I understood.)

He was always saying stuff like....

"You're old. Disc is in the air, just me and you, you're not coming down with it. I mean, come on, you have to admit that."

And....

"I mean, I'm not saying you aren't fast. It's just that I'm faster."

Gettysburg was our second game of the day. It was going to be the first time Rambo and I ever met on a real field with both of us going all out. He couldn't wait to show everyone how dominant he was. And I couldn't wait to kick dirt in his face like a loving older brother.

The first pull went out of bounds. I went to pick it up. He came sprinting over beside me as I walked it back to the center of the field. "Looks like we're gonna finally find out who's better," he said.

I casually reached the disc out for him to tap into play. "Don't take it personally buddy…." I said, surveying the field.

He started stalling. "One….two…

"But I'm about to destroy you."

"Three…"

I fired a hammer like forty yards to White Afro Mike and took off. He was going to have to chase me everywhere.

We were up 4-1 when I caught a swing pass and wound up to fire a backhand huck. He sprinted in and jumped in front of me as I was about to release it. Truthfully, it was a ridiculously athletic play by a ridiculously athletic kid. It really should've resulted in a spectacular kick block. I'm not sure how I did it, but I adjusted, pulling the disc in toward my body, dipping low, and shortening my follow through. The huck went between Rambo's legs 65 yards to White Afro Mike for the goal.

"How the hell did you get that off?" Rambo said, slack-jawed.

I just grinned and patted him on the back.

When I got to the end zone, White-Afro Mike flipped me the disc. "That throw looked like it came straight out of Rambo's ass."

"Ha," I said. "Make sure to tell him that."

That play frustrated him to no end. He was sure he had the monster foot block that he'd be reminding me about for months and it just didn't materialize. From there, I shut him down. He caught nothing. I thought he was going to have a stroke. But with all the trash he'd talked, there was no way I was letting up.

We were up 12-5 in a game to 13 when I knocked down a pass they'd thrown from the goal line to the center of the field. Rambo reacted and shifted over to mark me before I could pick up the rolling disc.

I could've waited for an easy throw to open up. But this was my girl-friend's team. She was watching from the sideline. I kind of wanted to impress her. Also the kid who wouldn't shut up about his superior skills was standing right in front of me. I wanted one last dagger, one lasting bitch slap of a play that would prove once and for all that when it came to Harrisburg Ultimate, I was still the king. I was going off the grid.

Out of the corner of my eye, I saw White-Afro Mike sprinting across the center of the end zone with his guy about a step behind him sprinting to catch up. One of the Gettysburg guys was poaching at the goal line as we scrambled to set up an offense. If I was going to hit Mike for the quick transition goal, the window was closing fast. I needed to surprise them. Rugby Mike was cutting to the force side cone but was covered. I faked a flick toward him causing Rambo to lean just enough....

I planted, turned my wrist over, fired my left knee toward the ground and rotated my hips backwards. My right arm whipped behind my back and I let go of the disc just in front of my left thigh. And man, I gunned the damn thing. The disc rocketed past Rambo's elbow, past the poacher at the goal line, and right toward Mike's face about 22 yards away. The throw came from a release point nobody was expecting and thus none of the defenders managed to react, not even the guy right on Mike's hip.

What really topped off the play was that I accidentally fooled Mike as well. He didn't see the disc until the absolute last second. Sprinting from left to right across the end zone, he jumped in the air and without looking fired his left arm up to snare the disc behind his head after it had already sailed by him. He landed, clutching the goal that ended the game and nobody- I mean nobody knew what to do. It was a behind the back bullet to a no look behind the head catch to seal the game. If we had it on video, it'd be one of the best ultimate highlights of all time. But we don't so you'll just have to take my word for it. All seven players in Gettysburg orange just froze in place. For a good three seconds, the field was dead silent.

The guy poaching at the goal line was flabbergasted. "What the.... how did... what the hell was...."

Rambo hung his head. "Cramer, you're a dick."

"Yup," I said, extending my hand. "It was the only throw you were giving me. Good game, buddy."

He slapped my hand and hugged me. "Next game I'm shutting you down. I know how to play you now."

"Uh-huh."

Barnacle Julie came running off the sideline to give me one of her barnacle hugs. "Wow!" she kept saying over and over. "Wow! I'm not even mad we lost cause I got to see that."

It was the last time any of the Gettysburg kids ever attempted to talk smack. Goddamn right, punks.

The party was once again incredible, over a hundred people packed into a two-story house just off Dickinson's campus. They made giant strawberry Jell-O shots in the back of Frisbees and our team won the subsequent race to see who could clean their Discraft first. It was a wild night that ended in quite a satisfying manner for me in a way or three that I won't delve into further in an attempt to keep this book at least marginally family friendly.

A front came through overnight and what was a brilliantly sunny and moderately warm late October Saturday turned into a damp and bone chilling Sunday morning. We'd finished 4-0 the previous day and earned ourselves a bye in the ten-team tournament. Unfortunately, Gettysburg had to play at 8:00 in the morning and Julie was my ride. I ended up sitting on these frigid metal bleachers watching her and the rest of her Gettysburg teammates take on Juniata College. You know how you can be perfectly warm until you start shivering just a little bit? Then five minutes later the wind is passing right through your soul and your teeth sound like a typewriter? Honestly, my next move only makes sense in the context of a frozen guy that was desperate to get warm by any means necessary.

Around halftime, Rugby Mike showed up with the gallon of orange juice that was about to be his breakfast. I unscrewed the top of a Nalgene bottle I happened to be watching for Julie and tipped it toward him.

"Dude, can I get a little hit of that?"

"You bet," Mike said, pouring and pouring, and pouring until the bottle was nearly full.

"Never let it be said that you're not a generous man, Mike."

"All they had at the store was gallons. But I really wanted OJ this morning so I ended up with all this."

So we sat there, shivering and chugging orange juice, wishing we were out running around to get our blood pumping. As the second half was about to begin, I chuckled at Mike and held up the orange juice container.

"Too bad we don't have any vodka, huh?"

Mike squinted. He turned around and looked to the parking lot. "Actually, I have a full bottle in my truck. I bought it for the party last night and then forgot about it."

"You're kidding."

"No. It's in a brown paper bag under the passenger's seat."

We sprinted for the parking lot. There was indeed a bottle of Absolut on the passenger's side floor mat. We eagerly disposed of the paper bag and each took one good chug of orange juice out of the Nalgene bottle. We replaced the empty space with the vodka, shaking it up to mix it around. Needless to say, the second half of the game was a lot more fun to watch. And the two of us sure quit shivering.

I'm sure I don't have to point out the major flaw in our long-term plan.

Gettysburg beat Juniata for the right to play us in the semifinals. When the game ended, Mike and I happily hopped out of the stands and went to begin warming up. We started off about twenty yards away and he flipped me a backhand. I stuck my hand out and - missed it entirely.

Uh-oh.

The rest of warm ups didn't go much better.

Before the game, Rambo came over to shake my hand and once again assert that he knew how to play against me now. He was certain that he knew all of my tricks and this game would be different. I just nodded. He had three eyes and two haircuts. And he was correct. He had no idea how different this game was going to be.

I was doing everything I could to hide the fact that I was plowed. I kept my shades on even though it was completely overcast. I tried not to say much. It was ten in the morning. My complete obliteration was the last thing anyone was suspecting.

Before the game, Barnacle Julie came over and hugged me tight like she always did. "Good luck, but we're going to beat you this time," she said, kissing me on the cheek. She let all her weight fall against me. It knocked me off balance. I stumbled and caught myself.

"Yeah, you play good too," I mumbled, brushing her hair. "You're all pretty."

She lifted my shades and beamed a surprised smile as she looked into my eyes. "Holy shit, are you drunk?"

"Shhhh," I said putting my finger over her lips. "Mike and I were really cold. We may have made a giant screwdriver in your Nalgene bottle to cope with….the wedder, weath….wea-ther."

"Oh my god, you're sooooo drunk," she laughed. "Now I really can't wait for this game to start."

Now playing ultimate while drunk has many drawbacks. Nonexistent depth perception comes to mind. But for me, it also came with one distinct advantage. When I'm drunk, I will run. Everywhere. And I won't stop. The little voice in my brain that tells me I'm tired doesn't activate any more. One time I was at a party in St. Augustine and a girl who wasn't particularly hygienic was flirting with me despite no obvious sign I wanted her to continue. As she leaned in to kiss me, I hopped off the couch, took off out the door and sprinted the entire way to the other side of town. I found out too late that had I been blasted for all of my collegiate cross-country races, I probably would've won the conference.

Rambo got open on me a bit more in this game - mainly cause I didn't know which one of him to cover. I think he actually caught a goal or two. But he didn't have a prayer of covering me - because not only would I not slow down, my cuts made absolutely no sense. One second I was clogging the lane, the next second I was wide open in the end zone and the next I was retreating forty yards to be a second dump option. He had no idea what the hell to do. I ran him ragged as I happily zigzagged all over the field.

I ended up with a goal and five assists in an 11-7 win. It would've been two goals except that I slightly misjudged the trajectory of a hammer as I skied over Rambo. I can still see my right hand extended in the air, trying to close on a disc that ended up hitting me just above the armpit. By that time, everyone on the field had their suspicions I was intoxicated. That confirmed it.

I heard their sideline give a resigned sigh as I tossed one of my goals.

"Cramer is trashed and he's still kicking our ass."

I turned and laughed. "Nah, I'm just…..really tired."

"Dude, your sweat smells like vodka!"

"That's my normal…uh….musk. You guys know the score?"

Anyway, we went on to play Shippensburg University in the final. Like usual they had about twenty-four players in uniform in comparison to our ten. Also two of our better players were kind of smashed. We still played well, but I managed to sprain my LCL in the first half and the Dickinson alumni plus one fell 13-9, four goals shy of a tournament championship.

I had to rest for a couple weeks to get my knee back in working order but by early December, I felt as good as ever. And it was a good thing too. I was headed to a big time tournament where I'd end up playing in one of the most epic universe points in history. It was so epic it deserves more or less it's own chapter.

TWENTY-EIGHT

WE CALLED HIM MONKEY ARMS. HIS REAL NAME WAS MARK AND HE WAS probably Gettysburg College's best player ever. One of the main reasons he was so good was that he was built like no other human being I've ever encountered. He was my size, maybe a little bigger, but with a completely insane arm to body ratio. When I stand up straight and let my arms hang down, my fingertips reach a point just below the middle of my thigh. Mark's reached his socks. That's only a slight exaggeration. He looked like what you'd get if you combined a tall and good-looking young congressman with an orangutan.

Mark had graduated two years prior, now lived in Delaware and played a lot of ultimate in the Philly area. All I knew about him was that he was a legend who everyone associated with Gettysburg Ultimate couldn't wait to see me match up against some day. When we finally met head to head at a small tournament in the fall, I found out the guy was as good as advertised. Playing for Harrisburg, I got the best of him in a 13-7 victory but we were evenly matched on the field. What I liked about his game is that he played just as fast, fun, and reckless as I did.

A couple guys he knew from Philly were putting together a team for a tournament called Ultimaxx in Greenville, North Carolina. They were short on players and asked Mark if he knew anyone who might want to join them. Barnacle Julie convinced him to ask me. I said yes in about a half second and so one Friday in early December I put in a full day at the high school and then the three of us headed south.

It's a five hour and forty-five minute drive from Fawn Grove, PA to Greenville, North Carolina and that's without hitting insane DC Beltway traffic. When you do get stuck in that automotive quagmire, it's more like ten. We'd all been up since 6:00 AM for various reasons and didn't arrive at the Red Roof Inn until well after midnight. I've seen movie zombies that looked more alive than we did as we exited the car.

As we stumbled into the room and flopped to the beds without even bothering to kick off our shoes, I mumbled into the comforter. "Why the hell do we do this again?"

Monkey Arms Mark was all but talking in his sleep when he answered, "I have no idea."

When the alarm went off early the next morning, I was perfectly content to drive 400 miles only to see the inside of a Red Roof Inn. If Julie hadn't tickled me out of bed, I'm positive I'd never have made it out the door.

Ultimaxx was a big tournament hosted by East Carolina University. It was a nice mix of the top club and college teams from the Mid-Atlantic and Southern Regions. The team I played with that weekend was aptly named "The Nomad Whores." Technically we were based out of Philadelphia, but in reality we were just random guys from all over the damn place who'd never played together before. In fact, I have zero idea how the team actually came together in the first place. It very well may have been part of someone's sociology thesis.

Along with Mark and I, we had a club player from Toronto named Alex, a mountain man from Appalachian State named Andrew, a fast, baby-faced kid from Chapel Hill named Ian, a crazy dude named Vlad who I thought was foreign but probably wasn't, and a carload of nondescript guys from Philly that I can't remember.

The team was captained by this slick dude named Clayton who had the look and personality of a nightclub DJ. I have no idea what he actually did for a living. He probably worked in IT for a bank, but he just had the vibe of a dude who saw a lot of fog and lasers.

And so on a chilly but sunny Carolina morning, twelve guys who'd just met took the field together to play a club team out of Asheville called Flying Snatch. I couldn't wait to play on the same line as Monkey Arms Mark. Turned out he was pretty damn excited about playing on a line with me. We both had the same unsaid feeling that we were going to make some jaws drop out there between the lines.

The Whores were down 1-0 when Mark caught a pass about 25 yards from the goal line. My defender shut down my cut to the back left corner so I faked to the center and quickly jitterbugged to the corner again. Before I even turned my hips, a beautiful hammer was in the air to the back cone. I boxed out the defender to catch a goal that tied the game.

Mark jogged across the goal line with a big smile. "I knew you were going back to the corner cause that's what I would've done."

I grinned. "This is gonna be fun."

With the two of us leading the charge for Nomad Whores, the first few points were quick, crisp, and hotly contested. I only wish I could've been around to see how it ended.

We were down 4-3 when Mark and I returned to the field on the O-line. We'd taken the pull and worked it to midfield or so when I faked deep out of the vertical stack and made a hard cut in on the break side. Toronto Alex was facing a tough mark and couldn't get the throw off, so I planted and turned to get the hell out of the lane.

Everyone on the field said it sounded like a gunshot. I dug my instep into the turf and whipped my shoulders and my head around to take off deep. Then an unexpected wrecking ball blasted into my forehead with a sickening, brain-rattling crack.

Smash to black.

I'm not sure how long I was lying there in the brown December grass. Apparently the other guy stumbled awkwardly to the sideline as I slowly worked my way to my knees with my forehead still pressed to the ground. My head felt like a kettlebell.

One of the nice things about Ultimaxx was that they'd marked the brick. (The brick mark is a term used to describe where you put the disc in play after a pull goes out of bounds.) Normally, you just take ten rather imprecise strides from the center of the goal line and tap the disc in from there. For this tournament, however, they'd done the measurements and made small circles in the grass with red field paint. As I slowly pulled my head up and regained some semblance of focus, I thought it odd that I happened to land directly on the brick mark.

One of the dudes from Flying Snatch was the first to get to me. He extended his hand to help me up. "Hey man, are you alright?"

I pulled my head off the turf and looked up at him. I was about to nod. I was about to say, "Yeah, I'm ok. Just give me a second."

But I didn't get the chance because of the next thing out of his mouth.

"Eeeew…." he said with the exact inflection of a little girl who'd just touched a booger. He motioned to our sideline. "Someone really needs to get over here!"

Turned out I hadn't been lying on the brick mark after all. That red circle on the field was wet. That red circle on the field was all me.

It was indeed nasty. When we hit heads, the other guy drove my shades back into my eyebrow so hard that it split open my forehead nearly to the skull. Blood was pouring down into my left eye and dripping from my cheek onto my shoulder. Monkey Arms Mark and Appalachian Andrew helped my wobbly ass to the sideline where they gave me a mirror so I could assess the damage. Let's just say I wasn't as handsome as I'd been when I got up that morning.

Barnacle Julie was playing for the Philly women on a team called Ho Stack over at the main fields. We thought we should probably fill her in as to what was going on. Monkey Arms Mark volunteered to miss the rest of the game and drive me to the emergency room so they could close the gaping wound in my head. Julie was on the sidelines cheering on her teammates when we got her attention and waved her over.

"What's up?" she said, nervously looking back toward her game.

"We're headed to the hospital," Mark answered.

I pointed to my face. "I lost some blood. It's back at the other fields."

"Oh, ok," she said quickly. "I'm supposed to be in on the next point, so…."

I turned to Mark. "Is there no blood on my face anymore?"

"No, there's lots of blood. You are saturated in blood. It's a horror show."

Julie wasn't paying attention at all. "Guys, I really have to go," she said, briefly grabbing my hand. "Feel better love you," she uttered before sprinting back to her sideline.

"Ya know I very well might die!" I yelled toward her back. If she heard me, she chose to ignore it.

Mark squinted toward the game. "That was a lot less concern than I anticipated."

"I'd nod in agreement but I'm afraid my brain would slip out of my head."

I guess I didn't blame her. She was six points into her first ever game with a high- level women's team. She tried to hide the fact that she was a bouncing, shivering, nervous, excited wreck, but it was pretty obvious. They could've dropped my ice-cold corpse in front of her and it wouldn't have registered.

So Monkey Arms Mark and I got a fun tour of Greenville, North Carolina. We missed the rest of the Flying Snatch game as well as the full second game as we sat in the ER watching college football pregame shows and waiting for someone with a medical degree to reattach my left eyebrow. It was maddening not knowing what was going on back at the fields, not being able to help my new teammates, and more than that, knowing Monkey Arms Mark was spending two hours flipping through old magazines for no good reason.

There are some interesting folks in the Greenville, North Carolina ER on your typical Saturday morning. Two sweaty guys in dirty soccer shorts were pretty damned out of place among the fat people with oxygen tanks and the skeezy rednecks jonesing for a smoke. As we waited, we swapped ultimate stories and laughed at our predicament. But the funny thing about the experience was the more we talked, the more we revved ourselves up.

"When we get out on that field again, there's no holding back," I said. "If you see me open or hell….even not open. Don't holster anything. Just launch it."

"I've been waiting for someone to say that my whole career," he laughed. "Where the hell are the doctors?"

We couldn't wait to haul ass back to the fields and storm triumphantly into the next game. This was an awful idea considering how much blood I'd lost and the fact that I most likely sustained a mild concussion, but I hadn't traveled that far to sit on the sidelines. Eventual dementia be damned.

Two hours later, I had a bunch of stitches in my face underneath a Band-Aid that could've housed a bird. And after half a morning out of commission, I was like a cooped up dog ready to be let out of its cage.

Virginia had just scored to close our lead to 14-11 when we skidded into the parking lot, slammed our doors and sprinted for the sideline.

"What's the score?" I yelled from a few yards away, doing a baseball slide to the sideline, trying to put my cleats on so quickly I nearly sprained my ankle in the process.

"We score, we win," Carolina Ian said.

"Sweet," I said, running out to the line with one cleat untied. Monkey Arms Mark ran in after me.

We got a big cheer from the line as we hustled onto the field. "Welcome back!"

As Virginia prepared to pull, DJ Clayton looked at us. "Anything in particular you guys want to run?"

"How tired are you guys?" I asked.

"Pretty tired," he answered. "With you guys gone, we were down to three subs."

"All right then," I nodded. "Just rest. Mark and I will punch it in."

"Yeah?" Clayton said.

"Yeah," Mark answered.

The caged dogs were about to be set free.

I picked up the pull and hit Mark ten yards out into the field. Then in a ballet of passes, the two of us worked it up the right sideline. It was a precise array of baby hammers, scoobers, push passes, and flicks. Nearing the end zone, Mark flipped one backwards over his shoulder and peeled around his defender. I caught it and popped a tiny high release backhand to space as he ran by me. I immediately cut behind him to the center of the field to run down a push pass he'd left out in front of me. He took off for the end zone where he stopped, lost his defender and came back to grab a flick I put right in his stomach. Goal. Two guys, ten passes, we win.

"Damn," DJ Clayton said as he ran in to high five us. "Whatever they gave you at the hospital, go back and get some for the rest of us."

It was great to be back.

In our next game against Duke, we picked up right where we'd left off against Virginia. I had three layout D's including one where I came flying from three yards behind a guy to get my hand in between his for a tip away. I had five assists and two goals and Mark had five goals and two assists as we easily got past them 15-9.

I'm not sure what it was with that tournament, but I felt completely unstoppable. I'm sure a huge part of it was playing on the same team as Monkey Arms Mark. We were just eternally on the same page. I think the other part was that at 27 years old, I was as good as I was ever going to be. Running around out there, it was like I was a foot taller than everyone else, sprinting on a cushion of air. If you ever get that feeling on the ultimate field or anywhere else, take it in. Enjoy it. Trust me, it doesn't last forever.

Our first game the next morning was against the host team, East Carolina, the same school that dominated college ultimate a decade earlier. While they weren't quite as elite as they used to be, this East Carolina team was still pretty damn good.

As we met a very hung over DJ Clayton and trudged our gear to the sideline, we had no idea that we were in for one of the most intense and exciting games any of us would ever be part of. It was a brilliant sunny day for ultimate and the first half was like a lot of Sunday first halves as two sore and sleepy teams tried to run themselves awake. After going down 1-0, I put up a long flick to Monkey Arms Mark for our first goal to tie it as the whole sideline yelled, "Hospital connection!"

From there, we forced a turn and I went deep, skying a guy to catch a huck that DJ Clayton had gotten off with a massive fake against a hard mark. After tossing the goal, he swerved down the field toward the end zone.

"That was a hell of a break," I said, patting him on the back.

He nodded and stared at me with bloodshot eyes. "The more hung over I am, the better I play," he said, his face turning green. "I could puke at any second. I'm gonna be spectacular today."

The first half went back and forth. Their offense went through their captain, this quick, lanky kid named Dieter. He was tearing us up, making spectacular play after spectacular play even with me or Mark draped all over him. It was frustrating. We kept missing big D's by an eyelash. Even with one more hospital connection, ECU took the half 8-5.

We came out rolling in the 2nd half and scored two straight to cut it to 8-7, then pinned them back in their own end zone on the pull. On their second pass, Appalachian Andrew suffocated the handler with a stupid good mark while I shut down the force side cut and DJ Clayton wore the dump option's pants. Panicked on stall nine, the thrower turned and threw it straight into Clayton's chest for the Callahan goal. We'd come back to tie it.

The rest of the half came in chunks. They'd score two and we'd come back and answer with two. They were up 12-11 when Mark's monkey arms allowed him to get a fingertip on a disc that was headed to my guy on an in cut just out of the end zone. The tip slowed rotation just enough to allow me to lay out over top of the dude and pin it to the grass. I stood up and flipped it to DJ Clayton to tie it 12-12.

On the next point, I thought for sure I had the big play we needed to change momentum and finally take the lead. Monkey Arms Mark was guarding their big guy Dieter while I was matched up on this other quick dude. They got a big chunk of yardage on a 25-yard flick to the center of the field to one of their deeps. The guy I was guarding took off for the end zone and I was right at his hip until I saw Dieter stop and go back toward the disc. Their whole offense flowed through him so I knew exactly where the deep wanted to throw it.

As we sprinted past the thrower, I dropped off my guy, slashed to the right and dove, sailing in from behind get a full hand on what should've been an easy two-yard reset. For a second there, I was really damn proud of myself. I'd made a sneaky little ghost D that was going to swing the pendulum squarely in our favor.

That was until Dieter reacted quick enough to snatch a bullet out of the air. He threw his hand out, accidentally knocking it straight down his own leg until with equal amounts skill and dumb luck, he kicked the edge of the disc back up with his toe and pinned the damn thing to his thigh.

"Really?" I managed to mumble from the ground.

As I scrambled to my feet, I was going to yell for Monkey Arms Mark to switch guys until I realized he was standing right next to me. We were like two dudes who got to the bus stop a minute too late as we watched the inevitable huck to my wide-open guy sail through the air. I swear

Mark rested his elbow on my shoulder as we followed it through the sky.

"Well, shit," I said as the guy caught the goal to put them up 13-12.

But we were resilient Whores. We scored the next goal, then got a turn and used about forty safe, crisp passes to work it the length of the field to go up 14-13. It was our first lead of the game. Channeling their championship history, ECU didn't let the pressure get to them and came back to score the next goal setting up universe point. And this universe point was everything a universe point should be. It had drama, stupidity, excitement, controversy, heroic injuries, and a couple of awesome hat spikes.

As we retreated down the field to receive the pull, I was hopping around like a jackrabbit. "Beautiful day, boys! Universe point. It doesn't get better than this. It doesn't get better than this. Let's go!"

That moment represented the very best of what ultimate can bring into your life. It was 9:30 on a beautiful morning that I otherwise would've slept through back in Pennsylvania. I was on the line with new friends who I was going to share an early beer with win or lose. And we were all about to get the opportunity to be heroes in this small little corner of the world.

The problem with universe point is that you also assume the very real possibility of morphing into a goat. They sent a high, hanging pull that I picked up a couple yards out of the end zone. As the defense charged down and set on us, I turned to see Vlad coming in hard on the break side so I stepped around my mark hoping to start a series of up-line breaks. Unfortunately, Vlad wasn't aware of my plan and changed his angle at the last second. I tried to hold up but couldn't. What came out of my hand was the equivalent of a wet fart. The disc sailed high and behind him and just like that, ECU had it twenty yards from the winning score.

I hung my head. Beautiful points on beautiful days aren't supposed to end that ugly. After having the tournament of my life, I was going to have to live with pissing away the opportunity for an exciting comeback victory. All I could hope for now was one more chance.

Amazingly enough, I got it. ECU swung it across the field and my guy made a cut to the front cone that I shut down. With a couple of choppy steps, he turned and headed for the back corner. I thought I had it covered until the handler put an outside-in backhand over my head. I tracked it and leapt, but it was just out of reach. I whiffed and tumbled to the ground. In front of me, the East Carolina guy dove and made a fingertip grab just off the top of the grass.

Kneeling there on the field, I pulled my visor the whole way down over my birdhouse-sized bandage. I'd blown it. Not only had I turned it over with my worst pass in months - I'd topped it off by getting burned for the score. It was an inglorious ending to an otherwise amazing - wait, nobody was cheering. Out of the corner of my eye I noticed the back cone a couple inches behind me. Which meant…..

The kid popped up and dropped the disc with a disgusted grunt. He was five feet out the back of the end zone. I'd gotten a temporary reprieve. Our disc. I intended to take full advantage.

On our second go, we got *two* passes completed before Vlad turfed a flick. Once again, ECU got the disc twenty yards from the winning goal. As we tried to march out of our end zone, they'd switched up their defense and now this very short but quick little dude with a red beard and backwards cap was guarding me. Off the turnover, I matched up against him as they set a vertical stack play in the end zone.

He was the second to last guy in the stack as Dieter picked up the disc. We were forcing flick. When the disc was tapped into play, Redbeard took two steps toward the flick side, then stopped and jetted around the back of the stack for the break side. I can't stress this enough – I wasn't fooled. Coming back through the stack, I was close enough to give him a wedgie if I felt like it. He was not going to be open. Not even close.

That all changed when the last guy in the stack put a shoulder directly into my sternum. He saw me coming and lowered his scapula straight into my chest. It stopped me cold and while I didn't fall down, all the air temporarily abandoned my lungs.

I tried to yell "PICK" as loud as I could, but it came out a deflated, "pih…"

Admittedly, Redbeard was wide the hell open. Dieter threw a sweet break that hit him within a yard of the goal line. The kid's eyes were manhole covers when he turned around and realized no one was marking him. There were so many options. This was a sure goal.

"Pick!" I finally managed to yell from the back of the stack.

It took the little dude a second to find the source of the sound, but when he did, he shot me a glare like he'd caught me taking a dump in his hat.

"No! No way! No! Three yards. You have to be within three yards! No way!"

"I was three *inches* behind you when your guy put a shoulder into my chest!"

"You can't decide it's a pick just because I burned you!" he yelled. "Three yards! You are nowhere *near* me!"

"I called pick as soon as it happened," I said, trying to remain calm. "Your guy here just knocked the wind out of me and it....didn't come out for a second."

(To be honest, I realized how lame it sounded as soon as I said it.)

Redbeard was not going to be persuaded. This was going to be his Butt Foul. He ripped his hat off and two-hand slammed it to the goal line. "You can't call a pick just cause I burned your ass!"

Now I was starting to get annoyed. I pointed at the kid in the back of the stack. "Ask your boy here. He knows what he did."

The son of a bitch just shrugged. He put his head down and stared at the grass.

"Dude, have some integrity," I said to him. But for him the grass was *really* interesting.

Finally Redbeard realized there was nothing he could do, so he fired the disc back at Dieter and came steaming back toward the stack.

"Just cause you can't keep up with me doesn't mean it's a pick," he grumbled.

Now I was full on ticked. There have been a select few times in my career when a guy said something that set off a seething, competitive concentration that took my normally scatterbrained mind to a level I can only describe as "Now you're fucked," mode. If I could've somehow played a majority of my career in that zone, I'd have been one of the best players of all time. But the thing about "Now you're fucked" mode though, is it's really, really damn hard to sustain. So I wasn't.

I took a deliberate step in front of him, leaned in, squatted down slightly and looked directly into his eyes. "You're so damn good, burn me for real," I said, facing him like a defensive back.

Behind me, I heard Monkey Arms Mark yell, "Coming in on three!"

As soon as I heard the smack of the disc, Redbeard tried the same move. I jabbed in front of him and cut off his route to the force side. As he stopped and went the other way, he tried to push off, allowing me to knock him off stride with a well-placed forearm. I jumped his break side cut. He had nowhere to run, his pride taking him to the same spot, but I had him smothered like a grease fire.

Keep talking, superstar.

As satisfied as I was at stuffing the little motor mouth, I turned around to see us once again on the verge of catastrophe. After Dieter looked off the break side cut, he turned back toward the force side and saw the kid who'd picked me a minute earlier running wide open near the front cone. An easy flick and the game was theirs.

What happened next almost defies belief. Carolina Ian wasn't even coming up on radar as Dieter let go of the pass. And then like something out of Area 51, a tiny blip appeared. Suddenly everything slowed into Matrix-style bullet time. For a second all natural laws were suspended. Sound and light warped around him as he flew like a superhero over the guy's shoulder, hovering for multiple frames as his left hand slowly ripped through space and time.

When he hit the ground, the world resumed. The disc was rolling toward some gym bags on the sideline. It took all of us on the field a second to recognize what had happened. Carolina Ian had appeared from another dimension to save us. We were still alive.

As I wiped my brow and ran out to the vertical stack, I realized that Redbeard was still on me. He may have been quick, but he was also like 5'6." I knew all I had to do was drift to the back of the stack and wait. I wasn't moving until someone was in position to hang one downfield.

East Carolina was angry at having their chance at victory taken away by Carolina Ian's ridiculous D and my unfortunately legitimate pick call. They were buzzing around like hornets. Monkey Arms Mark picked up the disc and had nowhere to go with it, flipping it back into the end zone for DJ Clayton. Another nine seconds without an opening and Clayton had to flip it sideways to Mark just to reset. Two more passes and we were still in our own end zone. Their defense had turned stifling. Mark spun to dump it back to Clayton but this time the DJ was stuffed. On stall eight Mark rotated to look upfield. Nothing. Now desperate, he cocked his arm back. Here came the punt I'd been waiting for.

He's thrown better hammers in his life. It was sky high and drifting way off to the left, but I wasn't too concerned. The higher the throw, the better my chances were. Unfortunately, it hung so long that it allowed Appalachian Andrew's defender a chance to run back and join the party. At midfield, I slowly drifted to the left with it, keeping Redbeard in front of me as he tried his damnedest to box me out. As the other defender spun around with a futile, dizzy jump, I leapt above both of them, casually popping the disc toward the sideline. I landed, boxed out Redbeard and caught it, sticking both feet in bounds just before the line.

Appalachian Andrew was wide open. Because Mark's crappy hammer had drawn his defender to me, I turned to see him streaking down the field completely and totally alone. I lofted a high release flick toward the end zone. Victory was ours.

Then the disc kept going. And going. And going. I was so excited that I accidentally ripped the damn thing much harder than I wanted. Andrew went from a run to a jog, back to a run, and then into an all out sprint as he realized it wasn't going to simply float into his chest for him to pancake like it should've. I put my hands to the sides of my head and dug my nails into my scalp. I was about to blow universe point for the second time in five minutes.

It's hard to let out a relieved sigh and an overexcited cheer at the same time, but I managed to do it when he laid out and grabbed it about two feet off the grass. He went sliding on his chest out the back of the end zone, but he was clearly in bounds when he caught it. I pumped my fist and went sprinting down to jump on him.

When I arrived, I expected him to pop up in celebration, but he just sort of remained on his back staring at the sky, sporting a gigantic smile crossed with a bit of a grimace - henceforth to be known as a smimace.

"Hell yeah! Way to run that down! Way to get there. Way to fuckin' get there!" I shouted, reaching down to smack the hand he held up for me to high five. It was then that I noticed his other hand clutching his left hamstring.

"Oh yeah, that's a popped hammy," he grunted. "That is *on* fire."

"Oh shit," I said. It was an injury I was way too familiar with. "I'm sorry, dude. I just didn't want to leave it short of the end zone."

"It's ok. Always wanted a layout to end a game on universe. I gotta shred my hamstring to do it, I'm fine with that. Cause now people will ask why I'm limping. And I get to tell them about the layout. Oh yes… believe me when I say I'm fine with it."

I slapped his hand again. "Andrew, you are a badass motherfucker with his head on straight."

As the two of us celebrated, it struck me as odd that none of our teammates had mobbed us yet. It was long past the point that we should've been tackled or at least man hugged. Curiously, I turned around. Everyone was frozen in place on the field exactly where they'd been standing when Mark let go of the hammer.

Well this isn't good.

From the entire way down the field over a hundred yards away, Mark cupped his hands around his mouth. I could barely hear him. "Contested stall! Gotta send it back!"

"What?" I yelled back.

Everyone started waving their hands gesturing for me to throw it back, allowing me to figure out what Mark's distance-muted message had been.

"Aaaarrrghhhh," I grumbled.

"What was that?" Andrew said from the ground.

I dropped my head. "Your hero story just took an unwanted turn."

Andrew had torn his hamstring so badly that he couldn't even walk off the field. Toronto Alex and I threw his arms around our shoulders and helped him hop to the sideline where he was immediately given liquid medicine in the form of a Coors Light.

As he popped it open, he looked at me. "Don't let my sacrifice be in vain."

So after thinking we'd won the game, we had to return the disc about as far as a disc has ever been returned. It was more than a bit deflating.

I casually strolled back to my position at the back of the stack. To my surprise, they didn't switch defenders. Even after I'd easily skied him, Redbeard still wanted to stuff me and gloat. This was fine with me. It was going to make things a lot easier. They tapped it in and I truly thought Monkey Arms Mark was going to float another shit hammer into the void. Instead he faked it and quickly dumped it to DJ Clayton, who swung it to Vlad. After damn near ten minutes of real time, we were finally out of our own end zone.

I probably should've done more cutting on that point, but my match-up was so favorable that all I did was hang out and wait for a chance to go deep. I ended up just milling around as I watched the rest of the guys weave it upfield. The disc was swinging virtually unimpeded from sideline to sideline. Next thing I know we're at midfield. A few more swings and we're encroaching on the goal line. By now I'd drifted back into the end zone.

Toronto Alex swung it off the left sideline to DJ Clayton. I saw the play developing and accelerated toward the front corner. Redbeard was two steps behind me. DJ Clayton caught it, turned, and saw me. He lofted a backhand high into the air.

The throw wasn't crisp. As I leapt, it drifted behind me. I was reaching back when I felt a shoulder come up through the back of my legs. Redbeard was trying to flip me from underneath. I should take that back. I don't know if that was his actual intention, but he was frustrated enough that I wouldn't have put it past him. Either way, I thought I was going over backwards onto my head.

But I wasn't missing that disc. Not on universe point. Not when my overexcited throw had already popped a guy's hamstring. Not when the guy who'd told me I couldn't keep up with him was currently fouling the shit out of me. My back was nearly parallel to the ground as I reached up across my face and caught it with both hands just behind the crown of my head. Now all I had to do was hang on.

It didn't feel pleasant when my spine bent the wrong way over Redbeard's shoulder. I'm sure it didn't do wonders for his neck either. My legs swung down, miraculously planting me on my feet instead of my head. Not only was I upright – I was holding the winning goal.

Nomad Whores 15

East Carolina 14

I wanted to turn and spike the disc at Redbeard's feet but that would've been about as classless as it gets, so instead I totally ignored him. I just held the disc in the air and walked off to the sideline as the rest of the Whores rushed in to pound on my back.

Redbeard punted his hat. They didn't shake our hands. Three or four of them were bitching the whole way off the field. And I was smiling from ear to ear. There's nothing quite like catching the winning goal of a hotly contested universe point. It's ultimate's walk-off homer.

The victory felt good. We enjoyed it for five entire minutes because one look at the bracket told us our ride through the tournament wasn't going much further.

Next up was Raleigh Ring of Fire, the perennial nationals contender. And uh, like you might expect, it didn't turn out so well. They identified what matchups they could take advantage of and exploited our weaknesses with ease. Monkey Arms Mark and I made a couple of big D's early in the game so they just adjusted and quit going to the guys we were guarding. We spent most of the game standing beside our decoys watching hucks fly over our heads to wide-open guys.

On the bright side, we did have four or five hospital connections. Our final one came when Mark threw a hammer dump that I had to lay out for. I scrambled up as he shot to the back of the end zone with his defender all over him. How I knew the exact second he was going to stop and turn around, I have no idea. It's probably because it's what I would've done. I zipped a flick before he even turned around that hit him in the stomach the moment he did. It cut the score to 14-10.

The Ring guy marking me laughed. "Ya know we can get the two of you jobs in Raleigh." I'm sure he was kidding, but it made my day. And don't think Mark and I didn't discuss it on the ride home.

After another virtually uncontested huck, the Whores were out of the tournament. But despite the trench in my forehead, the whole thing was an amazing success. We all hauled our coolers a couple of fields over to watch Barnacle Julie and Ho Stack play in the women's championship game. I think they won. I can't remember. All I recall is Julie's happy little bunny hops after both of her goals. She was so thrilled that I'd been there to see them that after the game she barnacled me for about two hours.

She kissed me on the cheek and wrapped herself around me. "Let me know if I'm squeezing too hard."

"Oh, you're concerned about my health now?" I said with a smile. "This is new."

"I was always concerned. I was!" she whined. "They needed me in the game."

"My boyfriend has a gaping head wound," I laughed. "I'm sure he's fine. I'll pay it no mind."

She buried her face in my chest and giggled. "I've said I'm sorry like fifty times."

"No mind at all. There's plenty of fish in the sea."

After a chilly morning, it was surprisingly warm as we sat around sipping on cold beers with DJ Clayton, Toronto Alex, and Appalachian Andrew telling the story of Julie's lack of distress the day before. We still had a seven-hour drive ahead of us but for that moment, our weary legs and bodies were enjoying the sun and the company.

As I cracked open another cold one, (hell, I wasn't the one driving) I nudged Monkey Arms Mark. "Remember back on Friday night when I asked you why the hell we do this to ourselves?"

He leaned back to relax as we all laughed around him. "Yeah," he said, looking up at the clear blue sky. "It's all starting to come back to me."

TWENTY-NINE

Until January of 2005, I had never heard of the University of California at Riverside. Didn't have a clue that such a place existed. For a guy born and raised in Pittsburgh's shitty eastern suburbs, California might as well have been a foreign country.

Barnacle Julie had done her research. Apparently UCR had one of the finest graduate programs in Shakespearean Literature on this side of the pond. And she really, really wanted to go - which we both realized pretty quickly was going to be a major obstacle to the future of our relationship. So we just sort of coasted along ignoring the problem until a list of zany things happened almost concurrently.

I lost my school counseling job in York County because my buffoon of a principal had become convinced I was a warlock. I really wish I was kidding. He thought I got along "a little too well" with the Goth kids and made up an insane story about how I was traipsing off into the woods at night to perform spells with them. (Which is ridiculous because if I really had been off performing spells, I'd have killed off his cranky ass long before he had a chance to confront me about it.) Apparently I was supposed to scold and ostracize students for being weird and different instead of helping them graduate and get into college. My fault entirely.

The week I found out my contract was being terminated, Julie tried to cheer me up by researching graduate programs in creative writing. One of the most interesting was the exciting new playwriting program at UCR, the school she was hoping to get into. (I wrote plays on the side and by that time my work had been seen at a few big festivals.) Truth be told, I had no desire to return to school. But she was insistent. The application deadline was fast approaching, so one day she printed out all the materials I'd need to apply and brought them over to my apartment in a little packet.

"We could go to school together in California," she said sweetly. "It would be amazing."

I just smiled and kissed her on the forehead. I only applied because she was so excited about it. Also, I figured it could buy our relationship another month or two before we had to make any concrete decisions. It was worth a shot. I applied, sent in the application and promptly forgot all about it.

I forgot about it mainly because a stroke of luck had the 6th grade counselor at Gettysburg Area Middle School taking a sudden sabbatical for the last half of the school year. Staring down unemployment as January approached, I applied and mainly since no one else with any experience had shown interest - ended up getting hired. And it was the complete antithesis of my previous job. The administration was supportive, the teachers and staff were welcoming, and they actually (gasp) cared about the welfare of the kids. I loved it.

On nice days after lunch, the kids were allowed outside to run around, play, make fun of each other's clothes, and scoff at authority. On the first sunny and warm day of the semester, I saw one of the skater kids stroll into the cafeteria with a disc. And it wasn't a piece of junk from a car dealership either. It was a Discraft 175.

I walked up to his lunch table. "Is that an ultimate disc?"

His eyes lit up like I just told him he'd won a free brownie. "You know about ultimate?"

"I've played a little bit," I laughed. "Is it cool if I toss with you guys when you head outside?"

"Sure. Yeah!" he said excitedly before realizing he was in 8th grade. "I mean, whatever, man. It's cool."

As soon as the skater kids finished their lunches, they waved to me and I followed them out into the afternoon. Technically I was supposed to be watching out for kids punching each other and stuff. And I did - in the moments I wasn't launching 70-yard flicks in dress pants that had the kids completely dumbstruck. Which was a good thing. When you work at a middle school, the students assume you're a useless lame ass whose sole purpose on the planet is to ruin their fun. The burden of proof is squarely on you to prove otherwise. My Frisbee wizardry helped the kids realize I was an actual human. I was no longer the new guy they didn't know anything about. Afterward there was a marked uptick in students voluntarily knocking on my door to talk about their problems before things went haywire in the hallway.

The cool thing was that as the recess game got popular, the kids wanted a chance to play for more than ten minutes a pop. So they asked me if we could start an after school ultimate club. And of course there was no debate. The administration gave me their full support, I got permission slips from parents and next thing I knew, I was the coach of a middle school ultimate team. Once a week, we practiced and scrimmaged for ninety minutes on the football field out behind the school. And just like the program that Havelock Ben and I ran in West Virginia, the kids loved it. Every Thursday they ran, threw, dove, and discovered. They were Internet-era kids who grew up inside staring at a screen all day. And yet because of ultimate they were outside running around on nice afternoons like kids have been doing since the dawn of time.

One of the 7th grade science teachers ran the Gettysburg High School team. He was a big lumberjack of a guy everyone called Coach Scott. Seeing how well the middle school program was going, he invited me to help out up at the high school as well.

The great thing about sports in general is that they always seem to figure out a way to break barriers and create incredible, uniquely human moments – moments that help us realize that in all this insanity, perhaps there really is something out there greater than ourselves. I was lucky enough to have one of those profound moments on the field at Gettysburg Area High School.

Most of the kids who played with us were pretty damn good athletes - fifteen to seventeen year olds, track stars, soccer players, and even the semi-coordinated band kids. All of them were the picture of health, right on the verge of entering their physical prime. Their entire lives were ahead of them - except for one kid. He was a wisecracking, intelligent, kind of geeky senior who I'll refer to as John. Sometime during the previous year, John had been diagnosed with ALS. If you're unfamiliar, it's the neuromuscular disorder that struck down Yankees Hall of Famer Lou Gehrig. At that point, John was relegated to a wheelchair but still had limited use of his arms and could still jabber like nobody's business. The kid's attitude in spite of his condition was bafflingly upbeat.

Aside from only being able to go as fast as his mechanized wheelchair would allow, the kid wasn't bad. He could throw a decent flick and backhand. Unfortunately, as we neared the end of the season, he still hadn't scored a goal.

"Today's the day," he'd say to his friends. "Today's the day I take one of you punks deep and you'll smell something odd…something different in the air. You'll sniff and sniff and wonder, 'John, what's that?' And I'll be like, 'It's toast. What you're smelling is toast.'"

And to their credit, they never let him get behind them. Cause he'd have known. He didn't want any bullshit charity. We were near the end of a closely contested scrimmage when I got the disc on the right sideline. John kind of snuck up the opposite sideline without anyone seeing him. He was probably forty yards away and the entire way across the field when I saw him put his arms up to let me know he was open.

This was his chance - his one great opportunity at a legitimate goal. If I'd have taken any time to consider the significance of it, I probably would've psyched myself right into an overthrow. Luckily I didn't. I faked a flick to draw in the backside defense, then pivoted and let go a high, hanging backhand. A yard out of my hand, I knew it had a chance. It was right on target.

It played out in slow motion like the critical moment in a cheesy teen sports movie. Inspirational synthesizer music filled my brain as the disc descended towards him. One of the kids on the other team jumped but couldn't reach it. John read it, backed his wheelchair up a couple feet and pancaked the disc in the back corner of the end zone.

It took the kids a second to realize who'd scored the goal but when they did, they went berserk. His teammates sprinted over and mobbed him, slapped him on the back, humped his wheelchair, and did all the things overzealous high school kids do. Even the guys on the other team walked over to slap his hand, congratulate him, and mess up his hair. John had caught a huck. For a goal.

"Does anyone else smell toast?" he yelled. "Anyone? I think the cafeteria's getting an early start on tomorrow's breakfast."

The kid was *beaming* as I strolled over to high five him. "Nice catch, dude. Way to read the disc."

"You put it straight in my lap. I didn't do anything," he said, deflecting the credit.

"You could've let it donk off your crotch. And you didn't."

He was desperately trying to not make it a big deal, but we all knew it was. And the cool thing was that when all the seniors hung out by the cars with us recapping the games, John wasn't just ripping on the other guys and providing comic relief. He had his own story to tell. I have no idea if John's still alive. I'm sure I could find out, but to be honest, I don't want to. In my career I've thrown tens of thousands of passes. And that right there is my absolute favorite one.

I had no idea my life would change so drastically that spring. Julie and I broke up after an ill-fated ski trip in March only to get back together and break up for good at an ultimate tournament that April. She wanted to experience her last semester of college uninhibited and I didn't particularly want to wait for her on the other side of it. The breakup sucked but I guess every relationship, no matter how good is always a bit shaky when you're young. (Or uh, 27 for me in this case) But even though forever wasn't in the cards for us, Barnacle Julie ended up being a central figure in my life for one very big reason - making me apply to UC-Riverside.

I'd totally forgotten I'd even applied. Without Julie around to mention it, the whole thing completely slipped my mind. They called on a Monday afternoon. Unfortunately, I was out in the woods - literally. Every year Gettysburg Middle School's 6th graders spend five days and four nights at a camp just off the Appalachian Trail outside of Waynesboro, PA. It's an amazing week where they do science lessons in the forest, make art projects out of acorns, and learn about astronomy at night. It's a fantastic experience for the kids. As you might expect, it's also an absolute zoo for the teachers, especially for a counselor like me who was basically on duty 24/7.

A bunch of my middle school ultimate players were up there during the week and wanted to put a game together each recess. This would've

been simple to set up except the camp itself was on the side of a mountain. The only flat space around was an abandoned barn next to the
nurse's cabin. So we made due.

"Ok, guys, one rule," I said. "No laying out. I'm serious. There's a lot
of weird stuff in here. Rusty paint cans and pitchforks….and I'm thinking that thing in the corner might be a dead goat, so…"

"You got it Mr. Cramer. No laying out."

And of course three passes into the first game, a kid lays out into a
tractor. Which, let's face it, after years of playing ultimate, I should've
seen coming. You can't just let a disc hit the ground without making a
bid. Otherwise the terrorists win.

Anyway, that camp was awesome for one other ultimate-related reason as well. My Harrisburg teammate Shameless Wyatt had started the
Appalachian Trail that March. He was walking north from Georgia and
on the occasions when he made it to some random mountain town, he'd
find his way to a public computer and blog about the experience. One
day after school, I checked on his progress only to find….

*Worst news of the day? I was tossing with Snacks and one of my throws got past
him. My disc rolled into a ravine. No tossing until November? I don't know how I'm
going to survive. This might be the thing that keeps me from finishing!"*

The moment I realized the trail was less than half a mile from our
camp, I knew what I had to do. I dug in my trunk for one of my old road
discs and hiked over, taking detailed mental notes of my surroundings as
I plunged down the mountain. Once I got back to town, I emailed him.

*Right after you cross into Pennsylvania, you'll go down a mountain toward PA
Route 16. Just before the road is a creek. About fifty yards up from that creek is a
huge fallen tree just off the trail to the left. Check underneath it.*

Luckily no one else was checking for treasure underneath fallen trees
that spring and he found the disc sometime in mid-June. I can just imagine him throwing down his pack and dancing the minute he saw it. Wyatt
had it with him when he scaled Maine's Mt. Katahdin that October to
complete the 2,180 mile journey. And because of him, I can now say I've
completed nearly a *half-mile* of the Appalachian Trail.

I got back to my apartment in York that Friday and checked the mes-
sages on my machine. (Yes, I *still* didn't have a cell phone) As I stood

there staring at the wall, anticipating nothing of any importance, I heard the following….

"Hi Kevin, this is Janice from the University of California at Riverside. Please call us back. You've been accepted to the program and we'd like to offer you some money."

I squinted at the wall for a good minute. It was the last thing I expected after arriving home from five days in the wilderness with a bunch of 6th graders. In reality, all I wanted was a nap. Bleary-eyed and half delirious, I called them back, having to first explain that I hadn't been ignoring them, I'd just been on the side of a mountain since Monday morning. Turned out, the playwriting program at UCR had recently decided to aggressively recruit people from outside of southern California and I happened to be a great fit. They offered me a full ride - a free degree.

Damn, I was headed to California.

That September, my dad and I packed everything I owned into my two-door Chevy Cavalier and took off across the country. My father was 58 at the time and had never seen the Mississippi River. He'd never seen the Rockies. He'd never seen the Pacific Ocean. We spent five awesome days pointed west on I-70 and I-15 stopping in gorgeous places like Glenwood Canyon, the San Rafael Reef, and Zion National Park. The whole way through Utah, my dad's face was pressed to the window like an eight year old kid. It was the best five days of my life.

We crossed into California on a hot, disgusting Sunday morning that made the smog loiter above the desert, but I couldn't help it – even my appalled lungs were excited. The trouble was school didn't actually start for three weeks - so after my dad flew back to Pittsburgh, I found myself 2,000 miles away from home without much to do. Outside of the lovely folks at the Riverside DMV, I wasn't privy to much human interaction. The whole time I was thinking, "I'm only a fourth of a mile from a college campus. There *has* to be an ultimate game nearby." So one day I drove around town to identify all of the soccer fields in the area and gerrymandered my nightly run to pass by all of them hoping that by some random miracle I'd happen upon people tossing a disc.

Ten days into my California adventure, my miracle arrived. I was jogging past the intramural fields when I saw a guy drop a bag on the sideline and start changing into his cleats. Next to him was a round white object approximately the size of a….*holy shit!*

I sprinted through the gate with a grin that could've swallowed a canoe and accosted the guy. He was a balding dude in his early 40's with the wiry athletic body of a college kid.

"You have a disc and you're putting on cleats," I said hyper-excitedly. "Please tell me you're about to play ultimate."

(I resisted the urge to tell him, *"You don't know it, but I've been stalking you since I arrived from Appalachia."*)

He looked up, calm as could be and said. "Yup. Seven-thirty. Everyone else should be getting here soon."

"Sweet," I said, shaking his hand. "Cramer."

"Neill," he responded just before I turned and sprinted down University Avenue to grab my cleats and a disc.

And thus began my west coast ultimate career. Most of it was spent running around on Tuesday and Thursday nights under the lights in the middle of the UCR campus. In Southern California, the area around Riverside and San Bernardino is called "The Inland Empire." Players came from all around, east from Pomona, south from Redlands, and sometimes in the whole way in from Palm Springs. It turned out to be nearly as great a pickup scene as we'd had back in Jacksonville.

There were great characters here as well. Neill was a freak of nature who at 42 was still one of the fastest players on the field. In complete contrast was Les, a slow, old hippie professor who'd played on the original team at the University of Arizona. He had long gray hair and a beard and was pretty much made of wiseness. Our grad student contingent included Rob, a history major who sported a different Civil War-style beard each month, Albert, a Chinese guy with a buzz cut who chucked hammers all over the field, and George, an Oregonian surfer who'd played at Willamette University and was so damned handsome everyone just assumed he was in LA to be an actor even though he was actually getting his PhD in Spanish.

Our women were amazing players too. We had Kim, a pale, vegan redhead who'd played at the Carleton College ultimate factory, Theresa, an impossible to cover doctor who'd played at the University of Florida, and Robin, a stunningly beautiful botanist from Idaho who was such a perfectionist that any throwaways or drops ate at her for hours despite never having played before.

In a freaky coincidence, there was also a balding guy with a thin beard who looked exactly like Receding Eddie from Jacksonville – just stretched out a foot or so. Except for the height difference, they were *perfect* doppelgangers. And just like Receding Eddie, this was the guy on the field who did everything wrong nearly all the time. He was the guy who'd unabashedly fire a wobbly hammer into triple coverage, swear he'd never do it again, and then throw a worse one into quadruple coverage on the next point. He was the guy who'd drop four wide open tosses in a row and then be cranky that you looked him off. He was the guy who everyone tolerated but loved at the same time because he was such a character.

And the cherry on top of the whole thing? His name was goddamned Eddie. To this day I've never been totally convinced that Receding Eddie from Jacksonville wasn't part of a genetic experiment gone wrong and placed in witness protection on the west coast.

The night I found the game, I knew my time in the Golden State was going to be all right. Near the end of that first night, Wise Les got way behind everyone and Freak Neill put up a bomb to the end zone. Les had ten yards to cover and I had forty. And uh - I got there first. Wise Les was as crafty as they come but even veteran savvy couldn't mask the fact that he was in his fifties. I jumped over him to snag the disc and took it back to the goal line to tap it in. As Wise Les shuffled over to mark me, I happened to look up at the sky and almost dropped the disc. Above everyone in the dying sunset, a giant orange and red missile trail snaked through the dusk. It looked like a neon python from Mars. I pointed to the sky.

"Not to alarm anyone, but it seems like the world is ending."

Our carefully positioned vertical stack fell apart as everyone looked up, slack-jawed. None of us had ever seen anything like it. Above us seemed to be the fissure that the horsemen of the apocalypse were about to burst through. We'd been so focused on the final few points of the game that no one had noticed the beginning stages of Armageddon.

"What the hell is that?" War Beard Rob shouted.

"Oh good," Handsome George said. "The sky is on fire. I hope nobody minds but I'm going to sub out and hide under the bleachers."

I pointed upward. "I take it this is abnormal? I just got to California last week. For all I know this could happen a couple times a month."

"Being nuked by the Russians?" Handsome George answered, hustling to the sideline. "Not an everyday occurrence. If you're smart, you'll join me over in the fallout shelter."

Carleton Kim started chewing on one of her long, red pigtails. "Yeah, I'm fine with a tie game. I'm following George."

"We're tied with one point to go," Idaho Robin said. "Don't you think we should finish? Aren't we being a tad bit dramatic?"

"Fine," George yelled. "I guess it'll be up to me and Kim to repopulate the Earth. We'll tell the grandkids stories about all of you."

"Oooh, George," Kim said. "Dirty apocalypse sex in the gravel under the bleachers. How could a girl resist?"

I was walking briskly toward the sideline when it occurred to me, "So am I still invited or…"

"Hmmm," George said. "I don't know. That might get weird. We'd be friends at first but after a while we'd start arguing about whose turn it was to impregnate Kim. I don't want things to get complicated. Hate to do this but I retract my invite."

Beside me, Wise Les stared at the sky. "It's ok," he said to me. "You seem like the type of guy who'd rather die on the field than huddled under some bleachers anyway."

"Wow, Les. You're right. You're a very wise man."

"So I've been told."

Kim stopped and turned around. "Yeah, Les is right. I'd rather die on the field. And I'm not sure that those bleachers could survive a nuclear blast anyway."

"Blasphemy!" Handsome George yelled, jogging back onto the field. "If humanity goes extinct, it's on all of your heads!"

I don't remember who won. But I do know that even in the face of what could've been the beginnings of a nuclear war, we decided to finish universe point. Turned out it was simply a satellite launched from Vandenberg Air Force Base reacting in a very odd way with the pollutants in the Riverside sky. Sorry if I caused any alarm. No need to panic. You're still alive.

That night was the first of many nights that I'd gather with that sweaty crew of people for a beer or five at The Getaway, the only bar within walking distance of campus. It turned into a tradition over the next few years. Done with ultimate? It's time for a $10 pitcher of Sierra Nevada and a lot of laughing with friends out on the patio. Ultimate had delivered exactly what I hoped it would. I'd moved the whole way across the country not knowing a soul and within two weeks I was sharing beers with friends I swore I'd known much longer than a few hours.

My ultimate experience changed in California. No longer was I practicing or playing for a particular team whose goal was regionals or nationals. No, we just played hard amongst ourselves on Tuesday and Thursday nights - great spirited and incredibly fun games under the lights. We weren't very organized until one night when War Beard Rob put up a flick to Carleton Kim along the sideline. Doctor Theresa undercut her. What followed was one of the sickest double layouts I've ever seen. Both women cut through the air at the same downward angle. Somehow Kim made the grab over Theresa, who must've flown in from three yards behind her. I was guarding Handsome George at the time and when it happened, we shared a stunned glance.

"We should really put together a co-ed team."

The team ended up being named IESB. (Inland Empire Strikes Back) Yet again, I ended up on a great team that no one knew about, mainly because it was hard for us to travel. The main crux of our team was made up of professors, doctors, and grad students doing critical research. It wasn't like we could all just head up to San Francisco for the weekend to sling around a disc. We were all off running theaters, curing disease, and cross-pollinating things.

Even so, we managed to win a tournament. It was a tiny co-ed tourney at the University of Redlands one warm and sunny December day beneath the San Jacinto Mountains. We rolled through the first couple games beating Redlands and then the club team from Palm Springs before meeting the other undefeated team, Long Beach State, in the final. Their big captain wound up and absolutely launched the opening pull of the game toward us – just ripped the damn thing. They were tall and athletic, but we knew we could exploit their inexperience. This was going to be an easy victory unless we did something like - start the game with a mystifyingly terrible decision.

I jogged out into the middle of the field and watched Receding Eddie II drift back for the disc, which was easily going to sail out the back of the end zone. I mean there was *no* way it was landing in bounds. Then as I settled into the stack, I watched in amazement as Eddie put his heels against the back line and inexplicably jumped up and tried to catch the disc over his head with one hand. It boffed off his fingers and skittered away.

In one collective breath, Long Beach excitedly yelled, "Turnover!"

Our whole team reacted as if we'd been slapped by the same wet newspaper. "Eddie, what the hell are you doing?"

"Hey, get off my back. Things like this happen, ok?"

"No," Handsome George yelled. "They don't." He turned to me. "Cramer, you've played a lot. Ever see something like that happen?"

"Not a once."

"Ok. C'mon, guys," Receding Eddie II responded. "Quit jacking around. Quit jacking me off, ok? Guys have dropped the pull plenty of times. You act like it's never happened before. Geez. I'm sorry. Shit."

His inability to comprehend his error was almost comically stunning. From then on, IESB had one rule - Eddie wasn't allowed to catch the pull. George and I were assigned to tackle him if he tried.

Luckily, it didn't affect the outcome. They scored to take a 1-0 lead but from there we took control. With the score 14-7, I caught an in-cut and turned to see Neill throw a sick fake on a kid over twenty years younger and break open across the back of the end zone. I lined up a flick and sent a laser that smacked into his chest just as the kid recovered and laid out, missing it by an inch.

I only mention it because I've just now realized it was the only time in my life that one of my teams actually won a tournament. The 2005 Redlands One-Day - the only tourney where I can actually say my team came out on top. If I'd known what a singular moment it was, I'd have celebrated a little more. As it was I just sort of pumped my fist and nodded.

That year I played a lot of ultimate. Much like Harrisburg, I ended up a big fish in a small pond. I was the best player in the Inland Empire, but I knew there was a whole ocean of players out there beyond the 605. It was about time to see how I stacked up to the rest of Los Angeles.

Every year LA hosts a huge hat tournament around St. Patrick's Day called (drumroll) St. Pat's Hat. It's one of the largest hat tournaments in the country, attracting players from all over California. In 2006, there were sixteen full teams, all given T-shirts with a different shade of green.

Early that morning, I picked up Idaho Robin in Riverside and we set off across southern California for the fields 75 miles west of us in the San Fernando Valley. Idaho Robin was very meticulous about a lot of things including her athletic preparation. That morning and during the car ride, she ultra-hydrated, drinking the equivalent of a trash can full of water in an hour. The trouble was, her bladder was considerably smaller than a trash can, a fact that became clear to her somewhere on the 134 west of Pasadena.

"Cramer, I'm going to have to pee soon, so next exit, can we pull off and find a gas station?"

"Ok. No problem."

Little known fact about Los Angeles. There's a wacky bathroom desert right outside of Glendale. We pulled off at the next exit and spent five minutes driving around an industrial complex. By this time Robin was getting slightly uncomfortable, but no problem, we'd just get back on the freeway and get off at the next exit.

"Ooh, there's a sign for the zoo!" Robin said. "There's got to be somewhere to pee near the zoo. Kids go to the zoo. Kids have to pee all the time."

It seemed like a perfectly reasonable assumption. But we ended up on a nice drive in some green hills with lots of trees. It was beautiful. But it wasn't what we needed. We were smack in the middle of LA and somehow unable to locate urban sprawl. Now Robin was squirming and leaning forward, practically ripping out her ponytail.

"Cramer, I'm going to pee myself right here in your car if you don't find a gas station."

"There's a perfectly good culvert right there."

She slugged me in the shoulder. "I'm not peeing in a culvert!"

"That's what culverts are for!"

"I'm not pulling down my pants next to a freeway!"

We continued on that road only to find a nice park, another industrial complex, and like three consecutive residential developments. When we finally hit Burbank, it was all homes. Block after block of homes. By this time, Robin's face was as pale as a cloud. Her nails were digging into my forearm.

"Cramer, I'm going to explode if you don't find a gas station!"

"I'm not Burbank's city planner! What do you want me to do?"

Her eyes were filled with fire as she screamed like a demon into my ear. "Find... me...*a bathroom*!"

Finally after fifteen minutes of futile searching, we turned a corner to find a small mom & pop grocery store. I slowed down. "Hey, I think that's a..."

She was out of the car and sprinting before I even came to a full stop. Once inside, she apparently had to beg one of the cashiers to let her use the employees' only restroom by threatening to let loose right there at the register. Anyway, with traffic behind me, I figured I'd just go up to the next light to turn around. So I did. At a Shell Station. That was next to a Chevron. Across the street from a Texaco. Diagonal to a Taco Bell.

We got to the fields at Balboa Park to find ultimate everywhere - two hundred fifty people slinging discs around on a gorgeous Saturday morning. I got put on the Kelly Green team with Wise Les and a bunch of people from around Los Angeles, San Diego, and Santa Barbara. For a hat tournament, I was a little nervous. I'd been dominating a pretty good game out in the Inland Empire, but now I was going to be matched up against some of the top players in SoCal. Guys who played for the Santa Barbara Condors were there. Here came my first real test in the west.

Our team was pretty good. We had three guys who played for Monster, LA's club team at the time. I gelled with them immediately. Early in the second game, I went deep and leapt over the 6'3" club guy covering me, landed off balance and immediately hit one of the Monster guys in stride with a quick behind the backer for the goal. The whole field roared. I'd brought a bit of the Flagler Courtyard to the west coast. The

Monster guys came sprinting down to smack my hand.

"Cramer, where are you from?"

"Out in Riverside."

"You're playing for Monster this year, right? You don't want to drive the whole way to Santa Barbara. That'd be a pain in the ass. You want to play with us."

Holy shit, the LA club team is RECRUITING me! Away from a team I never thought I could play for in the first place!

I would've loved to play for Monster. But the day after the tournament my father called and told me he had kidney cancer. I wasn't going to stay in LA between semesters when I could be back home with my family.

There was also one more rather large factor as to why I didn't try out that April. And it happened in the very next game.

I was having another great game. I had a huge huck for one goal, and a bullet flick to one of the Monster guys for another one. We were rolling toward our second victory when I cut to the goal line and stopped quickly to come back to the disc. There was a burly but athletic dude covering me. One of the Monster guys threw one a bit low and to the right, but it was a pass I could easily lay out and snag. As I came out of my break, the burly guy bumped me just enough to send me stumbling. Still, I rotated in the air to extend and get my right arm under the disc for the catch.

Unfortunately, the burly guy had stumbled too. Next thing I know, there's 200 pounds or so on the outside of my left shoulder. This would've been fine if it hadn't driven my right shoulder into the ground. The force didn't have anywhere to escape. For a half second, I could feel all that energy desperately trying to leave my body until….

CRACK!

My right collarbone snapped. I knew it was bad immediately. I let out a guttural roar and flopped over.

The burly guy was genuinely apologetic. "Oh shit, I'm sorry, man. Are you alright?"

"Actually, I think I need a doctor if we can find one."

I was done for the next eight weeks or so. The field medic crafted a makeshift sling. I stayed around as our team played our last two games, cheering them on and drinking a lot of beer with my left arm as I tried to temporarily forget how much it hurt to breathe. Later, Robin and I skipped the tournament party and had a fun date night in the Riverside ER.

The team was great. At the end of the tournament, they voted me team MVP and most spirited. (Purely out of pity, but I'll take it) For sacrificing my collarbone, I got a sweet "I (Shamrock) Beer" T-shirt that I still have to this day.

But the great thing about St. Pat's Hat was even thought I got hurt, I at least proved I could hang with all the big boys in the big city. And that felt pretty damn good. And once I healed, I was on my way back to Pittsburgh for what turned out to be a very eventful ultimate summer.

THIRTY

STANDING ON THE SIDELINE AT EASTERNS THE DAY I SCORED THE ONE BIG goal I ever scored for Penn State was a skinny twelve-year-old kid from Little River, South Carolina. The youngest of my three cousins on my mother's side, Chris was athletically gifted if not particularly motivated. He was the type of laid back beach kid who played sports for the fun of it and not necessarily to win. He loved when I'd come to visit because I always brought a Frisbee. We'd spend hours in his backyard or down at the beach just chucking the thing back and forth in ridiculous ways where he could show off his athleticism without anyone barking at him to hustle.

My Aunt Diane had brought him up the King's Highway to Wilmington that morning to watch me play. Aunt Diane was a proud Penn State graduate and couldn't wait to watch her nephew play a sport she didn't understand for the university she loved. And while my other two cousins didn't seem particularly interested in anything other than lunch, my tiny cousin Chris hung on every pass. There was something about the intensity and precision of our game versus Ohio State that spoke to him in a way that basketball and soccer didn't. As I walked off the field after our zone had forced a turnover to help us take a 10-9 lead, the little goofy kid who barely ever showed emotion was cheering his head off.

"What do you think, buddy?" I said, jogging by him.

He didn't have an answer ready but something in his eyes said, *I want to do this someday.*

After we lost, I invited him out onto the field. And it was obvious he'd been practicing. He was tossing 40-yard flicks, hammers, scoobers - you name it, he threw it. And he caught everything I put near him, diving all over the place, turning his khaki shorts into a giant grass stain. In fact he was so good, Duffy yelled out to him from the sideline....

"Damn, kid, you could play for our B team right now."

Chris just shrugged. "Yeah, probably."

By the summer of 2006, that tiny kid was 6'4" and going into his senior year at North Myrtle Beach High School. Inspired by Easterns, Chris started a pickup game at a local park. Five years later, he was completely abusing the high school kids he played with, but he'd never seen any real game action. I knew that needed to change.

After driving across the country from California that June, I picked up on a local team called "Little Green Men" for the Mars Tournament that 4th of July weekend. Knowing Chris was going to be in town, I asked if there was room on the roster for my little cousin.

How little? Was the email response.

Well, he's only sixteen, but he's six-four.

Six-four? Yeah, there's room.

Our first game that morning was against a team of University of Michigan alums from Ann Arbor. We were up 2-0 when Cousin Chris entered the game and looked like a cross between a dog chasing after a tennis ball and a kid lost in the mall. On defense, he overran everything as he tried to get a block on every throw. On offense, he was zipping around with no particular purpose or direction. After getting burned for a goal because he'd wandered way out of position, Cousin Chris sulked to the sideline. He was used to dominating his little pickup game and not in any way prepared for the whooping he just took.

I walked up to him and laughed. "Ya know it just dawned me that you have no idea what you're doing."

"That occurred to me right in the middle of the point as well."

"Don't feel bad. All these guys either played for or still play for Michigan. They're not your chunky little buddy from down the road who can kind of throw a flick sometimes."

"No. No, they are definitely not Kyle."

I patted him on the back. "All right, man. You sit out the rest of this game. You watch me. Watch my positioning on defense. Watch my cuts on offense. Pay attention to where I go and at what times. You have any questions, you ask."

Amazingly enough, when I dove to pancake a hammer in the middle of the end zone, our scrappy little pickup team beat Ann Arbor 13-10. We were 1-0 at Mars. For me, this was uncharted territory.

At the beginning of the second game against Edinboro, I tapped Cousin Chris on the elbow. "You ready?"

"Uh, not quite yet," he answered.

He sat out the entire first half, still observing, still nervous to enter the game. But in the second half with many of our guys tiring out, he really had no choice. With a lot of encouragement from our sideline, he jogged in, ready to give it another try. To tell you the truth, I wasn't expecting much of a contribution from him. All I wanted was for Chris to experience the speed and precision of a real game – to get him used to the action. That all changed when I got trapped on the left sideline and put up a lob to one of our handlers, this greasy little dude named Cheese.

It would've been a perfectly fine throw except a gust of wind decided to hold it in the air at midfield about two yards from the sideline. Cheese stopped underneath it. So did his defender. And another defender. Damn thing morphed from a nice backhand lob into a total hospital pass. In fact, it hung so long it afforded me a second to check on Chris, who was chilling in the middle of the stack trying like hell to stay out of everyone's way. But the longer the disc stayed in the air, the more time he had to psyche himself up. I could almost read his thoughts through his eyes.

Ya know I bet I could get that.

He even gave a tiny nod to himself to confirm his idea. He took about five loping strides, planted his foot and took off. I can barely describe this catch other than to say that if there'd have been a camera on the three players huddled beneath the disc, Chris would've jumped from completely off screen. He caught it ten and a half feet in the air, a full torso above everyone else, curling his wrist like a swordsman as he grabbed it. When he landed, the game stopped - literally stopped to let the whole field exhale.

"Whoooaaa...." was the general consensus.

He totally forgot what he was doing as he simply grinned at the disc in his hands. With that one leap, his confidence gauge went from near zero to completely full. He turned and fired a precise 20-yard flick and took off.

When he got back to the sidelines, our whole tent mobbed him, everyone telling him, "You don't worry about anything else but going deep."

"Ok. I think I can do that."

I excitedly punched him in the shoulder. "That's what they used to tell me."

"That felt pretty good."

"Ya know, I'm starting to wonder what Grandpap's vertical was."

"Or Grandma's."

"Oh, she could dunk. There's no doubt about that."

We lost that game 15-7 but finished off the day with a 13-10 victory over a team from southern Maryland. Chris used his newfound confidence to score three goals. The kid was so happy that a bunch of critters came out of the forest to sing with him.

Our first game of the following day was versus Yank My Doodle, a team of club players from North Carolina that would end up winning the tournament. Of course, it's the only game that our family can attend the entire weekend. By this point my father was fully recovered from his kidney surgery and his cancer was gone - which meant he could do things like drive to Turner Valley to watch his son and his nephew get trounced 15-2.

Seemingly after every point, Chris or I would apologetically pass by them on the sideline. "I swear we're a lot better than this...."

"Oh, of course you are. No, we believe you. We really do."

"Next game won't suck as bad."

"Ok, but we can only stay for the first ten minutes."

Ten minutes into the second game, we were down 4-0 to New York Traffic. We actually scored our first goal at the exact moment they were getting into the car to leave.

We smiled and waved to them as they pulled out of the lot. "Good riddance," we mumbled under our breath.

Now that they were miles away, we came back to win 11-9, setting up a very interesting scenario for our final game against Dartmouth. If we could manage a victory, for the first time in seven appearances at Mars, I could actually be on a winning team.

Since the Weasels disbanded, I'd picked up on a few teams that were uh…really fun. One year we were so fun we finished dead last in actual competition. But the weekend was always a blast, a three-day respite from life that I looked forward to every July. During the early 2000's, a tent city would develop around the Turner Valley pavilion and 400 people would crowd in there, swarming the picnic tables for the Saturday night karaoke party. Every year I sang "The Devil Went Down to Georgia." And every year I felt like a fucking rock star. The energy was amazing as 32 teams sang, drank, played flip cup, had boat races, and spilled out into the night to watch the illegal fireworks that a bunch of Carleton College alums always snuck into Pennsylvania.

For five years, that party was the pinnacle of what ultimate parties should be. Fun, loud, and unrestrained - a singing, dancing, sweaty, half naked mob surrounded by stupid games and random fires, more ridiculousness and bad decisions packed into one pavilion than should've been humanly possible. So fun definitely wasn't the issue. Success on the other hand….

If Little Green Men could somehow beat Dartmouth, I'd have no idea what to do with myself. I could be somewhere other than the D bracket on the tournament's final day.

We promptly came out and went down 3-0 before gradually working our way back into the game, trailing only 11-10 when the cap went on. Game to 13. It wasn't looking good when Dartmouth scored to take a 12-10 lead. On the next point, I caught one at midfield and gunned a flick toward this really good Australian dude named Ian. We were going to be set up right at the goal line until one of Turner Valley's famous gusts caught it and sent it over his head. Luckily for me, one of our women, a fast, petite brunette named Caryn was making a similar cut to the end zone about ten yards behind him. It ended up hitting her right in stride. The throw looked so good there was absolutely no way to tell that she wasn't my target all along. I was laughing to myself the whole way to the line.

"Great throw," Caryn said. "What's so funny?"

"Ah, nothing. That *was* a great throw, wasn't it?"

At 12-11, Dartmouth worked it the whole way downfield only to have Cousin Chris come the whole way across the end zone for a catch block that sent us rushing the other way. I caught it nearly the same distance from the end zone as the previous point and saw Caryn on a similar cut. This time I actually meant to hit her with the backhand that tied the game 12-12. I was one good point away from finishing Mars with a winning record.

Our line was on a roll so we decided we'd all stay in for universe point. We may have been a little tired because they worked it downfield rather easily against our zone, swinging it from one side of the goal line to another, looking for any way to puncture our defense. Thankfully, they passed up a few decent looks in search of the perfect one before one of our guys leapt to knock a swilly lob to the corner out of bounds. And just like that, we had the disc and a chance to win the game.

Three passes later, I bailed out Caryn, who was trapped against the sideline about twenty yards out of our own end zone. Unfortunately because of it, I was now the one trapped on the sideline. And my mark was doing things to me that would've been universally condemned by Southern Baptists everywhere. There was nothing open in the middle. The dump was covered. At Stall 8, I didn't have much choice. Fifty yards away, I saw Cousin Chris standing at the back of the stack.

It wasn't the best huck I've ever thrown. Far from it. The mark was tight and I didn't get the follow through I wanted. As it crossed the goal line, it started to tail toward the opposite sideline, eventually heading more horizontally than forward. I'd overshot everyone, but it was ok. It was an effective punt and we'd be able to reset our zone, hopefully get a turnover and win the....

As it was rapidly blading to the ground, I saw Cousin Chris begin to accelerate. Everyone on the field was expecting that throw to hit the grass. Again, if a camera had been on that disc, Chris wouldn't have even been in the picture when he left the ground. A step across the goal line, the kid shot forward, sailing through the air waist high. His full 6'4" inch frame stretched to its maximum length, he twisted like a screw being drilled into a wall. The disc angled down from the sky into his upturned palm. He curled his fingers around the rim. When he landed, he skidded five yards on his back before hopping up with the disc in his hands and a jubilantly stunned expression. On the sideline, water and bits of granola were chucked into the air.

"Holy shit," I muttered to myself from 60 yards downfield before taking off sprinting toward the mob that was currently swallowing my cousin. I was the last one to him and when I got there, I tackled the chuckling chucklehead and started punching him in the back. "Dude, that was sick!"

"I learned it all from Grandma."

"You realize the family is never going to believe us when we tell them about this, right?"

"Not a single word," he laughed as I continued to punch him.

"Cousin connection!" I yelled. "Cousin connection!"

So many things made that moment amazing. I'd taught him how to throw when he was seven years old and now I'd just hucked one to him to win a hotly contested game. There are just some things that are made better when they're shared with family. That day, Cousin Chris and I found out that universe point is one of them.

Geography prevented Cousin Chris and I from ever stepping on the same field for the same team again, so that moment – that huck to layout against Dartmouth is forever etched in both of our minds. There's not a time we hang out when we don't tell the story. He went on to found and captain a scrappy little team from a tiny school in the south much like his older cousin. He played four years for Coastal Carolina and every time I saw him, he couldn't wait to show me a new video of the no look scoober he completed against UNC-Asheville or the weird overhead lob he pulled off against Liberty. And I beamed with pride every time I watched him emulate one of my charming bad habits on the field.

Just before our blowout loss to the team from Edinboro on the first day of Mars, I was introduced to the 20-year-old kid that was the captain of my new summer league team. His name was Tad and he was a short, muscular handler with curly blonde hair who looked like he'd teleported in from WrestleMania III. (He may or may not have written the forward for this book.) Tad had named our summer league team "Rigor Mortis –

The Friendly Tortoise" based on a children's show character he'd come up with one night while on mushrooms. Actually, I wasn't there, so I have no idea if he was on mushrooms or not, but c'mon, look at that name and try to come up with an alternative explanation.

After every victory, we'd all circle around Tad and pretended to be the kids in Rigor Mortis's studio audience. With the gravelly voice of a creeptastic public access turtle-man, he'd crawl from a pretend shell.

"Hey kids!" he'd yell.

"Hey Rigor!" we'd respond.

"I got some life lessons for you today. Like this little gem. Don't let your brother in law handle your finances. When he makes shitty investments and loses you 10 G's, it makes for an awkward Christmas."

"Thanks, Rigor!"

"That's all I got today. So how about you give me a 'Fuck yeah!'"

"Fuck yeah!"

"I can't hear you kids!"

"Fuck yeah!"

Hell, maybe we were all on mushrooms.

When Barefoot Ben introduced me, Tad shook my hand with the vigor of Hulk Hogan. "Cramer, here's what I know about you. I was told, 'He gets there.' That's all I know. 'He gets there.' That's all I need to know."

"Well, I do get there," I said.

"Fuck yeah," he replied, dislocating my shoulder with a hand slap.

Rigor Mortis went undefeated in the regular season that year – the first time it had happened in Pittsburgh Summer League in a decade. Obviously the wins were nice, but if I asked Tad, I know his favorite story from that summer came in a competitive game against some team dressed in yellow whose name I can't remember. This dude in a Detroit Tigers cap tried guarding me all game but couldn't quite keep up, so he started calling fouls anytime I got near him. I believe he was a Miami of Ohio graduate.

Just after halftime, one of our small, quick handlers got the disc and saw me running stride for stride with Tigers Cap near the goal line. He put up a hard backhand about nine feet off the ground. I had the angle and leapt across Tigers Cap's shoulders to momentarily snag it two hand-ed. He made a late play on the disc and jumped up, plowing into my chest and punching me in the elbow. The disc popped out of my hands and I flipped over him, keeping my eye on the disc as I hit the ground, reaching out flat on my back to catch it next to the cone for a spectacular goal.

When he inevitably called a foul on me for getting punched in the elbow all I remember is a red flash of anger followed by the disc I'd just caught blading high and deep into the parking lot. The way Tad tells the story, it hit the ground with the force of a mortar, blowing chunks of gravel and dirt so high into the air, the sun was blocked until the follow-ing May.

Tad strode up to me laughing. "It seems you….disagree with his call."

"Did I make it that obvious?"

"Three people in the parking lot are dead, so…yeah," he said looking toward the cars. "But I blame him. That call was bullshit."

Once we got a disc that wasn't tacoed and covered in cinders, we resumed the game. And Tigers Cap was anything but deterred by my unhinged reaction, calling two more questionable fouls. By this time I was boiling, so I approached Tad as we lined up.

"When you get the disc, you huck it to me. I don't care if their whole team is in the end zone. Put the damn thing up. I'll come down with it."

"Are you sure? We're tied here. What if…"

"What's the first thing anyone told you about me?"

"That you get there."

"Put it up. I'll get there."

There were times in my career when I suffered from acute bouts of overconfidence but this time I was pissed enough to back it up. We end-ed up working the disc to midfield. I was almost parallel with Tad on the opposite sideline when he yelled my name and let one go for the end zone.

There were at least four defenders between me and Tad's overexcited huck. I was so angry and focused that I didn't care. I shook off Tigers Cap and shot between two of his teammates, leaving only one dude with any chance of keeping me from that disc. He'd dropped off his guy near the back of the stack as soon as the throw left Tad's hand. Now he was all alone in the end zone, casually tracking the disc with no one around him. The guy was at least two steps in front of me when he peeked over his shoulder at the sound of my footsteps and left the ground. I was out of time. I had to jump too.

It felt like an eagle taking a fish from a seagull. He leapt straight up from underneath and got his fingers around the middle of the rim as I soared in from behind and simultaneously clamped my right hand down next to his. We landed going full speed, both in possession of the disc. But he didn't want it as much as I did. Every rep I'd ever put in at the gym paid off at that singular moment as with one hand, I ripped the disc out of both of his and sent him comically spinning out the back of the end zone. I held up the disc, silently pointed down the field toward Tad, and let it fall to the ground.

Tad came jogging down the field, his wild 80's wrestler eyes staring at me like a madman on speed. "I will never question you again."

"I told you I'd fuckin' get there."

That play combined with a break mark behind the backer I threw for a goal in a torrential downpour later in the season led Tad and the other kids to think I was some sort of living legend. (They were young, impressionable, and hadn't seen real legends play yet.) Because of it, they invited me to be on their team for a beach tournament on the shores of Lake Erie called "Don't Give Up the Disc." Other than Caryn, the girl from my Mars team who was also 29, our team was totally comprised of kids who hadn't yet reached legal drinking age. Now I was in grad school and still doing my share of partying, but the partying was somehow different. We were drinking bourbon and wine and making jokes about Film Noir until 5AM. I'd forgotten what undergrad parties were like. I was about to be reminded.

After Tad got off work that evening, we took off for Erie. With us were Caryn and Tad's big redheaded friend Tom. Tad drove his "car." I use this term loosely. The thing wasn't a car so much as a collection of random parts floating down the interstate on a miracle. It was some sort of white Oldsmobile from 1991 with one maroon door. Along the way, we had this conversation….

"Hey man, I can't roll down my window."

"Yeah, the button's broken," Tad said. "Don't worry though, I made a tool that works sometimes. Tom, see if you can find….there's a twisted paperclip in the glove box."

"Don't worry about it, man," I answered. "I don't suppose this thing has air conditioning."

"Yeah, it's called rolling down the window. Which like I said you can do on occasion with this little tool I created."

It was one of the most fun and harrowing drives of my life, mainly because Tad was one of those guys who needs to be looking at whomever he's talking to at all times. Eighty miles an hour and he's trying to read your nonverbal cues.

"And he like severed a tendon," Tad said, watching the trees go by behind Tom. "At the party. Stepped on a beer bottle at the *party* and missed regionals."

"How much of a dumbass do you have to be to get hurt at the party?" Redhead Tom answered. "Get through a whole day of ultimate perfectly fine and then get hurt at the *party?* What a dumbass."

At this point, Tad is staring right into Tom's eyes with one hand on the steering wheel. "I know, right?"

RUMBLE RUMBLE RUMBLE RUMBLE RUMBLE…..

And without saying a word, Tad would jerk the car back into the lane temporarily before launching into one of his many theories on life.

RUMBLE RUMBLE RUMBLE RUMBLE RUMBLE….

And so on and so forth.

Then came the most amazing part of the drive. I'm in the middle of a story….

"…..so Duffy comes running back with the mop," I chuckle, "barely avoids the dog again as up in the kitchen the hillbillies are reaching for their shotguns…."

"No way. No way that happened. No fuckin' way!" Tad laughs, gasping for air.

He finds it so funny that he pounds his fist on the dashboard. And all of the lights in the car immediately go out. It was the kind of instant, all encompassing blackness that happens just before a chainsaw roars in a horror movie.

"Ah, shit!" Tad screamed. "I don't know how fast we're going any-more! Oh fuck! Are the headlights still on?"

Redhead Tom squinted, leaning forward. "I think one of them's still on. I can't tell. Your headlights suck."

"Hit the dashboard again!" I yelled from the back.

"That seems logical, but what if I hit it and the brakes go out? I'm nervous."

"There's no mechanical way that can happen."

Tad turned around in his seat to look at me as we sped down the road in darkness. "With this car, you can't rule out any possibilities."

Caryn's hand was covering her eyes. "Tad, could you please look at the road?"

If he heard her, he chose to ignore her. "If I hit the dashboard again, the whole car might blow up. That's a desperate, last chance option."

Caryn nudged me. "Is he looking at the road yet?"

"Not as of yet. Although out of all the things wrong with this car, the alignment doesn't seem to be one of them."

"I'm not ready to hit the dashboard again. There are a lot of other things to try before…"

Redhead Tom reached over from the passenger's seat and thumped down on the dashboard. Immediately all the lights came back on.

Tad whipped back around. "What was that?"

"You're welcome," Redhead Tom said.

Now Tad had somehow sweet-talked a girl he knew from Edinboro into letting us stay at her house for the weekend. We were about twenty minutes out of town when she called to tell us her parents had gotten wind of the plan and weren't exactly thrilled about it. Which let's face it, was a pretty sensible reaction. (See Kosher Josh) But her mom suggested one alternative – the Crawford County Girl Scout Headquarters. So before I knew it, I was surrounded by ten of my much younger teammates (and Caryn) trying to go to sleep on a mattress designed for the comfort of a ten-year-old girl.

Our team was called Elephant Concubine (again, I'm assuming mush-rooms) and we had a pretty damned respectable showing. We knocked off the number one seed in our division, a team from Ithaca 13-11 when

I let go a two-point end zone to end zone backhand that I knew won the game as soon as it left my hand. We went 4-2, barely losing to a couple of other teams from Pittsburgh on a steamy August day.

But the real stories of this tournament weren't on the field. They came later at a giant tournament-sponsored house party. To that point, I'd forgotten how undergrads drink. (Namely quickly and poorly) Before I could finish my first whiskey, Tad and everyone else on the team were plowed like a farm field. I walked up the stairs and into the kitchen to find Tad pissing in a drinking glass.

"Oh, hey Cramer," he said, filling the glass. "Could you check the freezer and see if there's any ice cubes?"

"What the hell are you doing?"

"I need to make this look like lemonade."

"A lot of that is going to depend on how much you hydrated today."

"I know," he answered drunkenly. "When yellow is your pee, hydration is key. Seriously though, see if there's ice."

I opened the freezer and found some ice, handing him the tray, which he cracked, placing the cubes in the "drink."

"Why are you making a piss lemonade?"

"Bob won't trade shorts with me. He has these awesome Iowa State shorts and I want them. But he said he wouldn't trade unless I got him a lemonade."

"So because he won't trade shorts with you, you're going to make him drink your piss?"

He stopped peeing and just for a second seemed to realize how ridiculous that sounded. Then he chuckled. "Yeah, that's what I'm doing," he said plopping in the ice cubes.

I felt compelled to warn Bob as Tad stumbled into the other room with the glass. Then it occurred to me that one of my main rules in life is never to interrupt the plans of a guy holding a glass full of piss.

Tad was pretty plowed, but still aware enough to know he was doing something that his friendship with this Bob guy probably wasn't going to survive. I mean you just don't recover from something like that. Serial adulterers have a better chance at reconciliation. Bob was lounging on a wicker couch when Tad handed him the glass.

"Ice cold lemonade, just like you asked," Tad said.

Bob nodded. Tad stared at him with the conflicted grin of someone ashamed at the payoff he was anticipating.

The glass was within a hair's width of touching Bob's lower lip when Tad's conscience finally intervened. He leapt toward him with his hands up. "Bob, don't drink it, it's my piss! Seriously, it's my piss!"

Bob, who was sort of a burnt out professor in his early 40's just blinked. "What?"

"Yeah, it's my piss. My actions here are very regrettable. Bob, you should punch me in the face."

"I'm not going to punch you in the face."

"Bob, I'm an asshole. I deserve it. Seriously. One punch. Right to the teeth."

At this point, I intervened, gently pushing Tad toward the door. "I think it's about time to head outside for a few minutes, buddy."

"Ok, but Bob owes me a punch in the face. Don't let him forget."

"I won't dude. I'll print up a reminder card."

When we got outside, Caryn came up to us sipping on whatever was in her red Solo cup. "Hey, what were you guys up to?"

"Uh, well Tad wanted someone else's shorts and to be honest you probably don't want to know the rest."

Tad's eyes were spinning. "Man, I really wanted those shorts."

Then, suddenly Tad lurched forward and did what guys who drink too much too quickly tend to do.

Seeing it, Caryn immediately grabbed my hand. "Come with me," she said.

"Ok....where are we...."

We'd gotten about ten yards from the garage when she leaned to the right, chucked to the grass and kept walking. It was the most nonchalant puke I'd ever witnessed.

"Did you just puke?"

"Yeah," she said. "The smell of puke makes me puke. It's a horrible cycle. I'm sorry, I know that was gross."

"Sorry? Don't be sorry. You didn't even break stride."

She laughed and dragged me toward this country road out behind the party. "I need some air."

And so the two of us spent the rest of the night on a nice platonic walk in the moonlight while in the distance all of the kids (and Bob) threw a rager that we both realized we were a little too old to fully enjoy.

A few minutes later, we were leaning on a fence beside a barn in the middle of nowhere. "Two years ago, I'd have torn up that party," I told her. "Now all I'm thinking is how I just played six games in the heat and I can't wait to lay down on a crappy mattress that's six inches too short for me."

Caryn slid off the fence. "Oh my god, thank you. I was afraid I was being old and lame and keeping you from the party."

"Oh, you're being old and lame all right. I appreciate it."

"I'm so tired."

"Fuck. There might be a bingo game we could hit on the way back."

She laughed with her eyes half closed. "I don't have the energy for bingo."

Our insane tournament Saturday night ended around midnight when we hitched a ride back to the Girl Scout Headquarters. We'd both been asleep for a couple hours when the rest of the crew came barging in like a horde of Mongol invaders. It was fifteen minutes of confused shouting and the sounds of hips accidentally banging against furniture before they all fell asleep covered in half-eaten Pop Tarts.

The next morning, Caryn and I woke refreshed in the middle of what it must've looked like the day after the Battle of Antietam - just bodies strewn everywhere.

The two of us played well enough to win our first game Sunday morning - but with the rest of the team as nimble as your average camel and Redhead Tom out with a separated shoulder, we dropped our second game and headed home.

And why was Tom out with a separated shoulder? To find out, I approached him as he sat on the sidelines with a towel over his head. "Ya know, I don't remember seeing you get hurt yesterday," I said. "All six games you seem to have gotten through just fine. And now…"

"I hurt it at the party."

"At the party, huh? So *you* were the dumbass."

He sheepishly looked up from under his towel. "Tad threw a bagel at me. I couldn't let a good bagel hit the ground."

"You separated your shoulder diving for a bagel?"

Tom sighed. "Yes. Yes I did."

Now Tom was a pretty good player for our summer league team and he managed to put himself out for the playoffs. Rigor Mortis won our first round game, but Tad tweaked his hamstring on a layout in the first half. Early in the second game, I caught a huck for a goal and rolled an ankle trying to keep my feet in bounds. With our two best players hobbling around, we dropped our second round matchup to the #10 seed. Our undefeated season was no more.

I was disappointed in the result, but the one personal bright spot was that I was nominated for league MVP. If I'm being honest, I really thought I was going to win. I'd absolutely taken over the league that year, leading us to that undefeated record. Despite not being able to will us to the final like I'd hoped, I still thought there was a damn good chance I'd take home the uh, trophy. Or trinket. Let me rephrase that. I thought there was a damn good chance I'd take home whatever someone from the league had bought at the Dollar Store on the way to the fields. We were all sitting on the hill after the final game when the commissioners made the announcement.

"And finally, the male MVP for Pittsburgh Summer League 2006 is Kevin...."

Tad and all of my teammates leapt up and screamed their approval. Inside I smiled. I was finally getting the recognition that years of hard work had brought. Finally, I was being recognized as one of the best, if not *the* best player in the city. I even lifted my ass from the ground in anticipation of walking down there to shake everyone's hand.

"....McCloskey."

I sat back down. Who the hell was Kevin McCloskey? I'd never even heard of him. Tad and all the rest of my teammates voiced their displeasure. I just laughed into my hands at the irony of the dude who won MVP being named Kevin as well seemingly for no other reason than to give me a nice jolt of excitement before being smacked with the cold hand of reality.

In the end though, it was a great summer. I played a lot of ultimate. And I'm glad I did because in a couple of months, things were about to change dramatically.

And I still wonder on occasion what the hell Bob did with that glass of piss.

THIRTY-ONE

Ultimate has brought me a lot of great things in life – stories, friends, and some pretty awesome scars. But nothing – absolutely nothing compares to what it brought me at the end of September 2006. Two weeks earlier, I'd driven my Cavalier back across the country and rejoined the Tuesday night pickup game at the intramural fields underneath Box Springs Mountain. The game was so full of personality, fun, and skill that a few of us decided to bring it to the next level. And so ten years after I'd started my first college team, I helped start my um….third.

We called ourselves the Highland Bears because for some reason UCR's actual mascot was a bear in a kilt – which I always suspected came about after they passed on other animals in human clothes.

Dog in a sports bra?

Gopher in a jump suit?

Bobcat in really tight jeans?

No? Well how about a bear in a kilt? *Folks, we have a winner!*

We were going to be named "Faultline" due to the fifty or so fissures underneath Riverside that are eventually going to annihilate the place. Then at a party before our first tournament, Handsome George handed me a beer and said, "Ya know, I'm not digging the name Faultline."

"Really? I think it sounds pretty bad ass myself."

"That's the problem," he said. "I don't know if we're good enough to have a bad ass name."

I put my beer down and squinted into the blinking lights of the dance floor. Half the team was there gyrating with the rhythm of a leaky faucet. "We are not bad ass enough for that name, no. You have any suggestions?"

George smiled wide. "Grrrowwwwllll," he roared in a Scottish accent. "I am the Highland Bear! Stay away from me' cubbies!"

I raised my beer and mimicked the accent. "You thought I was hibernatin' but I was just a wee bit pissed!"

This went on for hours. Days. Weeks. The Highland Bear pretty much narrated everything the team did. We had an identity.

Due to a miraculous clerical error at the UPA, I was informed that at twenty-nine, I still had one more year of college eligibility - to which I simply said "thank you," and didn't ask anyone to examine further. I'd first appeared on a roster in 1997 with Flagler but apparently those years didn't count because we never went to sectionals or something. In the end, it's not like it mattered much. UC-Riverside wasn't going to come out of nowhere and sweep through the southwest anyway. Or were we?

The short answer is no – no we weren't.

But we did have a hell of a good, if not incredibly deep team. With me, War Beard Rob, Handsome George and a huge 6'3" redheaded bruiser named Rollie, we had some superior talent. Throw in three super fast freshmen who'd all played high school ultimate in the Bay Area and I'd have put our starting seven up against any college in southern California. In early November, we were going to find out if I was right. For the first time ever, UC-Riverside was going to play the local powers at a tournament hosted by UCLA.

Playing without Rollie at a small tune-up tournament in Pomona, we beat Cal-Poly and Azuza Pacific, while barely losing to a very good Claremont team 13-11. Handsome George and I were by far the best and most experienced players on the field. Any time we desperately needed a score, I'd tap him on the shoulder.

"Me and you on this point," I'd say.

George would nod. "Let's show the kids how it's done."

And we'd promptly pass it back and forth to each other, weaving and slicing our way down the field for the goal.

After we'd done just what I'd described to take half against Claremont, Idaho Robin approached us on the sideline.

"Ya know, it would be nice if you let some of the other guys touch the disc. Aren't we trying to get the freshmen some experience here?"

Handsome George turned and gestured at them. "They're learning by watching. There are a lot of respected studies out there that back up what we're doing."

I laughed. "We're demonstrating greatness, Robin. They have to know what it looks like in order to emulate it."

"You realize you guys are both almost thirty," she laughed.

"Are you suggesting that we should be spending the weekend mowing the lawn and debating our investment strategies instead of dominating a small college ultimate tournament?"

"Well no, but now that you mention it…."

Whether she was right or not is totally beside the point. After showing that we weren't too shabby even without a couple of our better players, we couldn't wait to take on the bigger schools. UCLA, USC, UC-Irvine, Cal, Arizona State, UC-San Diego – they were all going to be in Westwood at the end of the month. UC-Riverside Ultimate was ready to surprise the hell out of the regional powers. We couldn't wait. And then two weeks before the tournament, the director emailed a couple of the smaller teams.

We've gotten more interest than we thought and with our field space as limited as it is, we have to cut a couple teams that we've already accepted. Being that this is an elite tournament, we're sorry to inform you that UC-Riverside….blah, blah, fuuuuuck.

Now even though I'm not a big fan of how they handled it, I completely understand what happened. UCLA got more interest than they anticipated. When more well-known teams like San Louis Obispo, Arizona, and UC-Santa Barbara decided at the last minute they wanted to come as well, the tournament organizers had a problem. So teams like UC-Riverside and Cal Poly were pushed aside. They weren't trying to be dicks, they were just victims of their own poor planning. Unfortunately, it also led to a craptastic series of events that ended the "dominant athlete" portion of my career.

Since we weren't going to UCLA, we decided we needed to fill the void. In its place, we decided to quickly throw together a small hat tournament just before Thanksgiving at the UCR intramural fields. War Beard Rob organized the whole thing, posting it on the LAOUT (Los Angeles Organization of Ultimate Teams) website. As it turned out, we got a pretty decent response from all around southern California.

The Saturday of the tournament, I woke up early, spent an hour directing people into the parking lot, then got assigned to my team with a bunch of kids who'd made the trip over from Cal-State Northridge. I was excited. A few of the top players from San Diego and LA were on my home turf and I knew I was going to have a big day.

On the second point of the first game, I leapt in front of the guy I was guarding to pick off a pass in the end zone. One of the top female players in California was on my team, a speedster named Nicole Belle Isle. As I ran to the goal line to ground check the disc, I saw her flying down the right sideline with no one on her. A few seconds later, she ran down my 80-yard backhand huck to tie the game 1-1. It was a beautiful day and everything was going right. And as any Californian will tell you – that's when the earthquake hits.

Two points later, I was playing defense on Handsome George when Receding Eddie II put up a long hanging flick along the sideline. George leapt. I sprung in from behind him, soaring way over his head to emphatically swat it out the side of the end zone. I'd prevented a goal. Like normal, I was flying. At nearly 30 years old, I could still leave the ground like a bird.

From the first day I stepped on the field at the fort, the one real talent I possessed was the ability to rise up over anyone to make a play. Other guys were more precise, more technical - better players. But the air was my home. I remember realizing just how far above George's head I was as I watched that disc sail off toward the chain link fence surrounding the fields. If I'd have known what was coming, I'd have taken a mental snapshot of what it was like to be free and totally unbound by gravity - for the last time.

As George landed, he stumbled and stuck out his leg to catch himself. My right cleat came down out of the air and landed on the top of his foot. My ankle rolled outward. All my weight came down on it.

POP!

If someone had shot me from the top of the bleachers, I don't think the pain would've been any more intense. My ankle felt like a tiny bomb exploded inside of it. And in some ways it had. All three fibular ligaments (all the ones in and around the ankle bone) snapped like rubber bands. It hurt so bad when I hit the ground that I couldn't move, not even to scream and roll around clutching it like a soccer player faking his own death at the World Cup. I just laid there at an awkward angle, totally still, trying to meditate it all away. It caused Idaho Robin and Carleton Kim to rush over to me, thinking I'd broken my neck.

"Oh my god. Cramer. Cramer, talk to us. Cramer, can you hear me?"

I can still see their faces against the blue sky. "Of course I can hear you."

"Don't move. Don't move. We're going to call an ambulance. Just keep your head immobilized. Can you wiggle your fingers?"

"My fingers are fine. What I need you to tell me is if my foot's still attached."

"Your….oh….holy shit."

It ballooned to the size of an orange almost immediately. I got helped to the sideline and bathed it in ice the rest of the day. Luckily for me, my roommate forgot to pay the gas bill that month, so I got two weeks of beneficial ice-cold showers. I spent the next few weeks hobbling around campus on crutches, the next month visiting the campus doctors, and the next four months tracing the alphabet in the air with my big toe.

By early March I was jogging again. By mid-April I was back on the field. In June I watched a couple minutes of my graduation on my way to the gym to do plyos. I was happy to graduate with my Master of Fine Arts in Screenwriting, but the end of my time at UCR was bittersweet. I now had to somehow find a job in a crowded Hollywood market that was a lot better set up for 22 year olds who went to Yale, Harvard, or USC than 30 year olds who went to UCR. My health care was running out at the end of August. I couldn't imagine trying to play high-level ultimate without it - especially with my track record. I figured I'd better try to squeeze in as many games as I could.

Unlike Pittsburgh Summer League, which played back-to-back games on Saturday afternoons, the LA Summer League played Wednesday nights under the lights. (On the same fields out in Encino where I'd broken my collarbone) I played in the men's-only league and was drafted onto the Brown Team (that was as creative as our name ever got) with a bunch of guys I'd never seen or played with before.

The summer was fun. We had a great group of guys I don't really remember very well. But it was a skilled and spirited team. And seven months removed from destroying my ankle, I was feeling great again. I was launching contested hucks 60 yards for goals. I was making layout D's. I was diving behind me to catch wobbly tosses. I was stuffing cuts and forcing turnovers. A case could be made that I was one of the four or five best players in that entire league.

But there was one problem I just couldn't shake. In 1971, Pirates pitcher Steve Blass won Game 7 of the World Series after tossing five shutouts in the regular season. For a few years, he was one of the best pitchers in baseball. But by 1976, he was a jewelry salesman because of a sudden, inexplicable inability to throw the ball over the plate – something he'd done literally tens of thousands of times in his life. Out of nowhere, like aliens had infiltrated his arm, his control simply vanished.

How is this relevant? Early on in the year, we were playing the White Team. (That's as creative as their name ever got) I was guarding a guy that ten months prior couldn't have scored on me if I'd been wearing a baby. He faked in and took off deep. He had a step. Their handler put up a long backhand huck. The guy was surprisingly quick, but after forty yards, I caught up. All I had to do was spring over top of him and tip it out of bounds like I'd done hundreds of times in the previous twelve years.

I tracked the disc. He went up. And I – thought better of it. A second grader would've snickered at the bunny hop I attempted. It was pathetic squared. As I went to leap, all I could hear was my ankle whispering, "*Whoa, hold on a second. Let's think this out.*" Needless to say, he celebrated and I jogged back to the sideline. The dumb thing was that I had zero problem jumping when no one was around me. I have a picture of me leaping for a disc on the beach in Carlsbad that August where I'm damn near three feet off the sand. But when another player was in the vicinity – here came the yips. I did *not* want to land on someone else's foot again.

I gave up more contested deep goals in seven summer league games than I had in the previous seven years. It was beyond frustrating. The amount of times I'd tell myself, "*Jump, dummy! When it's there, just go get it.*

That's what you DO!"

And the next time a disc went up, I'd stand there and watch my guy catch a pass I could've easily tipped away. I suddenly felt a kindred connection with Steve Blass.

The season ended well. I missed a day of moving sandbags around a movie set in the 118 degree heat of Palm Springs to drive to Long Beach for summer league finals. Playing on a bunch of fields next to a mountainside that overlooked the ocean was sort of amazing. In the first games I played after turning thirty, I helped us make the championship game where we lost to the Black Team. (That was as creative as their name ever got) I laid out to snag hammers, made more than a few run-through D's, and fired bullet flicks for goals. But I still couldn't jump. Not like I used to.

Driving back to Palm Springs that night, I knew August 31st was barreling down on me. The expiration of my health insurance was the end date for my ultimate career - at least until I found a real job. And what real job in Hollywood was going to give me enough time to travel to tournaments every weekend? And even if I had the time, what club team was going to want a deep receiver who couldn't jump? I had invites from LA Monster and San Diego's co-ed team, but I knew it was futile. One more ankle roll, one more busted collarbone, one more concussion would be the end of my savings. I was thirty and had to grit my teeth and make an adult decision. After the summer league final there in Long Beach, I tossed my spikes in the trunk of my car. Except for a few small pickup games, they'd remain there for four years.

Now I started this chapter talking of how ultimate brought me something inconceivably amazing in September of 2006. But I never got around to what it was. So here it is.

Because UCR Ultimate was now an actual club, we were allowed to have our own tent at the "Block Party," this huge street fair in the middle of campus. Basically all the new students wandered around, ate funnel cake, and listened to local bands as all the clubs wooed them with key chains, lanyards, and other assorted shit they found sitting in boxes next to the bookstore dumpster. War Beard Rob brought his collapsible Fris-bee golf hole, and as captain I stood there in my Jacksonville Ultimate visor shouting at anyone who looked athletic. Most of the conversations went like this…

"Hey you in the blue shirt! C'mon over here!"

"Oh wow, do we have a disc golf team? That looks cool."

"Uh, no actually," I'd say. "We're the ultimate team."

"Then why do you have a disc golf basket?"

"Well, we couldn't really get an ultimate game going in this tent, so…"

"Well uh….let me know if you guys ever start a disc golf team…."

Thirty or so people signed up. All the freshman who'd played in high school were really stoked to see us. But the best thing about the whole night had nothing to do with ultimate. The previous day, a girl had emailed our creative writing listserve. Her name was Alexis. She was a poet from New Jersey who'd been in town for two weeks waiting for class to start and was bored out of her mind. I knew the feeling from the previous year.

"Come to the Block Party tomorrow night," I emailed back to her. "Show up at the Ultimate Frisbee booth. Ask for Cramer."

Halfway through my seemingly eternal four hours manning the booth, a girl who looked like she played bass in a progressive rock band nervously approached. "Um, I was told to ask for Cramer?"

I knew it was that Alexis girl, so like normal I couldn't resist being a bit of a jag. I laughed. "What the hell do you want to talk to that jackass for?"

"Um….he emailed me. We're like….in the same program."

"Seriously, if you know what's good for you, you'll stay the hell away from that dude. He's bad news."

Her shoulders slumped. She looked so disappointed. "Oh. That sucks. He sounded really nice in his emails."

Beside her stood a cute brunette who thus far hadn't said a thing. She was ghost pale, wore glasses, and had a giant tattoo of a rose covering her right shoulder. She looked me dead in the eye and laughed in a voice that was only truly at home using dry sarcasm.

"You're Cramer, aren't you?" she said.

I laughed. "Nice to meet you."

Alexis breathed a sigh of relief. "Ya know that really was kind of a jackass move. I'm thinking you weren't lying."

The girl next to her smiled. "I thought it was kind of funny."

Alexis gestured to her friend. "This is Jessi. We met at orientation yesterday."

Three years later, Jessi and I were married at a little train depot in her home state of Wyoming. She's sleeping in the next room as I write this, tucked in next to our little boy. We were in the same program, so I'd have met her eventually even if I hadn't been out recruiting players for UCR Ultimate that night. But we might not have met so soon. She and Alexis might not have stayed at my apartment just about every night until school began. We might not have gone on to do all the things that let two people get comfortable enough together that they wake up one day and realize they're staring at their future.

And if I don't get cut from the baseball team at Flagler my freshman year – if I don't run into Principal Phil outside the gym– if I decide not to head out to the fort that Sunday in 1995 where I got hooked on some weird hippie sport I barely remembered from gym class, I wouldn't have gone looking for the Harrisburg Pleasure Van once I ended up in York. And if I don't do that, I don't meet Tour de France Todd. He doesn't ask me to play for his Wildwood team. I don't duck into a hotel party to find Barnacle Julie sitting there on a couch. If I don't play two frustrating years at Penn State, I don't meet Duffy. He's not there to pull an amazing Duffy wingman job and I probably don't end up with Julie for a year. Without her I don't apply to a school in California I'd never heard of. I'm not manning a booth in the middle of Aberdeen Drive recruiting freshman to the new club ultimate team. A mill-trash yinzer from Pittsburgh never meets an intellectual ranch girl from Casper, Wyoming. My son is never born.

I can't think of an ultimate player who doesn't have a similar story. So many of the things we have, our memories, and even many of the people in our lives are there because of our desire to run after that silly piece of plastic hanging in the wind.

And that's why we're willing to drive 400 miles to get sunburnt and bruised for something most people think involves dogs.

THIRTY-TWO

IN THE FALL OF 2007, I WON A PRETTY MAJOR SCREENWRITING AWARD. IT WAS an award that launched the careers of Francis Ford Coppola and novelist Jonathan Kellerman among others. The fame and fortune that were no doubt in my future would easily allow me to once again afford health insurance. I was going to be back on the field in no time.

Unfortunately, six days after I won the award, the Writer's Guild of America went on strike. For a hundred days from October through the next March, I walked around in front of different studio lots holding a picket sign instead of getting paid for various projects. It was a very odd time in my life. I met and hung out with famous actors once or twice a week. I ended up traipsing around town having beers with Oscar and Emmy nominees. The beautiful star of the top rated TV show at the time made me a whole tin full of homemade cookies. It would've been truly amazing if I wasn't rapidly running out of money in a tiny house in Pasadena with no heat and no air conditioning. Even after the strike ended, Hollywood didn't recover. By July, I was down to my last seventy dollars.

Before Jessi came to UC-Riverside, she'd promised a friend that she'd apprentice at his tattoo shop. This wouldn't have been a big deal if the shop was say in Los Angeles or San Diego. But it wasn't. It was in Laramie freaking Wyoming. At that point we'd been dating for 18 months. If we wanted to continue, I was going to have to follow her. With the economy teetering on the brink of a cliff and no real job prospects in southern California, I realized it wasn't much of a decision. I soon found myself driving all of my things to the least populated state in America.

Fun fact about Wyoming - there are *two* seasons. They are winter and

July 27th. One night in February of 2011 the air temperature hit -39°F.
For some perspective, that's so cold it had to warm up 71 degrees just
to get to freezing. And the wind never stopped. The three windiest days
I've ever experienced were during Hurricane Iris, Hurricane Irene, and
a random Tuesday in Laramie. So let's just say it wasn't an ideal place to
foster an ultimate community.

Even so, the University of Wyoming was only a few blocks away and
after doing some Internet stalking I found they actually had a club team
and practiced on Tuesdays and Thursdays at 4:00.

Finally one dude got winded and I found myself back on the line. I
hadn't played in over a year. The collection of nineteen and twenty year
olds on the field looked like they were in about fourth grade.

"Hi," I said, waving. "I'm Cramer."

"Thanks for coming out," their captain said. "Always good to see new
people. Have you ever played before?"

I didn't mean to let out a chuckle, but I did. "Yeah. A little."

The pull went up. I was excited – even to be playing in a pickup game
with a lower tier college team. I absolutely sprinted down to cover my
guy. Shut him down. He ran all over the place but it didn't matter. He
couldn't get open. I had him smothered. I had him...*wow, my lungs are
really burning. Really, really burning - like they're filled with kerosene. Yeah, man,
you go ahead and catch that in cut. I'll be back here wheezing.*

After two points, I reluctantly stumbled off the field wondering what
the hell was wrong with me. I came to the sideline and put my hands on
my knees, huffing and puffing. I now knew how Savannah Ron felt in
Flagler's polyester baseball uniforms.

"I haven't played in a year," I said to the kid beside me. "But (inhale)
goddamn, I thought I was in (inhale) better shape than this. I can (inhale)
barely breathe."

"Did you just move here?" he asked.

"Yeah. A week ago. (Inhale) From LA."

"You know we're at 7200 feet, right?"

In fact I did know that, but the full ramifications of the information
didn't hit me until that very moment. It was then that I realized the top
of Mount Mitchell in North Carolina (the highest point east of the Mis-

sissippi) was 600 feet *below* my apartment. We had to drop *down* 2,000 feet to get to Denver. Realistically, the whole town should've been pressurized. Yet another reason Laramie wasn't exactly a hotbed for ultimate.

I ended up playing with the University of Wyoming kids for about a month as my rusty throws and catches gradually improved and my oxygen deprived lungs started to adapt. They even asked me to coach them for the fall season, an offer I gladly accepted until I got a job teaching at an automotive school. I didn't get out of work until after their practices ended. So once again ultimate went away.

Without ultimate, it was a long three years. I got married. I went hunting. I worked out. I got a job as a bouncer at a bar on the weekends. Other than that, I spent a lot of it shivering. Jessi completed her apprenticeship, becoming a pretty damn good tattoo artist in the process. But it was Wyoming. There are high school football stadiums in Pennsylvania that could comfortably fit Laramie's summer population. There simply wasn't enough skin to ink.

"Ya know Pittsburgh has lots of people," I said to Jessi one day over dinner. "With shitty Steeler tattoos that need fixed."

She thought about it for a good month before flopping on the couch next to me one night and asking, "Will I still get to wear my sweaters in Pittsburgh?"

"Trust me, that will not be an issue."

I was headed back home.

The first time I met the dude I'm going to call Demo Jared was during my first summer league game back in town. I showed up at Turner Valley, a place I knew so well from a decade of playing Pittsburgh Ultimate - and yet every single face running around the fields that day was blindingly unfamiliar. It was like going back to your high school ten years after you graduate. The familiarity actually makes it feel strangely alien. In fact, I was so anonymous I ended up a ninth round draft pick.

The first pass I ever threw to Demo Jared clanked off his hand like he'd reached for it with a shovel. It was a hard flick up the middle at about shin height as he was busting straight in. After the other team scored off the turn, the 6'2" 230 pound former tight end came off the field cursing and kicked a backpack about fifteen yards.

"Shit, damn, motherfuck my hands," he grumbled.

"Don't worry about it, man," I said. "I gunned it at your ankles."

"I always make that catch!" he roared.

"I put that in your stomach and it's not even an issue."

"Let me take the blame here!"

I thought for a second. "Yeah, you're right. You should've fuckin' caught that."

For my first game in three years, I played pretty well. But even as my teammates lauded my unexpected 9th round talents, certain aspects of my game were making me cringe. I tried to gun a 60-yard flick to one of our deeps before the defense could react. In my head, I saw one of my patented rockets that smashed into the receiver's chest like a laser-guided bomb. This one looked more like a paper plate getting blown off a picnic table. After twenty feet, it flopped over and curved out of bounds.

Demo Jared turned to me. "Well that was ambitious."

"I used to have that throw. I swear to you I had that throw."

"Well you don't seem to have it now."

"I do not seem to have that throw anymore, no."

We'd go on to win that game as well as half of our others that summer. And aside from our captain not bothering to show up for the playoffs, it was an awesome season. Demo Jared turned out to be a pretty cool guy. We'd sit on the sidelines and bullshit about Civil War generals and baseball strategy as the young'uns on our team talked about how much PBR they drank the night before. And when the season was over, Demo Jared provided me with a pretty cool opportunity.

In 1987, three smaller schools in Pittsburgh's rough eastern suburbs were forced by a judge to combine into one giant mega-district called Woodland Hills. It included Swissvale, the town where I'd played battle disc with my cousin Eric when I was younger. My father taught chemistry and announced the high school football games there for over thirty years. Demo Jared was Woodland Hills's ultimate coach. He needed an assistant. I loved coaching and I loved Swissvale. I said yes in about a half second.

Now Woodland Hills is a nationally known football powerhouse. In

2010 they had nine guys in the NFL including Hall of Famer Jason Taylor and Patriots All-Pro tight end Rob Gronkowski. To get an accurate picture of the state of their ultimate program, just picture the opposite of that.

The actual high school mascot was a wolverine. We called ourselves the Woodland Hills Beaverdogbears - mainly because the wolverine is by far the toughest member of the animal kingdom to depict via cafeteria mural. Honestly, if you told Van Gogh to paint a wolverine on a cinder block wall outside the gym, it's going to come out looking like a furry brown meatball with teeth. Later on in the season, the kids got pretty awesome turquoise and black uniforms with the wolverine logo on the front and their names and numbers on the back. As Demo Jared told me later, "I spent like five days drawing that damn logo and it still came out looking like a skunkosaurus."

We spent a lot of winter nights trying to teach the kids how to throw, catch, and cut in the gym as they half paid attention and asked in whiny voices when we were going to let them scrimmage. We lost about 40 discs beneath the bleachers, all of which the physical education department would scoop up later and mark as their own. Late in the season, we actually had to send the kids on covert missions into their own gym classes to steal our discs back so we could do basic drills.

And perhaps the best story from our winter practices came one night when Jared sprained his ankle demonstrating how to pivot.

In tennis shoes.

With no one marking him.

On a smooth, perfectly even gym floor.

Which is why I'm calling him Demo Jared.

I absolutely loved that team. They were great kids. Not particularly good at ultimate, mind you, but great kids nonetheless. Our one really good player was a junior named Soup, who was the only kid on the team who understood the game well enough to hang with top competition. Other than him, we had a lot of great athletes (all named Jake or Adam) who couldn't throw. Or we had kids who could throw but moved as fast as spilled caramel. Or we had guys that could do both but always got stuck babysitting or decided academic probation seemed like fun.

There were some real characters on that team. One of the most memorable was an exchange student from Vietnam who actually told us to just call him "Nam" because saying his real name out loud would cause most Americans to bite clean through their tongue. He barely spoke English and had no idea how to play the game in February, but by late April, he was launching hammers downfield like his diploma depended on it.

We had a junior we all called Ollie. Now most times your best cup zone defender is a stick of a kid who can run forever, but at 5'8" 220 pounds, Ollie was ours. He'd hustle and get in the face of everyone he marked, counting louder than the Blount Island Marines. The handlers on the other team would invariably waste two or three seconds just making sure they weren't about to be picked up and body slammed. And he was more committed to the sport than anyone I've ever seen. When the season started he'd been on academic probation. He loved playing the game and loved his teammates so much that he studied his ass off and pulled his GPA up to a 2.80. Partly because of ultimate, I'm proud to say Ollie was accepted to the University of Akron's accounting program. When he told me, I actually jumped about five feet in the air with excitement. I've never been so proud of a kid in my life.

We had the only girl in the all boys league because there weren't enough interested girls to field their own team and Hayley *really* wanted to play. It helped that she had better throws than most of our guys so we told her that if anyone questioned her to just act appalled and start talking in a deep voice.

And probably the most enthusiastic and purely awesome kid on the team was a 19-year-old from the special needs classroom named Paul. He was amazing because even when we were getting our brains beaten in, he'd run onto the field like it was universe point, clapping and yelling, "Let's go guys! Let's go!" At minimum, five times per half, he'd ask me or Jared if we were buying the team ice cream after the game.

"Well, Paul, if we manage to come back and win this game we're currently trailing 12-0, we will treat you guys to all the Dairy Queen you can handle."

And he'd get all excited. "Ice cream if we win, guys! Let's go! Let's run hard!"

Amazingly enough, after that we'd typically go on a remarkable three goal run before losing 15-3.

We didn't realize how completely overmatched we were until our second game of the season. When Demo Jared and I showed up after work to meet the team, thirteen players were there waiting for us to head up north to Pine-Richland High School.

"Alright, guys," Jared said. "It's a forty minute drive, so let's get on the road."

To which they all simultaneously called shotgun and proceeded to create a rugby scrum attempting to squish into his truck.

"Whoa, whoa, whoa." Jared said. "Some of you have to go in the other cars. Who else is driving?"

"Coach Cramer."

"Other than Coach Cramer."

The kids just stared at each other. Finally Soup spoke up. "Uh, my dad needed the car to get to work today. I don't think anyone else has one."

So there we were with a game in ninety minutes able to safely fit six of our thirteen players into our combined vehicles.

"We can just lay down in the back of the truck," Soup said. "There's plenty of room back there."

Jared wasn't amused. "Do I look like I have the money to deal with that lawsuit?"

It was a frenzied half hour trying to figure out who we were going to leave behind as we begged kids to call their moms and puppy dog them for a ride. After fifteen desperate minutes, one of the Jakes spoke up. "I think my uncle has a minivan."

"Call him! Call him now!"

And Jake's uncle rather reluctantly came through for us. He was a guy who looked like he just put in twelve hours at the mill and didn't particularly want to be driving forty minutes with seven high school kids to watch a Frisbee game. We thanked him profusely and set off on our way.

Now some of our kids were from the middle class suburbs of Churchill and Forest Hills, but a lot of our kids were from Swissvale, Turtle Creek, Rankin, and Braddock, some of the most economically depressed areas in western Pennsylvania. Braddock itself sits in the shadow of one of Pittsburgh's only remaining mills and is basically a national poster for urban decay. I only tell you this to set up the scene as we rolled up to the field in Pine Township that day.

The field was on a hill surrounded by million dollar houses with fairway-green lawns. In the driveways sat Audis and BMW's. Fountains spat crystal clear water into the sky. For our kids, it would've been less of a culture shock if we'd driven them to Bolivia. Although none of them would admit it, the affluence was definitely intimidating. I knew if we could just get them warming up, concentrating on something other than the mansions, we'd be ok. So even though we were running late due to the lack of rides, I headed over to find their coach. He seemed nice enough until I shook his hand.

"Hey, we had a little trouble getting rides for all our guys, but we got here," I said. "Just give us about ten minutes and we'll be ready to go."

"Game starts at 4:30," he answered. "It's 4:28."

"It's a long way up here from Churchill, buddy."

"My players are going to be on the line in two minutes."

Our guys were barely cleated up when we gathered them together. If we'd been allotted some time to warm up, I'm pretty sure my pregame speech would've been about having fun, staying calm, and making good decisions. Instead, their coach's arrogant diss got the Swissvale city boy in me riled up. As we gathered in a circle before the game, Demo Jared talked about not clogging the lanes and making smart throws.

He turned to me. "Coach Cramer, you have anything to add?"

"Yeah," I said making eye contact with every one of them as I spoke. "When you go out there and you look at the guy across from you, he might be bigger - he might be faster - he might live in one of these gigantic houses down there. But no matter what happens, just remember that not *one* of them could survive a *minute* in your neighborhood."

And suddenly, they were a pack of dogs ready to tear the Pine Richland kids limb from limb. Standing there in the middle of one of the wealthiest zip codes in Pennsylvania, we all put our thumbs on the disc. I told them what to yell.

"On three," I said. "One...two....three...."

The resulting cheer roared down the valley and rattled the windows of every Jaguar, Bentley, and Cadillac. "*WELCOME TO BRADDOCK!*"

And while I'd love to say my fiery speech inspired them to victory, it didn't. In fact, we got shut out in the first half. But we did score five goals in the second half - which was a hell of a momentous occasion for the Beaverdogbears.

Just before halftime, we put Hayley in the game and after a turnover, Demo Jared yelled out to her. "Hayley! Don't just force it to Soup. Adam was open through the middle!"

One of the Pine-Richland parents heard him. "Hayley? You're playing a girl? Girls aren't allowed in the boys league."

I butted in. "He said 'Hey Lee.' Her name is….I mean, his name is... Lee."

When she came off the field later, we told her about it and in the deepest voice she could muster, she yelled at the Richland parents, "Boy, are my balls itchy!"

As a high school coach, there are a thousand things during the season that you feel guilty laughing at as you realize you're failing miserably at being a positive role model. But the guilt on that one was totally worth it - as was my guilt at approving the following….

Sometime in the second half, one of our African-American kids, a skinny, near-sighted trash talker named B.C. came up and tapped on my shoulder.

"Coach, I got a defense I know will work."

"I'm listening."

"It's called the black zone."

"Sounds interesting. How do we run it?" I asked, thinking he'd come up with some crazy amorphous defense only a high school kid could conjure up.

Instead, he grinned. "We put me, Ollie, and Darnell in the cup. One of these rich white kids surrounded by three black dudes? Guaranteed turnover."

I almost fell on the ground laughing. I also knew he was probably right. "Why the hell not?" I answered. "Go use our country's strained race relations to our advantage, B.C."

B.C. pumped his fist and turned around, excited as hell. "Ollie,

Darnell, we're running the black zone!"

True to prediction, Pine-Richland turned it damn near immediately and Darnell ran down a floaty backhand from B.C. to score our fourth goal of the game. Realistically, it probably had more to do with the gale force winds that kicked up during the point than any trepidation they may have had about our diversity, but it was still fun to watch.

We went 0-10 that year, finishing dead last in the league, never scoring more than five goals in one game. I desperately wanted them to get one victory so they could be rewarded for all the hard work they'd put in. But in the end, the other teams just had more athleticism, skill, and money. And as disappointed as we were after losing our final game 15-5 to the other winless team in the league, the kids piled in the school van, (yeah, we wised up) blasted a bunch of bands I'd never heard of and acted like we'd just been crowned champions as we drove back across town.

In the driver's seat, I was still pissed off about the loss until I looked in the rearview mirror, saw them all laughing together and realized the Beaverdogbears would forever be their Fightin' Amish. I'm willing to bet that none of them remember any of the scores of our games, but they remember stealing all the change from my cup holder to go buy beef jerky when I stopped for gas. They remember Ollie's stall count. They remember Nam shrugging his shoulders and smiling after completing one of his crazy crossfield hammers. They remember Paul sprinting off the sideline to high five them after a goal. Sometimes after playing for seventeen years, you need a little reminder what it's all about.

And yes, Paul, if you're reading this, I realize I still owe you an ice cream.

THIRTY-THREE

I ONCE SAW HIM CLOSE A THIRTY-YARD GAP IN A NANOSECOND TO MAKE A ridiculous lay out catch D between two players in the end zone. His name was Fish and he was a Pittsburgh Ultimate legend, an unstoppable athlete with every throw imaginable. One of the top players in the mid-Atlantic region, Fish was a key member of the New Jersey Pike team that consistently went to nationals in the early 2000s. He was also a huge reason that Max Power once beat the Pittsburgh Weasels in under an hour.

A few Mars tournaments later, I picked up on a team from Philly called Germ Circus with Tour de France Todd. In our third game, we ended up matched against Fish and a bunch of his old Pike mates.

"Ah, crap," I said to Todd. "That's Fish. He's going to shred the hell out of us."

"In that case, you want to guard him?"

"I guess I'll take a stab at it. Don't expect much."

We pulled. I went down to cover Fish, mentally preparing to get run around and broken.

He cut and – I stuffed him. He tried to cut again and I wore him like a jacket. He got a half step on me and they put one out to space that he couldn't quite run down, stumbling as the disc glanced off his fingers.

Turnover.

It was like an alternate dimension. He still looked the same – maybe a few pounds heavier, but whereas he used to turn on a dime, he could now barely turn on a truck tire.

Now admittedly, he may have been stoned out of his mind and that could've contributed to it, but I'm pretty sure he was stoned out of his mind when he laid out to make the insane catch D that I described earlier. Something was off. I walked off the field that day wondering what the hell happened to Fish. More on this later.

It was in my damn Facebook feed. That's where the whole idea came from. At thirty-five, I thought I was done with high-level ultimate. I hadn't played in a club game in going on six years. But there sandwiched between annoying political rants from someone I hung out with once at a wedding was….

Dire Wolf Ultimate Tryouts – Player Information Form

Founded in 2010 by my old friends Tad and Barefoot Ben, Dire Wolf was Pittsburgh's only men's club team that was truly open to anyone who wanted to give it a shot. There was also a team in town called Oakland but they were basically the University of Pittsburgh's college team so the doors were all but closed to the rest of us in the city. Seeing the tryout form there on my computer, a dumb idea started to take shape in my head. I stared at the form for a good ten minutes. And finally clicked on it.

As I completed the form, Jessi came home, lugging her roller derby gear into the kitchen.

"So, uh, I might be playing ultimate again," I said.

She dropped her bag and gave me a sweaty hug. "Oh? Like summer league?"

"No. Like the Pittsburgh travel team."

She lovingly searched my eyes for signs of seriousness. "Won't you be a lot older than everyone?"

I sighed. "Uh. Yeah. That will probably….be the case."

She kissed me on the cheek. "Just don't get hurt."

"You play roller derby. I've seen you get smashed off the track and into a row of folding chairs."

She began walking up the stairs. "I fail to see how that's relevant."

In mid-May, I showed up with about fifty other guys to try out for one of the twenty-one spots on the team. More than anything, I just wanted to see if my old ass could still compete in a fast-twitch sport that realistically I should've given up on years earlier. I plopped my backpack and my water down on the sideline next to Barefoot Ben and looked out at a field full of much younger guys whose bodies weren't yet beat to shit.

"What's up, Ben?" I said. "Good to see you, buddy."

"Cramer," he said, shaking my hand. "Thanks for coming out. We were surprised to see your name on the tryout list."

I laughed as I laced up my cleats. "Yeah....so was I."

I was as nervous as I'd ever been on an ultimate field. I tried to project the confidence of the muscular, tattooed old veteran that I was, but in my head I had no idea if I realistically still belonged out there. What if I was just in the way?

After warming up, we ran some sprints. I wasn't last. That was a good sign. We did some drills. I didn't fuck up too badly. I wasn't turfing throws or dropping easy catches or standing out for sucking. So that was good.

Two hours into the tryout, we broke off into a scrimmage and I got immediately sent out onto a defensive line. This was the test. I was going to have to ya know - cover guys without my hamstrings exploding. We pulled. The other team weaved it up to midfield as I hovered around my guy, giving up an in-cut but otherwise sticking with him. I hadn't gotten immediately torched – a fact I was definitely thrilled about. Then they turned it. It got swung to the sideline to one of Wolf's main handlers, a DC native named Jay who could've easily passed for the ambassador to Ecuador or some other tiny South American country. Consequently, the guys on the team always jagged him about living in a mansion and owning a fleet of Rolls Royces even though he showed up at practice every day in an old Volkswagen Passat. Seeing Beltway Jay get the disc, I cut toward him. He looked off my in cut, so I released up the sideline. Jay saw it. He wound up a backhand and let it fly.

Oh shit. Someone actually threw it to me.

For the first time in my life, I felt as if the word "lumbering" could accurately describe the way I was propelling myself forward. After a forty-yard sprint, I dove to pancake a goal that I'd have easily caught in stride in 2007. But I'd caught a goal - the first goal of the first scrimmage of the first day of tryouts. Maybe I wouldn't simply be in the way after all.

Everything had changed. I wasn't a deep anymore. There were guys out there that were 6'3" and fast and I could no longer outrun and out jump them. In the six years since I'd last played club, the vertical stack offense was replaced almost exclusively with a horizontal stack that spread the receivers wide across the field instead of clustering them in the middle. I had to figure out new angles on defense and new cuts on offense. It was like seeing a remake of your favorite movie. The plot's still the same, but the actors, scenes, and shots are totally different. It was very unsettling.

So I realized the only thing I truly had in abundance was a calm mind and a veteran presence. Without the confidence to launch the disc all over the place and the athleticism to go up, over, and around guys, I finally had to become something I swore I'd never be on the field – smart and boring. The Jacksonville wild man in me puked a little every time I had the opportunity for a wacky thirty-yard scoober and took the safe swing pass to keep possession. We played five scrimmages in the two days of tryouts and I didn't throw the disc more than ten yards down the field at any point. But in a miraculous reversal of personality, I also didn't turn it over a single time. I felt like a comedian trying his hand at a serious role. I felt dry. I felt sober. And as long as I was still on the field, I didn't really mind.

The call woke me up from a nap I desperately needed after two exhausting days of running. I answered the phone. "Hello?"

"Hey, Cramer, it's Tad."

"What's up, man?"

"So we're going over the roster here and we got an offer for you if you want to take it."

"Ok."

"There's a six or seven guy taxi squad. It's usually for young guys with a lot of talent who aren't quite ready to get in the mix yet but we could really use like - a veteran on the field at practice. I mean, you'd be on the team, get a jersey and all that shit, but not rostered for most of the tournaments. We'd call you up if we had injuries or guys were being lazy dicks, not showing up to practice - being fuckin' nutsacks. We'd love to have you out there, but we also understand if that's not what you're looking for. If you wanted to go play co-ed or whatever."

I let out a sigh of relief. It was the perfect scenario all around. I could still play ultimate at a high level three or four days a week but didn't have to travel to Chicago and Boston with a bunch of twenty-three year olds I no longer had much in common with. And Tad and Barefoot Ben didn't have to grit their teeth and cut one of the guys who'd helped teach them the game as teenagers before they became leaders of the Pittsburgh Ultimate community.

"Sounds good," I said. "Let's do it."

"Sweet," Tad said. "Congrats."

"Hey, man, be honest. Am I still any good?"

"You're not what you used to be, obviously. Your straight-line speed needs work. But we cut like thirty guys, so – we wouldn't have kept you if you weren't still good."

"All right, man. See you at practice."

I hung up and smiled. I'd done it. It wasn't scenario number one in my head when I'd filled out the online form, but it was pretty damn close. I'd made the team. I was getting a uniform. I was eight years older than the next oldest guy on the roster.

Like most club teams, Dire Wolf's practices were just the right mix of intensity and complete goddamn clownishness. Tad always led the stretching circle with tales of some crazy exploit that could've only happened to him.

"So uh – you guys tell me if this is weird or not. Like I met this chick last night at Silky's. And she was really cool, right? But she kept herself turned away so I couldn't see the left side of her face. I mean she was making a conscious effort. I got her number but now I'm pretty convinced she only had one ear. I mean, I don't think I ever saw the other one. Otherwise, swimsuit model gorgeous. Funny. Got a PhD in neuro-fuckin'-biology. She can like rebuild brains. But uh, the ear thing…. really bugging me."

Barefoot Ben would chime in next. "There's no way she only had one ear."

"All I'm saying is I can't confirm she had two."

Beltway Jay would turn around from doing leg kicks. "Was she wearing glasses?"

"Of course she wasn't wearing fuckin' glasses, Jay. Or I'd have known she had two ears."

"That's the point I'm trying to get across. If she was wearing glasses, you'd know. I'm trying to help you here."

"Jay, this is what happens when you have your servants do your homework for you. You end up saying dumb shit later in life."

"Ha. Yeah. My servants," Jay would say, resuming his leg kicks. "At some point you're going to need to get new jokes."

"If your family didn't have sixteen butlers, we wouldn't have to make the same joke all the time."

As for me, I'd just laugh and keep my head down, wanting to add to the discussion, but holding back because of one big reason. I'm a talker. I tell stories. In case you haven't figured it out yet, I can ramble a bit. Why is this relevant? Because as I stretched in silence, one of the younger guys would always speak up. We'll call this guy Coop. Since his name was Coop.

"I knew a girl in high school who only had one hand," Coop would say. "I mean, she was cute but...I think it was some genetic thing. Some disease called Murffel uh....Murffel-Pucker Syndrome or wait, that's not it. But it was something like that...."

Now here's why I kept my mouth shut. Beltway Jay, practically skipping at the fact that we'd quit focusing on his riches, would ninja creep next to Coop and yell as loud as he could into his eardrum from two inches away.

"BOOOOOOOORRRRRRINNNNNNNNG!"

And at this point, the whole team was allowed to just slap the hell out of Coop and pelt him with whatever we had readily available. Clumps of grass, bits of dirt, chunks of gravel, muddy cleats, sweaty shirts, water, trash, forearms – it didn't matter. You were getting it all because you were a boring motherfucker. Getting Boringed was the ultimate shame of shames - a ten to fifteen second onslaught of mental and physical torture that I'm pretty sure violated the Geneva Convention.

Coop would be lying there in the grass like a wounded bird, picking cinders and worms out of his teeth when Tad would stand up and point to the other side of the field.

"Break mark drill. Let's go."

And it was time to get serious.

Mainly because I kept my mouth shut, I was only ever part of a single Boring. We had a guy on the team I'll call Awkward Kraig who was one of the most puzzling ultimate players I've ever seen. He was a hyper intelligent guy whose brain managed to simultaneously be three steps ahead and three steps behind everyone else at the same time. When he ran, his arms and legs were almost never synchronized so it was impossible for the defense to have any idea where he was going. This led to him being a totally unstoppable force of nature one day and a bumbling turnover machine the next.

Because of him, the only Boring I was ever involved in got nominated for 2013 Boring of the Year. We'd gotten a new guy on the team named Auble. He was a deep receiver for Carnegie-Mellon and one of those dudes who always looked like he was ready to storm out of a tunnel before kickoff – eyes wide, ready for the side of his head to blow out and cover Yakima in a layer of ash.

Awkward Kraig ends up in line behind me during a break mark drill. He handed me a disc. "Cramer, I have to get a Boring on Auble. Look at him. He doesn't smile. Ever. He's just begging for a Boring."

"I don't know the kid. This is the first time I've ever seen him."

"That's why you've gotta help me."

I stepped up to throw a mark, then grabbed a disc, fired a low release flick and sprinted off to catch a toss from the other line. Kraig did the same and caught up to me.

"You gotta introduce yourself," Kraig said. "And ask him questions about his family. And his major and…"

"You want me to corner him into a Boring? Isn't that slightly unethical?"

"There's no….ethics in Borings. C'mon, Cramer, I need your help."

"Fine, man. At the next break."

The drill went on for twenty minutes. We broke low, we broke high, we broke forehand, we broke backhand, we broke southeast, we broke northwest, we broke every direction on the compass. Every couple minutes or so, Auble would miss a catch or turf a throw and start swearing at himself. Seeing it would send Kraig into a tizzy. He'd tap me on the shoulder, shaking with glee in anticipation.

"You're gonna do it, right? Cramer, I'm counting on you."

"Yes, Kraig. I'm gonna do it."

A few rotations later, he'd tap me again. "We're gonna get a water break right after this drill. You could do it then."

"Kraig, I got it, man."

"Ok, so right after this drill."

"Kraig, I fuckin' got it."

We did in fact get a five-minute water break while Tad and Barefoot Ben set up the next drill. With Kraig nudging me in the kidneys the entire way off the field, I went over and grabbed my water, wandering up toward Auble. I planned on asking him what his major was, his favorite textbooks, facts about his hometown - stuff to really set up an A-number-one Boring. That was the plan, anyway.

I present the following conversation verbatim and in its entirety.

"Hey man," I said, shaking Auble's hand as Kraig snuck up behind him like a terrible pickpocket. "I haven't met you yet. I'm Cramer."

"Auble."

"They said you go to Carnegie-Mellon?"

"Yeah."

"BOOOOOOOOOORRRRRRIIIIIIIIINNNNNNNNGGGG!" Kraig screamed, pouncing on Auble, pointing in his face and showering him with water.

He'd spoken exactly two words, which meant that for all intents and purposes, Auble got Boringed simply for existing. It definitely pushed the boundaries of fair play. Even so, Auble was a rookie and no one gave it much thought. Until his eyes went black.

You ever see one of those wildlife shows where some unfortunate villager pisses off a hippo? Imagine that.

Kraig wore this dumb, gleeful smile the entire way to the ground, laughing his ass off until the horrifying moment he realized Auble was beating the shit out of him.

Auble grabbed Kraig's shirt, throwing short, powerful punches into his back. "What the fuck was that? Don't fuckin' touch me!" Auble yelled.

"Hey, it's a team thing," Kraig said, struggling to breathe. "It's a thing we do."

"Don't fuckin' touch me!" Auble yelled again, slamming Kraig's head into the hillside by the field.

"Auble, let him up," Tad shouted, coming back to get more cones. "Kraig, what the fuck, man? It's his first practice. Not cool."

Kraig got up with dirt and rocks stuck to the side of his face, astonished at the way it had all turned out. "He was being boring. Ask Cramer."

I shrugged. "I guess he wasn't being exciting if that's how you want to look at it."

Auble turned around, swearing to himself as Kraig straightened his shirt and searched the grass for one of his contacts. "It's a thing we do. I swear! Someone tell him it's a thing we do."

Unsurprisingly, not one guy told him it's a thing we do.

I turned to Auble. "Dude, he pestered the shit out of me for like fifteen minutes. I had no choice."

"Fuck off."

"All right then."

I played with Auble the rest of the year. Saw him at three to four practices a week. That was our final conversation.

It came in second place in "Boring of the Year," but only because one of the guys got a Boring on Tad at regionals that the site photographer caught at the perfect moment. The hi-resolution photo captured Tad laying face down in the grass surrounded by a circle of laughing, black-shirted teammates as he desperately tried to hold onto what remained of the man he'd once been. That photo gallery was shared to the entire ultimate community on the most read ultimate site on the Internet. And nothing was beating that. It was like the moon landing of Borings.

Heading out to three or four practices a week brought back my game awareness, agility, and endurance. I slowly turned myself back into a pretty solid and useful club player. The team took trips to DC, Boston, South Carolina & Chicago without me, but I saw it as my job to help get them ready for those tournaments, mentor some of the younger deeps and be ready to step up whenever an opening arose.

That first opening was a tiny, four team tournament hosted by Oakland. (The University of Pittsburgh's club team) Nearing the end of the season, they realized they hadn't played enough games to qualify for the club series, so they threw together a small round robin inviting Dire Wolf, Rochester Zebra Muscles, and Columbus Madcow to Turner Valley. Due to the quick nature in which the tournament was put together, a lot of our guys were going to be out of town. So grandpa got called up to the show.

Right out of the gate, my first club game in five years pitted me against Pitt, the team who only two months earlier had won the collegiate national championship. Some of the best players in college ultimate were lining up on the other goal line. Lord knows we couldn't have played some cream puff to let me get my feet wet. Nope, I was getting tossed to the dragons.

Our O-line received the pull. From the sideline, I watched them march down the field with crisp passes to take a 1-0 lead. An auspicious start.

Tad walked off the field for a sub. "Cramer!" he yelled. "Let's go."

I jogged out there, slapping his hand on the way. And suddenly, I was once again on the line in a club game, staring down at the tiny figures seventy yards away. The pull went up. I sprinted down to cover one of the wing handlers. The deep shot they wanted took too long to develop. At stall nine, Oakland tried to dump it back into the end zone, but pressure from the mark forced a bad pass. Suddenly, we were getting it on the goal line with a chance for an early break.

Oakland set their defense quickly as I slipped into the middle of our vertical stack, watching Beltway Jay pick up the disc and hop it back to the goal line. I planned take a few seconds to survey the play and be the bailout option should our younger, quicker guys have trouble getting open. Then I noticed my defender's head was turned, barking instructions to a teammate.

I didn't even have to throw a shoulder fake. I just stepped out break side and Beltway Jay lofted an outside-in flick that I hopped up to catch virtually uncontested for the goal. We were up 2-0. I'd scored a goal against the college national champions. I walked off the field feeling pretty damn good about things.

That feeling wouldn't last long.

We were up 3-1 when I went in for my second point, running down to cover the off side handler again. This time, however, the guy I was covering was a big athletic dude named Julian Hausman. (After he graduated, he'd go on to play for Seattle Sockeye, one of ultimate's legendary club teams.) He was the exact type of player who I'd have jumped at the chance to lock horns with back in 2002. Unfortunately, it was 2012. We stuffed their initial looks out of the end zone, so they swung it to Hausman. I threw on a confident mark that didn't allow him anything upfield, so he turned and dumped it back into the end zone. Then he did something I wasn't ready for at all. He took the fuck off.

The last time I was on a club field, this wouldn't have been a problem. As fast as he was, (and he was fast) I'd have just run him down. But in the time it took me to get my hips around, he got a step on me. That step quickly became two steps. And three. I stared at his back the entire way down the field until he had the disc in the end zone. I realized right then that no matter how many sprints you do, no matter the insanity of your plyo and core routines, no matter how many miles you put in every week – you can't outrun thirty-five. I walked off the field, for the first time hearing a clock ticking in my head. Tick, tick, tick, tick…..

Suddenly, I knew what happened to Fish.

We were up 12-11 when Tad laid out like he'd come off the top rope to snag a long flick in traffic that would've put us up 13-11. But he hit the ground so hard that his hand popped open and the disc rolled out. Oakland marched downfield to tie it. They got the break they needed on the next point to take a lead they never relinquished.

Against Zebra Muscles, I had my moments, on one point running my defender silly, getting the disc three times and completing a quick ten-yard backhand to the goal line that we punched in on the next pass. But again, my defense was shaky. As the game wore on, the captains started playing me less. We dropped a game we probably should've won 15-12.

Our final game was against Columbus Madcow, who'd been to nationals as recently as 2010. With our short bench getting tired, I got thrust in there a lot, sometimes against guys I could cover and sometimes against dudes I didn't have a prayer against. One tall fast dude just kept running and running and running in some insane geometric pattern that I'm pretty sure the world had only seen in a crop circle in the British Midlands.

I wasn't defending him so much as chasing him like a little brother who wanted his hat back. I knew he was going to score on me a full two minutes before he actually did. It was a really, really sickening feeling.

At halftime, Demo Jared showed up with a couple of the Beaverdogbears just to show them what high-level ultimate looked like. I dragged myself out of the shade to go talk to them.

"Oakland and Madcow, huh?" Jared said. "Those are tough matchups. We miss you doing anything cool?"

I took a desperate sip of water. "If you mean 1997 through 2007, then yeah. If you're talking about this morning, then no, you didn't miss shit," I said, laughing and heading back to our huddle.

Tick, tick, tick, tick, tick......

Over the fall, winter, and spring, I worked my ass off in the gym so I could play one last year. When I showed up at tryouts in 2013, I felt confident. Unlike forty or fifty of the guys there, I already had a uniform. That confidence showed. I was faster and more agile in the drills. I made more decisive cuts and quicker, more assertive throws. During the combine phase, I even managed to jump and reach to 10'2" from a standstill off of wet ground.

This is the point in the story where I conveniently skip right over my 40 time.

For the second year in a row, I made the team as a practice player. And while the Borings still held a sacred place in Wolfdom, a new piece of comedy gold emerged that would eventually sweep the ultimate world.

Until 2013, there was only one company that made official ultimate discs. That company was Discraft out of Wixom, Michigan, and the Frisbee everyone was familiar with was the 175 gram Ultra-Star. Basically, if you started playing any time after 1990, you probably never threw with anything else. Then suddenly, a company called Innova known for high quality disc golf discs entered the ultimate market with the bold new Innova Pulsar. And right out of the gate, they landed some pretty sweet partnerships in the burgeoning new pro ultimate leagues.

Somewhere along the line, one of the guys brought a Pulsar to practice. And while it still had the same weight and dimensions, the bowl was deeper and the edge slightly smaller. Now what you have to understand about ultimate players is that as wild and carefree as we seem to be - on a whole we're as resistant to change as your Republican Uncle Dave. So the new model was met with quite a bit of skepticism and derision.

Because of this, Tad picked up a football lying on the sidelines and pretended he was tossing it like a Frisbee. He later posted the pic to Twitter with the caption, "Hey guys, check out my new Innova Pulsar." And the joke took off from there. All season, guys took pictures of themselves pretending to throw all manner of things – dinner plates, waffles, manhole covers, go-kart tires, loaves of bread, Navajo pottery, pizzas, bedpans, dead birds - if it even slightly resembled a Frisbee, it probably ended up in a Pulsar pic. Other teams started getting in on the action posting Pulsar pics of their own. I think one dude from Baltimore posed with a beehive. Pulsar pics quickly became a semi-regional not quite national phenomenon.

During all the wackiness, I was showing flashes of my former self. At practice, I'd Superman dive to pick a throw that was way behind me or taco swat what would've been a seventy-yard backhand huck an inch from the thrower's hand. Not only was I better in my second year - I was infinitely more relaxed. I was enjoying it. I no longer felt I had anything to prove.

I only got into one game that year when Cleveland Lake Effect came down to play us one Saturday afternoon behind old Pitt Stadium. And I played relatively well for a guy who had almost no effect on the game whatsoever. Lake Effect moved the disc with little short passes up and down the field. We hucked it like ninety times to our top deep receiver, a kid we called Mike Pants. The battle of contrasting styles ended up a close game throughout with neither team getting much of a lead.

It was tied 13-13 when I shut down my guy's deep cut. As he rotated back toward the disc, one of their other guys slipped up-line with two steps on his defender. It was something I'd seen on the field thousands of times. Instinctively, I called a switch and dropped toward the open receiver as the Cleveland dude prepared to throw the easy backhand score. Here was my chance to come out of nowhere to make the game-changing defense that would propel us to victory. It would be a fitting end to my career.

But the handler saw me drop. At the last moment, he holstered his backhand, spun and lofted a hammer to my uncovered guy. It took so long to come down that when he let the thing go, I was eighteen, running shirtless and carefree underneath the palm trees at the fort. By the time I watched it brush past my fingers and settle in the receiver's hands, I was thirty-six with an arthritic hip and a kid on the way. Cleveland went up 14-13.

In baseball, there's a saying, "Careers don't end with home runs. They end with a ground ball to shortstop." It seemed fitting. My club career ended watching a hammer sail over my outstretched fingers. A hammer I'd have swatted out the back of the end zone in my 20's.

Tick, tick, tick, tick......BEEEEP!

Overall, my two years with Dire Wolf provided me exactly what I needed. I needed to prove I could still do it. I needed the camaraderie. I needed the blood on my knee and the sweat ring on my cap. At thirty-five and thirty-six, I got through two entire seasons without once missing a practice because of injury - a fact I'm incredibly proud of. But what I'll always remember – always appreciate was how the team came together at the end of a grueling practice - everyone exhausted, sore, and covered in tiny bits of rubber from the field turf at CMU's Gesling Stadium. As the sun set over the press box, we'd all crowd together and put our thumbs on the inner edge of the same disc. Our post practice chant would echo off the stands.

"One…two….three – WOLF!"

Those are the things you miss when you're done. Those are the things you wish your body would hold together for. So you can have one last year one last time.

Dire Wolf had a four-hour practice scheduled on the morning of Sunday, September 15th, 2013. Jessi had been due on September 8th. I was sitting on the couch watching the Pirate game that Saturday night when she came home from the tattoo shop where she worked, walked through the door and said, "I don't think you're going to practice tomorrow."

And that's how I found out my kid was on the way. The next day while my teammates prepared for regionals, I was helping my wife breathe and push. At 6:17PM, Henry Dalton Cramer entered the world. It immediately eclipsed Chickamauga Jeff's catch against Minnesota as coolest most, amazing moment of my life.

"Welcome to the world, buddy," I told him. "I'm your daddy. Your mama and I love you very much." Then like every new ultimate dad, I quickly did the mental calculation to see what year he could be up for the Callahan Trophy.

The next day my sister came over to see him for the first time. She took a picture of him with his eyes wide open, grinning like an old soul that we posted to all the social media sites to announce his birth. But in the second picture ever taken of him, I held his swaddled little body in my right hand, looking downfield as if I was about to rifle a flick. In the picture, Henry looks equal parts excited and suspicious about what the hell daddy's up to. I announced his birth to the team with that picture and the caption….

"Dirty diapers are *no match* for the Innova Pulsar."

Tad immediately wrote back to the entire Dire Wolf email thread. "That's it. Pulsar Pics are officially over. Cramer wins the Internet."

Damn right I did.

My son was exactly two weeks old when Dire Wolf went up 4-2 in the Mid-Atlantic Regional final against perennial power Truckstop out of Washington D.C. Winner went to nationals. Should they emerge victorious, I knew I could probably convince Tad and Barefoot Ben to let me round out an inflated roster as a favor to a veteran who'd never gotten to set foot on the nationals stage. Maybe I could even get into a game at the end of a blowout. I started dreaming of finally stepping across the sideline and out onto those pristine fields- to finally say I'd played on ultimate's biggest stage. (Convincing my wife to let me leave her alone with a one month old so I could fly to Texas for the weekend was another matter entirely.)

But alas, a few ill-advised turnovers swung the game in Truckstop's favor and Dire Wolf fell a mere five points short of crashing ultimate's biggest party. The season was over. The next year, I'd have a tiny little guy to look after. Four practices a week would be out of the question. So (after months of waffling) I finally decided to retire.

So my club ultimate career was over. And I really, truly meant to hang

it up. Until one last good reason to pull my cleats out of the trunk appeared out of nowhere.

THIRTY-FOUR

It was one of those days where simply walking through the grass soaks your socks through your shoes. After Beaverdogbears practice one Saturday afternoon in April of 2012, Demo Jared and I drove over to my hometown of Trafford to watch Western Pennsylvania sectionals at the superfund site beneath the bridge. It was the biggest thing to happen to Trafford since some guy robbed the 7-11 back in 1994. We slogged by Pitt vs. Carnegie-Mellon, Penn State vs. IUP, Shippensburg vs. Clarion, and finally settled on the sidelines of Edinboro vs. West Virginia. (Which Western PA had apparently annexed without anyone noticing.)

Tad was there rooting on his alma mater, drinking from a flask of "hot chocolate" to keep himself warm as he and his old Haggis teammates went berserk and stormed the field with a bagpiper (yes, an actual bagpiper) any time Edinboro scored.

At halftime as the two cold, muddy teams huddled up, Demo Jared and I joined Tad to analyze the first half.

"Dude, your bagpiper is sick," I said. "That's a three point swing in your favor out of sheer intimidation. The only thing West Virginia could possibly do to counteract it is find a bearded dude with a musket."

"And a coonskin cap," Demo Jared added.

"Well that's a given."

"Don't let them hear you," Tad said. "Fuck. I don't want to have to fight some guy who made a Bowie knife out of a deer antler."

"Who said you'd have to fight him?"

"Oh, I'd have to fight him," Tad said, taking a swig from his flask. "Pro league got nothing on us. They got cheerleaders? We got bagpipes. Tell me that's not sexier."

Demo Jared peered down the sideline at the hairy-armed bagpiper. "That is *not* sexier."

"Open your mind, Jared," Tad said, tapping on his temple. "For once, huh? Try opening your mind."

It took me a while to process what Tad had said a few seconds back. "Pro league? What the hell are you talking about?"

Jared turned to me. "You didn't know about that? Today is momentous. First pull should be going up right about now."

Somehow I did *not* know about that. When I got home I immediately hit my computer to find out that the American Ultimate Disc League (AUDL) had indeed launched ultimate into the world of professional sports that very day. There were teams in somewhat odd places for ultimate – Indianapolis, Detroit, Lexington, Providence, and New Britain amongst a few others. To be honest, it seemed like it had been thrown together by two guys in a basement. But even so, people were *buying tickets* to go watch ultimate. Which meant that players were *being paid* to play. They were being paid per year what your average NFL player might drop on a steak, but that was beside the point. I knew right then and there that everything had changed.

What was it like to be part of the spectacle that was the very first professional ultimate weekend? Beltway Jay from Dire Wolf played in one of the inaugural games for the Buffalo Hunters against the Philadelphia Spinners in front of a raucous crowd at historic Franklin Field. I'll let him describe it to you first hand.

That first game was surreal - one of the most incredible experiences of my life. The venue was the University of Pennsylvania's Franklin Field, a massive 50,000-seat stadium. The Spinners had an announcer, a DJ, cheerleaders, concessions, and Spinners apparel for sale - a totally professional operation. They'd arranged for us to have access to the locker rooms, which was key because our owner mandated that we show up in business casual attire. (We were professionals now!) When we got to our locker room, the Hunters staff had laid out our hot-off-the-presses uniforms on the benches.

We went out to the field for a brief warm up. It was hard to focus without taking occasional glances at the growing crowd in the stands. A few minutes before the scheduled start time, both teams gathered out of sight in a tunnel on the far side of the field waiting for our cue to come out for the national anthem. I was physically ill with anxiety. Well, either anxiety or the sketchy chicken sandwich I ate at the podunk middle-of-Pennsylvania diner we stopped at on the way to the game. Whatever it was, I'd never felt that way before in my life. I shot the breeze with some of my friends on the Philly team while we waited, and waited, and waited and….holy shit, when is this thing gonna start?

Turned out they had to delay the game because there was still a bottleneck of fans waiting to get into the stadium. By the time we walked out for the anthem, the crowd was way bigger than it had been during warm ups. Something like 1,600 people had shown up. That may not sound like much for a stadium that seats 50,000, but trust me, it was a lot. And in keeping with the tradition of Philadelphia sports, they were very, very loud.

The game started and we were totally overwhelmed. The Spinners were more skilled, more prepared, and more athletic. We only had a couple practices to familiarize ourselves with new teammates, the bigger field, and refereed play, so we were completely out of sync. Between the short time allowed between points and the noise of the crowd, we struggled to even get the right line on the field - it was THAT loud. I spent a lot of time imagining how this first pro game would go, but it never occurred to me that crowd noise would be such a huge factor. But here I was, straining to hear our coach scream out the line at the top of his lungs from just twenty feet away. When (Mike Pants) scored and celebrated with an audacious spike that one of his Pitt teammates had invented, he was met with a cacophony of boos.

The Spinners took an early lead and beat us handily, 26-14. I didn't play well and the team as a whole didn't play particularly well, so the game itself isn't one I really like to think about. But I'll never forget that atmosphere.

Thanks, Jay! I saw highlights of that game on the Internet and my jaw dropped seeing an ultimate game with that many butts in the seats and that kind of festival environment. I can't imagine what it was like to see it through Jay's eyes as he came out of the tunnel.

The inaugural AUDL championship was even played at the Pontiac Silverdome, the former home of the Detroit Lions and host to Super Bowl XVI. Here's an interesting snippet of what Jay wrote about playing there in a regular season game against the Detroit Mechanix.

Because of the old school 70's Astroturf surface, our locker room at halftime was like a medical ward: blood and gauze and sterilizing wipes everywhere. By some miracle I made it through most of the game without too much carnage, even though I'd

played a majority of our D points. I thought I'd escape unscathed until I laid out for
a goal at the final buzzer. (We were down by four but I was still looking for my first
AUDL goal.) So much for that - blood pouring out of both elbows and knees. I was
still oozing at work on Monday.

The Silverdome was abandoned and the roof collapsed in January 2013, just a
few months after the end of that AUDL season. I felt kind of conflicted about it
because, on the one hand, I had the privilege of playing there; but on the other hand,
fuck that place and its blood-sucking turf from hell.

Jay contributed some great stories about that season including how he
frustrated Rhode Island's best handler with some admittedly questionable tactics, how cool it was to score a professional goal in front of his
dad, and the ups and downs of playing for a squad that ended up 3-13 in
an upstart league that still had a lot of bugs to work out. Unfortunately, I
don't have the room to include them all in this chapter. Maybe I'll include
them all in the 900 page "Universe Point – The Super Deluxe Author's
Special Edition" somewhere down the road.

The Spinners beat Indianapolis 29-22 in front of a rather sparse
crowd in the championship game, but in many ways the experiment had
worked. If done correctly, pro ultimate seemed (at least potentially) vi-
able.

The next year brought a civil war of sorts as a bunch of legal battles
raged on that I don't particularly want to dedicate any time to. (Because
I'm terrified half of Dire Wolf will charge into my house and Boring me
to death.) Long story short, the Philadelphia Spinners took their championship trophy and formed their own pro league - Major League Ultimate. (MLU) So suddenly there were *two* competing pro ultimate leagues,
a fact that was as ridiculous as the most ridiculous thing you can come
up with. Personally, I'm thinking of a bullfrog with a mullet. Having two
professional ultimate leagues is 47% more ridiculous than that.

Each league seemed to have its own strategy. The MLU carefully
branded and marketed their league with slick logos, cool merchandise,
and their own Internet channel that broadcast live games and highlights.
They had awesome team names like The San Francisco Dogfish, the
Vancouver Nighthawks, and the Seattle Rainmakers. (The Rainmakers
logo is this mysterious guy in a cloak and is seriously one of the top

five coolest logos in all of professional sports.) The league signed TV deals with local cable providers. I was sitting on my couch in Pittsburgh one night flipping through the channels and found a replay of the Philadelphia Spinners vs. Boston Whitecaps game. I stayed up until 2AM watching ultimate *on my own television* with announcers and sideline reporters and coach interviews and instant replays and everything. I swore I'd fallen asleep and just didn't know it. It had to be a dream.

Overall, the MLU smelled professional as hell. But they only had eight teams - four along the I-95 corridor and four along I-5 in the Pacific Northwest. So while the game was sleek, exciting, and well marketed, their reach was somewhat localized.

The AUDL on the other hand gave out franchises to whoever won bingo on Tuesday night at the local senior center. Four of the original eight teams folded after the first year. They didn't care. They went out and got nine more. And just as it seemed the fledgling league was teetering on the brink of failure, they signed a bunch of ultimate's biggest stars. Next thing anyone knew, they were announcing a deal with ESPN to broadcast a game of the week on ESPN 3. They expanded into Canada and as far west as Minneapolis. Western and Southern divisions followed in 2014 & 2015. A mere four years after a couple dudes brought the league out of their basement, there were twenty-six teams stretching all the way from Ottawa to San Diego. The next few years will almost assuredly see the AUDL feature the same number of franchises as the NHL, NBA, and Major League Baseball. (Especially since the MLU ceased operations about two months prior to the publication of this book.) And while some teams struggled to find a fan base, the 2016 semifinal between the Madison Radicals and Seattle Cascades brought well over 3000 fans to Breese Stevens Stadium in downtown Madison, Wisconsin. I've been to Pittsburgh Pirates games with less people.

Highlights from MLU and AUDL games started making it into Sportscenter's top ten plays, beating out NBA dunks, crazy NHL saves, and towering home runs. The 2014 MLU championship between the DC Current and Vancouver Nighthawks was even played at the Major League Soccer stadium in Philadelphia - and for the first time ever featured a field lined specifically for ultimate. No distracting football yard markers, no soccer goal boxes, no orange cones that were sorta kinda lined up. They played on a field with painted brick marks and lined end zones with the correct dimensions. When I saw it, I'm not afraid to say I wept a little. It was a minimalist's dream. It was beautiful.

Combined with the fact that the USA Ultimate championships (both college and club) were now being streamed live on ESPN 3, it could be argued that ultimate's arrival was no longer pending. It had crushed a beer can against its head and kicked down the door.

On July 4th, 2014 as the country celebrated our independence, I was laying in a hospital bed, completely unable to move. Each individual muscle felt as if it was being squeezed by a vice from the inside out. Two days prior my body started yelling at me, but I thought I'd just overdone it at the gym so I ignored it. By the 4th, the pain was so intense that I was all but paralyzed. I couldn't lift any of my limbs. I had to be helped in and out of the car. I couldn't sign my own name at the hospital because I wasn't able to grip the pen. Suddenly my vertical and my bench press were the last things on my mind. The guy who'd dedicated a majority of his life to outworking and out-training everyone else was confined to a bed, wondering if he'd taken his final steps. It was fucking terrifying.

They never figured out what it was. The doctors and specialists were absolutely baffled. Could've been from a mosquito bite I got in the backyard. Could've been a random virus I picked up from a doorknob. Hell, maybe I knocked over a vial at the CDC and just don't remember. Whatever it was, after two days of near total immobility, the pain subsided enough to allow me to walk again and even swallow without flinching. But it took damn near a month to get the strength in my hands and forearms back. All through July I couldn't open a jar on my own, let alone throw a disc. It took over three months for the headaches to finally subside. Whatever the hell Neptune Pox invaded my body, I don't wish it on anyone. But I guess in the end I lucked out. It wasn't permanent. It passed.

As I struggled to get back on my feet (literally) I ran across a very interesting announcement. Out of nowhere, an AUDL franchise had been awarded to Pittsburgh. The owners were accomplished medical professionals from Ohio who apparently had a hell of a good Tuesday night at bingo. There'd be an open tryout in early 2015.

If I hadn't been weak, helpless, and bedridden, I probably wouldn't have done it. But I remembered the frail powerlessness of July all too vividly. I needed a goal to motivate me to throw up those extra reps, climb one more set of stairs, and run that extra mile - something more than simply the hope of returning to normal. Looking at that announcement, I knew exactly what that motivation would be. I was going to be the oldest guy on the field at that tryout. And I was going to belong out there amongst all the young kids in their athletic primes. I had five months to rebuild my body.

Around the end of September, I was ready to start pushing myself. I sprinted the bridge over the Allegheny River. I ran the giant Pittsburgh hills. When the winter came I did shuttle runs, plyos, kettlebells, stairs, pushups, pull ups, burpees, and core work. Every time I wanted to quit early, I told myself, *"Everyone you're going to face on the field is going to be a decade younger. And they won't be trying to fight back from Neptune Pox."* And I'd put my head down and do one more set.

My initial test came during the first ever Pittsburgh men's winter league. The Community for Pittsburgh Ultimate had managed to snake some extra space late on Friday nights at a local indoor soccer arena. So we took advantage of it with a six-team league. Everyone in the league was put on random teams, hat tournament style. It was five on five speed ultimate, drop and go - fast paced, six second stall count, hockey style substitutions, end zone to end zone two point throws, and your occasional body check into the riser boards.

The league itself was incredible. My team included three guys from Pitt including a stupidly good athlete named Trent Dillon who'd later win the 2016 Callahan, along with a fast, lanky leaper named Anson who'd finish the 2016 AUDL season with the second most D's in the league. Also we had Demo Jared who uh….had a reliable truck.

All the teams sported similar talent. In fact, over the summer I'd watched a machine named Rob Dulabon score a goal in the MLU championship for the eventual champion DC Current. On my first point in my first game, I went to pick up the disc and he came over to cover me.

I laughed. "There are a lot of other guys to guard out here. Just so you're aware."

He chuckled and tapped the disc into play. I knew it was going to be a fun couple of months.

In our sixth game of the year, Demo Jared charged in to attempt a D against a guy that also looked like a former football player. Jared didn't get there quite fast enough, missing the disc by an inch or so, his momentum carrying him into the netting along the side of the fields. And this would've been the end of things had the netting not cartoonishly slingshotted him back into the playing field to crack heads with the guy who'd just caught the disc.

At that point I realized the phrase *"Oh shit, does anyone have a towel?"* never indicates anything positive. Three minutes later, Jared came off the field with an old shirt pressed to his nose. I walked out from the bench to meet him.

He lifted the bloody cloth away from his face and squinted. "How's it look?"

"Well," I said, noting that his nose had shifted quite a ways toward his left eye, "From what I remember, it's not where it's supposed to be."

"Shit. I have a date tomorrow night."

"Yeah, I'm thinking you're gonna have to win her over with your personality."

Anyway, we lost that game to start the year 3-3, but apparently the ultimate gods were appeased by Jared's blood sacrifice. We finished the year on a seven game winning streak and at 10-3, found ourselves in the championship game against a team captained by Tad, whose team came into the game 12-1.

With two minutes left, we were up by three and trying to kill the clock when Lanky Anson got trapped on our goal line. I faked out my defender and cut horizontal across the field to bail him out. His throw floated way out in front of me. Out of the corner of my eye, I saw Tad leave his guy. If he arrived at the disc before I did, they had a chance to score quickly and only be down two points with plenty of time left to come back. I knew he was barreling down on me. When Tad locks his eyes on the disc, he might as well be in a tunnel. He's not slowing up. He's steaming toward you like a train.

I leapt. I extended my right hand as far as I could reach, twisting in the air, exposing my ribs. I curled my fingers around it just as Tad bulled through my hip. He undercut me. My ass came down on the back of his shoulder. I rolled to the turf, kicking up bits of rubber. But I still had the disc. I stood up and looked at the clock. It ticked down under two minutes. I knew I'd just sealed us the championship. I'd been one of the better players in a league peppered with nationally known stars. My hard work was paying off.

I woke before dark on the day after New Year's 2015 and drove down I-79 to the Southpointe Fieldhouse. It was the first ever event hosted by the expansion Pittsburgh Thunderbirds and though the pro team got a bit of a frosty reception from the local community at first, you could feel the excitement from the players and staff as soon as you walked in the door. All the guys filling out forms beside me seemed to be realizing that if they did well, they could legitimately call themselves professional athletes.

There were a lot of familiar faces, but also a bunch of guys from Cleveland and Columbus that had made the trip over to PA. Eight guys had already signed contracts, so the fifty or so players at Southpointe that day were all fighting for somewhere around seventeen roster spots.

The head coach was a Pitt alum named Dave Hogan who had apparently been a hell of a college player from 2006-09. (Which made the *coach* a decade younger than me. Sigh.) After warm-ups, he gathered us in a circle and fired us up, letting us know the schedule for the six-hour tryout. We split up in groups of twelve to hit the various combine events – shuttle run, vertical, 40-yard dash, and serpentine.

A cool thing happened along the way. In essence, we were all competing against each other, but through each event, we couldn't help but yell encouragement and root each other on.

"Dig, dig, dig, push through. Push through!"

It's a rare kinship that lets a group of athletes cheer for the other guys that are fighting for the same prize. But it's what ultimate players do.

Hilariously, somebody forgot the tape measure, so the volunteers in charge of the forty-yard dash had to eyeball it and guesstimate. It was a bit long. As guys came back to the start line for their second attempt, I yelled to them....

"Let's go! Let's go! Make this your best forty-three and a half yard dash time ever! You've never run forty-three and a half yards this fast!"

Later I was told that all my measurables fell somewhere in the middle of the pack, which at thirty-seven felt like an outright victory.

The morning was filled with four-on-four and five-on-five games as the coaching staff and general manager evaluated the talent. I played ok, making a few D's and scoring a few goals, but I also kept getting beat up-field on handler cuts, which I knew wasn't particularly impressive. None of the coaches were saying, "Man, that Cramer sure can get burned up-line. I wanna see more of *that!*"

By far the best part of the tryout was what happened around noon when we came back from a half hour break. Based on what the coaches had seen during the morning session, they split us into two equal teams of 21, a dark team and a light team. Each team was then subdivided into lines of seven that would rotate in every three points regardless of what happened on the field. Drop the pull and get scored on? Go sit down. Play an epic point with seventeen turnovers? Cool, you got two points to rest. Game to 25.

I wasn't quite prepared for how strange the game would seem. The scrimmage was played under the new pro rules. The field was much, much wider to accommodate the sidelines of your typical soccer or football field. It was like playing on a cruise ship. The field seemed *huge*. Also, unlike regular ultimate, double-teaming the disc was legal. The stall count was only seven. And in the strangest departure from normal, there were referees making calls and counting your stall for you. No more self-officiating. It was the same game...kinda. It felt like ultimate's jacked up cousin.

The line I got put on included Lanky Anson from my winter league team, a kid named Trucks who was on the U19 national team, Jack Slevin, a local product who handled for Oregon, and three of my former Dire Wolf teammates, Weiss, Kummer, and a dude I'll call Wandering Adam. (Because he once stumbled away from a Dire Wolf party and wasn't seen or heard from for two days.)

As we discussed strategy, we realized that somehow we ended up with a seven handler line. There wasn't a single weak thrower. We were going to do some damage. And we did. On our first point, Lanky Anson charged up the middle to make a diving two-handed layout D on the second pass out of the end zone. He picked it up and hit Wandering Adam for the score. We'd barely been on the field.

"Well that was quick," Weiss said as I followed him off the field.

Weiss was a Woodland Hills graduate who was elusive as hell for being built like a tiny, balding tomato can. I'd never seen a guy who was so infinitely better than his body type. He was also a law student who led Dire Wolf in getting Boringed because he just couldn't help bringing up random case studies all the time.

"Ya know," he'd say, "in relation to your discussion, there was actually a precedent set in Gurgles vs. Dirthammer back in 1988."

Tad would look around. "Whose turn is it to Boring Weiss? Like seriously, we should just make a permanent rotation."

On our second point, I leapt to catch one on the left sideline and with nothing upfield, flipped a high release flick back to Weiss. He swung it wide across the field to Slevin who quickly punched it in before the defense had a chance to shift.

On the way off the field, Weiss socked me in the elbow. "Way to stay calm and beat that double team. That's a veteran play," he said.

"I was getting double teamed?"

"Yeah. On that high release dump you threw me."

"I didn't notice," I said. "If it was a veteran move, it was only because I'm so old I've become oblivious to my surroundings."

Kummer, a wiry handler with a 70's mustache looked up from the bench. "Is it weird to anyone else that you're standing there marking a guy and not saying anything?"

"Yeah!" Wandering Adam exclaimed. "The silence is killing me."

"You can have a conversation now," I said. "Guy's looking downfield, you can ask him anything – *So what do you do for a living? You know anything about cold fusion? Got any thoughts on the afterlife?*"

"It's like an awkward date," Wandering Adam said. "It's creepy."

"*You know any good restaurants around here? You like those cleats? Fucked up what's going on in Syria, huh?*"

We'd been right. Our line did some serious damage. We played seven points in the first half and scored on six of them. Just before halftime, we came out on defense and I got assigned to cover the break side handler wing. He picked up the pull and tossed it to the apex. As I arrived to cover him, he shot past me to make a scooter cut into the middle. Trailing him by a step and a half, I saw the play developing. The opposite handler was busting up the sideline, using the ridiculous width of the field to his advantage. There was no doubt my guy was going to catch the disc and loft it out for the handler to run down in a power position looking for a deep shot. So instead of slowing down to mark him when he caught it, I leapt across the front of his body. What he thought was going to be an easy little backhand flip skimmed my thumb and fluttered sideways.

Off my tip, Wandering Adam made a spectacular neck-high dive, catching it halfway to the surprised handler. Adam landed on his stomach and slid a few yards toward midfield, then popped up and turned around. By then, I was already behind my guy and heading for the end zone.

My cut cleared a lane for Kummer. Wandering Adam spotted him and hit him with a fifteen-yard flick. Now it was my turn. Seeing Kummer get the disc, I took two hard steps to the center of the end zone, then stopped, put a hopping swim move on my defender and tore back to the corner. Kummer floated a pretty no step backhand that I leapt for, toeing the line with both feet, scoring the goal that put the dark team up 13-7 going into half.

At 37, I forced a turnover, threw a sick fake, and scored a goal in a scrimmage that featured some of the best players in the area, if not the country. If the pro leagues really do take off, I can always tell my son, *"Yeah, I was at the first ever pro tryout in Pittsburgh. I was way older than everyone. Some of the top players in the game were on the field with me. And I scored a goal."*

And that's what I have. It's not Tiny Alex tossing a ten-yard pass to his younger brother win a college national championship. It's not Kosher Josh catching the final goal to win club nationals. It wasn't Captain Ian's Callahan to send Penn State to the big dance. But it's what I got. And that's enough.

The game itself became an instant classic as the white team stormed back from down 20-13 to eventually tie it 22-22 as the entire arena started to fill with spectators, injured players, parents, and random people who were looking for the gas station down the road. It got *loud* in there as both teams shouted their heads off, our voices reverberating off the ceiling to create a giant echo chamber that made the fieldhouse seem packed with fans. With forty-two of the best players around all battling for spots on the roster, it became one of the best, most exciting games I've ever witnessed.

Tied at 23, I was out there defending a guy that Coach Hogan had specifically matched me up on for most of the game. His name was Haser, a 6'4" kid who'd started at wide receiver for perennial state powerhouse North Allegheny High School. The kid ran the fastest shuttle time of anyone at the combine and his vertical was right around eighty-six feet. Also, he'd just turned eighteen, which meant he was approximately as old as the Fightin' Amish jersey in my closet.

I'd done well against him so far, using his relative inexperience to my advantage. Despite being a freakish athlete, he'd really done nothing all game on me – until that point. After I shut down his deep cut, Haser was drifting around in the back of the end zone when the disc got swung to the one dude on the field who maybe shouldn't have been there amongst all the elite players. He was a really nice kid. I'm sure he was a solid summer league player. But he was tiny. He was somewhat spastic. He was getting pushed around out there against the big boys. Knowing this is what shot me in the ass.

Seeing him with the disc, I crept into the middle to help out, trying to get a sneaky poach D should he panic and float something into the end zone. The mark was all over him. The stall was getting high. We were a half second from forcing a turn when out of his hand came the most insane twenty-yard lefty hammer I've ever seen. I still have a snapshot of it in my head as it left his fingertips, going straight up into the air like a NASA launch, nearly skimming the lights hanging from the ceiling directly above me. Its apex had to have come a half inch from one of the I-beams on the roof. I'd have expected to turn around and see Bigfoot before I expected *that* throw from *that* kid. It was damn near incapacitating in its audacity. For a full second, I actually stood there in awe at its impossible trajectory before yelling loud enough for the entire fieldhouse to hear....

"Awwwww shit!"

I turned and tracked it like a center fielder running down a fly ball toward the wall. In front of me, I could see Haser sprinting in as the disc fell straight down between us. We arrived at nearly the same time. I left the ground with a half leap, half layout and got my entire palm flat against the disc. I crashed face first into Haser's thigh before flipping onto my back as I hit the turf. As I lay there, I nodded confidently. I'd just made one hell of a defense. Maybe that was the moment that pushed me into the running for a roster spot. Maybe I had a chance to make this team after all. I looked around to see where the disc had gone. I didn't see it anywhere. That was odd. *Wait a minute.....*

I looked up to see Haser holding the disc in the air celebrating the goal he'd just scored. All I could do was stare at the rafters. He told me later on the sidelines that I'd managed to push the disc about a foot or so straight into his hands.

"And then you punched me in the mouth," he said, rubbing his jaw.

"Serves you right for stealing my big D," I said patting him on the back. "Great fuckin' catch, man. Great fuckin' catch."

I guess in the end, it was appropriate. My generation of ultimate players spent two decades building up the game that the founders had created. It was time for the next generation to take over. It was as if the disc itself was an extension of the hands of time. I'd done my part. Now it was time to move on. *"Here, kid. You take it from here. Sorry for punching you in the mouth on my way out."*

Our next line managed to stop the bleeding, scoring to tie the game 24-24. It brought on universe point, something we all really should've anticipated from the opening pull. Coach Hogan called out the top players on each team to match up in one final epic point. (Not surprisingly, I wasn't one of them.) The energy and the camaraderie around the field that day was something I'll always remember as both teams yelled, shouted and cheered for our temporary teammates like we'd all been playing together for years.

Almost immediately a giant backhand huck went up from the white team. The sidelines exploded as one of the guys from Columbus Mad-cow tracked it and left his feet in a full layout. For some incomprehensible reason, he reached for the tailing disc with the wrong hand and swatted the winning score away from himself. The roar of anticipation quickly turned into an "Ooooohhh."

We got the disc back and two passes later one of the Cleveland guys launched a huge flick for Trucks, the kid on the U19 National team. Both sidelines leaned forward. Trucks went up over his defender. Picked the disc. Tryout over.

I realized watching that point that in twenty years, I'd truly seen it all. For better or for worse, ultimate had become the sport I'd envisioned back in 1997 when I dreamt of fans storming the field at Flagler. There were no slacker hippies in that handshake line. There weren't any fat kids. No one was barefoot. It looked more like a professional soccer tryout than something that spontaneously happened at a Phish concert. The sport I loved was a little less quirky. A little more mainstream. And it's truly hard to say how I feel about it other than I'm glad I got the chance to experience both ends of the evolution.

Two days later the Thunderbirds posted a few videos on their Face-book page. My son Henry was fifteen months old at the time. He scrambled up into my lap with one of my ultimate discs as I clicked on "play" to show Jessi where I'd been for six hours on Friday. In the video, one guy catches the disc and tries to squeeze a backhand into the end zone. The defender runs over, lays out and tips it into the air only to have it act like a falling leaf and float straight into the receiver's hands behind him.

Henry held up the disc and pointed at the computer. "Fribby!"

"Good, buddy. That *is* Frisbee! That's where daddy was on Friday morning."

Jessi smiled a knowing smile. "If you don't make it, are you really going to hang it up or are you going to keep using your book as a reason to limp up the stairs twice a week? I know you're only writing it so you have an excuse to play ultimate forever."

"Nah, this time I'm really done," I said, cringing at the words. "Maybe. I mean. I played ok." I looked down at my son who held a disc in his hands that was almost bigger than he was. "Now that I think about it,

I *could* make the team. There's an outside shot. I mean it's definitely not zero," I said imagining the possibilities. "But if I don't make it, I'm retiring. I swear this time. Probably."

"Uh-huh," she said rolling her eyes. "Why do I have the feeling this isn't your last chapter?"

Like usual she was right. Turned out there was one more chapter after all. But that's it, I swear.

THIRTY-FIVE

The scoreboard clock at Cupples Stadium on Pittsburgh's Southside showed eight seconds left in overtime when the throw went up. Two-time AUDL MVP Jonathan "Goose" Helton of the Chicago Wildfire was tracking the floating disc into the end zone. And I was sprinting with him stride for stride. As he leapt, I was in absolutely perfect position. The whole game was riding on me.

The game itself had only gone into overtime because Chicago's star deep receiver AJ Nelson had come down with a desperation flick into the end zone, grabbing it between two defenders on the sideline with one second left. Then with thirty seconds remaining in the extra period, a pass went right through Helton's hands, somehow caught air off his stomach and zipped right into the chest of former Pittsburgh Weasel Dave Vatz to give the Thunderbirds a slim 27-26 lead. As our announcer told the crowd, "The pass turned Helton into a hologram," which is both the truth and the best live description of a play I've ever heard.

Whoever won this critical late season contest was almost sure to lock up second place in the Midwest Division, meaning a home game in the playoffs. Whoever lost would finish third and have to travel. There was a lot riding on that hanging disc.

No doubt looking to atone for his defensive miscue, Helton left the ground about two strides from the back of the end zone. I was the only one anywhere near him as he grabbed it about nine feet in the air and stretched to get his right foot down. It was close. Really close. If I hadn't sprinted my ass off to track him down, I'm absolutely sure it would've been a goal. Behind me, I heard the hometown crowd groan thinking they'd been snake bitten by another last second Chicago score.

But I didn't see any green turf between his toe and the white line. I blew my whistle and signaled him out the back of the end zone. Game over. Pittsburgh wins. The crowd went nuts.

A truly exhausted Helton hung his head and looked at me. "I was out?"

I patted him on the back. "You clipped your toenails today, that's a goal."

As Pittsburgh started to celebrate and Chicago began to realize that their hard fought effort came up a hangnail short, the other three refs wandered over with skeptical looks.

"He sure looked in from where I was standing."

"I thought for sure he tied the game."

"I was already preparing for double overtime."

"His toe was out," I said. "Right on the line."

They continued to stare at me.

"Actually now that you jagoffs are asking about it, I'm not sure anymore." A feeling of dread overtook me. "Oh shit, I hope I got that right."

As expected, the Thunderbirds just didn't have room for a former deep who was as close to fifty as he was to twenty-five. I was disappointed but realistically I knew that ultimate's explosion had come a decade too late for me. As the season approached, I'd anticipated buying season tickets to watch a bunch of guys I knew well – guys like Tad, Lanky Anson, Tiny Alex, Viking Darren, Mike Pants, and a few of my other Dire Wolf teammates represent Pittsburgh as professional athletes. I planned on drinking beer, getting loud and heckling – until I got an email from the Thunderbirds general manager.

Kevin, we were hoping you might be interested in being a referee for the Thunderbirds this season. You wouldn't have any problem keeping up with the game, and the rules won't be that difficult to learn for someone who's played so long. We're looking to add a few more guys to the crew.

At first I dismissed it. Refereeing? Sounded to me like a lot of needlessly getting yelled at by people I couldn't just tell to fuck off. Also, I wasn't sold on refs being part of the sport. Many players still considered self-refereeing and "Spirit of the Game" as integral to ultimate as the disc itself. By donning the stripes I felt a little sinister, like I'd be helping to "Ides of March" half the people who taught me how to play. It wasn't a chance I jumped at by any means.

I'd rather help in some other way, but if you're in absolutely desperate need, let me know.

They were in desperate need. Two days later I was trying to memorize the rulebook.

The Thunderbirds were set to make their debut as a team at a pre-season mega-scrimmage in Cincinnati soon thereafter. So about a week after receiving the rulebook, I found myself in a minivan headed west on I-70 through wild, wonderful Ohio. The players had crammed themselves into a 15-passenger van that I'd stupidly promised our head referee, a snarky, beer-loving dude named Heim that I'd drive home after the tournament. This gave me a chance to hang with the twenty-three year old college buddies who ran the team.

"I couldn't believe the level of talent at the tryout," said Andrew, the team's general manager as he tried to keep up with the speeding passenger van. "It was so much higher across the board than we expected."

Elliott, the assistant GM turned back to face me. "After the combine, we looked at each other and we were like, 'We have to cut *this* guy? Are you kidding?' We knew we'd have some top end talent but like, when we started seeing the guys we had to *cut*, that's when we started getting pretty excited."

Andrew laughed. "Cramer, let's just say if we made a team of the dudes that we had to get rid of, you guys would get five or six wins this year. Seriously, fifteen guys that didn't make it would've been the best player on my college team."

"Oh yeah," I laughed. "Where'd you play?"

"Miami of Ohio."

I swore we smashed into a construction barrel.

"Are you….Miami of….are you goddamn kidding me?"

"No," Andrew said. "I played at Miami of Ohio. Why?"

"I'm going to have to ask you to pull over so I can get out and walk the rest of the way."

Andrew laughed. "Oh no, did you play them when they were assholes?"

"Seriously, there's a rest area coming up here in a half mile."

"I heard they used to be the worst," he laughed. Then with a sincerely apologetic tone, he continued. "I did everything I could the last couple years to clean it up. I swear we were really cool."

I felt like I'd been blown out the back of the van, my limp body careening down the interstate. *What did he just say?*

"Wait, you're telling me *Miami of Ohio* was cool and fun to play against?"

"We tried to be, yeah."

"You realize that's like telling me dinosaurs are still alive, right? It throws off my entire worldview."

"Oh shit," he laughed. "You gotta tell me stories."

"It all started on a rainy day in Gainesville…..."

A former Miami of Ohio player had hired me to make sure that ultimate games were being contested fairly and honestly. I can now say I truly understand the definition of irony.

We arrived at the giant bubble that had been inflated over the University of Cincinnati's football practice field about twenty minutes before the first game was to begin - which meant that Heim and I had virtually no time to prepare. They sent us to the referee's locker room where some guy named Waffles did a bang up seven-minute job of prepping us for being on the field. And then it was time to go.

The scrimmage featured the Thunderbirds, Cincinnati Revolution, Indianapolis AlleyCats, and expansion Nashville Nightwatch. Each team would play four 12-minute games from 10:00PM straight through until 4:00AM. When the scrimmage began there was a real sense of excitement amongst the teams who were hopping, screaming, and jumping at the chance to get the season started. Music was blasting and 200 or so fans lined the field. I'd seen enough ultimate in my life that I wasn't even slightly intimidated by it – until the first pull went up.

I quickly realized that simply reading a rulebook leaves you woefully underprepared to put your knowledge into action. Acting decisively was something I had no problem with when I was playing - but put a whistle in my hand and I was like a nervous kid peeking over the high dive. After being the sideline ref in the first game between Cincy and Indy, they moved Heim and I onto the field itself for the Pittsburgh vs. Nashville game. Suddenly, we were the ones right in the middle of all the action – the ones who did strange, alien things like count the stalls, mark penalty yardage, and control the clock.

With a disc in my hand, the game itself had long ago slowed down. Ten seconds seemed like thirty. But as I stood behind the thrower watching for infractions, I felt like my cousin Chris in that first real game he'd ever played - suddenly and surprisingly overwhelmed.

Ok, stalling one….two….three…..oh shit, they're trying to dump it - get out of the way. Was that a travel or did the mark bump him? Am I supposed to call that? Nah. I'm not supposed to call ticky tack little….oh fuck, I'm not stalling. I should be on six by now, right? Uh…..six…… …seven. Wait, seven's a stall in this league. I should blow the…..eh, he got the pass off. Fuck it. (Fifteen-yard sprint) *One…. two…..*

There was so much to keep track of, it felt like I was watching a game on fast forward. And the running, holy shit, the running. There were only four refs there for the entire scrimmage. Which meant that we were on the field for all eight games that night. And every time a huck went up, guess who had to chase it down to get in position? By the time the last game rolled around at 3:30AM, I was deliriously losing my peripheral vision. Luckily, so were Cincinnati and Nashville, who managed to go over ten minutes tied 0-0. When the game was over, I couldn't wait to just mash my ear against the window and pass out as nighttime Ohio zipped by outside. Then as we're walking out of the bubble, Heim flips me the keys to the 15-passenger van.

"Glad I drove on the way here," he snickered. "I'm fuckin' dead."

"Son of a bitch. I promised I'd drive, didn't I?"

"Hey, you have a one-year old, right? You should be used to getting no sleep."

I blinked. And held it for ten seconds. "That is an unfortunately accurate assumption. Get in. Let's go."

With the entire team dozing off and relaxing after running half as much as I did, I slammed a Red Bull and threw the van into drive thinking how regrettable it was that the Thunderbirds would never get to play another game after most of the team perished in the fireball that was assuredly in our future. But through a lot of slapping myself and peeling my eyelids open, I got the team safely back home. When we pulled off the Parkway, most of the team began to wake up. A couple of the guys behind me started complaining that due to the cramped nature of the van, they'd only gotten about forty-five minutes of sleep.

"I feel you," I said, turning back to them. "I only got ten, fifteen minutes tops."

They all chuckled uncomfortably, unsure whether I was serious or not.

"Thank God Ohio's flat and straight, huh?"

The Thunderbirds inaugural game was at Indianapolis in early April. I'd been getting reps in each Saturday morning at practice until I was much more comfortable blowing the whistle. And I'm glad I did because guys constantly had weird questions.

"So what happens if the pull rolls out of bounds and then gets kicked by a dude on the receiving team back in bounds off one of their teammates and then is intercepted by the defense?"

"It goes back to the point where the pull originally rolled out of bounds."

"Really?"

"Yup."

I didn't fuckin' know, I just said shit that sounded correct with lots of confidence and then looked it up when I got home.

Apparently for the first weekend of the season, Indy was having trouble fielding a full complement of referees. So a few days ahead of time, I got an email from the team asking if I had any desire to head to Indiana to call my first official game. Once I cleared it with Jessi, I once again found myself heading west on I-70. After seven hours of travel, we arrived at a high school south of the city.

Now professional league or not, it was ultimate after all, so more than a few things were bound to be patched together with gum and splinters. As I walked over to meet with the owner of the AlleyCats, I was about to find out just how much of the night was balanced on a precarious pile of rocks.

"Hi. I'm Cramer," I said, shaking his hand. "I'm here from Pittsburgh to help out your ref crew tonight. Do you know where they are? I'd like to meet them, go over a few things, find out what the plan is and all that."

"Well they aren't here as of yet," he answered. "I told them to show up a half hour before the game."

"Oh," I said. "A whole thirty minutes. Awesome."

When they finally arrived twenty-seven minutes before opening pull, I hustled over to introduce myself. One guy was a big, confident dude who'd played briefly at the University of Indiana and the other guy was an incredibly timid kid who I swore was still in high school.

"Hey, I'm Cramer," I said. "I'll be reffing with you guys tonight. Is there anything I should know? Anything you guys found that worked well last year?"

The two guys shared a frightened glance. The big one spoke up. "We didn't do this last year. A friend of mine asked me at spring league a couple days ago."

"Yeah," said the shy kid.

I'm pretty sure my face started twitching. "Have either of you ever reffed an ultimate game before?"

"No," they answered.

"Practice? Anything?"

"I just got the rule book yesterday."

Just then, the owner came up to us. "So I assume we're all set then?"

I looked off toward the parking lot. "Is there….another guy showing up? So we have ya know…..four guys like we're supposed to?"

"Should be, yeah," said the owner.

"Any way you could you call him? Anthem starts in like ten minutes."

"Oh, I don't have his number on me," he scoffed. The guy seemed much more interested in whether anyone was buying AlleyCats merchandise. "Ok, you guys are good to go then, right? You brought whistles, ref jerseys and all the stuff you need?"

The big guy shook his head. "We were under the assumption those would be provided."

"No, that's on you. Why would *we* provide that?"

The three of us stared at the guy with open mouths as he quickly turned and walked off toward the merchandise table.

The big Indiana kid nodded. "I referee intramurals. I think I have a whistle in my car."

The shy dude shrugged. "I don't have a whistle."

"Fantastic."

So for my first official game, I became the de facto head referee on the field with two dudes with zero experience, one of whom didn't even have a goddamn whistle. And none of us had referee shirts. I actually took the field in my old Dire Wolf jersey since we all managed to have black shirts handy.

Fifteen seconds before the coin toss, I realized I didn't even have a quarter. I actually had to bum one from someone in the stands to prevent the two teams from having to play bear-ninja-cowboy at midfield. Now because the other two guys didn't have any experience, we collectively decided that the easiest course of action would be for them to take the sidelines and for me to be the single on-field ref. It stood to reason that if they both handled the duties of the deep ref while I acted as the trail ref, we'd be able to triangulate everything and keep the whole field covered. It was an incredibly rushed plan that I didn't have much time to think through, but as the first pull went up directly into the setting sun, it seemed like a great idea. Especially after the Thunderbirds received the opening pull and worked it right down the field for a score.

Ok, cool. I think this is going to work.

I went down and lined up behind the AlleyCats and soon the pull was heading toward them. They received it and slowly worked it downfield for about eight or nine passes before they zipped a twenty yarder wide of the mark - which immediately highlighted the major flaw in my plan.

Oh fuck, I forgot about turnovers.

I had to sprint my ass off weaving in and out of players to try and get behind the handlers to count the stall. Pittsburgh hucked it downfield. Turnover. Another sprint. Indy fired it downfield. Turnover. Yet another sixty-yard sprint. Finally, Pittsburgh got the disc and worked it in for the score to go up 2-0 - after which I had to sprint seventy yards back to the other side of the field to line up behind the receivers again. The AUDL has strict requirements for the time between when a goal is scored and when the next pull has to be in the air. Fifty seconds. That's it. That's all I had to rest between points.

After the first quarter, I chugged half my water and flagged down the big guy.

"All right, now that you have a whole quarter of experience under your belt, how about you rotate off the sideline every time there's a turnover and become the trail ref? Keep in mind if you don't, I will be leaving behind a wife and child."

He laughed. "Yeah, I think I can handle that."

And truly, the big guy did a hell of a job. He picked it up quickly and confidently, showing zero sign that he'd never done it before. He absolutely saved my ass.

Pittsburgh went up 4-0 and Indy never could quite close the gap. Early in the second half, one of the Thunderbirds caught a goal and in celebration, punch spiked it to the ground. Indy wasn't too pleased about it so when they scored on the next possession, the fiery little dude that scored punted the thing right past Tad's ear. Never one to back down, Tad said something to him and next thing you know they're jawing at each other from ten yards away. The big Indiana dude had to step in as I hustled in from midfield to assist him. The game was starting to get chippy and with only two and a half refs, I wasn't in the mood to let it go any further. I walked with the Indy guy off the field.

"Hey, no more of that. Kick it again and I'm going to have to call you for an unsportsmanlike." I said calmly.

He acted like I'd just flung dog shit in his eye. "What the fuck? They're allowed to do it but we're not?"

"You kicked the thing at a guy's head and I'm only giving you a warning. That should be fifteen yards already."

"That's bullshit, man! You better tell them to knock it off too."

I shivered at how this dude might react if something legitimately terrible actually happened to him. "I'm going over there right now," I said. "No more of that shit. You hear me?"

And he pouted and stomped his way across the field. I warned the Pittsburgh bench and the Indy bench but forgot to mention it to the guys on the line, so when Indy forced a turn and scored to bring it to within three, the dude that caught it punched it straight down at the feet of his defender and shouted like he'd done a backflip and caught it in his teeth instead of making a simple clap catch near the sideline. Pittsburgh's bench goes nuts yelling at me that it should be fifteen yards.

"Hey, hey, I didn't get a chance to talk to that line," I yelled, which of course didn't satisfy them at all. So I go up to the Indy kid. "Hey, you guys were already lined up when I warned both benches about spikes, but next time it's an unsportsmanlike."

And this dude lost it even worse than his buddy. "That's not even a rule! I can do whatever I want after I catch a goal. You can't tell me what to do!"

You're right, kid. You catch a goal, anything goes. Punch a dog, throw grenades around, fuck your grandma, the rules of society no longer apply. Because you're a special little flower.

"Well it's a rule now for this game. The chippiness stops now."

"That's bullshit. Spikes are allowed," he yelled as he moped to the sideline.

"Trust me, kid, it's possible to score without acting like a douchebag," I said, not quite loud enough for him to hear before sprinting back to the line.

That seemed to calm things down. Luckily I didn't have any problems the rest of the way. Pittsburgh ended up winning their first ever game 28-20 and other than the spike war, it miraculously went smoothly despite the fact that it was set up to be a total shit show.

Afterwards, I shook the big guy's hand. "I don't know how the hell we pulled that off."

"Please tell me you're going to be at the rest of our games."

"Heh," I laughed with a touch of evil that I didn't mean to be there. "Good luck with the rest of the season."

Now the odd thing about refereeing professionally but locally is that you're not supposed to show any bias toward one team or another - which let's face it is tough when two players and the GM are on your summer league team and a couple of guys are friends you've known for over a decade. To be honest, I think I was so aware of it that I was actually searching for calls against the Thunderbirds just to make sure I didn't come across as a homer. I'd have much rather been doing DC or Philly games.

And while you're supposed to remain neutral about the entire experience, it's definitely hard to remain so when the city you cherish and the sport you love come together in a showcase that turns all the dreams you ever had into a reality. In late April, the Cincinnati Revolution came to town for the first professional ultimate game in Pittsburgh. The venue was amazing - picturesque Cupples Stadium on the south side of the Monongahela River, sandwiched between the water and a working class neighborhood on the side of a cliff. An old Orthodox church sat behind the west end zone, trains chugged by just above the far bleachers, three bridges were within eyesight, and the city skyline loomed over the press box. It was so very Pittsburgh.

And the line to get into the game went halfway down the block. Smoke from the burger stand wafted over the field as the PA blared. By the time pregame festivities started, just south of a thousand people were filling the stands.

They announced the team individually, the players running onto the field to loud music and large applause. And then they announced the refs. I got to tip my cap to a huge crowd. It was unexpectedly cool as I looked around at the people and the wild atmosphere and sucked it all in. I may not have been playing, but I was *on the field* for the experience. I had a view that not many people get. And it truly was magnificent.

As our PA announcer, a thirty-year ultimate veteran named Matt Weiss said in a speech before the game, "Those of us who built this game and dedicated our lives to it have never been able to truly give our non ultimate friends and family a glimpse into our world. For years we've wanted to invite them to the party. But what were we going to do - ask them to hang out on a sideline in Charlotte for two days? But today – today, we can finally share our sport with everyone. Enjoy it Pittsburgh. In just a moment, our national anthem."

I was standing with the other referees, Heim, Red, and Trevor at midfield when the DJ put on "Jump Around" by House of Pain.

"Pack it up, pack it in, let me begin...."

I turned to Heim. "I didn't know they changed the national anthem to 'Jump Around.' I can't believe that got through Congress."

The game was insane. Nine hundred people sounded like nine thousand as they stomped and cheered and heckled and generally went berserk.

For ultimate.

There were seven home games that inaugural year, some total blowouts, and some nail-biters. There was a game where the Thunderbirds broke the league single-game scoring record with 44 goals against Detroit. In that game, one of the Detroit players turned and randomly tried to dump it to me as I stood behind him counting the stall. I instinctively put my hands up to catch it, then realized, *"Wait a minute. I'm not playing."* I simply backpedaled out of the way– for which I got heckled mercilessly.

"Never let a disc hit the ground, Cramer!"

"The disc is as scared of you as you are of it, Cramer!"

"Cramer, you just tanked that guy's completion percentage you dick!"

In complete contrast to that blowout, there was a totally insane game against the previously undefeated Madison Radicals where the crowd was so loud during the 4th quarter, the players could barely hear our whistles. Pittsburgh won a thrilling game but what I'll remember the most are the four ice cold Sam Adams Lagers that randomly appeared after the game in the maintenance garage we were using for a referee locker room.

"Were those beers there at halftime?" Heim asked.

"They were definitely not there at halftime," Red answered.

"Are they for us?"

"Let's examine this, boys," I said. "There are four of us and four beers, which is a telling sign."

"Agreed."

"Now if we drink them and they were someone else's, it would be a dick move, but also an honest mistake. But if we don't drink them and they were indeed a gift, that's a slap in the face of whoever left them."

"And four cold beers go to waste," Red said.

"I say we drink the beers," Heim said.

"It's the only prudent thing to do."

We drank the beers. After running around on a hot, humid night, the word refreshing barely does them justice. Drinking the beers was indeed the right thing to do.

The great thing about our crew is that we were as professional on the field as we failed to be off of it. Right before the final home game, we almost missed the coin toss because for some reason we were in the locker room taking bets on whether there was a porno based on the story of Goldilocks and the three bears.

"C'mon – 'this one's too small, this one's too big, this one's just right?'" Heim said. "That's begging to be turned into porn."

"Everything in the world turns into porn eventually," Trevor said. "Goldilocks is too easy. I'd be more surprised if there *wasn't* a Goldilocks inspired porno."

"But are the bears actual bears or are they just hairy dudes?" Red asked.

"I doubt a porno is going to have the budget to train one bear let alone three," I said. "I'm going with hairy dudes."

Heim dug into his gym bag for his phone. "That's it, I'm looking it up."

Turned out there were like five, a fact that surprised none of us. But now we knew. And we could call the game with enlightened minds and a clear conscience.

As we came out of the locker room and into the stadium, one of the team representatives started chatting with us. "What do you guys talk about before the game? Do you study the rule book and quiz each other or what?"

The four of us tried to suppress grins. "Yeah, the rules. We mainly discuss the rules."

That game was spectacular for even more than the pregame knowledge I acquired. Sometime in the second half, Pittsburgh's lefty gunslinger Pat Earles caught a pass on the far sideline and tried to rifle a flick across the field to a wide-open receiver in the end zone. But Indy's Nick Hutton sprinted straight back, hit a horizontal trampoline and flew like six yards to make the absolute best catch block I've ever seen. For a moment, he became a human rocket. The play happened right in front of me, which was fortuitous when it later became #2 on Sportscenter's top plays. There gets to be a certain point in every athlete's life when you've given up the dream of appearing on a national highlight show for anything other than a foul ball landing in your nachos. But there I was on national television sprinting to get in position. Which was pretty cool. With a better angle the whole country could've actually seen me stop and mouth the word "God-damn."

Which brings us back to the Chicago game and the gigantic call I was no longer positive I'd gotten correct. There were enough eyes on that game around the ultimate community that if I'd blown it, it was going to be hard to remain anonymous. I was suddenly a bit nervous - until Beltway Jay found me in the crowd as I walked off the field. He'd been taking pictures for the team that day and tapped me on the shoulder.

"Cramer, look at this," he said.

I looked down at his digital camera. There on the screen, he'd zoomed in on Goose Helton's foot the moment it landed at the back of the end zone. And by the slimmest of margins, his toe was indeed out of bounds.

"You got it right," he said.

I hadn't blown it. I could officially call my first season as a referee a success.

The dream that I'd held for so long of someday being on an ultimate field in front of hundreds of spectators had actually materialized – just not in the way I'd expected. And I once again was a small part of helping to build something greater. And while Pittsburgh was making waves as an expansion team in the Midwest division, another expansion team down south was making everyone take notice as well. The Jacksonville Cannons (coached by Tuba) were tall, fast, and played a run and gun style, hucking the damn thing all over the place. Watching their highlights warmed my heart to no end. Squint a little and it wasn't hard to see me, Tall Andy, Big Tim, Clancy, and Black Tide Matt out there just putting it into the sky, trying to make something spectacular happen.

2016 saw the league get even crazier. In mid-July, the Thunderbirds played a playoff game versus the Minnesota Wind Chill at Highmark Stadium, home of Pittsburgh's pro soccer team. It was right on the water with riverboats cruising past and a spectacular view of the city on the opposite bank of the Monongahela. Every goal was immediately replayed on the Jumbotron. During breaks in the action, I'd occasionally look up and see myself on the screen – wiggling my arm or hopping up and down just to make sure it was all real. At one point in the 2ⁿᵈ half, the frenzied crowd began stomping on the bleachers, shouting the USA soccer chant, "I BELIEVE – I BELIEVE – I BELIEVE THAT WE WILL WIN! I BELIEVE THAT WE WILL WIN!" My back was to the stands as I straddled the goal line waiting to make sure the Thunderbirds weren't offside on the pull. When I heard it, every hair on my body stood up. My detached impartiality floated away and the pure energy of the moment enveloped me - consumed me. Only one word managed to cross my mind….

Wow.

And the expansion Dallas Roughnecks launched the sport into the stratosphere by going all Yankees and Manchester United on the rest of the league, raiding the defending champion San Jose Spiders of their top three players. How'd they do it? Money. Yeah, you heard me. Money. In ultimate. Rumor had it that heavyweight Beau Kittredge was being paid five figures for the season – which may not sound like much, but when you consider that in the sport's first forty-nine years, ultimate players all gladly took a financial hit just for the privilege of chasing a disc, five figures seems like a Gatesian sum. And it worked. The Roughnecks went undefeated, easily dispatching the Toronto Rush and Seattle Cascades on championship weekend to lift the trophy. Who knows what the other franchises will have to do to catch up. The forthcoming arms race is likely to be insane.

Seeing the pro leagues up close and personal was a remarkable experience. It was still the same game, just slightly bigger, faster, and crisper – the fate it was probably destined for all along. And despite ultimate's growing pains, unexpected explosion, and gradual drift toward the mainstream, it's still in my humble opinion the greatest damn sport on Earth.

And as long as we nurture the game and don't let it stray *too* far from its counterculture roots, it will remain so for a long time.

AFTERWARD

So that's the story of how a sport I started playing because I didn't want to be bored one Sunday afternoon took over my life. While this book might be done, I'm hoping my playing days aren't. I swear I have at least five more years in me. All right, ten more years. Maybe fifteen. Ok, realistically, I'm playing until an ambulance takes me off the field and straight into a casket. After years of badgering me about when I turned 40, I finally got to tell Black Tide Matt he could roster me with his southern California-based Grandmasters team in 2017. They finished fifth in the country last year so maybe, just maybe after all this time I'll get to set foot on the fields at nationals. Super old guy nationals, but nationals nonetheless. That'd be pretty cool.

Recently, Pittsburgh's two club teams, Oakland and Dire Wolf decided to patch up their differences and come together to form a mega team called Temper that could finally take on regional powers like Truckstop and Ring of Fire. And one night in the summer of 2015, Temper held a scrimmage that confirmed what I already knew. The sport I'd played for the last twenty years was now on a totally different plane of existence.

At Schenley Park above the city, Temper scrimmaged Raza Ultimate from Bogota, Columbia. That's right, Bogota, *Columbia*. Ya know, the country in South freakin' America. Henry was 22 months old when I took him over to watch the game, which ended up delayed by a huge thunderstorm for nearly an hour. As the teams and fans huddled inside a pavilion to wait out the rain, Henry ran over and grabbed an ultimate disc off a picnic table. Seeing such a little guy with the disc amused some of the Columbian players, so one guy put up his hands.

"Throw?" he said, urging him on.

And to the shock of their entire team, Henry fired a perfect five-yard flick right into his hands.

"I fro a fwick!" Henry yelled.

There was a slight language barrier, but the look the Raza guy gave me said, *"Are you kidding me?"*

For the next five minutes until he got bored, Henry threw flicks and hammers to guys from a completely different culture thousands of miles away.

And when he yelled, "Push pass!" and threw a legitimate three yarder, practically their whole team came over to high five him. Henry was having the time of his life.

And it occurred to me that if he chooses to take up this sport, he'll never quite understand the game as it was when his father played. His experience will always be pro leagues and television and playing catch with new friends from other countries. Hell, now that the IOC officially recognized flying disc sports, he could see it in the Olympics before he turns eleven years old.

And if it gets there, it'll be partly because of slap ass pickup games at places like the fort. As I wrote this book, I realized that the stories I was telling were (hopefully) a reflection of all of our stories – the tales of where we came from and the wacky road to where we landed. There are a million Havelock Bens, Tall Andys, Barnacle Julies, Duffys, and Demo Jareds out there whose anonymous shoulders the current players now stand on. In a world that now legitimately contains ultimate superstars, I hope the story of a bunch of pluggers who helped build something bigger resonates at least a little bit.

As the Raza guys held up their hands for the high fives and fist bumps that Henry excitedly doled out, he held up the disc, pointed at me and said emphatically, "Daddy play fribby!"

I laughed, picked him up, and swung him around. "Yeah, buddy. Daddy does play Frisbee. Maybe one day you will too."

I can't imagine what the game will be like then. But damn, I'm excited to find out.

Hope you enjoyed the stories and I'll see you on the fields.

Made in the USA
Las Vegas, NV
13 November 2022

59449110R00272